SOUTH AFRICANS VERSUS ROMMEL

THE UNTOLD STORY OF THE DESERT WAR IN WORLD WAR II

DAVID BROCK KATZ

STACKPOLE BOOKS
Guilford, Connecticut

To Jack and Miriam
To my daughter Jacqueline
To my compadre and l'amour de ma vie, Adina
My past, my future, and my present

Published by Stackpole Books
An imprint of Globe Pequot
Trade Division of The Rowman & Littlefield Publishing Group, Inc.
4501 Forbes Boulevard, Suite 200, Lanham, Maryland 20706
www.rowman.com

Distributed by
NATIONAL BOOK NETWORK
800-462-6420

British Library Cataloguing in Publication Information Available
Library of Congress Cataloging-in-Publication Data

Names: Katz, David Brock, author.
Title: South Africans versus Rommel : the untold story of the desert war in World War II / David Brock Katz.
Description: Lanham, Maryland : Stackpole Books, an imprint of Globe Pequot, 2017. | Includes index.
Identifiers: LCCN 2017033969 (print) | LCCN 2017035145 (ebook) | ISBN 9780811766081 (e-book) | ISBN 9780811717816 (hardback : alk. paper)
Subjects: LCSH: World War, 1939-1945—South Africa.
Classification: LCC D766.97 (ebook) | LCC D766.97 .K38 2017 (print) | DDC 940.54/1268—dc23
LC record available at https://lccn.loc.gov/2017033969

∞™ The paper used in this publication meets the minimum requirements of American National Standard for Information Sciences—Permanence of Paper for Printed Library Materials, ANSI/NISO Z39.48-1992.

Printed in the United States of America

Contents

Acknowledgments

I have been fortunate to meet many caring and informed individuals who have given generously of their time and knowledge. A large proportion of the research was undertaken using primary documents contained at the South African National Defence Force Documentation Centre (Military Archives) (DODA) in Pretoria. Deputy Director Louise Jooste heads up the archive and her kindness included the provision of tea and biscuits on many of my visits. Ms. Jooste took an avid interest in my progress and insisted that the assistance I received from her staff be first class. Steve de Agreila was always available and offered invaluable advice on finding the most elusive documents. His banter, command of many languages, and general accommodating demeanor makes a visit to the reading room at the documentation center a pleasure. Gerald Prinsloo, the custodian of an incredible collection of unpublished photographs, was unstinting with his time and patience. Ms. M. Borain, the librarian, provides another example of the friendly and helpful manner that one is greeted with on a visit to the documentation center. Evert Kleynhans, in his capacity as an employee of DODA, often furnished me with tidbits he had come across that he thought might be relevant to the topic. The flames of completing our master's degrees together at the Saldanha Military Academy have forged our friendship.

The reading room at DODA presents many opportunities besides that of rewarding research. I was fortunate to make the acquaintance of Dr. Anne Samson at DODA, who was also busily undertaking research at the time. Anne has generously provided archival material from the National Archives in the United Kingdom whenever she comes across something that she believes will be of interest. We share many common interests, and she has been extremely helpful in obtaining some vital documentation for the production of this book. The pursuit of research has transported me to many new places, including numerous visits to the South African National Archives in Pretoria, the Stellenbosch Uys Krige Archive, the University of Cape Town Library, the University of Witwatersrand Library, the University of Pretoria Library, and the National Archives of the United Kingdom. I would like to extend my thanks to all these excellent institutions, which not only make essential research possible, but through their professionalism make it a joy.

Hamish Patterson, a gentleman of immense knowledge from the Ditsong National Museum of Military History, was most helpful in allowing me the extensive use of their Sidi Rezegh archive. Ilze Cloete of the Ditsong National Museum of Military History Library generously gave of her time to assist me in locating many of the previously unpublished photographs that appear in this book. She was kind enough to go out of her way to provide photos, never before seen by the public and that now adorn some of the pages of this book. Lieutenant Jacobus van Aarde helped me with translating certain texts from English into Afrikaans, and Professor Deon Fourie took time out of his busy schedule to offer invaluable insight and guidance. Professor Paul Harris of the Department of War Studies at the Royal Military Academy Sandhurst sent me his only copy of a rare, out-of-print book that he had authored. He did this despite the fact that I was a perfect stranger from a foreign country, fully trusting that I would return the book when I was finished. Needless to say, I continued to make use of his generosity, and he has read some of my articles, once again offering important insight and guidance. My thanks again to Evert Kleynhans, Tony Garcia, and Will Gordon for reading some of my chapters and providing valuable insights and necessary editing advice.

The Dean of the Military Academy at Saldanha, Professor Sam Tshehla, believed in my commitment and generously opened the door to my academic pursuits, making good on the one force principle and affording me the same opportunity as my permanent force colleagues. The South African National Defence Force has provided me with a first-class education and has enabled me to undertake projects of this nature. Andries Fokkens ensured my smooth yearly registration at the academy and tackled his administrative task with humor and vigor beyond that demanded by his scope of work. Lieutenant Herman Warden took care of all the administrative tasks during my residential visits. The Saldanha Military Academy is a center of military history excellence and is truly a national treasure. Lieutenant-Colonel (Prof.) Ian van der Waag has dispensed invaluable guidance throughout my academic career as well as in the formulation of this book. Through his untiring efforts, I was able to obtain my master's degree with distinction and, during the program, produce three published academic articles. He guided me through three conference presentations, one of which, a personal highlight in my life, was at Royal Military Academy Sandhurst in April 2014.

Professor Andre Wessels of the *Journal of Contemporary History* afforded me the opportunity to publish a piece on Tobruk.[1] Professor Abel Esterhuyse took a keen interest in my article about South African Second World War historiography for inclusion in *Scientia Militaria*.[2] In June 2012 Professor Karen Harris of the Historical Association of South Africa approved my presentation paper on the Union War Histories Section as a historical source, and in April 2014 Dr. Simon Trew (Royal Military Academy Sandhurst) and Dr. Marcus Faullam (Kings College) approved my presentation paper on South African War policy in 1944. A thank you to the South African Military History Society for providing me with an opportunity to present a paper on the fall of Tobruk in 1942. My thanks to Professor Tim Stapleton for publishing two of my pieces in the 1914–1918-online International Encyclopedia of the First World War.[3] All these opportunities allowed me, directly or indirectly, to test and develop some of the ideas that appear in this book.

An enterprise of this nature requires a strong network of friends to facilitate its final production. A book is not a book unless published. I have been very privileged to make the acquaintance of Dave Reisch of Stackpole Books. I am indeed fortunate that from inception, he has believed in the project, and his guidance has helped shape the subject matter to be of interest to a wider audience. In Dave's words, he has assisted me with the aim of allowing me to produce the best book that I am capable of producing. Although we are separated by many miles and reside on two different continents, this has not stopped Dave from offering encouragement and advice on demand. He has done so despite being inordinately busy and subject to the strains and stresses of a business merger. I look forward to many more future ventures as proof that soldiers and soldiering are truly a universal language and the bond of comradeship between soldiers transcends politics and international boundaries.

Producing a book of this nature requires a huge investment in time and is impossible without sound backing from the home front. My dear wife

Adina has endured endless hours of me absenting myself to work on this book in my study. She has stayed up late at night reading my manuscripts and correcting them. She has faithfully accompanied me to venues near and far to listen to my presentations on the subject and offer advice on their improvement. She has listened attentively at many a breakfast and dinner to my latest theories on history and doctrine. Over the years, she has absorbed the subject matter and has even become an expert on some issues. She has been my greatest critic and also my biggest motivator. Her constant praise and encouragement have spurred me on even in the darkest hours. This book is as much a product of her unstinting support and encouragement as it is of any of my efforts.

Introduction

This book is the first of a kind in that it covers South Africa's war in East and North Africa in a single volume. However, it is by no means a complete history. Some events, especially those which involve the South Africans, are dealt with in detail, while other facets of the desert war receive less attention. The Union Defence Force in the Second World War made tremendous sacrifices, all but forgotten in South Africa and Britain. Britain owes a debt to the South Africans who voluntarily came to her aid during her darkest hour. Modern-day South Africans, who enjoy the fruits of a democratic country, should not forget that black and white South African soldiers took up arms and fought side by side against fascist tyranny in the hope that a better and freer South Africa would emerge as a result of their sacrifices. Fortunately, there is a small but perceptible shift within South Africa in recognizing the personal sacrifice of these men and women, and there are signs of reclamation of the memory of their sacrifice for the new national identity.

South Africa rendered service to the British Empire when it played a fundamental role in ridding East Africa of its Italian presence. The Union Defence Force's mobility, coupled with its maneuver style of warfare, demoralized the more numerous, but less agile, Italian defenders whenever they met on the battlefield. Their fully motorized infantry brigades, a modern version of their old mounted infantry, often outflanked and enfiladed the static Italian defenders. South Africa had deep roots tapping into maneuver warfare and could trace their military genetics to the Boer mounted infantry of previous centuries. Trucks, armored cars, and tanks replaced the sturdy ponies of yesteryear in East Africa, and by using some of the same military formulas of their forbears, they quickly overcame the Italian defenders at a relatively low cost in lives and material. The conquest of East Africa was a vindication for South Africa's way of war, and for the first time this book attempts to describe the evolution of South Africa's unique war doctrine by comparing it with that of its allies and enemies.

Unfortunately, the British had negligible use in North Africa for the South African penchant for mobility and often misused the Union Defence Force in a static role. The British failure to institute combined arms warfare left the sometimes hapless South Africans to their own devices. The natural role for the highly mobile South Africans would have been integration with the British armor formations, but this proved to be a step beyond British vision and command capability. Despite mismanagement, the South Africans played a significant role at the tipping point in Operation Crusader. The sacrifice of the 5th South African Infantry Brigade at Sidi Rezegh on November 23, 1941, blunted the armored edge of Rommel's *Panzer* Divisions. Again, the South Africans suffered a grievous loss when the 1st South African Infantry Division surrendered at Tobruk on June 21, 1942. They fell victim to a last-minute and poorly executed decision by the British to defend Tobruk. This decision was a political one and it took place against better military judgment. British failure at the operational level resulted in the commitment of a fully motorized South African division to a static defense. British obscuration further compounded the inept fumbling of an inexperienced South African general at the tactical level. The disaster at Tobruk gave Rommel his greatest victory and severely shook the confidence of the Allied powers. This book reexamines South Africa's role at Sidi Rezegh and Tobruk and seeks new insights into the grievous and needless losses suffered in these two battles.

Britain's clumsy operational conduct of the desert war, coupled with poor tactics, cost the South Africans dearly in both life and limb. In the wake of the Tobruk fiasco, ordinary South African soldiers and their commanders had scant belief in Britain's ability to beat Rommel. The British High Command also harbored doubts and believed that the South Africans were past their fighting best. Despite flagging morale and battered confidence, South Africans manned the front lines at El Alamein, and once again, they were at the tipping point that marked the end of Rommel's advance into Egypt. South African troops found their composure and held fast at El Alamein on July 1–3, 1942. They broke the spirit of the crack veteran German 90th Light Division, as they tried to bypass and cut off El Alamein, and caused a rare state of panic among the Germans. Surprisingly little is known about their contribution to the demise of Rommel's hopes to conquer Egypt. Even in the thick of battle, the South Africans were largely unaware of the devastation their artillery had wrought on the Germans. The extent of the German demoralization at the hands of the South Africans only becomes apparent after consulting German and Italian primary sources.

This book attempts to show how events unfolded, based on research of hard archival evidence rather than mere speculation arising out of a rehash of the secondary sources. The archives have provided many new insights, and as a result, some of the long-cherished myths that have survived for decades have been debunked. The book places heavy reliance on the use of primary documentation in reconstructing the events, with the emphasis on a South African perspective. Use has also been made of the excellent German and Italian official histories as well as translated German and Italian primary documentation, to gain a balanced view of all protagonists. The book is a military history in the sense that it does not examine the impact of the war on civil society to any great extent, but rather focuses purely on the military aspects of the campaign. Military history is probably not the most respected branch of history in modern times. There is an understandable aversion to the study of war due to the mistaken belief that to study it is in some way to approve of it. However, war is far too important a subject to ignore, even though its destructiveness and wastage make it an issue that many would prefer to avoid. Civilians and soldiers alike can learn much by studying historical campaigns, and good history can have a real and direct utility.

The approach to tackling the voluminous subject matter has been to concentrate efforts on the top three battles that defined South Africa's contribution to the war effort. The South Africans fought the battles of Sidi Rezegh, Tobruk, and the First Alamein under the command of the British Eighth Army. The South African contingent's fortunes followed closely those of the Eighth Army, and as argued here, on occasion, influenced the fortunes of the Eighth Army. Factors within and outside of the control of the South Africans directly affected the outcome of the various engagements. The brilliant and daring command style of Rommel and his leader group, and the tactical skills of his German divisions, often resulted in the demise of his less-gifted opponents. His robust and skilled military ability is only part of the story, and it is a part that has received the greatest amount of attention from historians since the war. Books on Rommel run into the hundreds, if not thousands, and the popularity of the subject seems to grow stronger as the years pass.

Less well served, especially in popular history as opposed to academic history, is research into the deeply flawed British military doctrine that placed the Eighth Army at a severe disadvantage in the operational and tactical levels of the desert war. The book seeks to analyze these battles by taking into account the conflict of doctrine between the participants. This doctrinal approach goes a long way toward explaining some of the battlefield decisions made and the results obtained as a consequence of them during crucial periods of the battle. It is not immediately apparent that South Africa had its own military doctrine and a unique way of war. The different military groupings that made up the Union Defence Force directly influenced the final format of South African doctrine. The South African doctrine was similar to the British in many ways, but it differed from the British in some fundamental aspects. For example, the South Africans had a long-standing aversion to sustaining "unnecessary" battle casualties, and this one difference was the cause of much misunderstanding and bitterness between South African and British commanders. The book attempts to demonstrate where the differences in doctrine led to friction on the battlefield and less than optimum performance. The first two chapters lay the foundations of the Union Defence Force and the third sets out a comparison of the doctrines of the major participants.

The second chapter of the book covers the South African campaign under the harsh, arid, and later mountainous conditions of East Africa. It is a campaign in which the South Africans excelled due to their mobility. The campaign served to cement the South African doctrine of maneuver and there were high hopes that the South Africans would perform a similar role in North Africa as part of a combined arms formation, as had been the case in East Africa. Chapters four and five describe the events leading up to the loss of the 5th SAI at Sidi Rezegh on November 23, 1941, and chapters six and seven follow the same format in recounting the events leading to the fall of Tobruk on June 21, 1942. The last chapter examines the South African role in the First Battle of El Alamein, July 1–3, 1942.

Thousands of books on the subject of the desert war have served history well. Works have appeared on nearly every aspect, down to the minutiae of uniforms worn and equipment used by the participants. This book seeks to fill a gap in the vast body of knowledge available, by presenting a South African viewpoint of the battles and the conduct of the campaign. The South African perspective is refreshing in many ways and provides a unique and critical angle that will be presented alongside other, better-known viewpoints in order to bring us closer to the truth.

A Note on Sources

Researchers interested in locating sources relating to South Africa's desert war can look to a vast collection of primary sources and a somewhat sparser assortment of secondary sources. The Union War Histories Section (UWHS) has collected and archived the most readily available and comprehensive collection of primary sources available. The UWHS published the most comprehensive secondary sources available in the form of official histories dealing with two of the battles, Sidi Rezegh and Tobruk.[1] Most of the South African secondary sources, as well as the British, New Zealand, Australian, German, and Italian official histories, have made extensive use of the works of the UWHS when dealing with Operation Crusader and the Gazala battles. Ideally, the primary purpose of official history is to offer an unbiased treatise of the events that took place, to provide a platform on which subsequent historians might build. However, much of the production of official history is for nation-building purposes. The official histories of the UWHS remain the last word on Sidi Rezegh and Tobruk, due to a general failure by historians to investigate historical matters further and come up with up-to-date accounts based on new evidence and ideas.

John Keegan held that the worst types of official history are peculiarly desiccated and didactic, while the best are conscientious and inspired. It would seem that the efforts of the UWHS fall into the latter category.[2] The much-underrated Professor J. A. I. Agar-Hamilton, a professional historian with links to the Universities of Pretoria and South Africa, headed up the UWHS.[3] The motivation behind the formation of the UWHS was to ensure that South Africa's war efforts be documented accurately, to facilitate the formulation of a serious historical account after the war.[4] Armed with a team of highly qualified academics and appropriate government funding, the UWHS managed to collect an abundance of official and unofficial documents, together with translated documents from the Axis forces.[5] This book draws upon the trilogy of published work[6] and unpublished manuscripts, together with extensive accumulated documents, which form a rich seam of historiographical material.

The UWHS's first book covers the fall of Tobruk and the First Battle of Alamein.[7] Agar-Hamilton deals with the reasons for the fall of Tobruk and the resulting surrender of the South Africans. The book has a twofold purpose in seeking an academic explanation, in light of the Australian success in holding the fortress the year before, and it offers something in the way of lessons learned.[8] The second book deals in great depth with Operation Crusader and the destruction of the 5th South African Infantry Brigade.[9] It seeks to resolve the controversy around the destruction of the 5th Brigade and the issues surrounding the Crusader battles.[10]

The published UWHS official histories provide a rich source of research material on Sidi Rezegh and Tobruk, including a detailed campaign history of the events leading to the destruction of the 5th Brigade and the 2nd Division. However, the official histories do have limitations and have disclosed little in the way of insight into the various political forces at play in the demise of these South African formations. The books were subject to the same political constraints, such as the sensitivity and classification of individual documents, that stymied the official board of enquiry into the surrender of Tobruk. The UWHS published the books when political considerations and relations with the United Kingdom took precedence.

More extensive, and perhaps subject to less political influences, are the vast unpublished manuscripts and documents of the UWHS housed at the South African National Defence Force (SANDF) Documentation Centre (Military Archives) (DODA) in Pretoria. These deal with issues of the history of South Africa in the Second World War beyond the published works. The archives are a fruitful source of information readily available for research purposes, comprising first-class primary and secondary material.[11] The extensive collection consists of 391 boxes of narratives and reports, grouped under twenty-four headings. There are 54 boxes containing narrations and documents about the campaigns in East Africa, Madagascar, the Middle East, and Italy.[12] The narratives and documents dealing with the Middle East campaign include personal eyewitness reports, regimental histories, relevant documents, and narratives on all aspects of South Africa's desert war.[13] This section has seen the most amount of fruitful publication, and it forms a good part of the UWHS source material for the two books on the desert war.[14]

There are a small number of published journal articles and dissertations from the last decade that deal either directly or indirectly with the subject matter. This book profitably consults these sources, to gain insight into their research and conclusions. The book makes extensive use of further secondary sources including the semi-official histories, regimental histories, and some biographies and campaign histories on the subject produced both locally and overseas. British accounts of the early desert battles of Crusader in 1941 and Gazala in 1942, published some two decades after the war, had as their primary objective the protection or boosting of individual reputations rather than the details of the battle or the real reasons for the Eighth Army's setbacks. Adding to the general dearth of information was the fact that politics and military etiquette barred prominent military figures from rendering their accounts when they were serving officers, and furthermore, most military records were not available for consultation. When official records were finally released for research purposes, some of the myths born in the years after the war were already firmly entrenched. Some aspects that pertained to the early defeats involving South African forces were ignored or glossed over.[15]

Contributing to the dearth of information is the fact that the destruction of the 5th South African Infantry Brigade at Sidi Rezegh was somewhat shrouded by the eventual victory achieved in Operation Crusader. South African losses were, to some extent, vindicated and ameliorated as having had a significant role in grinding down the irreplaceable tank forces of the *Deutsches Afrika Korps*. The bigger picture of the Crusader battles almost obliterated the memory of a major South African catastrophe, together with all the expensive lessons learned. The celebrated victory at Alamein and the successful conclusion of the desert war as a whole put paid to a balanced history about the ignominious surrender of Tobruk. Tobruk was too politically hot to handle for years after the war, as both the British and South Africans sought to suppress the truth in an exercise of political expediency. Many forgot these events and they paled into insignificance once political sensitivities began to wane decades after the war.[16]

The historiographical hiatus regarding Sidi Rezegh and Tobruk has come about due to a lack of research on the subject in the years following the closure of the UWHS in 1961. There has been a general failure to build on the foundation of official histories and expand the pool of knowledge on the subject further. Historical works on the topic in the intervening years, including the South African semi-official histories, have tended to rehash the available secondary sources or ignore the events entirely. Most overseas publications, including the official histories of the Allies and those of Germany and Italy, have also placed a heavy reliance on the work of the UWHS when referring to these two battles. The lacuna remains substantially unfilled despite a late spike in historical work produced by way of a few dissertations and academic articles in the first decade of the twenty-first century.

Fortunately, the primary sources available for research purposes are vast. Because of this, there has been a need to identify those that are pertinent to this study at an early stage. The book makes extensive use of the Brigade and Divisional War Diaries housed at DODA. Further relevant primary sources consulted, which supplement the official sources and involved archival work, are the George Brink papers, the personal file of H. B. Klopper, and individual items in the Smuts Papers. In addition, documents from the United Kingdom National Archives as well as the elusive board of enquiry documents on the surrender of Tobruk, of which the authorities made only seven copies, have been accessed. Collections of private papers were added to the primary sources, the brigade and divisional war diaries, and other pertinent documents held in local and overseas archives.

It has also been necessary to seek out and consult the documentation of those on the "other side of the hill" to produce a balanced examination of events taking into consideration the perspectives of all participants. The Italian viewpoint poses a real challenge because unpublished material is difficult to obtain. Despite the difficulty, one cannot afford to ignore the Italians, as has been done in many historical works. Historians have overlooked the *Regio Esercito* (Royal Italian Army) because of their supposedly inferior military performance (another myth that deserves reexamination) and the fact that many of the primary and secondary sources do not have ready English translations. Use has been made of the excellent Italian official histories and, where necessary, they have been translated to get a better understanding of the battles.[17] The official German histories are an excellent source and no study is complete without consulting them.[18] They are more accessible than the Italian official histories partly due to their almost complete translation into English. The UWHS has translated further valuable Italian and German documentation and the book has made good use of it where possible.

This book hopefully contributes to filling the gap in the historical knowledge of South Africa's role in the desert war, and specifically her role at Sidi Rezegh, Tobruk, and First Alamein. The official South African histories have provided the foundation and this book, using the available primary and secondary sources, builds upon their sterling work through a reexamination of the battles.

Chapter I

From Unity, Strength

To be antiwar in South African society—either at the start of the conflict or for its entire duration—was to be a member of an exceptionally broad church. Naturally, the Union had its little knots of Quakers, antimilitarist socialists, war-hating liberals and nonviolent Christians, but these came nowhere close to resembling the campaigning antiwar constituencies of Europe, especially in Britain. Those in South Africa who were against war opposed it in their own local ways, based as much on their own old grievances as on any body of common beliefs.[1]

The Interwar Years 1919–1939

Before 1910 "South Africa" was merely a geographical expression. The Union of South Africa came into being as a political entity on May 31, 1910. Her designated borders resulted from the amalgamation of the former Transvaal and Orange Free State Boer Republics and the British colonies of the Cape and Natal. The Union emerged from the ashes of a bitter war fought between Britain and the Boer Republics from 1899 to 1901. The Boers gave a good military account of themselves, but the economic and numerical might of the British war machine eventually and inevitably proved overwhelming. In the aftermath, bitter foes set aside implacable differences in a quest to create a single entity. The hope was that a unified South Africa would facilitate and coordinate the different aspirations of Englishmen, Afrikaners, and the British Empire. An emerging Afrikaner nationalism would challenge dreams of a politically unified South Africa, forged under one banner. Adding to the political complexity was the reality that Afrikaner nationalists were neither homogenous nor united in their objectives. Some yearned for the restoration of the Boer Republics while others sought an independent unified South Africa distanced from the United Kingdom.

In the Union, almost 33 percent of thc 2 million white South Africans were English-speaking and of British descent, while 55 percent of whites were Afrikaans speaking.[2] A large proportion of these English-speaking South Africans considered themselves British, strong supporters of the concept of Empire and more than willing to take up arms in its defense. English-speaking South Africans dominated the economy in most areas and enjoyed considerable influence over the military, government policy, and culture of South Africa.[3] Therefore, South Africa differed substantially from the other dominions in its political and demographic makeup. Of a population of 11 million, only 25 percent were of European origin and less than half of these were English-speaking, unlike Australia and New Zealand, where 90 percent of the population was of British descent. The British connection in South Africa was tenuous and mostly belonged to a small minority who felt a strong affinity with the United Kingdom.[4]

When the Union came into being in 1910, there was consensus on the need to form an independent unified defense force. At the time, South Africa was garrisoned by 3,500 imperial troops—which the United Kingdom would withdraw in the event of a European war—and three colonial organizations, namely, the Transvaal volunteers, the Cape Colonial Forces, and the Natal Militia.[5] The formation of the Union Defence Force (UDF) in 1912 owes much to its chief architect, and the Union's first Minister of Defence, Jan Smuts (1870–1950). He was determined to create a modern defense force based on Western methods. Lord Methuen (1846–1932),[6] commander of the military forces in South Africa, and Major General Sir Henry Timson Lukin (1860–1925)[7] influenced the committee that prepared the South African Defence Bill. Both proposed a Swiss-style military system where all adult males were members of part-time reserve and could be quickly mobilized when required.[8]

The UDF, like the Union, was an amalgamation of former enemies. British instructors tutored Republican Boers, Englishmen, Afrikaners, and British Colonial forces after they merged (or were submerged) into the new army. The UDF adopted a new coat of arms with the motto "Ex Unitate Vires"—From Unity there is Strength. In reality, this was more an exhortation than a statement of fact. Many in the new defense force resented the British uniforms, comparatively stern discipline, and strict dress code. The former Boer armies wore mostly civilian clothes, elected their leaders, and had little time for parade-ground discipline.

> The Boer army fought with guns and gunpowder, but it had no discipline, no drills, no forms, no standards, and not even a roll-call. It was an enlarged edition of the hunting parties which a quarter-century ago went into the Zoutpansberg in search of game—it was a massive aggregation of lion-hunters.

And:

> The most conspicuous feature of the Boer forces was the equality of the officers and the men, and the entire absence of any assumption of superiority by the leaders of the burghers. None of the generals or commandants wore any uniform of a distinctive type, and it was one of the most difficult problems to distinguish an officer from the burghers.[9]

Nevertheless, most adapted to the hated British khaki uniforms, pith helmets, and square bashing. Former enemies put aside their differences in a remarkable feat of reconciliation and nation-building. Much of the success of combining four different armies with three military traditions and two languages was due to Smuts. The UDF could not offer posts on ability alone when, in the interests of nation-building, the overriding consideration was representativity. The UDF achieved equilibrium to a large extent, between Afrikaner and Englishmen, in an exercise of political expediency, albeit arguably at the expense of military efficiency.[10] Smuts built a defense force based largely on consensus and compromise—the foundations of nation-building. Ian van der Waag adequately describes the process as, "[The UDF] . . . was a product of a combination of systems, but nonetheless a thoughtful combination."[11]

The UDF's first deployment reflected its primary purpose—the suppression of internal strife. Law and order took priority, rather than the protection of territorial integrity against the threat of an external power. The UDF posted soldiers on January 7, 1914, to protect key points in a general miners strike on the Witwatersrand. The UDF's first real combat challenge came with the advent of the First World War. Its first task, even then, was to stabilize internal ructions. An Afrikaner rebellion in 1914–1915 threatened the very existence of the fledgling Union and would have to be put down before its nationalist-separatist message took root.[12] The UDF, despite a shaky start, went on to conquer German South West Africa in 1915 and after that, under the leadership of Smuts, removed the Germans from the territory of German East Africa in 1916. The Germans in East Africa would continue to resist under the direction of General Paul von Lettow-Vorbeck (1870–1964) until a few weeks after the war ended in 1918.[13] South Africa fought these two campaigns with a degree of mobility and an art of maneuver unheard of on the Western Front. South African forces served in France and the Middle East, and the UDF emerged from the First World War with battle experience and a unity forged in the flames of war.

The First World War involved more than a quarter of a million UDF soldiers who served in the different theaters of war. This effort saw 10 percent of the total white population in uniform. The 1914 Afrikaner Rebellion almost split the nation, threatening to undo all the tentative prewar steps toward conciliation.[14] The rebellion, combined with the horrors of trench warfare, conspired to unite most South African politicians to confine military support for the empire to the continent of Africa. After the war, Major General J. J. Collyer (1870–1941),[15] Chief of the General Staff in 1920, and much of the general staff did not foresee the eventuality of South Africans fighting in the European theater again.[16] The UDF geared itself for a possible conflict in sub-Saharan Africa and intended to steer clear of a European conflict. Collyer's didactic official history of the conflict in East Africa published in 1939 is indicative of this "not beyond Africa" thinking. His work highlighted the disadvantages of mechanization and practically dismissed the role of the tank and airplane in any future sub-Saharan war.[17] The identified threat facing the UDF was that of internal unrest, which took the form of sporadic black uprisings and industrial action, for which there was little need to field a sophisticated mechanized army.

After the First World War, South Africa faced three potential military threats that challenged her political integrity. Aspects of these threats, existing before the First World War, had considerably receded due to South Africa's seizing of German South West Africa in 1915 and Germany's final eviction from her African colonies in 1919. The first threat was that of a seaborne invasion, hardly credible in light of the almost complete hegemony the British enjoyed in the southern oceans. There was simply no other sea power to challenge the British in this part of the world. The second threat of a landward invasion was even more remote, and except for Portugal, no European power controlled colonies near South Africa. Britain and Portugal enjoyed a close relationship, demonstrated by the oldest alliance in the world dating back to 1373, which ensured that a threat to South Africa from the direction of the Portuguese colonies of Angola and Mozambique was highly unlikely.[18]

The major threat to South African stability, and the third threat perceived, was that of internal unrest. The very real fear of domestic disturbances dominated the thinking and shaped the preparation of the South African military in the interwar years. In a country riven with disparate political agendas, the threat could emanate from black or white disaffected communities, for political or economic reasons. The possibility existed that a wily foe could combine the incitement of internal strife with a landward invasion. South Africa and its defense force would face a serious challenge if this scenario transpired.[19] It goes without saying that a force designed to suppress internal unrest or embark on mainly policing activities has a very different combat structure to that designed to meet a conventional army threat.

Besides these direct threats to the security of South Africa, segments of the population, mainly from the English-speaking community, foresaw a role for the UDF beyond that of merely policing South Africa's borders and countering internal uprisings. These parties envisaged that South Africa could deploy beyond its borders in Africa and, together with Commonwealth forces, meet a European enemy threatening the empire. The Defence Bill in 1912 introduced this possibility and underlined the importance of defense as an imperial matter. Those who sought greater independence from Britain, as opposed to those who felt an obligation via an imperial duty and were desirous to remain "faithful to the vision" of a united and a free South Africa within the Commonwealth, contested military deployment beyond the South African borders.[20]

There were attempts in the interwar years to standardize training between the United Kingdom and its dominions and to provide staff courses for military leaders across the empire. The 1921 Imperial Conference gave the question of imperial defense high priority and sought, unsuccessfully, to install an Imperial Defence Council and to standardize establishments, equipment, military thought, and intelligence.[21] The South Africans were unable to maintain quotas for training courses in the United Kingdom due to the inability to pass physical and literacy tests. Two future generals that were able to take advantage of these training programs were Lieutenant General George Brink (1889–1971), who commanded the 1st Division at Sidi Rezegh, and Major-General Dan Pienaar (1893–1942), who commanded the 2nd Brigade under Brink in the same battle.[22] Brink attended a staff course at Camberley in 1920, having as his chief instructor Brigadier-General John Dill (1881–1944)[23]; his classmates included the future Field Marshal Viscount Montgomery of Alamein (1887–1976) and Lieutenant-General Sir Richard O'Conner (1889–1981). Brink considered that Camberley had been of estimable value and there is no doubt that had more South Africans availed themselves of the opportunity, the UDF would have put their knowledge to good use in East and North Africa during the Second World War.[24] Lack of general staff training negatively influenced the UDF's fighting power. An early practical example was the campaign in East Africa, where South African forces initially struggled to coordinate their attacks on enemy objectives effectively. In contrast, staff training in the German Armed Forces was the highest priority, and excellent staff work was the reason for most of their early victories.[25]

The Imperial Conference tasked South Africa with the entire defense of the Union and the suppression of any "native insurrections" in the Portuguese colonies, Matabeleland, Mashonaland, and in the High Commission Territories (HCT) of southern and central Africa—Swaziland, Basutoland, Bechuanaland, and Barotseland. The UDF was to accomplish this onerous task despite the lack of an intelligence arm (subsequently reestablished in 1923), the absence of decent maps, nonexistence of brigade headquarters, and a defense force that had dwindled in numbers from its peak in the First World War of 254,666 to 39,667.[26]

Smuts, a staunch supporter of Britain and the empire, had assumed the premiership of South Africa after the death of the Prime Minister General Louis Botha (1862–1919). Smuts lacked the charisma and the popularity of Botha and lost the election to the pro-republican Nationalists in 1924. The National Party, in coalition with Colonel F. H. P. Creswell (1866–1948) of the Labour Party, assumed power under the new Prime Minister, General J. B. M. Hertzog (1866–1942). The Pact Government was an unlikely coalition, united in their dislike of Smuts. Hertzog's election in 1924 ushered a new dimension into Anglo–South African relations. The British found Hertzog's Afrikaner nationalist leanings, lack of finesse, and unpleasant modus operandi to be distasteful. Britain confronted South Africa's move toward Afrikaner nationalism with distrust, driving them to protect black interests from this new wave of republicanism. Captain Bede Clifford (1890–1969), imperial secretary to the South African High Commission from 1924 to 1931, saw blacks as ". . . one of our biggest allies in the country." He believed that everything possible should be done to retain their loyalty and confidence, "as a buffer against the process of secession by attrition which is going on now."[27]

The 1926 Imperial Conference resulted in the Balfour Declaration, which repositioned the dominions, together with the United Kingdom, as autonomous communities within the British Empire. They were united by common allegiance to the Crown, but freely associated and equal in status to one another in all matters domestic and external. The Statute of Westminster gave effect to the Balfour Declaration in 1931. British world power was largely dependent on the economic resources, manpower reserves, and political fidelity of the dominions, while commerce, migration, and shared ideals kept the dominions bound to Britain.[28] The conference effectively placed Great Britain and the dominions on an equal footing within the empire, with each dominium having independent control over its foreign policy, especially in the event of war. Britain could no longer expect of her dominions an automatic declaration of war in sympathy with herself, and indeed, the expectation was that Canada and South Africa would remain neutral in any future European war.[29] The Canadians were extremely cautious and adopted a policy of "no commitments," to protect the unity of a severely divided country. In 1936 Mr. W. L. Mackenzie King (1874–1950), prime minister of Canada, declared in Parliament, "Our country is being drawn into international situations to a degree that I myself think is alarming."[30]

Under the National Party, the UDF's purpose was to protect South Africa's neutrality rather than further the aims of British imperialism. At the 1926 Imperial Conference, Cresswell, the new Minister of Defence, plainly stated South Africa's role in imperial defense.[31] The priority of defending South Africa in any part of southern Africa gave the UDF its structure. He did not provide for deployment outside of southern Africa, and no South African citizen other than a volunteer would be sent to aid the empire. In the event of South Africa's involvement in a war outside the

Union, the UDF would recruit and intensively train special units before their deployment, as was the case in 1914. The policy of restricting the South African Permanent and Citizen Force to internal duties and using only a volunteer force for duties outside of the Union inhibited the modern development of the UDF. This policy ensured conflicting equipment requirements for the two types of force. It also caused a long-term lack of modern equipment and as a consequence, a resulting hiatus in training with modern equipment.[32]

Post–1924 governments considered sub-Saharan Africa as being within the area that South Africa was prepared to defend and the only theater outside of South Africa to which the government would be willing to send South African troops. South African politicians showed a distinct reluctance to subject their citizens to the "horror" of trench warfare as experienced by 30,000 South African soldiers in the First World War.[33] This limited role envisaged for the UDF also shaped the extent to which it was modernized and mechanized by developments in Europe. Poor infrastructure, inaccessible terrain, and budgetary constraints, together with the nature of a potential enemy, precluded the development of a modern mechanized army, despite South Africa possessing the industrial capacity to do so.[34] In addition to the limited role foreseen in the event of a European war, the severe worldwide economic crisis, caused by the economic depression of the 1930s, ensured that military expenditure was low on the list of priorities.[35] Political lethargy, coupled with the Great Depression, decimated the UDF. As a result, forty-nine Active Citizen Force units and a multitude of Defence Rifle Associations ceased to exist. All continuous training for the Citizen Force stopped between July 1930 and June 1934.[36] Rationalization of manpower and drastic defense expenditure cuts precluded the acquisition of basic equipment, let alone much-needed modern weapon systems.[37] Strong government tendencies toward neutrality in any future war, coupled with a reluctance to deploy beyond South Africa's borders and a poor economic climate, steadily eroded the fighting power of the UDF.

Economic necessity was the primary driver behind Hertzog, leader of the Nationalist Party, and Smuts, leader of the South African Party, forming a coalition called the United Party in 1934. The "Fusion" government was the result of the amalgamation of two unlikely bedfellows.[38] The Fusion government appointed Oswald Pirow (1890–1959), son of

German immigrants, as the Minister of Defence. His affinity for all things German went beyond his lineage, and he held a deep empathy for the Nazi regime. Indicators of his pro-Nazi fascist leanings included a visit to General Franco's headquarters during the Spanish Civil War and a later confidential meeting with Hitler, whom he declared was "perhaps the greatest man of the last thousand years."[39] Pirow's appointment aided and abetted South Africa's rather lackadaisical military posture.[40] His anti-mechanization attitude was infamously manifest in the anachronistic procurement of bush carts drawn by Malgache oxen. Pirow supposedly relied on the advice of the Chief of the Imperial General Staff, no less a figure than General von Lettow-Vorbeck, the legendary master of bush warfare.[41] Pirow contemplated the bush carts for a police action and not a full-blown conventional war, and in his words,

> The type of intervention eventually decided on by General Smuts in Abyssinia, North Africa and Italy was not only not contemplated by General Hertzog but was subsequently condemned by him as an unnecessary shedding of South African blood.[42]

However, Pirow's appointment signalled a significant budgetary increase for defense and with that, the UDF's dire situation began to partially reverse.[43] His proposed expansion of the UDF took the form of a five-year plan, envisaging, among other things, an air force of three squadrons, a reserve of 100,000 men, and a mechanized battalion.[44] The government proposed a census to determine what armaments were viable for local production.[45] The five-year plan promised much in the way of revitalizing and modernizing the UDF. However, good intentions did not translate into any meaningful procurement of modern equipment. The government remained reluctant to procure modern arms before a declaration of war, in an exercise designed to avoid obsolescence.[46]

Smuts believed South Africa's first line of defense lay outside the country. In contrast, the government policy toward defense at this time favored an expansion of the UDF for South Africa's defense and not that of the British Empire. South Africa's reexamination of defense policy was more due to concerns at Italy's bellicosity in invading Abyssinia in 1935 than with any desire to coordinate defense policy with the United Kingdom.[47] Defense policy did not include the formation of an expeditionary force, and Pirow remained adamant that the UDF would not be available for service outside of Africa.[48] He was not prepared to commit the UDF in advance and he refused to bind South Africa in a war that was not directly in her interests.[49] The government's supposed concession of moving the wartime frontier beyond South Africa's borders did not result in the formation of an expeditionary force.

The policies of the Fusion government gave structure to the UDF around the premise that in the event of a European conflict, South Africa would remain neutral. This policy persisted right up to the outbreak of the Second World War. Influential elements within the government and the opposition parties were adamant that the central role of the UDF was to protect South Africa's neutrality.[50] Neutrality would certainly be the case should the United Kingdom initiate a declaration of war. However, South Africa would come to Britain's aid should the Axis declare war. Smuts himself supported this neutralist stance before the Munich crisis of 1938. After these events had demonstrated the naked aggression of Germany, he changed his mind and saw the Axis as a threat to world peace.[51] Given South Africa's predisposition to neutrality, the Fusion government imagined a role for the UDF of protecting South Africa against internal threats and any other threats emanating from Southern Africa.[52] The Chief of General Staff, H. A. van Ryneveld (1891–1972),[53] was concerned about the possibility of an invasion by the black masses to the north of the Union. He expressed his apprehension about the policies of France, Belgium, and Portugal to arm blacks in their colonies, seeking thereby to strengthen their military capabilities in Africa.[54]

In 1935, the European power that posed the greatest threat to South Africa was Italy and her colonial possessions of Abyssinia and Somalia. South Africa found rare political unity around the issue of Italy and the mischief she had caused by invading and conquering Abyssinia in 1935.[55] South Africa was one of the louder voices calling for hard-hitting sanctions against Italy in the wake of her aggressive grab for Abyssinia. This was in direct contrast to the general ambivalence surrounding the support of the United Kingdom against Germany. South Africa took a harsh view regarding Italy and its threat to peace.[56] The Italian Air Force had the capability to reach targets in northern South Africa with some of its long-range bombers, magnifying South Africa's insecurity in this regard.[57] However, the poor to nonexistent infrastructure north of South

Africa's border lent little to support a major landward invasion, giving further impetus to those who made light of this possible threat.

Afrikaner nationalism and disaffection among a significant percentage of blacks shaped South African defense policy in the interwar years. The military viewed the real threat as one coming from disaffected sectors of the population within the country's borders. The possibility of a European enemy posing a landward threat was remote, as geography separated South Africa from large European forces by thousands of kilometers.[58] South Africa, in a quest for greater independence from the United Kingdom, chose a path of neutrality in any future European war. South Africa's ambiguous defence policy and its ambivalent attitude toward the empire at the highest levels of government, combined with general military neglect due to financial constraints during the depression, left the country with a token defense force on the eve of the war.

South Africa on the Eve of the Second World War

South Africa's declaration of war on Germany on September 6, 1939, was anything but a simple matter. For the other dominions, the entry into the Second World War signalled an abatement or cessation of party politics. Not so in South Africa, where it marked an escalation in domestic strife and bitterness.[59] The divisions in her society resulting in an ambiguous defense policy preceding the war were about to play out in the house parliament. Hertzog had always taken the stance that South Africa would only participate in a European war if its interests were at stake.[60] He had always adopted the position that the interests of the Union of South Africa took precedence over imperial sentiment, which in any event appealed to a minority of the population.[61] In fact, in September 1938 the whole cabinet, including Smuts, had agreed to a policy of neutrality should Britain and France declare war on Germany over Central European issues.[62]

Now that war had finally arrived, Hertzog and a significant portion of the South African population did not consider the invasion of Poland, nor the steady rise in Axis power and bellicosity, to be a direct threat to South Africa.[63] Hertzog viewed Germany's actions as an attempt to right the injustices imposed by the Treaty of Versailles.[64] He saw no difference between the present situation and that of the Munich crisis of 1938, during which South Africa signalled its intention to remain neutral. He expected his thirteen cabinet members, of which Smuts was one, to adopt the same position.[65] The British offer of a security guarantee to Poland materialized without genuine consultation with the dominions. Failure to consult caused deep unhappiness among them.[66] At a cabinet meeting on September 2, 1939, it was evident that the issue of neutrality had divided the government. In the face of Smuts leading a split cabinet, Hertzog had no option but to place the matter before parliament on September 4. The elected representatives would have to decide between Hertzog's neutrality and Smuts's proposal to join the war.[67]

In a somewhat bizarre turn of events, some plotted to overthrow the government in the case of a decision to remain neutral. Brigadier E. P. "Scrubbs" Hartshorn was part of a triumvirate who saw Hertzog's demands for neutrality as "virtual lip service to Germany."[68] Hartshorn was a charismatic one-armed soldier (an injury acquired as a result of a First World War wound) who would later see action with the UDF in East Africa and North Africa. The plan entailed the calling up of all members of the Active Citizen Force based in Johannesburg. The optimistic Hartshorn believed this process would gather 8,000 to 9,000 men sympathetic to the United Kingdom. From there, once all the citizen force members had been assembled and provided transport, the convoy would make its way toward Natal, which was a province of the Union of South Africa most predisposed toward the British Crown. It is unclear exactly what the conspirators hoped to achieve by this demonstration. Hartshorn expected that such a spectacular demonstration by the country's fighting men would exert massive moral force and win the day.[69] Happily for Hartshorn and perhaps the rest of South Africa, this pro-imperial rebellion was unnecessary.

Hertzog committed a tactical error by attempting to justify Hitler's actions in making his case for neutrality, and immediately opened himself up to the accusation of being pro-German and anti-British. He harmed his appeal for neutrality, which would have stood on firmer ground had it been based on real constitutional considerations.[70] Smuts took the opportunity to dismiss the call for neutrality as unsustainable with little chance of friend or foe honoring it. The dissension in the United Party cabinet was reflected in the party itself, resulting in a split between proponents of neutrality and those favoring war. After a heated debate lasting the whole day, the Smuts faction triumphed with a majority of eighty to sixty-seven, narrowly defeating Hertzog's motion of neutrality. Hertzog had no option but to resign in what amounted to a vote of no confidence, leaving Smuts to take over as prime minister. It is debatable whether South Africa would have gone to war had the Governor-General, Sir Patrick Duncan (1870–1943), granted Hertzog's wish to dissolve parliament and call for a general election. In any event, this was not put to the test as the Governor-General asked Smuts to form a government. The historian Giliomee draws attention to an authoritative journal, *Round Table*, which considered it likely that the antiwar faction would have won an election. Stewart agrees with this viewpoint, concluding that if Governor-General Sir Patrick Duncan had granted Hertzog a dissolution and a chance of a new election, he may have won, resulting in South Africa's neutrality.[71]

The streets of Johannesburg reflected the political divisions of parliament. Ugly scenes developed as police with drawn batons and ample tear gas charged the crowd of 700 surrounding the German club in the center of town. Active Citizen Force members gathered at the Drill Hall, tensely awaiting the decision of parliament. The authorities ordered German nationals to stand by in readiness to leave for Germany, and anxious Italian and German citizens, seeking South African citizenship, inundated the offices of the Department of the Interior.[72] No doubt those close to Hartshorn were relieved when South Africa chose a path at the side of the United Kingdom. For Afrikaner nationalists, it amounted to nothing less than a betrayal of the years of conciliation and nation-building under Hertzog.

Reconciliation in the interwar period all but buried the internecine conflict between Nationalist Afrikaners and those mainly English-speaking South Africans who supported the empire. The coalition Fusion government of the opposing sides had busied itself with building a South African nation and forgetting the past.[73] The arrival of war had once again rent open the old animosities in a large section of the white population.[74] In the first instance, those who had political power fractured almost immediately along language lines when deciding to remain neutral or go to war.[75] In the main, English-speaking white South Africans saw it as their duty to support Britain and the empire wholeheartedly in its hour of need. A significant portion of the Afrikaners were indifferent or opposed to entering the war.[76] Smuts's enthusiasm for the empire led to South Africa's wholehearted support of the war. Churchill and Smuts enjoyed a special bond based on their shared belief in empire. The two countries enjoyed excellent relations while under the premiership of both leaders, but this was not to survive once Churchill left office in July 1945. Andrew Stewart goes further and suggests that the Anglo–South African alliance owed its existence to the personal and respectful relationship between Smuts and Churchill.[77]

Many Afrikaners greeted Hertzog's resignation with joy, and they treated him as a hero and champion of the Afrikaner cause. On his trip back from parliament, from Cape Town to Pretoria, thousands cheered him. Afrikaner enthusiasm for Hertzog continued unabated, resulting in spontaneous demonstrations involving thousands of Afrikaans women who delivered demands that the government make immediate peace with Germany. Encouraged by this support, Hertzog, as the leader of the opposition, introduced a motion to parliament on January 23, 1940 calling for peace with Germany. According to Hertzog and many of his followers, "South Africa's participation in the war is the greatest blunder and most fatal mistake ever made by a responsible statesman."[78]

South Africa's domestic issues seem insignificant when measured against the immediate dangers posed by a world war. However, South Africa's entry into the war rocked its foundations, and for many weeks after the declaration the Nationalists who represented nearly 40 percent of the white population organized massive demonstrations.[79] There was a real threat of an Afrikaner rebellion along the lines of that which occurred at the outbreak of the First World War. South Africa's importance to the United Kingdom at that hour was one of real significance. Had South Africa remained neutral, it may have had dire consequences for the unity and morale of the Commonwealth. Consequences such as the denial of strategic resources for the Allied cause could have resulted in serious repercussions.

South Africa Goes to War September 1939–June 1940

Hertzog's defeat and Smuts's assumption of the premiership resulted in a sudden change of defense policy. The long-regarded policy of neutrality gave way to active participation in a European war in support of the Allies. South Africa found herself with a military force unsuited for the tasks set for it. The core of the three divisions eventually sent to meet the Axis in the Western Desert existed only on paper. One indicator of the pervasive neglect the military institution had suffered in the interwar years was the abandonment of physical training in 1923. Its reintroduction was only partial in 1937 and then full in 1939, a few months before the outbreak of the war.[80] Stringent cutbacks and neglect in the interwar years meant that the country went to war with a Permanent Force of 352 officers and 5,033 other ranks, together with an Active Citizen Force of 13,490 members. The UDF armored component consisted of two hopelessly obsolete tanks and two armored cars with next to no artillery pieces and eight antiaircraft guns.[81] The South African Air Force boasted a meager strength of two high-speed bombers, twenty-six obsolete general purpose planes, and forty training aircraft.[82] Apart from coastal defenses, South Africa possessed no navy. The army found itself poorly trained, underequipped, short of modern arms, and possessing mostly obsolete equipment.[83]

The Military Secretary, Collyer, furnished Smuts with a full report on the general conditions of the UDF soon after the declaration of war. In every respect, the fighting power of the UDF had fallen to abysmal levels. The most severe issue, and one that was perhaps unique among the Allies, was that South Africa had no defense plan. The lack of a coherent plan meant that there was no basis for calculating manpower, logistic, or equipment needs for any given course of action or event. There were only four fully trained and eleven partially trained staff officers in the UDF, and a further fourteen who had received elementary training.[84] The military was unable to conduct anything more than low-level internal security operations.

Adding to the woes of a derelict military were deep-seated political fissures. South Africa was unique among the Allies in having an official opposition entirely opposed to the country's participation in the war and obstructive to the war effort. Opposition to the war effort included vociferous attacks through the Afrikaans press and demonstrations, of which some were not peaceful. Subversive organizations flourished, some of which resorted to physical sabotage. Afrikaners daring to join the UDF faced the prospect of their kinfolk labeling them as traitors, and the same people often celebrated Allied battlefield defeats.[85] South Africa's declaration of war split the white population. Many Afrikaners sympathized with the Nationalist camp and found it contemptible to fight for the British. More than a few had open sympathy for the German cause and admired Germany for its racial and anti-Communist stance. An Afrikaans language poet, N. P. van Wyk Louw, thought it despicable to fight "for those who have conquered your own people."[86] Another example of Afrikaner resistance to participation in the war was the refusal of some Dutch Reformed Church ministers to allow soldiers in uniform to attend services.[87] This split in the white community would certainly diminish the fighting power of the UDF.

Smuts faced a dilemma in mobilizing South Africa's military machine. He gave way to political expediency and decided to recruit purely on a volunteer basis rather than rely on the Defence Act that provided for conscription of all able-bodied men below forty-five years of age. Smuts had assumed the premiership without a general election and had no indication as to the extent of his political support. A large proportion of the country was resolutely against the war and this left him with little other option than to build a pure volunteer force. Volunteers were required to sign a special attestation, and to distinguish them from other soldiers who refused to serve beyond South Africa's borders, they were required to wear a red tab on their shoulder straps.

The government policy of identifying volunteers for duty outside of South Africa with red tabs on their uniforms made those opposed to the war easily identifiable and their life within the military tough, with few prospects of employment if they resigned.[88] The fear of adverse consequences resulting from identification as "antiwar" must have provided an added negative incentive for many Afrikaners to take the "oath of loyalty." Afrikaners were not homogenous in their political viewpoints, but the motives of a significant number of those who eventually joined the UDF were unlike those of their English-speaking comrades who considered it their duty to assist the British Empire.[89] For Ike Rosmarin, a South African Jew, the red tabs were a ". . . golden opportunity to demonstrate a willingness to defend what was near and dear to me."

> In the beginning of 1940, I proudly signed on the dotted line. It was a great honour to wear the "Red Tabs" on my shoulder straps. Those red tabs indicated a readiness to serve anywhere in the world. Anti-Smuts and pro-Nazi supporters, however, took great delight in nicknaming us "Red Lice."[90]

The loyalty of a significant number of Afrikaner volunteers was rooted in a less than enthusiastic solidarity toward the British cause.[91]

Approximately half of the volunteers in the UDF were Afrikaners. A significant number joined up for purely financial reasons rather than any sense of duty to the defense of the British Empire.[92] The UDF provided a source of income for these Afrikaners, who, as a group, had been especially hard hit by the economic depression. As Grundlingh puts it, "their political convictions took second place to their material wants."[93]

If Afrikaners had mixed reasons for supporting the Allied war effort, then the black population of South Africa had every reason to tend toward reluctance. Blacks, denuded of political representation and treated everywhere as third-class citizens, had no lofty ideological incentive to participate in the war. Those blacks who eventually joined the UDF did so mainly for economic reasons, such as an opportunity to earn money and perhaps acquire a skill, their situation being grimmer than that of the Afrikaners.[94] The black grassroots level did necessarily share their leadership's expression of loyalty and support for the war effort. The African National Congress (ANC), traditional chiefs, and church groups saw the war as an opportunity for blacks to gain equal rights and ease racial policies by squeezing concessions from the government during wartime.[95] The experience of those blacks participating in the First World War did little to enhance black attitudes, as they sacrificed much in that war for small gain. Bill Nasson describes black attitudes:

> By the end of the 1930s, loyal, patient, and dutiful men had acquired a painful sense of the deception of voluntary service in wars not of their making. Neither the South African War (Anglo-Boer War) nor the Great War had brought the marginalised black majority civic reward or a political dividend for their pro-Empire patriotism. At a general level, the hindsight of history influenced attitudes to a further war. Certainly, thousands of individuals served in the Union Defence Force, but very many more were alienated, sceptical, or just too lethargic to be bothered.[96]

A writer for the first black newspaper, *Imvo Zabantsundu*, best summed up the feeling among blacks with these words,

> Why should we fight for you? We fought for you in the Boer War, and you left us to the Dutch. We also fought for you in the last war.

> Our lives were sacrificed for you in France as well as in East Africa. When that time was over, did anyone care about our future . . . was there ever concern about us? Truly, what have we to fight for?[97]

The government was initially reluctant to recruit any blacks for fear of antagonizing the active antiwar Afrikaner community.[98] When recruitment of blacks became unavoidable, due to the demands of the war, the UDF excluded those that enlisted from fighting duties and restricted them to unarmed support service roles, such as drivers, stretcher-bearers, cooks, clerks, and orderlies.[99] The re-forming of The Cape Corps went ahead on May 8, 1940, despite deep-seated reservations in certain quarters of the Afrikaner community. Because of a limited white population, necessity overcame prejudice and took precedence.[100] The formation of the Native Labour Corps on June 1, 1940, soon followed, providing essential noncombatant services for the UDF. Initially, there was no shortage of volunteers, but South Africa's inability to resort to conscription and restrictions in arming black troops would result in severe manpower shortages in the later stages of the desert war.[101] Blacks did serve with distinction in the Second World War despite the extremely adverse conditions in which they found themselves.

Black recruits faced appalling conditions of service at many levels.[102] They received different and fewer rations than their white comrades. Poor accommodation and less uniform issue were the norms for a black volunteer. The indefensible excuse was that due to their lower living standard their needs were comparatively less. Orders given in May 1941 ensured that black NCOs were to wear their badges of rank inverted so as to avoid friction with their white NCOs of the same rank. Initially, blacks received twelve days annual leave, compared to the thirty days for white soldiers. The highest rank held by a black soldier was staff-sergeant. That rank had worth only when commanding black troops, and black NCOs had no authority over "European" members of the forces. The iniquitous situation was no different when it came to remuneration. Black soldiers received a fraction of what white servicemen earned, even when performing the same duties.[103] Despite tremendous manpower shortages, political considerations took precedence in ensuring that the UDF denied blacks a real combat role. Lack of trained manpower manifested in the South Africans being able to field only two brigades instead of three at Sidi

Rezegh, which was a major contributor to the overrunning of the 5th Brigade on November 23, 1941.[104]

South Africa's economic position was in a better state than her threadbare military. The government had prepared South Africa on the economic front and, with rare foresight, the Department of Commerce and Industries had constructed plans to impose official controls to protect economic assets in the event of war. The National Supplies Control Board extended its control over imports and exports, wastage management, raw material management, price control, rationing, labor, production, distribution, and other critical economic factors. The Union Treasury introduced a wartime monetary policy that would ensure that the flow of vital war goods and essential services would remain uninterrupted.[105] The Union set about a rapid mobilization of the population, together with an overhauling of the country's industrial infrastructure to enhance the military capacity of the UDF. South Africa was the only industrialized country on the continent, and the country immediately began a manufacturing program to meet the demands of the war and equip the rapidly expanding military. Many factories that had been established to manufacture peacetime implements changed their structure to produce equipment for war. So successful was the transition to a war footing that South Africa was able to equip its units and even export some of its military material.[106]

The authorities decided to undertake the indigenous manufacture of artillery pieces when faced with few prospects of importing military necessities. The situation with small arms was equally disturbing, with shortages of 833 Bren Guns, 548 mortars, and 780 antitank rifles.[107] Collyer stated in his memorandum that "War material, arms and ammunition are scarce in every direction."[108] South Africa was fortunate in having a relatively well-developed mining and explosives industry that redirected its efforts into producing items such as mortar bombs, hand grenades, shells, and mines. The production of TNT increased sevenfold and innovations in the process of explosive manufacture produced new efficiencies. South Africa possessed vast quantities of the purest iron ore, with a well-established iron and steel industry and an abundance of coal and electrical power. A growing wartime industry manufactured other items, which included boots, socks, uniforms, blankets, beds, mattresses, medical supplies, and much more. The army equipped its soldiers almost exclusively with South African resources. Active Citizen Force units busied themselves with accepting volunteers and training 137,000 of them at various camps throughout the country.[109] The UDF cut instructor courses by half and prematurely commissioned officer cadets to meet the enormous demand for training and to swell the ranks. Therefore, through a combination of innovation, skilled mobilization of scarce resources, improvisation, and sheer determination, South Africa was able to build her military from scratch.

While Smuts waged a successful war on the economic front and began to rebuild the UDF, he faced ongoing resistance from the Afrikaner nationalists. Smuts faced a smoldering political situation fraught with uncertainties. Some past members of the Fusion government used a variety of parliamentary and extra-parliamentary methods to try and stymie the war effort. Oswald Pirow and Hertzog both began to agitate against the government.[110] Disapproval of the war effort would take many forms, from benign critical comments in parliament, to open hostility. Increasing incidents of antagonism to "red tab" members of the UDF occurred, and even some desperate attempts at sabotage took place, in addition to other treasonable activity by some members belonging to the disaffected rump of antiwar Afrikaners. Smuts took the precaution of ordering the handover of all privately owned rifles to the government, thus reducing the chances of rebellion. He ordered the internment of enemy aliens, together with Union citizens suspected of acting suspiciously or of conducting unlawful actions against the state.[111] Whatever the form of antiwar activity and the measures taken against it, from the more severe to the nonthreatening, the disgruntled attitude coming from a significant portion of the population would contribute to reducing the effectiveness of the fighting power of the UDF.

Despite the general clampdown on dissidents, thousands of young Afrikaner males were compelled to join the overtly neo-Nazi *Ossewabrandwag* (OB), which at its peak claimed a membership of hundreds of thousands.[112] The militants in the OB were hostile to Britain and sympathetic to Germany. Their leader, Hans Van Rensburg (1898–1966), envisioned a future based on National Socialism and made no secret of the National Socialist convictions that he held. His Nazi sympathies were disseminated throughout the OB, and his principles gained traction within the movement with every German victory.[113] The OB's paramilitary wing, the *Stormjaers*, committed numerous acts of sabotage against government installations and private property. They dynamited electrical power lines and railroads and cut telegraph and telephone lines. Beside sabotage, the regular OB members also harassed off-duty soldiers in uniform.[114]

In an almost miraculous fashion, under the implacable leadership of Smuts, South Africa mobilized its economy and manpower and managed to place the country on a war footing. Transformation of the military from its state of unpreparedness occurred in a relatively short period. Smuts's dogged resolve and South Africa's industrial sophistication ensured the UDF was able to oust the Italians from East Africa and after that to deploy three divisions to North Africa in time for Operation Crusader. It offered testament to the unbending determination of Smuts and his supporters, and to their unmitigated enthusiasm for the British Empire. The British held great store in Smuts's leadership being essential for good relations between the two countries and for the contribution that South Africa could make to the Allied cause.[115] However, the political divisions in South African society meant that Smuts would always have to cast one eye back on the home front in conducting the war.

South Africa's Changing Role with the Fall of France June 1940

It was fortunate for South Africa that Italian neutrality at the outset of the war, together with the remoteness of the European battlefields in relation to southern Africa, afforded the UDF approximately ten months in which to prepare for their first campaign in East Africa. The relatively isolated South Africans were distant from the first catastrophes that befell Europe. South Africa's role, because of her diminutive military and remoteness, was limited to the provision of strategic resources and moral support to the British war effort. This situation dramatically changed when France surrendered in June 1940 and the Vichy regime effectively became a German ally. Germany's easy defeat of France occasioned Italy's belated entry into the war and added to the shift in power. These two events fundamentally changed the balance of military power on the African continent toward the Axis.

Great Britain counted on France as an essential military partner not only in Europe but also in Africa. Britain did not envisage, by any stretch of the imagination, fighting a war against Germany or Italy without the aid of the sizeable French military.[116] The sudden demise of French military power placed Great Britain in a precarious position, creating a conspicuous lacuna in her defense policy that necessitated the immediate deployment of South African and empire forces to meet the impending Axis threat. The British, in the absence of France, were reliant on the resources of the dominions and their considerable economic, manpower, and military support to bolster her defenses. South Africa was required to play a significant role in aiding the United Kingdom in neutralizing the Italians in Africa. The French surrender, together with Italy's declaration of war, suddenly placed the British East African colonies and Britain's presence in Egypt in immediate danger. The Italians hopelessly outnumbered the British in manpower and fighting equipment in North and East Africa. Although numbers alone are not the sole constituent in determining fighting power, there was hardly any reason for the British to feel complacent.[117]

The false image of a courageous Britain facing the might of the rampant Axis powers alone was very far from the truth. The British enjoyed access to the massive manpower and economic resources of a vast empire. France's surrender immediately catapulted South Africa's strategic importance. Up to that date, the Union was dependent on Britain for most of her military needs. She would have to become self-sufficient and give way to Britain's priority of reequipping her devastated army in the wake of the disastrous Dunkirk evacuation. It was a task that South Africa embraced energetically, and she not only achieved self-sufficiency militarily but was able to become a significant producer of arms and munitions for the Allied war effort.[118] South Africa's importance to the Allied cause went beyond that of providing a strategic base, vital raw materials, and military hardware. Churchill, a longtime friend and admirer of Smuts, often took Smuts into his confidence; this was unlike his treatment of the other dominion leaders. Smuts became politically indispensable to Britain, being a great supporter and friend to Churchill and somewhat of a military expert. He became a Field Marshal in the British Army in 1941 and served in the Imperial War Cabinet, sharing a strong common belief in the concept of empire.

However, South Africa's support of the United Kingdom was not entirely altruistic nor based purely on loyalty. Although the strategic threats to the British Empire and those facing South Africa did not coincide perfectly, there was a close strategic congruence when it came to imperial designs on Africa and South Africa's latent expansionist interests. South Africans, in general, regarded East Africa and especially Kenya as being in their backyard. Smuts among others had grand imperial designs of incorporating much of East Africa into a greater South African state.[119] At the heart of British–South African relations lay the general expansionist aims of the various South African governments who coveted the British HCT and other territories farther to the north. Smuts sought to form a united state stretching possibly to the equator, including South West Africa and southern Mozambique. Pretoria would be the actual geographical capital of the "Greater South Africa." Smuts saw this expansion as part of an imperial plan, whereas Hertzog and his Nationalists shared these same objectives but more as an Afrikaner entitlement. Therefore, the differences lay in their motives and not their aims.[120] The British were reluctant to feed South African expansionist aims by turning over the HCT in the face of the blatant racist attitude of successive South African governments and Afrikaner nationalist aspirations for an independent South Africa. This denial of expansionist aims was one of the leading causes of political conflict between South Africa and Britain in the run-up to the Second World War.[121]

One of Smuts's goals on entering the Second World War was his intention to formalize South Africa's territorial claim to South West Africa. Failure to annex the territory peeved Smuts and Hertzog, and instead they had to make do with a mandate. Smuts gambled on a reward for South Africa's impeccable war record in the form of the formalized incorporation of South West Africa into the Union. None other than Churchill encouraged him to annex the territory, but India dealt any chance of incorporation a final blow when they blocked the transfer at the United Nations, based on South Africa's unacceptable racial policy.[122]

A resurgent Smuts was behind the most extraordinary of all the bids to obtain Swaziland on the eve of the Second World War. He attempted to resuscitate prospects for a Greater South Africa. One of his first acts was the request to transfer Swaziland to the Union. His prime motivation was to strengthen his hand against the nationalists, by taking advantage of Britain's preoccupation with the war and gratefulness for South Africa's support.[123] His act of brinkmanship diplomacy met with a sharp rebuff from Anthony Eden (1897–1977), the Secretary of State for Dominion Affairs in October 1939. Eden sent a message through Sir William Clark (1876–1952), Britain's high commissioner to South Africa.

> It has come as an unpleasant surprise to me that General Smuts wishes to raise the transfer question again at the moment. It would certainly be wrong to assume that Parliament would be indifferent to the matter if there was any suggestion of trying to make use of the present preoccupation of public opinion with the conduct of the war to force through transfer of any of the Territories, if there should be strong opposition from the native inhabitants.[124]

Smuts, not easily deterred, sent Deneys Reitz (1882–1944), the Minister of Native Affairs, to once again broach the subject personally in London. Eden again issued strong words in an attempt to end the problem: "It would be a grave mistake to underrate the public interest in this matter at the present time. Nothing could make a worse impression than if we were to hand over these Territories in a time of war when we were fighting for the interests of small nations."[125]

The British sharply rebuffed Smuts's attempts to force a hand over the HCT during the war years. Smuts took the opportunity, on the occasion of the fall of France and Italy's entry into the Second World War in June 1940, to advance to Churchill his understanding of the strategic role of South Africa in the defense of the British Empire in Africa. Smuts saw Africa as the next logical target for the victorious but largely idle German army. He saw the Germans joining the Italians in first conquering French territory in North Africa and then moving inexorably southward, down to the southern tip of Africa. Smuts considered South Africa crucial to the British retaining India, Australia, and New Zealand. In his words, "To save the Empire and the Commonwealth it is, therefore, necessary to hold Africa South of the Equator at all costs in this war." He continued to request a "number of British and Dominion divisions to be deployed to East and West Africa to assist the effort of South Africa." Smuts saw Southern Africa as, ". . . not a sideshow but a vital area of Empire."[126] In his reply Churchill politely disagreed with Smuts and insightfully considered that Hitler's next move would be in an eastward direction in Europe.[127] One must contextualize Smuts's opportunistic attempt to centralize the empire's strategy toward the African continent in terms of his desire to expand South Africa's territory in an exercise of sub-imperialism.

In 1938, Portugal's African colonies barely survived Hitler's dismissal of a British appeasement attempt to offer Portuguese African territory in order to satiate Germany's European territorial demands. If Portugal's entry into the First World War saved her African territories from being divided up between the United Kingdom and Germany, then her neutrality in the Second World War almost resulted in the Union Defence Force invading Mozambique, soon after South Africa's declaration of war.[128] The Union Defence Force had not been idle in the interwar period and had drawn up an elaborate plan for the invasion of Southern Mozambique and the securing of the port of Lourenço Marques. Major Leipoldt undertook the formulation of Plan Z[129] after the armistice. The UDF tasked Leipoldt, while he still served on the South West Africa Boundary Commission, to evaluate whether South Africa might become involved in military operations in Portuguese East Africa.[130]

Given the long previous history of South Africa's acquisitive desires for Delagoa Bay, it would be naive to assume a purely military role behind Plan Z. The need for a plan evolved from a perceived threat from Portugal in the interwar years. There was a possibility that an Axis intelligence and military force would use Mozambique as a base. During the interwar period, Portugal strengthened her garrisons in her African possessions and made a topographical study of her borders with South Africa. The activities of Portuguese intelligence officers and cartographers made Pretoria nervous. The fact that the Portuguese were soon to reinforce their seven military aircraft in Lourenço Marques with an additional seven added to the general disquiet. The establishment of some radio stations in Angola was of particular concern, as this had been the primary casus belli regarding German South West Africa (GSWA).[131]

The Second World War brought its insecurities regarding Mozambique and a possible Nazi takeover of Lourenço Marques. The UDF tasked Brink with making a plan involving at least one motorized brigade to invade and seize Lourenço Marques if the need arose. The controversial decision to go ahead if Italy entered the war was confirmed on June 10, 1940. The UDF ordered the brigade commander of 1st South African Infantry Brigade, Colonel John Daniel, to invade within an hour. A breakdown in logistics and an inexplicable unavailability of fuel caused the delay of the operation. A shortage of vehicles and persisting fuel problems caused a further delay. Despite all the problems, which included wireless sets not working and reckless driving, elements of 1st Brigade began to assemble at Komatipoort on the border by June 12. The original bold plan of sweeping through to Lourenço Marques diminished to one of taking up defensive positions in Komatipoort. This change of heart occurred in the face of overwhelming disorganization, and perhaps, intervention from a higher source.[132]

South Africa came within a whisper of invading Mozambique and occupying Lourenço Marques, and had the operation not faced logistic issues, the long dream of acquiring Delagoa Bay would have been a reality. Nasson is not only dismissive of South Africa's plan to invade and secure Delagoa Bay and Lourenço Marques in 1940, describing it incorrectly as "never more than an idea," but also prefers to draw the more obvious conclusions. He ignores South Africa's and the United Kingdom's long history of acquisitive desire for the Portuguese territory.[133]

With the immediate threat to southern Africa receding, Plan Z remained mostly dormant, until once again it received stimulus with Japan's entry into the war in December 1941. The UDF felt that the Japanese (or Vichy French) threatened Lourenço Marques due to its proximity to Madagascar and the alleged enemy military interest in that island.[134] The Allies also linked the securing of Portuguese assets in Africa to the necessity of securing the Azores and the Cape Verde islands should Gibraltar become unusable, or in the event of Spanish or Portuguese hostility.[135] Churchill was anxious to coordinate his seizure of the Azores and Cape Verde islands with South Africa's seizure of Portuguese East Africa and other Portuguese African territories, but not at the expense of bringing Portugal and Spain into the war against the Allies.[136] However, South Africa's intervention in securing Portuguese assets, whether unilaterally or as part of a joint operation with the British, was a strong possibility in the early stages of the war. South Africa continued to apply pressure as late as December 1942, in the form of expressing her distaste at the hostile activities of notorious German agents in Lourenço Marques, and Smuts threatened that he would not tolerate any sinking of troopships in the close vicinity of Delagoa Bay.[137]

Smuts was not averse to applying a political solution to acquiring Mozambique, and he considered the possibility of making "tentative" approaches himself to the government of Portuguese East Africa to offer Union "protection." Smuts made it quite clear that, should the Portuguese accept the Union's "protection," he would be unwilling to return the colony to the *status quo ante* after hostilities had ended, stating that

"Their fate would be decided by the issue of war." According to the High Commissioner for the United Kingdom in South Africa, Sir Edward John Harding, Smuts wanted a much closer association developed after the war between the Union and neighboring territories in southern Africa. According to Harding, Smuts imagined something akin to a "Pan African Union" with very close economic relations.[138]

Conclusion

South Africa's entry into the Second World War was unlike that of any of the other dominions, due to a large proportion of its population harboring extreme hostility to the war effort. Many Afrikaners had not fully recovered from the effects of the Anglo-Boer War, and those who had a nationalist bent wished to distance themselves from the United Kingdom. Blacks too were wary and hence apathetic as the promise of more political freedom never materialized as a result of their support for the United Kingdom in the Anglo-Boer War and the First World War. The interwar years under Hertzog saw a growth in determination not to subject South Africa to the same internal acrimony in the event of another European war. A clear policy emerged, which envisaged a neutral South Africa or one that would only enter a war if directly threatened. The likelihood of this threat remained remote and consequently, South Africa prepared its defense force to meet an internal rather than an external threat. The government gave low priority to defence expenditure and military preparation in the face of tough economic times and a very remote external threat.

South Africa dispensed with its neutrality on September 6, 1939, by only the narrowest of margins. The country's declaration of war was, in fact, a reversal of the government policy of neutrality that had been in effect for many years. The price paid to support the United Kingdom was immediate political polarization. South Africa managed to avoid rebellion on her entry into the Second World War, although politically, the decision was no less divisive than entry into the First World War. Afrikaner nationalists joined forces in opposition to the war effort and the country once again divided on language lines. Years of nation-building in the interwar years lay in tatters, and once again attitudes hardened and political fissures widened.

South Africa was ill-prepared to meet the demands of a modern European war. The policy of neutrality and the emphasis on suppressing internal disorder robbed the UDF of the equipment and training to fight a modern conventional war. The UDF was in an abysmal state on the eve of the war, after years of neglect and downsizing. The UDF was devoid of a war plan or staff that could construct one. Despite the obvious difficulties and political risks, Smuts was determined to get South Africa into the war firmly on the side of the British. Smuts did not base his support for the United Kingdom purely on loyalty or altruism. Despite the glaring deficiencies in the UDF, Smuts saw in the war an opportunity of furthering South Africa's expansionist aims. The final annexation of South West Africa, the incorporation of Swaziland, and the long-cherished occupation of Portuguese Delagoa Bay were an important part of what fuelled Smuts's war ambitions.

Good fortune allowed Smuts a period of some ten months grace before the surrender of France and the inclusion of Italy in the war in June 1940. These two events changed the balance of power in Africa firmly toward the Axis powers and brought the war considerably closer to South Africa's borders. South Africa would have to deploy forces to aid the substantially stretched British Empire in Africa. The evacuation of the British Expeditionary Force from Dunkirk, with the consequential loss of massive amounts of equipment, ensured that South Africa would have to rely primarily on its own resources to pursue the war. Dogged determination coupled with a modern industrialized economy ensured that South Africa was able to mobilize considerable forces and equip them. This remarkable achievement took enormous skill and determination in placing South African resources on a war footing. The mobilization of South Africa's war economy stands out as a great success, and at its peak it was able to supply its armed forces with a good proportion of the essential materials needed to conduct the war, as well as some of the key items needed throughout the empire.

The UDF remained the product of an ambiguous and divisive political system despite the enormous progress in building a credible army. The three divisions eventually fielded were primarily light motorized infantry, and were therefore highly vulnerable to the mechanized and armored might of the Axis forces. Training was deficient due to years of lacking modern mechanized equipment, and experience in handling brigade- or divisional-size units was negligible. The divisive nature of South African politics filtered into the military and precluded conscription and the deployment of blacks as fighting troops, significantly diminishing the ultimate fighting power of the UDF. Fortunately the UDF's first test of combat would be against a less formidable foe, in the form of the Italian colonial forces in East Africa.

Chapter 2

The East African Campaign July 1940–June 1941

From personal experience, I know what awaits you. I know what war means—seven years of my life have been spent in wars. They were among the hardest years of my life, but they were also full of the richest experience that life can give. I would not exchange my war experiences of the Anglo-Boer War and the last Great War for all the gold on the rand. You are going to face danger, hardship and sacrifice—perhaps death itself—in all its fierce forms. But through it all, you will gather that experience of life and enrichment of character which are more valuable than gold or precious stones. You will become better and stronger men. You will not return the same as you went. You will bring back memories that you and yours will treasure for life. Above all, you will have that proud consciousness that you have done your duty by your country and rendered your contribution to its future security and happiness.[1]

France Surrenders and Italy Declares War June 1940

Mussolini declared war on France and Great Britain on June 10, 1940. Italian opportunism placed the British colonies in East Africa and their forces in Egypt and the Middle East under immediate threat. The French surrender on June 22, 1940, exacerbated an already precarious situation. The Vichy French government, predisposed to Germany, made redundant the defensive plans of the British in East and North Africa. Britain factored in France's strong African colonial army in her defense estimates at the outset of the war. French forces were no longer available and were now hostile, leaving Britain's African possessions exposed. South Africa was remote from the war initially and her significant contribution to the war effort was one of moral support for the United Kingdom. Italy's declaration of war and France's surrender were game changers. The once distant conflict moved uncomfortably close to South Africa's doorstep.[2]

In the absence of the French, Britain would rely heavily on South Africa to protect her overseas assets in East Africa. South Africa, in turn, could no longer rely on Britain for essential war supplies. The British were preoccupied with garnering all their resources to rebuild their depleted army, much of whose equipment lay strewn on the beaches of Dunkirk. South Africa used the ten months from the start of the war to Italy's entry profitably building up the UDF and placing the country on a war footing.

The UDF Departs for East Africa July 1940

South Africa officially declared war on Italy on June 11, 1940, after the Italian declaration of war on the United Kingdom the day before. Hostilities opened with an air raid. Four South African Air Force Junkers (Ju 86) took off from Nairobi in Kenya and bombed a large Banda[3] camp at Moyale, a border town in Abyssinia.[4] The UDF had busied itself with the formation and preparation of the 1st SAI Brigade for deployment to Kenya before the declaration of war. The brigade's first inauspicious action was a rush to Komatipoort, a town on South Africa's border with Portuguese Mozambique. The operation was part of the dubious Plan Z (see chapter 1) and the exercise, fraught with accidents and mechanical breakdowns, had not proved an outstanding success. For unexplained reasons, unresolved some seventy-five years after the event, South Africa refrained from seizing Portuguese territory and the bulk of the brigade withdrew back into the interior.[5]

On June 19, 1940, Colonel D. H. Pienaar received an appointment as the officer in command of the 1st SAI Brigade. Pienaar was a proud Afrikaner, descended from generations of farmers. He was born in 1893, and shortly after that, his father and his two elder brothers went off to do battle with the British on the occasion of the Second Anglo-Boer War of 1899. The latter part of the war saw Pienaar interned together with his mother and four other siblings in one of the infamous British concentration camps. He emerged from the concentration camp less embittered than most other Afrikaners subjected to the harsh and sometimes deadly conditions of internment. After the war, Pienaar's father and two brothers reunited with the rest of the family. They returned to their derelict farm, victims of the scorched-earth policy of the British occupiers. Pienaar struggled for years with difficult farming conditions and only obtained a rudimentary schooling, after which he joined the Natal Police in 1911.[6]

He trained to be a gunner, under the terms of the new Defence Act of 1912 that allowed the police an artillery section. Pienaar soon transferred to the UDF and saw his first action as a gunner in the Northern Cape against his kith and kin who took part in the Afrikaner Rebellion of 1914. In a bizarre turn of fate he met his rebel uncle, a new prisoner of war, and the two exchanged recriminations. Pienaar served as a corporal in the German South West African campaign of 1915. Promoted to sergeant in 1916, he went on to serve in the German East African campaign. There he fought bravely, was mentioned in dispatches and, like so many of his compatriots, became seriously ill with malaria. After convalescing back in South Africa, he again served in Palestine, Egypt, and Syria in 1917. He saw action against the Turks as battery sergeant-major and narrowly escaped death several times. He received his commission in 1918 and continued to serve with the British in the Senussi rebellion of 1919. There he gained his first experience of the Egyptian desert, where he was destined to fight on the same battlefields during the Second World War. He qualified, on course in England, as an acting battery major, coming a credible fourth in his class. Returning to South Africa in December 1919, he reverted to his rank of corporal. His time on the campaign had given him valuable experience in bush and desert warfare and honed his skills as a capable artillery officer.[7]

Pienaar found time to marry and attend an advanced artillery course at Salisbury Plain in England in 1920. Returning to South Africa after a year, he received a promotion to a substantive lieutenant and served at the Military College, where he lectured in gunnery. He obtained his captain's rank in 1926 and transferred to the Staff Corps at Defence Headquarters. He remained there for five years and eventually transferred to become a battery commander with the rank of major. He once again served time at the Military College and in 1934, took over command of Free State Command with the rank of lieutenant-colonel. Pienaar's wife died in 1937, a significant blow from which he took years to recover. In evident despair, he spent an inordinate amount of time at work, which included spates of heavy drinking in the officers' mess. He drank so heavily that it became a problem for his fellow officers and friends and the situation steadily worsened up to the outbreak of the war. In 1938 he transferred to become an officer commanding Transvaal Command and became a full colonel two months before the outbreak of the war. Fortunately for himself and those he commanded, he was able to get a grip and overcome his problem. He did not touch another drink for the duration of the war.[8]

The 1st SAI Brigade received a warning for a possible deployment to Kenya on June 27, 1940. The brigade set sail from Durban on July 17, 1940.[9] The 1st SAI Division was formed on August 18, 1940, under the command of Major-General George Brink and consisted of 1st SAI Brigade, already in Kenya, together with the 2nd SAI Brigade (under the command of Brigadier F. L. A. Buchanan) and 5th SAI Brigade (under the command of Brigadier B. F. "Billy" Armstrong). Lieutenant-Colonel W. H. E. Poole received an appointment as the divisional staff officer. The 2nd SAI Brigade reached Mombasa on July 17, 1940, followed by the 5th SAI Brigade on November 27, 1940. The 2nd SAI Division, commanded by Major-General I. P. de Villiers, the former Commissioner of Police, was to remain in South Africa, seeing its first significant action at Tobruk in June 1942.[10]

The departure of 27,000 South Africans via the 1st SAI Division to Kenya bolstered the meagre 8,500 British defenders facing an Italian army many times its size.[11] The British had to defend a frontier of nearly 1,600 km with these same paltry forces. This situation had considerably improved by December 1940, and Lieutenant-General Alan Cunningham (1887–1983), General Officer in Command (GOC) East Africa Force (1940–August 1941),[12] had a force at his disposal of 77,000, of which 27,000 were South Africans, 6,000 Europeans, 33,000 Native East Africans, and 9,000 West Africans.[13] The British faced His Royal Highness (HRH) Prince Amadeo of Savoy, the 3rd Duke of Aosta (1898–1942), and the Viceroy and Governor-General of Italian East Africa,[14] who had at his disposal 291,176 Italian troops, 39 light tanks, and 126 armored cars. Of the Italian troops and paramilitary forces deployed in East Africa, 70 percent were colonial troops, which varied considerably in quality. The vast majority were of an irregular nature and had no stomach for the conventional war about to descend on them. The Italians recruited, trained, and equipped East African irregulars, collectively referred to as the Banda, to do no more than carry out policing duties and maintain order in the colony, rather than fight a European army. Significant parts of the colonial army deserted at the first sign of the approaching enemy, while only some fought bitterly and bravely in isolated actions.[15]

The best of the Italian force were the regular units of the Savoy Grenadier Division, the *Alpini* Regiment and a Blackshirt Legion. They gave a great account of themselves at the battle of Keren (February 5 to April 1, 1941) some months later. Fortunately, the South Africans found none of these elite units on the Kenyan border.[16] The Italian forces facing the British had further problems besides a lack of mobility and questionable military training. They lacked sufficient medical facilities to treat the diseases, especially malaria, endemic to that area of Africa. In similar fashion to previous campaigns fought in this field, the majority of casualties suffered on both sides came not from the clash of belligerents, but from a neutral but lethal third party—disease. The most common ailments were snake and scorpion bites. Many soldiers carried small containers of permanganate of potash to treat bite wounds instantly.[17] The Duke of Aosta fell victim to disease during the siege of Amba Alagi, succumbing to tuberculosis and malaria on March 3, 1942, barely a few months after his capture.

Lack of mobility impeded the massive Italian army, proving to be a fatal flaw. The Italians lacked the required motorized transport needed to cover the vast distances in their territory. The South Africans, by comparison, were lavishly equipped with motorized transport. South African industry had gone to great lengths to supply enough vehicles of all descriptions to ensure the motorized transportation of every member of the brigade into battle. An SAI Brigade required 672 trucks in first-line transport, as against only 120 for the King's African Rifles, and trucks were crucial to their mobility in Africa, supplanting the thousands of porters used in the previous war. The South African Ford Company alone assembled 18,349 trucks for the South African Forces during the first year of the war.[18] The South African motorized brigade was in many ways the successor to the highly mobile Boer Commando, which was essentially mounted infantry.

In the Boer War, the Boer commando developed a doctrine of maneuvering to fight, which was different from the British who, due to logistical constraints, fought to facilitate movement. General Louis Botha's rapid and successful First World War campaign in German South West Africa in 1915 cemented the South African doctrine of maneuver warfare. Smuts, with much controversy, applied the same principles a year later in German East Africa when he managed to dislodge the Germans rapidly from the territory. He used maneuver to outflank the well-entrenched

Germans, compelling them to abandon their chosen and well-prepared positions. He forced them to fight on ground less suitable for the defense by dislodging them from their prepared positions. These tactics were born out of a Boer aversion to expensive frontal assaults and battles of annihilation, a strong preference of the British and Germans in many battles.[19]

The war started tentatively for the Italians, who opened proceedings on June 13, 1940, by bombing the Rhodesian airbase at the fort located at Wajir, Kenya. Despite enjoying an overwhelming superiority in numbers, the Italians remained mostly inert. Most of the activity on their part occurred on the northern border with Sudan rather than the southern border of Kenya. Lack of mobility and poor logistics restricted Italian efforts to seize Sudanese and Kenyan border towns. The British, having nothing more than three companies in the Sudan, had few options but to fall back.[20] The Italians went over to the defensive in the Sudan after capturing the railroad junction at Kassala and the small British fort at Gallabat. They occupied Fort Harrington in Kenya, and by the end of July Italian forces reached the villages of Dabel and Buna—their deepest penetration of the campaign. The Italians invaded British Somaliland on August 3, 1940. The ill-equipped British contingent of 4,000 men, possessing very little artillery and no antitank weapons, faced 25,000 Italian troops equipped with armor. The British successfully evacuated their forces from British Somaliland by August 17, 1940, after being numerically overwhelmed with little chance of forming an effective defense. It is noteworthy that the conquest of British Somaliland was the only example of a victory achieved by Italy without the support of their German allies during the Second World War. Italian war efforts elsewhere in the latter part of 1940 met with military disaster.[21] These initial victories in East Africa forced the Italians to adopt a defensive posture.

Brink, the commander of the 1st SAI Division, was known affectionately as "Uncle George" to his troops and his colleagues. He was born in the Orange Free State in 1889 to a family of two sisters and a younger brother. He, like Pienaar, would experience the bitterness of British occupation, among other indignities suffering eviction from his home, the arrest of his father, and a spell in a concentration camp with his family.[22] In similar fashion to Pienaar, he emerged from the Boer War experience with relatively little dislike for the British. His family crest bore the Latin motto "*Aequus in Arduis*," translated to "Calm in Adversity," and he displayed this trait when faced with military adversity.[23] Brink, a strapping six-foot-four and twenty-five years old, took a commission in the fledgeling UDF in November 1914, having served as a military clerk for a number of years.

He received his baptism of fire in the Afrikaner Rebellion of 1914 and went on to serve as a staff officer in the successful German South West Africa campaign of 1915. His impeccable conduct as a brigade major in that campaign ensured that he was thrice mentioned in dispatches and awarded both the French *Croix de Guerre* and the Distinguished Service Order.[24] Brink became a staff captain in the 1st Mounted Brigade on April 12, 1916, during the German East African campaign. He returned to South Africa at the end of 1916 suffering heavily from malaria. He came back to East Africa in 1917 as a major, serving as a staff officer under the new South African Commander in Chief, Lieutenant-General Jacob van Deventer (1874–1922).[25] There he remained until the end of the First World War.[26]

After the war, he reverted to the rank of a substantive captain and in 1919, he married. As mentioned in chapter 1, Brink attended the staff course in Camberley under Brigadier-General John Dill. On his return to South Africa, he accepted a post at the South African Military College as adjutant and officer instructor. Brink was an avid reader of military history. He was assigned as staff officer Van Deventer (1874–1922) in the Rand Revolt of 1922, another of those internal insurrections that plagued the early life of the Union. Brink was back at the Military College after the revolt and became its chief instructor in tactics. Promotion prospects were slow in peacetime, and Brink, a father of three daughters, became a major at the age of forty-one in 1931. The following year he took over the command of the college from Van Ryneveld, Chief of the General Staff from 1933, with the rank of lieutenant-colonel. During this period, Brink was instrumental in forming the Special Services Battalion, which mopped up desperately jobless young men and provided them with discipline and purpose.[27] It was a highly successful venture and men recruited to this battalion served in the Second World War with distinction. His superiors tasked Brink with reviving the decrepit Cape Command in 1934, a job he performed with distinction. Oswald Pirow sent Brink abroad in 1937 to study the organization, equipment, and training methods of the British and continental armies. He visited the armies of Great

Britain, Germany, France, Italy, and Denmark and attended German and French maneuvers.[28]

Major von Poppenheim, of the Attaché Group at the German War Office, questioned him closely as to the purpose of his staff visit in Germany. Brink stated in no uncertain terms that his visit to Germany was of no political significance and that he was merely visiting the Third Reich to "learn as much as possible about the organization, training and equipment of the new German Army."[29] Brink found himself attached to an infantry regiment (the equivalent of a South African Infantry brigade) for three weeks, and he attended a two-day, full-scale field exercise. He witnessed, first hand, the German method of air cooperation and night exercises. Brink left Germany with a favorable impression of her military prowess. He had been particularly impressed with the fitness of German youth, honed by compulsory six-month service with the *Arbeitsdienst* before a two-year stint of national service. In stark contrast were the poor fitness levels found in the UDF. Brink went on to visit the Italian Army and there was able to witness the *Regiment Genoa* and other units on maneuvers. He carefully took note of Italian abilities, with an eye to facing them as a future enemy in Abyssinia. He was unimpressed with their physique and training regimen. There was a tendency to bunch up in the attack and the frontal area of 800 m seemed too narrow for a battalion. His attendance in France of armored maneuvers left him with the indelible impression that the French had little chance against the *Wehrmacht*. Over the period September 25–27, 1937, Brink was fortunate enough to be able to attend the British Army's yearly Infantry and Tank Maneuvers on Salisbury Plain.[30]

Brink had gained valuable insight into the motorization and mechanization of the major continental armies, and better informed and motivated by what he had seen in Europe, he returned to South Africa and took up the position of Director of Military Organisation and Training.[31] On his promotion to brigadier general in 1938, as the Deputy Chief of Staff, he busied himself with applying some of the lessons learned in Europe, especially those from the *Wehrmacht*. The formulation of his doctrine found its roots in his experiences as a staff officer in East Africa, and he sought to create a brigade group with integral supporting arms, able to operate independently of the division. Motorization of the troops and artillery would facilitate mobility in a war of maneuver, and they would drive right up to the battlefront, where they would dismount at the last moment.[32] The coming battle against the Italians in East Africa would test the effectiveness of Brink's foresight and planning.

The British, hopelessly outnumbered, were everywhere on the retreat before the arrival of the South Africans in East Africa. Bolstered by the South African 1st SAI Brigade under Pienaar, it was time to go on the offensive. British plans consisted of an attack on the northern front emanating from Sudan, commanded by Lieutenant-General Sir William Platt (1885–1975), GOC of the Sudan Defence Force.[33] This northern front would be the main offensive effort. The secondary effort would be an offensive launched from Kenya under the command of Cunningham. The third offensive effort would take the form of an amphibious assault in British Somaliland, followed by an advance into Abyssinia. The northern and southern offenses began in January 1941, with Cunningham launching his first attacks across the Kenyan border into southern Abyssinia.[34]

FIRST BLOOD AT EL WAK FOR THE 1ST SAI BRIGADE DECEMBER 1940

Before the general offensive got under way, the 1st SAI Brigade launched an attack on December 16, 1940. The focal point of the assault was El Wak, one of many stone forts that marked Italian-controlled Somaliland and the British-controlled Kenyan border. The operation combined the South Africans and the 24th Gold Coast Brigade, and together they faced the Italian 191st Colonial Infantry Battalion. Pienaar went to great lengths to ensure that the operation would result in success. He had a replica of the battlefield laid out some 60 km down the road from where the action proper was to take place. The exercise orders were as close as possible to those in the actual operation. Rehearsals of the plan, including air cooperation and approach march, took place according to a strict timetable.[35] He built a large-scale model of the battlefield, enabling the officers and NCOs to study the operation in detail. Demonstrations as to the importance of cooperation between infantry and tanks, especially when dealing with machine-gun posts, took place in the preparation phase.[36] Pienaar trained his men extensively before the attack on El Wak, including debussing from vehicles, movement through the bush on compass bearings, camouflaging vehicles and equipment, as well as digging trenches. The brigade practiced mass movement using transport vehicles at night with no lights to retain the element of surprise. It is interesting to contrast this doctrine with Pienaar's later reluctance to move at night in the North African desert war. This reluctance was to cost the South Africans dearly.[37]

The plan called for an enveloping movement to cut off and block the anticipated retreat of the Italians.[38] The thick bush surrounding the objective inhibited a quick envelopment while affording the Italians a concealed escape route. The attacking force divided into three columns, Dickforce, Pinforce, and the divisional troops. These columns moved up to the British landing ground close to British El Wak before first light on December 15. Troops rested for the remainder of the day and no further movement would take place before the onset of evening. Dickforce split into columns A and B, having their objectives as Areas X, Y, and Z, respectively. Pinforce, under Pienaar, was to follow in the rear of column A, finally splitting off to cover areas V and W in an enveloping movement. The attack would proceed after a half-hour artillery bombardment on area X commencing at 0745, thereafter rolling to area V for half an hour. Air bombing raids would take place at the same time as the artillery barrage. The infantry would attack once the gunners lifted the barrage, and the armored cars would then exploit in a northerly direction from the objectives.[39]

The approach march from the base to the objective was some 180 km, of which the last 60 km was under the cover of dark.[40] Approximately 1,100 vehicles made the journey over appalling road conditions that reduced the convoy to less than 8 km an hour over some of the worst sections. The slow-moving and dense columns relied upon air superiority for cover. As it happened, the Italians managed to launch a single Caproni bomber, which released anti-personnel bombs and strafed the landing ground on December 16 at 0615. Fortunately, the Allies suffered no casualties as a result of this attack.[41] That only two vehicles broke down on the approach march out of 1,134 assigned to the operation was a testament to their high level of maintenance. Assigned engineers improved the road wherever possible to ease the advance.[42]

It was the first engagement in which the South Africans fielded light tanks and armored cars. The formation of the South African Tank Corps took place in May 1940. The South Africans received twelve (five ton) British Mk III Vickers Light tanks in Kenya in June 1940, shipped from Egypt. Imperial Army tank instructors trained the South Africans in

Kenya. The Tank Corps expanded to two battalions by the end of June 1940 and consisted of five armored cars and two motorcycle companies, together with the No. 1 Light Tank Company already serving in Kenya. The first-line establishment of each armored car company was twenty-two armored cars, fourteen motorcycles, seven motorcycle combinations, one motor car, and twenty-one trucks. Three armored and two motorcycle companies soon joined the No. 1 Light Tank Company in East Africa.[43] Initially South African doctrine precluded the use of armored cars in the role of the infantry tanks in a frontal assault. Their primary function was that of reconnaissance and in the attack, they made use of their mobility rather than brute force.[44] South Africans found that it was best to combine motorized infantry with the armored cars in a combined arms fashion, the one supporting the other in the dense bush of East Africa. Armored cars were called on to fulfill this role in the absence of tanks. The South Africans made good use of their armored cars as part of their doctrine evolved from First World War experiences in German East Africa. The armored car solved a problem of extreme vulnerability to ambush in the dense bush of East Africa. The South Africans found the wheeled vehicle to be much more robust than a tracked vehicle in the vast distances of this theater. The maintenance units also travelled with the armored cars to ensure continued mobility and on-the-spot support.[45]

The No. 1 Light Tank Company played a decisive role in the battle of El Wak. The South African tanks led the dawn attack on Italian El Wak, and despite receiving copious amounts of fire from the Italian positions, advanced up to 20 m from the Italian positions and delivered withering fire among them. Once the engineers blew holes in the defensive wire, the infantry rushed the surprised defenders under cover of the supporting tanks. The tanks had a morale-boosting effect on the attackers and an opposite demoralizing effect on the Italian defenders.[46] In this initial battle, the South Africans made use of a combined arms approach. The motorized infantry, artillery, armored cars, and light tanks, together with support from the air, succeeded in working together to achieve positive results, especially the demoralization of the Italian colonial troops.[47] Circumstances a year later at Sidi Rezegh did not grant opportunities such as this for the South Africans to combine arms, with disastrous results. The British, as was their manner, purloined the South African armored car companies and the engineers for their own purposes and would not allow the South Africans to operate an infantry tank support component.

The two Allied brigades heavily outnumbered the Italians and the result was somewhat of a foregone conclusion. The South African's lost 2 soldiers, their first casualties in the war, while the Italians lost 7 Italian officers, 18 NCOs, and 118 Italian colonial troops.[48] Although the first clash of arms resulted in a victory, the South Africans failed to cut off the Italian line of retreat, allowing the escape of several hundred troops.[49] Although this action amounted to nothing more than a raid with an overwhelmingly superior force, it had a demoralizing effect on the Italians, robbing them of the initiative in East Africa. The success of the operation confirmed to General A. R. Godwin-Austen (1889–1963), commander of the 12th African Division, his confidence in the South African troops. He praised their leadership, dash, and enterprise in a message to Pienaar. Pienaar received his Distinguished Service Order (DSO) for his exploits and leadership at the battle of El Wak, becoming the first member of the South African land forces in the war to win a decoration in the field.[50]

A troubling feature of the British system of command exposed itself at the outset of the East African campaign. The South African 1st Brigade had been detached from the South African 1st Division and assigned to the 12th African Division for the purpose of the attack on El Wak, leaving the division one brigade short for its operations in Abyssinia. Brink attempted to recover his "lost" brigade for the attacks on Moyale and Mega, only to receive a rebuff. The 1st Division was again destined to operate with only two of its brigades at Sidi Rezegh in November 1941, with disastrous consequences.[51] The British practice of "borrowing" formations from the South Africans on an ad hoc basis would play a role in diminishing South African fighting power throughout their campaign in East and North Africa.[52] One of the early run-ins, the first of many that Pienaar would have with those in authority, occurred when General Dickinson wanted to split the SAI brigade and use its battalions as the foundations for new brigades manned by native troops. Pienaar was furious and was not prepared to accede to the request. The splitting of South African forces was to pose a major problem for the UDF in East Africa and North Africa. The Australian and New Zealand governments did not allow the British to split their units and demanded that they fight as a composite force.[53]

It is important to highlight the role of the South African armored units during all their offensive operations against the Italians in East Africa in keeping South African casualties to a minimum.[54] The South African armored cars played an important part in demoralizing the enemy, especially the colonial troops who made up a large proportion of the Italian forces. The South Africans tended to deploy their armored cars as tanks in an infantry support role on many occasions, leading and supporting the infantry in the attack. They provided long-range covering fire, close-quarter fire support, a means to outflank an enemy position quickly, and, on occasion, a tool to cut off a retreating enemy.[55] Mention must be made of the South African sappers who offered superb engineering services that were indispensable in assisting the British forces in East Africa. Among their other battle functions they removed land mines, built bridges, cleared obstacles, and provided and restored water resources.[56]

El Yibo: The 1st SAI Division Clears the Frontier January 1941

After Pienaar's credible performance, the opportunity fell on Brink and his 1st SAI Division, sans the 1st SAI Brigade, to show their mettle on a larger scale of operations. The British planned an attack to take place on January 16, 1941, on the border outposts of Kenya-Abyssinia, at the water holes of El Yibo and El Sardu. Brink made use of his 2nd SAI Brigade, commanded by Buchanan and supported by Ethiopian irregulars, armored cars, artillery, and aircraft. Astonishingly, the precise location of El Yibo was unknown to Buchanan or his staff.[57] This unnecessary fog of war could have been lifted somewhat if reconnaissance was actively used to determine the exact location of the enemy. A central feature known as Sugarloaf Hill dominated the entire ravine. Some entrenched Italian soldiers manned the hill and dominated all approaches to the wells at El Yibo and El Sardu from this strategic point. The Natal Mounted Rifles (NMR), commanded by Lieutenant-Colonel N. D. McMillan, together with five armored cars of No. 2 S.A. Armoured Car company, were to clear the El Yibo–El Sardu area on the Kenyan side of the frontier facing Hobok. The plan called for the 2nd Abyssinian Irregulars to co-operate by moving around the flanks and rear of El Yibo. It therefore, conceived an enveloping movement, followed by a frontal attack on the Italian positions.[58]

The South Africans set off at 0615 and were unable to find their objective due to incomplete reconnaissance. The enveloping force found itself conducting a frontal assault on the Italian positions while the offensive component, who were supposed to deliver the main attack, were not even in sight of El Yibo. All contact was lost, with the enveloping force leaving the main force with the incorrect impression that the enveloping force had occupied El Yibo. The main force proceeded at a snail's pace toward the Italian positions. The armored cars governed their speed and they, in turn, struggled over the nearly impossible terrain. By the time the frontal assault forces reached their objective at Sugar Loaf Hill at 1430, the irregulars of the enveloping force were spent and began to withdraw. Exhaustion, combined with a lack of water, put paid to the resolve of the main force as well, and they too began to pull out at dusk.[59] Douglas Baker, a member of the hapless NMR attempting to wrest El Yibo from the Italians, relates,

> The preliminaries to the final assault meant that almost the entire regiment dressed in scanty khaki shorts and shirts to lay out all day and half the night in temperatures that had reached 145°F, and a heat that scorched not only your skin but heated up the lava rocks on which you lay. [. . .] The actual target was unclear and was presumed to have been occupied in the first skirmish, which occurred between 10:00 and 15:00 hours. This alone had tired out our forces through heat exhaustion. Then it was found that El Yibo hadn't been attacked at all! The target lay a few further miles on. By now the regiment was exhausted and had run out of the most precious of all commodities at this stage which was . . . water.[60]

The attack resumed the following morning. The men moved cautiously forward in extended order with three armored cars in support. They were working their way forward by 1130, through thornbushes that tore at their skin and over scorching-hot lava rocks, while the sun beat down mercilessly. The attackers seized Harris Hill at 1300 and immediately came under fire from the Italians, 800 m to their north, on Sugar Loaf Hill. Despite air support, in the form of three Hartbeest bombers which bombed the Italian positions twice in the day, Buchanan considered the enemy's position impregnable to an unsupported infantry attack. He called off the attack at 1500 and decided to continue the assault, supported by artillery and aircraft, the following day.[61]

The attack would have profited greatly had it been executed via an outflanking maneuver as originally envisaged. The South Africans outnumbered the Italians significantly and a night attack on the defenders was a possibility not explored. Lack of imagination and aggression, coupled with the challenging terrain, oppressive heat,[62] and inexperience of the South African officers, inflated the battle into a three-day ordeal. Baker again describes the harrowing experience,

> The regiment spent a sleepless night in discovering that the extreme heat by day of semi-desert is exchanged in the night by freezing conditions. Worse! Water supplies did not get through until the next day. The following day was almost as frustrating. The enemy, 150 strong, counterattacked but were driven off after they had reached a point 100 yards distant from battalion headquarters. More "humming and aharring" around and after this further day of heat exposure the exhausted regiment had to spend a further night on the bare mountain. On the following morning, El Yibo was occupied by the NMR. In fact "the birds had flown" the night before.[63]

The attackers captured the position after the enemy abandoned their positions at night. Buchanan proved too cautious in not entertaining the prospect of cutting off their retreat in a more daring night maneuver. W. F. Ashburner, a South African journalist and an observer, described the operation: "The battle for the wells had been a shocking flop." He goes on, "Had a little enterprise been shown we could have easily surrounded the Sugar Loaf on the first day of the attack and forced its surrender."[64] The South Africans suffered no casualties, and the South African press, hungry for victory, proclaimed El Yibo a triumph.

The attack highlighted some shortcomings of the green South Africans. The Italians, consisting of 7 officers and 400 irregulars, managed to hold off a far superior force with artillery, air, and armored car support.[65] Brink also felt that Buchanan had been overly cautious in what amounted to nothing more than a minor task.[66] Cooperation between the armored cars and the infantry was distinctly lacking. Sundry infantry officers issued conflicting instructions, which resulted in the cars performing uncoordinated maneuvers and losing cohesion through lack of command and control.[67] The shortcomings highlighted in this operation did not pass unnoticed by Cunningham. He offered some keen advice, in a personal letter to Brink, as to the acclimatization of the troops as well as cooperation between the infantry and armored cars. Brink's bold use of the armored cars in an offensive capacity, to demoralize the enemy colonial forces, came in for harsh criticism. Cunningham favored the traditional reconnaissance role for the armored cars, and in the spirit of the old cavalry, he suggested that the South Africans also use the armored cars in a final maneuver to cut off the enemy line of retreat.[68]

With the water wells of El Yibo in South African hands, the 1st Division continued their advance into Italian territory. The 2nd and 5th Brigades crossed the Abyssinian border north of Dukana on January 31, 1941, as part of the southern offensive. Italian irregulars, led by a few Italian officers, defended Gorai, El Gumu, and Hobok lightly, and as a result the South Africans captured them in quick succession. The only casualties were two South Africans who died in action. One of them an Englishman, the other an Afrikaner, they were the first buried in Abyssinian soil.[69] The armored cars successfully attacked Italian positions at Hobok, unsupported by infantry, as they were encouraged by the unsteadiness of the Italian opposition thus far. In North Africa, the British would conduct the same type of unsupported attack with the lack of a combined arms approach, resulting in a more resolute opponent punishing them severely.[70]

The biggest obstacle in the East African campaign was climate and terrain rather than the fighting ability of the Italian soldier.[71] In this particular operation, the harsh nature of the terrain took the commanders by surprise. They expected open plains, but instead they faced a dense, nearly impenetrable bush, unmarked on the maps they were issued.[72] The lack of reconnaissance in East Africa became an unfortunate feature repeated on occasion by the South Africans in North Africa, with costly results in terms of casualties.[73] The armored cars, in the forefront of every attack, played a fundamental role in demoralizing the Italian irregular soldiers, who made up the majority of the forces encountered. Low casualty rates suffered by the South Africans were disproportionate to those inflicted by and attributed to the armored cars and the protection they afforded the infantry.[74]

The Battle for Mega February 1941

After the relatively cheap victories of El Wak and El Yibo, Gorai, El Gumu, and Hobok, Cunningham decided to capture the important frontier forts of Mega and Moyale. Expectations were that the Italians held these in some strength, as they overlooked the two major roads in Abyssinia. On February 15, the 2nd and 5th SAI Brigades of the 1st SAI Division launched a double flanking movement on Mega according to a confident plan formulated by Brink. He anticipated the capture of Mega by February 16. The intention was for 5th Brigade, commanded by Armstrong, to attack from the north while 2nd Brigade attacked simultaneously from the east. It became apparent, once the attack got under way, that Buchanan and the 2nd SAI Brigade did not fully grasp Brink's plan and his intentions. The 2nd Brigade made its way to its intended target of El Sod to the north of Mega, but contrary to the plan, dropped its C Company to block the Yavello–Mega road. Buchanan perhaps meant for the lone company left at the crossroads to guard the rear of the 2nd SAI Brigade. However, he had no instructions to detach any of his force.[75] His action was superfluous as the 5th SAI Brigade had already achieved this blocking action farther down the road. The remainder of the 2nd SAI Brigade proceeded to the intended target of El Sod.

Ensconced at the crossroads, C Company heard the rumble of vehicles approaching from the north at 0330. Within moments, a firefight broke out in which C Company engaged the enemy vehicles. The Italians regrouped at 0515 and, supported by fifteen light tanks that had been on the way to support Mega, launched a further attack on C Company. The South Africans were not immune to the psychological impact of attacking armor.[76] The Italian tanks caused consternation among C Company and their supporting armored cars. The South Africans, close to panic, began to retreat toward El Sod. Harrowing tales began to emerge of how the Italians had overrun the company and its virtual annihilation at the hands of the Italian tanks. The "tanks" in question were in fact not tanks but Carri Veloci, a turretless tankette armed with two machine guns and thin armor. The reports of a tank attack were erroneous and caused much consternation at the 2nd SAI Brigade headquarters.[77] South African casualties in this fiasco were two killed, four wounded, and ten captured. It was a relatively high loss rate for a single engagement compared to what had been experienced in the conflict thus far. It was a clear demonstration of what may have transpired had Italian resistance been uniformly resolute.[78]

Buchanan hastily assembled a strong counterattack force. Sufficient antitank guns and armored cars set forth to avenge C Company. The counterattack force met with stragglers who estimated losses at a company less a section (or about one hundred men). The 2nd SAI Brigade reported sighting tanks on the Yavello–Mega road at 0800, considerably adding to the already tense situation. Buchanan gained the impression that the enemy was converging on his position. The air force dispatched air reconnaissance immediately but failed to report any sign of enemy armor in the area. The South Africans sent another alarming signal confirming enemy tanks were moving south only a few miles east of El Sod. When the counterattack force eventually arrived at the crossroads, they failed to encounter any sign of the enemy. The Italians were beating a hasty retreat northwards, closely followed by the South African Air Force, who bombed the retreating column and the armored cars in hot pursuit. The South Africans were closing the gap with the enemy when the brigade headquarters, in an overcautious frame of mind, ordered the pursuing column to desist and turn around. This reprieve allowed the Italians to escape to Yavello, thereby narrowly avoiding capture and destruction, although harassed continuously by the air force. It was the first in a sequence of events which was to exasperate the officer in charge of the counterattack, Lieutenant-Colonel Engelbrecht. He was furious that his commander recalled him when the enemy was within his grasp. Engelbrecht grew increasingly frustrated with Buchanan's conduct as the attack on Mega progressed.[79]

While Buchanan was dealing with the consequences of a phantom full-scale Italian offensive on his C Company, the 5th SAI Brigade reached its objective 13 km north of Mega on the Yavello road. The brigade proceeded to dig in and duly sent out reconnaissance patrols toward Mega to locate the enemy. Buchanan gave assurances that 2nd SAI Brigade would be ready to attack the next morning (February 16) by 1130. The 1st SA Irish Regiment made preparations for the forthcoming assault that they would launch the next morning at 0800 once the 2nd SAI Brigade was in position. This coordination between elements of the 2nd and 5th SAI Brigades would result in a simultaneous attack on Mega from two directions.[80] The first objective was to capture the high ground of Kirby and Dobbs Ridge, and after that to pause and consolidate, allowing 2nd SAI Brigade to reach their assault positions.

On approaching the objective, the 5th SAI Brigade began to receive heavy artillery fire, which did little to impede their advance. The advance on the left flank and the 2nd SAI Brigade preparations for the assault were proceeding with far more ambiguity. The journey from El Sod to the objective on the east of Mega proved heavy going. Thick bush and deep sand covered the approach. The brigade apparently made an effort to avoid enemy artillery fire and this, compounded with a misinterpretation of the orders yet again, caused the brigade to make a 36 km detour from the route directed by Brink.[81] Adding to 2nd SAI Brigade's woes was an element of tardiness demonstrated by its failure to leave El Sod on time.[82] This delay was due to a suspected enemy convoy approaching from the northeast. These delays had the cumulative effect of pushing out the brigade's arrival time at the objective to 1445. In the end, extensive armored car patrols sent out ahead of 2nd SAI Brigade found no evidence of any enemy activity, thoroughly disproving reports of approaching enemy columns. Apparently, the previous day's calamitous engagement on the Yavello–Mega road caused extreme skittishness and hesitancy in maneuvering the brigade.[83]

Brink's clear intention was for 2nd SAI Brigade to attack Mega from the east. Buchanan instead prioritized the cutting of the Mega–Moyale road 6 km south of Mega in an attempt to prevent the enemy escaping southwards.[84] With this misunderstanding, 2nd Brigade's undertaking to be in a position to attack Mega by first 1130, then 1425, never materialized. An exasperated Armstrong had little option but to call off 5th SAI Brigade's attack when he had not yet received any signal from 2nd Brigade by 1800. Armstrong preferred to consolidate his position in readiness for both brigades to attack the following morning at 0700. He sought definite confirmation from Buchanan that he would press the attack at the designated time the next morning. The response Armstrong received was less than enthusiastic. Buchanan responded that he would do his best in the face of the "impregnable defenses" that now lay before him.[85] Not for the first time, the South Africans would be spending the night exposed to the elements. Lieutenant-Colonel Dobbs graphically recounted,

> There were no coats, no groundsheets, no blankets, no hot food or drink as the faint yellow twilight waned and the night closed clammily around us. Rations were down to a quarter of the usual scale—a few mouthfuls of bully beef with the rain pouring greasily

> over the dull white lumps of fat. With their flimsy tropical clothing the men lay down in stony, shallow trenches that looked, and felt, like graves. They made the most of the dank, damnable darkness. There was no smoking; lights were banned, and streaming trees and bushes masked those who sought their shelter. Vague wreaths of mist swirled out of the deepest gloom like uneasy ghosts. The whole of the black heavens seemed to be weeping over the huddled figures in their trenches. And it rained and rained and rained. Somebody said that this was our reward for starting an attack on a Sunday.[86]

The morning greeted the South Africans with the miserable and unrelenting rainy weather. Disgruntled troops spent the night near the enemy. They had left most of their unessential kit behind the previous day, in anticipation of an attack that never took place. The combination of rain, mud, and heavy enemy shelling made it impossible for the transport to reach the forward troops and they spent the night without blankets or raincoats. Faced with miserable conditions and considerably behind schedule, Brink urged both brigade commanders to press the attack without any further delay. Once again, Brink made it clear that he expected the 2nd Brigade to attack from the east and not from its current position to the south. It was reasonable to assume that Brink had cleared up any misunderstanding in Buchanan's mind and therefore he knew what Brink expected of his brigade.[87]

The advance of 5th SAI Brigade resumed, albeit at a very slow pace. Poor weather, difficult terrain, incessant enemy shelling, and the presence of land mines, which extracted some casualties, caused many delays. The sappers helped clear the way and by 1430 the SA Irish had occupied Hill A and repulsed an Italian irregular counterattack. Contrary to Brink's clear directives, Buchanan believed it unfeasible to attack from the east. An irregular native guide advised him that the eastern approach was impossible.[88] The 2nd SAI Brigade made a wide flanking movement on Mega, once again proceeding to demonstrate from the south, which was the opposite direction from what Brink had instructed. Brink, and now Armstrong, once again requested that 2nd Brigade should attack from the east. Buchanan answered at 1500 that this was impossible and would result in severe loss of life. At 1730 Armstrong called a halt to the attack, having reached within 3 km to the north-northeast of Mega.

The two-pronged attack had failed to materialize yet again. Armstrong requested that Buchanan launch an assault at 0700 the next morning to coincide with his attack on Mega.[89] Dobbs describes the second miserable night before Mega,

> The men who were up on the ridges overlooking Mega will never forget that evening and that night. Nearly everyone lost control of his jaws. Violent shivering is never a pleasant sight: when it grips a mass of men it is almost terrifying. Jaws were clattering with horrible machine like precision, and soon vigorous athletic youths were falling unconscious through hours of exposure to the bitter wind and the rain. Some of the men had to be unceremoniously undressed by their comrades and fiercely massaged as they stood naked on the storm-swept ridges.[90]

Now two days behind schedule, both brigades prepared to launch a simultaneous assault on the morning of February 18. Brink conceded that Buchanan knew better about the conditions on the ground and accepted his reasons for coming in from the south. Having wrung this concession from Brink, Buchanan demonstrated an incredible volte-face. He ordered one of his battalions to assist 5th Brigade in its attack by adhering to Brink's original plan and attacking east, necessitating yet another long drawn-out move by the unfavorably placed brigade. The 2nd SAI Brigade was reluctant to launch an attack in the east despite Brink's instructions. Buchanan insisted that the eastern approach was impassable. He gained this incorrect perception through the use of native scouts. Had 2nd SAI Brigade conducted its reconnaissance on this and other occasions, they may have captured Mega Hill a lot sooner, without wasting energy by moving to and fro pointlessly.[91]

The weather began to improve at 0730 and this time, both brigades proceeded with their advance on Mega. Buchanan requested the support of the 5th SAI Brigade, in the face of strong opposition, which placed the 2nd SAI Brigade in a precarious position.[92] The final irony was the reversal of roles of the two brigades, as the original intention was for 2nd SAI Brigade to play the supporting role. Transvaal Scottish captured Mega Hill with ease at 1420, notwithstanding these distractions. Lieutenant-Colonel Engelbrecht, who could barely conceal his frustration with Colonel Buchanan at an order group earlier in the morning, undertook the action. He demanded a free hand and promised to deliver Mega. Engelbrecht then "stalked off" from the order group and proceeded to scale up the "impassable" eastern cliff, capturing the key Italian gun positions and unlocking the entire Italian position and rendering it hopeless.[93] The 5th Brigade was in a position to attack by 1630 despite hard going through rain, mist, and enemy artillery fire, and lack of support from armored cars, which were unable to traverse the sodden ground. Torrential rain accompanied the attack and soon Italian resistance collapsed, resulting in the surrender of the entire garrison with little resistance.[94]

The South Africans captured Mega and Moyale after three days in heavy rains and freezing temperatures, amounting to a test of endurance rather than a hard-fought battle. Inexperience was all too apparent, and the battle was marked by unnecessary delays, coupled with poor coordination. The 2nd SAI Brigade was only able to reach its start line after the third day due to poor navigation and poor reconnaissance. The Italians suffered relatively few casualties and after a token resistance surrendered en masse.[95] The South Africans found the outpost of Moyale abandoned and they occupied it on February 22 after the Italians pulled back to their inner defenses. The fall of Mega effectively concluded 1st SAI Division's operations in East Africa. Cunningham preferred the advance on Addis Ababa to come via the invasion of the topographically easier plains of Italian Somaliland. As a result, the division was withdrawn into reserve in Kenya in support of Cunningham's thrust into Somaliland. The necessity of this never arose, due to the speed and ease of an advance that outstripped all expectations.[96]

The Conquest of Abyssinia

Two of Cunningham's divisions, including the 1st SAI Brigade, moved into Somaliland. It was the Italian intention to defend the entire 576 km of the Juba River. The fortress of Jumbo anchored the defense at the mouth of the river. The relative immobility of the Italians forced them to decide to defend the length of the river on a static basis. The Italians were effectively isolated and cut off from overland supply routes, and the closure of the Suez to the Axis precluded a naval resupply. The shortage of supplies, especially spare parts for vehicles, brought about the relative immobility of the Italian forces. Pienaar's 1st SAI Brigade made for the fortress of Jumbo and the strategic village of Gobwen on February 16, moving mainly at night and remaining motionless by day. Pienaar brought his brigade to their start line in a final night move of 32 km through the bush. Once started, the attack came under heavy artillery and mortar fire. The South Africans, who had taken up positions behind the river, were subject to incessant shelling for over two hours. When the bombardment ceased, they agreed to outflank Juba with a river crossing farther upstream, rather than a frontal assault on the town.[97]

The South Africans managed to establish a bridgehead farther upstream the next morning, threatening to cut off Jumbo from the road to Mogadishu. The Italians attempted to reduce the bridgehead using company-strength attacks over the next few days, resulting in the near destruction and dispersal of the Italian Army in the area. The South Africans were able to bring substantial reinforcements for the assault on the rear of Jumbo after building a pontoon bridge over the bridgehead. With the spirit of the Italian defenders flagging, the fortress surrendered. As a result, the entire Juba line began to unhinge and the defenses along the river crumbled. The SAI Brigade had taken 6,000 prisoners and vast amounts of war booty in the campaign, suffering very few casualties in turn. The South Africans spent a mere nine days in turning the defenses on the Juba line. The road to Mogadishu lay open, and although the South Africans took no further part in the action, British forces captured the town on February 25. A rapid pursuit of a stricken enemy now developed.[98]

The southern force found itself up against a thin Italian rearguard action covering the approaches to the capital of Addis Ababa. On the move again, the South Africans just missed the battle of Marda, although they managed to supply artillery in support of the Nigerian Brigade attack. The Marda pass fell quickly to the Nigerians against a token Italian defense. A more resolute foe could have held out much longer in terrain that clearly favored the defense. The South Africans and Nigerians then forced the Italians to abandon their defensive positions in front of Harar, the second city of Abyssinia. The action was a two-day affair, involving a Nigerian direct attack, followed by a South African outflanking maneuver. The same situation occurred again at Babilli. The Italian defenders fell back in good order to the Bisidimo River, 16 km east of Harar, once again outflanked by the South Africans. The Nigerians conquered the

Harar on March 5 after bearing the brunt of the attack. After Harar had fallen, the 1st SAI Brigade took the lead from the Nigerians on the road to Diredawa. Here, the South Africans encountered Italian demolitions, but there was a marked absence of any real contest. Diredawa fell with little resistance on March 29. The fight was rapidly disappearing from the Italians and their morale had plummeted in both the colonial and the Blackshirt infantry. The way to Addis Ababa lay open. The South Africans expected nothing untoward that would slow them down on their way to claim their prize of the Abyssinian capital.

The South Africans, poised to claim a major Axis landmark, fell victim to an unfortunate incident at the gates of Addis Ababa, which robbed them of their prize. Pienaar demonstrated an alarming obstructionist attitude, which marked the first in a long series of unfortunate episodes following his career right up to his untimely death in 1942. Pienaar complained that he was unable to proceed to the capital for lack of fuel. His contention puzzled General H. E. de Robillard Wetherall (1889–1979), General Officer commanding the 11th African Division, particularly since the South Africans had recently captured a valuable haul of Italian fuel.[99] Wetherall passed through the 22nd East African Brigade on his way to confirm the extent of Pienaar's lack of fuel. The 22nd East African Brigade was acting as a reserve and Wetherall cautioned them to be available should Pienaar fail to advance. In the end, Pienaar insisted that he lacked sufficient fuel and Wetherall wasted no time in instructing the 22nd Brigade to pass through the South Africans and move on to capture the capital. They formally occupied Addis Ababa on April 6. The South Africans eventually entered Addis Ababa in second place behind the 22nd Brigade, managing to do so despite not receiving any further fuel rations.[100]

Despite the disappointment of not being able to claim Addis Ababa as a prize, 1st SAI Brigade had advanced 1,500 miles in twenty-five days, in a campaign that had lasted only fifty-three days. The greatest challenges had come from the terrain, severe weather conditions in the form of torrential rain, and poor road infrastructure, rather than stiff Italian resistance. The Italians suffered casualties of 50,000 prisoners and thousands killed and wounded against less than 150 East African Force members killed.[101] The war elsewhere was not going as well as in East Africa. Serious problems developing in the Middle East put pressure on General Sir Archibald Wavell (1883–1950), Commander in Chief of the British Middle East Command, to remove the South African Division from East Africa as soon as possible for a deployment to Egypt. The Germans conquered Greece and Yugoslavia, and Rashid Aali al-Gaylani (1892–1965) seized power in Iraq and made prisoners of Generals P. Neame (1888–1978) and R. O'Conner (1889–1981), in an Axis offensive that recaptured much of Cyrenaica and brought the Axis back to the Egyptian frontier.

The next objective in East Africa was to advance north to open up the Addis Ababa–Asmara road, enabling the embarkation of troops at the coastal ports en route to Egypt.[102] Accordingly, Pienaar and his 1st SAI Brigade, together with a proportion of allotted divisional troops, were ordered to move north and capture Dessie as the first step to Asmara. Dessie blocked the way to the two remaining Italian centers of resistance at Amba Alagi and Gondar. The Northern Force under Platt had been somewhat denuded in reinforcing the Middle East, thus making assistance from the south essential to securing the remaining objectives. It was the occasion for a further spat between Wetherall and Pienaar. The British general was somewhat perturbed at what he perceived to be the hesitancy of the South African advance. Wetherall ordered Pienaar, who disputed British intelligence as to the number of Italian defenders, to attack at once. Pienaar is said to have responded, "Now, General, please go away and leave us to fight our own battle. We know what we are doing. We will take the position and we will report to you when we have done so." Wetherall threatened to relieve Pienaar of his command at this insubordination. This incident and others like it seemed to leave an indelible stamp on Pienaar's attitude toward British generals, and they, in turn, treated the South Africans with a measure of disdain.[103]

The South African advance in torrential rains and mist to Dessie was accompanied by the occasional air attack and the all-too-familiar demolitions and inevitable groups of surrendering native troops. The South Africans immediately put these prisoners to work restoring passages through the road obstacles. Blocking the South African approach in this mountainous region of Dessie was a formidable Italian Force numbering over 10,000, of which 6,000 were Italian. The South Africans suffered casualties as the two forces engaged at the Combolcia Pass on the approach to Dessie. Following artillery duels, the South Africans proceeded to seize the high ground and steadily work their way forward toward the enemy positions. In an action lasting seven days, the outnumbered South Africans steadily advanced on the Italian positions, capturing key points in turn and overcoming the defenders. It was a credible performance, and by April 23 the South Africans had lost 10 killed and 28 wounded against much higher enemy casualty figures of 400 dead and 1,200 prisoners. The Italians retreated in disarray toward Dessie, mostly unmolested by the exhausted South Africans who had to remove obstacles on the road to effect a pursuit. The Dessie Garrison of 5,000 Italians and 3,000 native troops surrendered to the South Africans on April 27 without putting up much of a fight. It had been a remarkably short campaign resulting in the capture of 8,000 enemy troops and a massive haul of booty in the form of equipment and provisions.[104]

The final task left to the South Africans in clearing the Dessie–Asmara road was the capture of the defenders of Amba Alagi. The Duke of Aosta led the well-ensconced Italians, who occupied prepared and formidable positions 3,410 m above sea level.[105] The Italians filled the approaches to the mountain redoubt of Amba Alagi with obstacles and demolitions in an attempt to slow down the attackers as much as possible. The South Africans advanced slowly but relentlessly toward their objective, employing the familiar tactics of seizing the high points that dominated the approach and covering the troops with a steady artillery barrage. Once the South Africans captured the surrounding hills by using interlocking fire from the artillery and machine guns in support of the infantry, they brought the artillery to bear on Amba Alagi itself. The prospect of launching the final assault on the well-defended fort against a determined enemy was one that was bound to incur many casualties. The fort itself was subjected to an incessant artillery bombardment causing many casualties and restricting Italian movement within the fort during daylight hours. On May 16, the Italians suffered water contamination due to the incessant bombardment, and this persuaded them to make efforts to discuss surrender terms. The final exploit of the 1st SAI Brigade was to occupy Amba Alagi on May 19.[106] Shortly after that, the brigade departed for Egypt from Massawa on June 12, 1941. The 5th SAI Brigade had been at Mersa Matruh in Egypt since May 23, and the 2nd SAI Brigade departed from Berbera on June 3.

LESSONS LEARNED FROM THE EAST AFRICAN CAMPAIGN

The South Africans emerged from the East African campaign having learned valuable battlefield lessons. More importantly, a clear combat doctrine had evolved that favored a combined arms approach to conducting battle. The South Africans developed a taste for mobile warfare and they preferred the art of maneuver over that of positional and attrition warfare. South African operational plans tended to contain flanking or enveloping tactics intended to force the enemy out of their prepared positions and obliging them to fight on ground that was not of their choosing.[107] Outflanking movements across the country of up to 120 km were the order of the day, and were sometimes delivered from angles that the enemy did not expect. These outflanking maneuvers, preferred over a frontal assault, provided the element of surprise and ensured success against an entrenched enemy with minimal cost.[108] The South African experience in East Africa built on a doctrine that found its roots in the mounted infantry of the Boer army, the UDF in the German South West African campaign of 1915, and again in the German East African campaign of 1916.

The UDF made extensive use of maneuvering their forces at night, resulting in successful operations such as those at El Wak. Those building the South African doctrine embraced mobility at night. Discussions include the usefulness of a full moon to facilitate movement as well as setting a figure of 60 km as the distance that motorized infantry could endure in one night over bad roads and rough terrain. At the same time, they cautioned that restricting movement to a full moon would be too predictable and that the correct training would facilitate a night maneuver under all circumstances.[109] Unfortunately, the South Africans failed to expand these sound doctrinal trends in North Africa, and the UDF was surprisingly reluctant to move at night in the desert environment. Reluctance to move at night cost the South Africans dearly, especially at Sidi Rezegh.

The South Africans learned to combine infantry, engineers, artillery, air support, and armored cars on the move and into battle. Each component gave the other valuable support while maneuvering and especially in the thick of the battlefield. The UDF mastered the art of moving large forces over long distances and challenging terrain, and skills such as traffic control and staff planning were improved. They found that aerial reconnaissance, especially over rough terrain, did not provide sufficient detail to the ground forces. It was essential to deploy ground reconnaissance to gain the proper details of the terrain the infantry were to traverse. There was a concern that the absence of enemy aircraft on campaign encouraged a higher density of units than desired when on the move and when on the halt. The practice of proper dispersal was essential against a more formidable foe.[110]

The South Africans were quite prepared to use armored cars in the absence of tanks. The armored cars exceeded expectations as to their cross-country ability, and they were used extensively to cross ground thought only accessible to tanks with tracks. In fact, armored cars encountering rocky terrain did better than tanks, whose tracks were particularly vulnerable to sharp rocks. African conditions seem to favor a wheeled vehicle over a tracked vehicle. The dense bush aided concealment as it acted as a permanent smoke screen.[111] The armored cars' ability to operate away from the established roads allowed the South Africans to exercise increased mobility by avoiding mines and roadblocks along the established routes. Combat conditions convinced the South Africans of the efficacy of armored cars in aiding an attack on entrenched positions, and they believed the deployment of armored cars against hard targets saved many an infantryman's life. The South Africans discouraged the use of armored cars singly and preferred to use them en masse where they could provide mutual support and undertake flanking maneuvers in the attack.[112]

The UDF used its engineering component to good effect in the East African campaign, requiring it for two main purposes. First to supply water to the advancing troops, and second to destroy enemy defenses. The engineer's training program was deficient in the areas of detecting and deactivating land mines and booby traps. A sound mechanical knowledge needed greater emphasis in sapper training.[113] It is interesting to contrast the South African experience in vehicle maintenance with that of the Germans in the desert war. The Germans had a formidable vehicle recovery and maintenance component which would often recover tanks and vehicles in the thick of battle to repair them and make them available for combat the next day. The South Africans lacked a similar forward vehicle maintenance facility but saw the benefits of having one. It is interesting that the requirement was for such a unit within 160 km of the front line, while the Germans operated such units within the battlefield.[114]

Signals were of great importance in maintaining momentum and cohesion during a rapid advance. The 1st SAI Division saw traffic of between 500 and 600 messages a day on occasion, an indicator of the advance in communication since the First World War. The South Africans had to confront the challenges of a highly mobile army raid over enormous distances and the resultant increase in the flow of messages from headquarters to the lower formations, and vice versa.[115] There seemed to have been a lack of liaison between the brigades of the division and the division with the higher structures. The holding of daily and weekly conferences between all branches of the formation staffs solved this lack of communication in the North African desert campaign.[116]

The South Africans had learned a great deal about the medical aspect of the conflict from their experiences in East Africa during the First World War. In that conflict thousands of UDF soldiers and animals became casualties due to sickness. The UDF learned from its experience and improved on their medical measures. One of the measures was to ensure the acclimatization of all ranks in the environment they were to operate in before operations commenced. Failure in this regard led to massive sickness and exhaustion.[117]

The South Africans favored a highly successful form of mobile warfare, but there were gaps in the operational and tactical doctrine that precluded greater success in inflicting damage on the enemy. There was a tendency to stand fast after winning the battle, and there was a lack of exploitation on the one hand and a failure to coordinate defensive measures in anticipation of a counterattack. Had the enemy been more resolute, they may have forced the South Africans to pay a higher price.[118] The UDF relied on the British system of issuing written orders or operational instructions. Therefore, although the army encouraged subordinate officers to show initiative, it was not of the same standard as expected in the German army, which preferred to issue verbal orders in the interest of speed.

Chapter 3

The Clash of Military Doctrine

There is an old mess anecdote which runs something like this: A British and German officer both partake in a quiz. The question is asked of each contestant in turn; "how much is one plus one?" The English officer, after much deliberation and using the fingers on his hands to make sure, answers; "two!" The German on being asked the same question immediately stands up, slams the table and screams loudly; "three!" The answer "three" being close enough for military business.

Previous chapters have highlighted the interwar military neglect pervasive in Britain and the dominions at the outbreak of the war. The relegation of military affairs in the interwar years goes some way toward explaining the often poor military performance of the British in the initial stages of the Second World War. However, neglect alone cannot explain German military superiority, especially when the British often outclassed the Germans both numerically and materially on the battlefield. A significant portion of British ineptitude was their adoption of a deeply flawed and significantly outmoded military doctrine that set them at a distinct combat disadvantage. British military doctrine proved disastrous in an era when modern warfare favored armies that embraced newfound mobility brought about by mechanization and were able to exercise a combined force approach. It is profitable to look beyond the purely political and economic reasons leading to inadequate force preparation to gain insight into the military disasters that overtook the British and South Africans in North Africa.

Military doctrine encompasses a fundamental set of principles and formal expressions of military knowledge and thought that guide military forces as to how they will conduct their operational art and tactics to achieve their strategic objectives.[1] It is descriptive rather than prescriptive, describing how the army thinks about fighting, not how to fight. Doctrine is a guide to military activity and, as such, does not replace initiative and judgment on the battlefield.[2] Armies must continually adjust the doctrinal lens to stay focused as science introduces new and improved technologies into warfare, throwing the relationship between the different arms (artillery, air, armor, and infantry) out of synchrony.[3]

The various opponents in the desert conflict brought to the battlefield their version of battle doctrine. The Germans, because of their military superiority, dominated their Italian allies and imposed their military doctrine on them.[4] The British, in a similar fashion, subdued the doctrinal approaches of their desert allies, including the South Africans. British military doctrine influenced British command and in turn the conduct of the desert campaign. Unlike the Italians, the South Africans, New Zealanders, Australians, and Indians fighting with the British did so as infantry divisions and did not possess armored formations. Armor was the principal weapon in the desert and as such, the employment of armored forces shaped the strategic and operational conduct of the war. The North African desert, mostly devoid of population and terrain effects, provided perfect conditions to test the efficacy of the opposing military doctrines.[5]

The South Africans possessed a distinct military doctrine of their own. It was born out of, and evolved from, the melting pot used to form the UDF from components of the former protagonists in the Anglo-Boer War. UDF military doctrine was further refined in a highly mobile war of maneuver in German South West and German East Africa during the First World War.[6] The UDF further developed the doctrine of maneuver warfare, using the mobility afforded by motorized infantry, in the campaign against the Italians in East Africa during the Second World War. There South Africa made good use of her armored cars and tanks, combined with infantry and artillery and supported by air power, in a favorable exercise of combined arms warfare. The British in North Africa, unfortunately and inevitably, submerged South African military doctrine, which until then was heading on a trajectory of its own. The subordination of command to the British was to cost the South Africans dearly. The South Africans who spilled their blood in the desert sands of Sidi Rezegh or went into ignominious captivity when Tobruk surrendered were as much victims of inadequate force preparation as they were of inferior British armored doctrine. What follows is an examination of the main protagonists' military doctrines for the purpose of gaining a deeper understanding as to the conduct of the desert war, and the reasons behind the ebb and flow of the individual battles.

The Development of German and British Military Doctrine

The South African official history draws insightful attention to the fact that British military thinking was underdeveloped and harked back to the tactics of the First World War.[7] The British exited the First World War with an abhorrence to trench warfare and its resultant waste of life. J. F. C. Fuller (1878–1966) and Basil Henry Liddell Hart (1895–1970) led postwar British intellectuals to seek technological answers to alleviate the carnage brought about by static war and the power of the defense. Fuller helped plan the tank attack at the battle of Cambrai in 1917 and the tank operations for the autumn offensives of 1918. He never got the opportunity to implement his Plan 1919 for a fully mechanized offensive against the German army.[8] After the war, Fuller collaborated with B. H. Liddell Hart in developing new ideas for the mechanization of armies. Along with Fuller, Liddell Hart became known as one of the leading proponents of mechanization, although his actual influence, particularly in Germany, is a matter of some dispute.[9] Some saw the tank as the war-winning weapon, which would restore mobility to the battlefield and bring to an end the senseless human loss of attrition warfare. They foresaw that the tank would dominate the battlefield, mostly unsupported (unhindered!) by infantry or artillery, its main aim to seek out enemy armored formations and destroy them. The trend in British intellectual military thinking emerging after the First World War stressed the independent action of armored fighting vehicles, downplaying the need for interarm cooperation.[10] Fuller, the leading and influential British military intellectual, went to the extent of calling for the abolition of traditional arms.[11]

In contrast, German doctrine remained little changed from that of the First World War, and demanded close cooperation and mutual support of all the arms of service, as a method to restore mobility to the battlefield. The influence of British military thinkers, especially Fuller and Liddell Hart, in the interwar years on German military thought and the so-called "*Blitzkrieg* doctrine" has been exaggerated and, according to more modern accounts, overrated.[12] In fact, there is substantial evidence to suggest that the term *Blitzkrieg* was an Anglo-American construct.[13]

The term is extremely rare in German literature before the Second World War. It became a piece of German propaganda journalism rather than the official military terminology of the *Wehrmacht*. Due to its misuse and overuse, the term *Blitzkrieg* is ambiguous, and the idea that it was new doctrine formulated by Hitler due to the vigor of National Socialism is false.[14] What was later to become famously known as *Blitzkrieg* was nothing more than the evolution of centuries-old Prussian military thought,[15] though refined through "flexible defence" and "infiltration tactics" in the First World War. German doctrine received enhancement with the introduction of the tank as a potent addition to a balanced all arms concept of warfare.

In the early 1930s few would dispute that Great Britain was the world leader in mechanized warfare doctrine. The so-called "tank radicals" such as Fuller and Liddell Hart heavily influenced this doctrine, and the Royal Tank Regiment (RTC) accepted some of their distinctly unsound ideas as dogma.[16] That the British saw the tank as a war-winning weapon, to the exclusion of the artillery and infantry, can be directly attributed to the thinking of Fuller. In his award-winning RUSI[17] paper entitled "New Model Army," he saw the tank playing the central role and downplayed the other arms. He insisted that all arms would be built around the capabilities of the tank. Fuller explains the lack of a role for the infantry and artillery thus:

> The question now arises, what can the infantry do? These troops can do nothing outside playing the part of interested spectators. What can the gunners do? They can do next to nothing, for, being distant from the field of action, upon which in a minute a tank may have changed its position by a quarter of a mile, they dare not promiscuously bombard any area; besides, in order to fire at all, they will generally have to employ direct laying, which, in most cases, will require them to be either with, or in advance of, the infantry. In such positions, as the gunners, in order to protect themselves, cannot lie flat like infantry, their pieces will soon be silenced by hostile machine gun fire.[18]

His proposal was that an all-tank army would eventually replace an interim measure of a tank-heavy division incorporating elements of other arms.[19] Liddell Hart, similarly in a RUSI essay competition entry in 1922 titled, "The Development of the New Model Army," suggested that

> The tank is likely to swallow the infantryman. [. . .] The logical sequence points to the land or rather overland forces being comprised primarily of tanks and aircraft, with a small force of siege artillery for the reduction and defence of the fortified tank and airfield bases, and of mechanical borne infantry for use as land marines.

Both Fuller and Liddell Hart envisaged a much-reduced role for the infantry, such as mopping up and policing conquered areas. It is only after the war that Liddell Hart attempted to distance himself from his visions of infantry, as opposed to Fuller. The fact remains that he continued to be a faithful disciple of Fuller during the interwar period.[20]

It is more than a coincidence that the tactics employed by the British in the Western Desert during the Second World War closely mimicked the operational concepts of Fuller and Liddell Hart. A close disciple of Fuller pioneered these new tactics. He was the commander of the Mobile Force (Egypt) between 1938 and 1939, Major-General Percy Hobart (1885–1957). He firmly believed in the ability of the tank to overcome all tactical obstacles unaided by either infantry or artillery support. He favored fast-moving, highly dispersed mobile columns that would find the enemy flanks and rear and engage them with the advantage of surprise. His tactics led to dispersion rather than concentration and were contrary to an all-arms-combined-warfare approach. The nexus of Fuller–Liddell Hart–Hobart carried the early intellectual, but misguided vision of an all-tank army right up to the Second World War. The influence of these like-minded "tank radicals" persisted and permeated the Eighth Army despite Wavell's dismissal of Hobart in 1940, ironically due to his unconventional ideas.[21] The eventual result was that the British entered the Second World War with two different tactical doctrinal approaches. Armored brigades believed that it was tactically unsound to combine with non-armored infantry and artillery units, even when they were an integral part of the armored divisional structure. The infantry, on the other hand, possessed a separate infantry-tank-artillery combined arms doctrine. These two doctrinal streams led to the deployment of infantry support tanks such as the Matilda, which was slow and heavily armored, to aid the infantry in an attack, and a lighter tank such as the Crusader, which the British designed to be highly mobile, for maneuver warfare.[22]

The Germans observed and debated this radical new British line of thinking, but their approach was less intellectual and more pragmatic. They respected Fuller as an originator of tank warfare and one of the few soldiers in any army who had any practical experience of using tanks in actual combat. J. F. "Hans" von Seeckt (1866–1936), chief of the Reichswehr from 1919 to 1920, was responsible for building the new 100,000-man Reichswehr out of the ashes of the old Imperial Army. He stressed combined arms warfare in a war of maneuver, in which the tank and other arms were merely components of a balanced combined arms group.[23] The Germans, unlike the British, did not invent a novel armored doctrine, but rather fused the wisdom gleaned from past battles, especially those of the last year of the First World War, with the current philosophy and knowledge prevalent at that time.[24] The German doctrine united Field Marshal Helmuth von Moltke's (the elder) (1800–1891)[25] concepts of *Schwerpunkt* (point of concentration) and *Auftragstaktik* (mission command tactics) with *Stosstrupptaktik* (storm-troop tactics), developed in the First World War. It finally incorporated Seeckt's *Bewegungskrieg* (war of movement) developed in the Reichswehr.[26]

German armored doctrine found its roots in far older traditional ground than the British, who came to see the tank as a war-winning weapon to the exclusion of the other arms of service. The Germans came to view the tank as merely a component of a balanced all arms force, using combined arms tactics. One can trace this combined arms approach all the way back to the reign of Fredrick the Great in the late 1700s. The Germans viewed the advent of new technology differently from the British. According to Vardi, the German approach to technology was ". . . practical and utilitarian: how can technology serve the Army in realising its current doctrinal goals?" New technology fitted in with the existing military doctrine rather than changing it.[27] Combined arms warfare is akin to conducting a philharmonic orchestra. The individual components of an orchestra each have their own sections of the music to play, but it is only in combination with all the other instruments that the concerto emerges. Individual orchestra members are required to practice their craft to gain proficiency in playing their musical instruments, which is similar to the task of infantrymen or artillerymen, who constantly practice their trade to develop their craft. The crux is that what makes an orchestra produce perfect harmony is continual practice as a group of musicians.[28] The successful execution of combined arms warfare requires a strict regimen of training in which infantry, artillery, armor, and the air force train together so that they can fight together.

The German tradition, usually in the face of overwhelming odds, favored fighting a war of movement (*Bewegungskrieg*) rather than positional warfare (*Stellungskrieg*). Historically, circumstances forced the Germans to devise tactics designed to gain an advantage over enemies who invariably enjoyed a numerical superiority. German generals invariably built into their planning the underlying assumption that German forces would be numerically inferior to those of the enemy. Frederick the Great demonstrated that it was possible to defy adverse strategic force ratios by maneuvering faster than the enemy at the operational level of warfare.[29] The Germans used maneuver tactics and sought to bring the enemy to battle at a place and time of their choosing, allowing them to gain local superiority in numbers through superior concentration at the chosen point of attack (*Schwerpunkt*).[30] The emphasis was on converting German strategic numerical inferiority into an operational numerical superiority. Friese relates the concept of concentration, referencing the French General Charles Delestraint, who described the difference between French and German armor tactics at the time of the fall of France in 1940: "We used [tanks] in a thousand packs of three, the Germans in three packs of a thousand."[31]

In conformity with Clausewitz, and embraced by Helmut Count von Moltke (the elder), German doctrine encouraged a battle of annihilation (*Vernichtungsschlacht*), best achieved by adopting a strategy of envelopment or encirclement (*Kesselschlacht*).[32] The German penchant for encirclement and annihilation was born out of necessity in having to face an enemy in a European war on two fronts simultaneously. Encirclement and annihilation were means to concentrate on, and defeat, one enemy at a time by fighting them in succession. The German way of war also encouraged *Fuhren von vorn*, or leading from the front. This practice yielded both tactical and psychological advantages in a war of movement. The ability to make fast decisions on the spot increased the tempo of the operation, in comparison with the Allied approach to leadership from the rear. *General der Panzertruppe* E. J. E. (Erwin) Rommel (1891–1944) was perhaps the greatest exponent of this doctrine, and at times he took it to the extreme, much to the exasperation of his staff and indeed, his enemy.[33]

The Germans possessed a unique way of dealing with the inevitable fog of war as well as what Clausewitz refers to as "friction,"[34] and this differed substantially from that which the British devised to combat the confusion and stress of battle. Contrary to the British, who sought to manage all aspects of the battle in elaborate prearranged written orders, the Germans acknowledged that even the best plans dissolved after the first shot fired.[35] In preference to the British system of directive type command, the Germans established a command concept in which even the most junior officers were required to make far-reaching decisions.[36] German officers higher up in the command chain would merely give subordinate commanders objectives (often verbal and on the spot), and subordinate commanders in turn passed these all the way down to the lowest ranks, whom they trusted (demanded) to make on-the-spot decisions, subject to ever-changing circumstances on the battlefield. Commanders would limit orders to general instructions outlining overall objectives and timeframes, leaving the tactical conduct of the operation in achieving those objectives entirely to the subordinate tasked with the mission. Mission command tactics were far from easy to achieve, requiring all the echelons and components of the army to be thoroughly familiar with and to comply with the operational goal.[37] The devolving of authority and encouragement of initiative to obtain objectives was enshrined in German doctrine and became known as mission command tactics (*Auftragstaktik*).[38] The German doctrine of maneuver warfare in itself demanded a high degree of initiative at all command levels.[39]

The German concepts of *Bewegungskrieg* and *Auftragstaktik* demanded an aggressive spirit within the German armed forces. German doctrine encouraged commanders to seize the initiative by resorting to the offensive, even when the situation was in doubt, rather than assume the defensive and surrender the initiative. The German default was attack.[40] The result of this was that the Germans conducted their operations at a greater tempo than their adversaries. Waiting for orders from a higher authority often hamstrung the Allied pace of battle, while Allied reaction time was further slowed owing to the general fog of war. It is worth bearing this in mind when analyzing some of the decisions made by German commanders, especially in the case of Rommel. The German preference to attack rather than to hesitate permeated all levels of command and could sometimes lead to absurdity. *SS-Oberst-Gruppenführer* Sepp Dietrich (1892–1966), commander of the 6th *Panzer* Army in the Ardennes in 1944, when asked the objectives for his *Panzers* in the assault, replied, "Objectives, objectives! If I had to give everybody objectives, wherever should I be?" When asked about his overall plan all he could say was that it was to push through to Antwerp "and then give the English a good beating."[41]

The First World War served to further condition and build German doctrine, especially in the development of combined arms warfare, which had been a cornerstone of German tactics.[42] The Germans resorted to a doctrine of flexible defense. This doctrine called on the local commander to withdraw his main forces out of harm's way when confronted with an Allied attack accompanied by massively destructive artillery barrages. In this way, the Germans absorbed the Allied attack by giving up ground. In a classic demonstration of *Auftragstaktik*, the local commander had the discretion of when to initiate a counterattack, at the time and place of his choosing. German combined arms doctrine reached its pinnacle when expressed in their infiltration tactics that so nearly won them the war on the Western Front in 1918. The Germans nearly defeated the Allied forces in France by using the tactics of bypassing points of resistance. The initiative of subordinate commanders on the battlefield, following the lines of least resistance and then reducing enemy strongpoints with a combination of infantry artillery and airpower, enabled tactical success without the aid of tanks.[43]

When tanks became available to the German Army in 1934, long denied by the terms of the onerous Versailles treaty, they slotted them into the German combined arms doctrine to serve alongside the other arms of service. The Germans sought to enhance their doctrine with new technology, rather than allow new technology to alter their doctrine. The Germans attempted to ensure that the other traditional arms were mechanized as far as possible in order to keep up with the tank and match its superior maneuverability.[44] They soon realized that the tank was most effective when used en masse instead of in small units, tied down to the speed of the infantry. The most effective way of gathering tanks was in a combined arms *Panzer* division, which was unlike the British all-tank brigade. The British tank brigade fielded almost the same amount of tanks as a German *Panzer* division, the difference being that the German *Panzer* division had a strong component of infantry and artillery, lacking in the British version.[45]

The British sought salvation from the battlefield carnage of the First World War by using technical innovation, and as a result began to experiment with the tank. The establishment of the Experimental Mechanical Force in 1927—which Fuller would have headed up, had he not inexplicably resigned from the position—signalled the British army's acceptance of new and innovative ideas and its receptiveness to the radical thoughts of Fuller and Liddell Hart.[46] The concept of an all arms combined force was lost in an underestimation of the role of infantry and the overestimation of what unsupported armored forces could achieve on their own.[47] Thus, the final composition of the Experimental Mechanical Force reflects the influence that Fuller and Liddell Hart had on the British military establishment in the interwar years.[48] The lessons learned from this experiment, endorsed by the Royal Tank Corps spokesman, Liddell Hart, resulted in a movement toward an all-tank army rather than balanced all arms formations.[49] Contrary to his postwar claims of identifying the need for close cooperation between all arms, Liddell Hart rejected the inclusion, except for a small component of land marines, of any infantry in a future armored force. The Germans obviously watched these innovative developments carefully. Although influenced by the British to a certain extent, they drew conclusions from the British tank exercises that were different, having viewed the proceedings through German doctrinal lenses.

In his *Lectures on FSRIII*, Fuller did not envisage a role for the indirect fire of the artillery, seeing it as impractical in a fast-moving tank melee. He did not foresee the cooperative role of tanks and antitank weapons that formed the backbone of German tactics in the Western Desert.[50] Fuller shared some basic assumptions with the other radical tank advocates, namely that armies would get smaller; all armored formations were necessary for mobile operations; the integration of infantry into a mobile armored battle was problematic, even impossible; and conventional artillery had very little place in an armored battle. The following quote from Fuller, written at the height of his influence, is an insight into British radical thought:

> I will, therefore, in order to supply the reader with the ammunition of argument, consider the power of tanks against the traditional arms, and the restriction of their power when attached to them. I will now show that the tank of the near future is likely to be as superior to the traditional arms as a modern destroyer is to a British coracle, and that to link the traditional arms to tanks will be as uneconomical as linking sailing frigates to a squadron of battle cruisers.

There are differences in opinion as to the extent this train of thought shaped British armored doctrine. Without a doubt, strong traces of it were evident long after Fuller expressed these sentiments, and certainly this line of thinking was manifest in the British conduct of the war in North Africa.[51] There is little doubt that British doctrine reflected the influence of these assumptions in the Western Desert in the Second World War. Lord Wilson of Libya, in describing his efforts to train the 7th Armoured Division in Egypt in 1939–1940, wrote:

> One had to check a pernicious doctrine which had grown up in recent years, aided by certain civilian writers that tank units were capable of winning an action without the assistance of the other arms. . . . The chief agents in debunking this and many other fallacies of our pre-war pundits were the Germans.[52]

The British envisaged that the main role of the tank was to seek combat with other tanks and eliminate them as a first step to the battle. The German armored units, unlike the British, were encouraged to avoid fighting other tanks or antitank guns, and instead, true to their doctrine, they trained to exploit areas of little or no resistance.[53] Where tank-versus-tank combat became unavoidable, the Germans preferred to withdraw their armor behind an antitank screen in an attempt to entice the British tanks to attack.[54] The Germans considered antitank weapons to be an indispensable component of the mechanized combined arms team. In the early part of the war, tanks carried small caliber guns, relatively inaccurate compared to towed antitank guns with large caliber, high-velocity guns. Antitank guns proved lethal against armor at ranges more than double those of a tank's guns. Harris brings attention to an important doctrinal difference between the German and British tactical doctrines. The British, due to thinking of their mechanized forces as akin to naval warships, put great store into the ability to fire on the move. The Germans adopted the opposite doctrine, as firing on the move was severely detrimental to accuracy.[55]

The antitank gun enjoyed a relatively small silhouette, making it extremely difficult to detect and engage, and rendering the tank particularly ineffective with its restricted view when deployed against this weapon. The antitank gun, in turn, was extremely vulnerable to artillery fire and infantry attack. The British allowed the Germans to deploy their vulnerable antitank weapons with relative impunity due to their general unawareness that German antitank weapons played a fundamental role in the destruction of British armor. The British failed, on most occasions, to concentrate their artillery effectively against the German antitank weapons. British doctrine encouraged a limited viewpoint of the tank as the primary weapon against enemy tanks. As a direct result the British carried armor-piercing rounds exclusively, and they failed to arm them with high-explosive rounds more suitable for anti-personnel and anti-artillery use.[56]

Major-General F. W. von Mellenthin (1904–1997), a staff officer in the Afrika Corps, provides an excellent insight into the differences between German and British thinking regarding armored warfare doctrine. He acknowledges that British experts did appreciate that tanks had a significant part to play in a future conflict. What they failed to identify, with the same vigor and depth of understanding as their German counterparts, was the importance of cooperation of all arms in the armored division. The Germans went to great lengths in their training to achieve proficiency in combined arms warfare. In exercises, the army attached representatives from different arms to units of a different formation to ensure that, "the various branches of the service must become acquainted with each other."[57] Von Mellenthin placed the British ten years behind the Germans in combined arms doctrine.[58]

The British doctrine, favoring tank-heavy divisions to the exclusion of other arms, would have negative implications for the motorized South African and other dominion infantry brigades placed at the disposal of the British Eighth Army.[59] The British had very little use for these pure infantry brigades, beyond that of occupying territory conquered by the tanks and providing a safe refuge for the tanks to withdraw to replenish and refit. They saw their primary task as the destruction of the opposing tank force with their own tank forces, and until they achieved this, the infantry brigades remained very much in the background. It was indeed unfortunate that the British achieved the reverse in the battles of Sidi Rezegh and Tobruk, where it was the German combined arms forces that destroyed the British tanks, leaving the infantry brigades alone to defend themselves against the German *Panzer* divisions. One of those unfortunate infantry brigades was the 5th SAI Brigade, which found itself left to the mercy of the Axis armored divisions at Sidi Rezegh after the Germans destroyed the British tanks in detail. Had the British shown greater foresight and availed themselves of the South African mobile capability, the disaster may have been avoided. It seems the British were oblivious to the possibilities of making use of the South Africans by giving cognizance to their distinct way of war.

THE EVOLUTION AND OTHERNESS OF SOUTH AFRICAN MILITARY DOCTRINE

The UDF could trace its roots back to three distinct military systems and, as such, the DNA it carried into the Second World War was imprinted, to a larger or lesser degree, with the Boer, Colonial, and British systems that preceded it. More than forty years had passed since the end of the Anglo-Boer War when the Second World War engulfed the world, yet despite the passing of time and the apparent embracing of and adherence to British military doctrine and equipment, there was a strong element of the Boer way of war coursing through the veins of the UDF. Perhaps the strongest Boer influence persisted in the higher echelons of the UDF and this manifested in a strong abhorrence to wasteful frontal attacks and a distaste for pointless heroic final stands.[60] The South Africans demonstrated a clear preference for maneuver rather than positional warfare, and their motorized infantry, the successors to the old Boer mounted infantry, gave the needed mobility to fulfill this doctrine. In East Africa in 1941, a single section of fourteen men made their home in one three-ton vehicle rather than loading the truck to its capacity of twenty men. This vehicle then became their home, carrying all their kit and enough supplies of food, ammunition, and fuel to last the section a week or longer. Therefore, each vehicle was self-sufficient to a large extent and could act independently, a practice not far removed from the Boer commando at the turn of the century.[61]

South African generals, especially Dan Pienaar, displayed an individuality harking back to that of the Boer generals, often to the alarm and dismay of the British command. Pienaar's relationship with the British was not always an easy one due to his individualism and informality and a clear preference of adhering dogmatically to his own plans. His men admired his comradeship, which extended through all the ranks. He honored the old Boer principle that it was a crime to sacrifice lives needlessly. He had contempt for personal danger and was prepared to undergo any hardships he asked of the men he commanded.[62] Close military ties to Britain had not completely submerged the South African way of war by the time of the Second World War, and an understanding of its subtleties provides insight into some of the decisions made by the South Africans in North Africa.

The Boer army of 1899 consisted of 30,000 farmers with little formal military training and oblivious to an accepted theory of warfare or the methodology of recent wars.[63] The battles they fought and the movements they made were not in accordance with any recognizable established set of rules that suggested a system. The Boers made war with an instinct for fighting and self-preservation, which was more a function of common sense and their environment than any formal military doctrine. Their methods were extremely rudimentary and not born of any system of discipline or training but rather owed their existence to a way of life. This inherent natural ability was as much a cultural trait as the German *Auftragstaktik*, a concept easier to define than to replicate.[64] The Boer soldier almost always acted on his own initiative. Boer generals were of more importance before the battle, for planning purposes and bringing their men to the battle, than in conducting the course of events during the battle. On the battlefield, the Boer soldier was his own general. He never waited for an order from an officer to take advantage of a favorable situation. He was flexible and resourceful and was able to find cover, if necessary; retreat, if the opportunity arose; advance, and reinforce spontaneously. Boer cohesion in battlefield conditions was a function of spontaneity and instinct, and an ability to grasp a situation rather than follow direction in accordance with set orders. Unlike most other armies, there was a distinct lack of formal orders among the Boers.[65]

The Boer burgher was essentially a law unto himself and he could eat, sleep, or fight whenever he wished. He was not compelled to rise at a certain hour in the morning, and he could go to bed whenever he wished. There were none of the thousands of petty details that soldiers of most other armies were compelled to perform. There was no work on Sundays or Church holidays, and the Boers were sticklers for the observance of the Sabbath unless forced by circumstances into combat. The officers and men enjoyed an equality not seen in other armies. Officers did not wear distinct uniforms and looked the same and carried the same equipment as their men.[66] Officers enjoyed a close association with the men on a daily basis and were able to call most of them by their first names.[67] Ordinary soldiers elected their officers, more appropriately called leaders, by way of a vote in a manner similar to which they chose their presidents and civil officials. Unfortunately, ability and military experience were not always the deciding factors in electing the best man for the job. Many leaders owed their election more to family influence and party affiliations rather than military prowess, and nepotism often sidelined the best military minds.[68] This situation did undergo a change in the second half or guerrilla phase of the Second Anglo-Boer War. The military leadership in control at the outset of the war consisting of "[men] arrogant and obsessed with their own importance, occupying as they did the pinnacle of the Boer societal pyramid" were replaced by "a younger, better educated and disciplined cadre of commanders, who changed to a guerrilla strategy."[69]

In addition to the freedom of action enjoyed by individuals, the Boer army enjoyed mobility. Every soldier owned and was mounted on a hardy horse or pony, and as a consequence, the Boer tempo on the battlefield was many times that of his adversary. Boer mobility enabled the army to execute swift maneuvers on the battlefield, and coupled with their instinct, they were able to disperse when in danger and concentrate on taking advantage of a battlefield opportunity. Boers were able to change their course of direction many times within a battle, whereas their enemies, once they had unleashed their forces, were committed to a set course of action. Unlike the Boers, they had neither the mobility nor the flexibility to modify the plan with the changing battlefield conditions.[70]

The Boers saw little advantage in seeking glory or making personal sacrifices to achieve a goal. Afrikaner society considered a Boer life to be precious and the needless loss thereof to be detrimental to the community as a whole. As a consequence, the British felt that the Boers were risk averse and not willing to sacrifice lives even in achieving a decisive victory. The Boers were not disinclined to retreat when in danger and this characteristic of self-preservation was to cost them some decisive victories when they left the battlefield prematurely within sight of victory.[71] It is a mistake to view the Boer sensitivity to needless casualties as a lack of courage on the battlefield.[72] However, John Collyer, an official historian of the First World War, tackled the Boer lack of aggression on the eve of the Second World War. Collyer pointed out that the Boers missed many an opportunity to deal a decisive blow during the Anglo-Boer War by failing to launch a timely counterattack. Collyer believed that the Boer viewpoint of merely being satisfied with repulsing an enemy attack from defensive positions was outmoded and that the UDF needed to adopt a more aggressive stance. He suggested that a doctrine of aggressive counterattack form a definite part of the training of South African troops.[73]

Discipline was not a feature of the Boer army, and no rule of law prevented a Boer soldier from retreating.[74] The army had no drills, no formal paperwork or standards, and no roll call. It was a bigger version of a traditional hunting party; an "aggregation of lion hunters."[75] It is a moot point whether the Boer army would have been more effective if it had been possible to introduce discipline and training to enhance a very rudimentary but intuitive military system. Van der Waag believes that the weakest feature of the Boer system was indiscipline, "the burghers disliked being organised and their officers could never count on all the men on the muster roll being present to go into action."[76] The fact that the Boer army was "not hampered by traditional military concepts and methods"[77] gave it an unprecedented flexibility in the tactical battle but may have led to its eventual demise at the strategic level of the war.[78]

On establishment of the UDF in 1912, the structure of the new defense force was that of an uneasy amalgamation of former enemies with deep doctrinal differences. The Boer military system was certainly a significant component of the newly formed UDF. In fact, the new structure went out of its way to ensure an equilibrium of representation in command structures. The composition of the UDF general staff from 1912–1950 was almost an even split between Afrikaner and Englishmen. Van der Waag sees the UDF as "a compromise between the determination of English speakers to maintain the British military connection and the desire of

Afrikaner nationalists for a restoration of Boer political and military traditions."[79] There was a drive led by Smuts, which encountered much opposition, to modernize the UDF to be able to engage a modern enemy on equal terms. Smuts recognized that the future of the UDF was not the re-creation and replication of the Boer army and its systems, but the creation of a modern defense force.[80]

The First World War accelerated the pace of the UDF's modernization. The UDF instituted the essentials of a modern military organization, such as the unification of command and the development of the general staff and administration.[81] However, the mounted infantry columns that marched into and conquered German South West Africa and later ejected the Germans from their colony in East Africa would not have been out of place in the Anglo-Boer War. It was more than a coincidence that the racial composition of the mounted infantry units emanated mostly from Afrikaner stock, many of whom served in the Republican armies during the Anglo-Boer War.[82] Louis Botha in GSWA and later Smuts in German East Africa (GEA) conducted their campaigns using their mobility in a war of maneuver that was unlike the stalemate experienced by the Allies on the Western Front. The Boer penchant for mobility and maneuver seemed to find a natural home within the campaigns of the UDF in the First World War in Africa. The Boers and later the UDF maneuverd to fight while the British, tied into their large logistic needs, fought to maneuver.

The UDF emerging from the First World War underwent a process of modernization, and the acute political differences of its members were somewhat stifled and then forged into something more homogenous in the searing flames of war. Modernization ensured that the lax discipline and flat leadership hierarchy of the old Boer military system belonged to the past. The organization and leadership structure of the UDF followed that of the British army closely. British weaponry almost exclusively equipped the UDF, which followed British tactical doctrine closely. However, the UDF differed from the British in its distinct sensitivity to unnecessary casualties and its preference for maneuver warfare over set piece frontal assaults. Hartshorn eloquently brings to light a pertinent example of South African distaste for the sometimes flippant waste of life advocated by the British. He describes Pienaar's dislike of General Ramsden, his corps commander at Alamein, whom the South Africans knew as "chuck-em-in" Ramsden. It was an unflattering title given to Ramsden, who had the habit of "airily" prefacing his orders to commit men recklessly into the assault with the words, "chuck-em-in."[83]

It seems that the UDF adopted and took to heart the doctrine contained in *Infantry Training 1902*[84], which favored flank attacks over frontal assaults. The British produced *Infantry Training 1902* as a direct result of the lessons learned in the Anglo-Boer War. However, the sentiments of avoiding expensive frontal assaults expressed in this doctrine began to erode steadily in the period leading up to the First World War. The Russo-Japanese war of 1905 proved to be the catalyst in swinging British military doctrine back to a more direct approach to warfare in which the British favored the "moral ascendancy" in using frontal assaults to overcome an enemy.[85] Judging by what transpired with the UDF in its African campaigns, this was an obvious point of difference between the British and UDF military doctrines.

The interwar years saw the further modernization of the UDF, although this did not keep pace with developments in Europe. The UDF did not fully embrace mechanization, although South Africa had the industrial capacity to do so. Government thought of defense matters in terms of meeting local policing requirements rather than fielding a fully fledged conventional army to meet a modern enemy. Some promising developments never saw fruition, such as the South African Field Force. In the early 1920s, the UDF developed a strike force in conjunction with the South African Mounted Rifles. Known as the South African Field Force, the UDF established it around a small mechanized nucleus, making for an interesting embryonic combined arms battlegroup. Prevailing circumstances geared it toward internal policing matters and allowed for its rapid deployment to trouble-spot areas within South Africa and its neighboring territories. It is ironic that South Africa established an experimental mechanized force two years before their British counterparts.[86] The UDF disbanded the Field Force in 1926 due to fiscal constraints. Collyer, who served as a mounted infantryman and had seen fifty years of service in Africa, saw no reason to modernize and mechanize the UDF and dispense with horse-borne infantrymen. The absurd "bush cart" policy of Oswald Pirow epitomized his way of thinking.[87]

The UDF suffered most in the area of junior officer selection. The selection panel attached primary importance to the appointment of

Afrikaners, particularly those with a rather anti-British background. These junior officers displayed all the characteristics of individualism of their Boer ancestors but apparently lacked their self-control and experience. The higher echelons of command possessed scant military education and expertise with an overemphasis on administrative expertise. Therefore, modernization of the UDF had not totally eliminated some of the doctrine of the old Boer Republican Army at the junior level of command at the outbreak of the Second World War.[88]

South Africa played a major role in defeating the Italians in East Africa in her first campaign of the Second World War. Her battle performance in that campaign was credible and the UDF learned many useful lessons in the art of war. The main adversary proved to be the formidable terrain and climate, rather than the demoralized Italians. The UDF suffered surprisingly few casualties in what amounted to a test of endurance rather than one of fighting abilities. In East Africa, the South Africans never strayed far from their maneuver warfare roots, described succinctly by Hartshorn as "turn the flank, crawl like snakes, and dash in like lions."[89] The South Africans gained valuable, if at times not entirely appropriate, experience. However, the trial of warfare honed their doctrine of maneuver, and their initially weak organizational capabilities strengthened under battle conditions. On occasion, the South Africans managed to deploy armor in a combined arms exercise with good results. The South African experiment with armor was on a miniscule scale, but they nevertheless made significant doctrinal strides in the right direction. They were destined to encounter a far more capable enemy in North Africa. The Germans used the unique desert conditions to exploit their highly developed tactical and operational skills in mobile warfare and demonstrate their mastery of combined arms warfare.

When the UDF transferred to North Africa to fight under the command of the Eighth Army, there was a pronounced clash of doctrine between them and the British. The South Africans had an intense dislike of defending fixed positions and preferred to remain mobile. Under the command of the Eighth Army, they found themselves having to defend fixed positions when the situation instead called for mobile warfare. Major-General E. E. Dorman-Smith (1895–1969), who later changed his name to Dorman O'Gowan and served as chief of staff to Auchinleck, had an affinity for the South Africans and their unique way of war. He saw a role for them as part of a mobile force in close cooperation with the British tank brigades. He stressed the need for a "far-ranging, hard hitting, quick moving force" instead of the "stodgy, orthodox, British-type Army Corps." What Dorman-Smith envisaged was much closer and more suitable to the South African way of war, and had the British implemented it with a bit of foresight, the course of the desert war may have been somewhat different.

> What I envisaged, and discussed with Auchinleck, was a couple of armoured divisions wedded to two tactically mechanised unarmoured divisions. The proper people for this sort of work, to my mind, were the descendants of the South African War riders who had so often run rings around the slow-moving slow-witted British. They had done so in the open veld which so closely resembled as a tactical problem the Western Desert.[90]

Dorman-Smith was not alone in lamenting the misuse of the South African motorized infantry in an undesirable role that undercut their mobility. Agar-Hamilton believed that the Eighth Army should have maintained the South African formation as a self-contained, heavily armed, and highly mobile force, fighting as a unit. He sees it as a "tradgedy" that the South Africans were never permitted or provided an opportunity of "functioning in the role for which they were devised."[91]

General H. B. Klopper, the commander of the Tobruk garrison, was intensely uncomfortable in having to operate the defenses within the boundaries of the Tobruk perimeter. He wanted his counterattack force to be mobile and to attack the enemy beyond the perimeter defenses as they were forming up. Contrary to his instinct, Major-General Neil Ritchie (1897–1983) instructed him to maintain his defense within the Tobruk perimeter, thereby effectively consigning the entire division to an operationally static defense.[92] The South African predilection for mobile rather than static warfare was again demonstrated when the British ordered Pienaar to man the El Alamein defensive "box." Pienaar was extremely resistant to the idea of being "shut up" in the El Alamein defenses and preferred not to occupy any fixed defensive position at all. Eventually, the South Africans held the El Alamein box with one brigade, and the other two were semi-mobile on the edge of the Ruweisat Ridge.[93] This clash of doctrine was a point of extreme irritation between the British and the South Africans for the duration of the desert war.

The Desert Environment and Its Influence on Mobile Warfare

The desert conditions of North Africa were vastly different from the temperate oceanic climate of Europe or even the arid and semi-arid conditions in East Africa. The desert offered an environment that was as strange as it was harsh. The desert, bereft of readily available water and lacking in natural defensive terrain features such as rivers, forests, and mountains, offered up a unique set of combat challenges. Desert warfare is similar to naval warfare in some important aspects.[94] Just as at sea, and unlike fighting in Europe, the lack of major terrain features eliminated their use as defensive multipliers. The distances traversed were enormous and the lack of any natural barrier to the south ensured that both armies always presented an open flank. Mastering navigation in the featureless terrain was essential, and again, it was more akin to that practiced in the navy than the army. The Germans demonstrated astounding ability when it came to mastering desert navigation. Rommel's feats of maneuvering entire armies with high precision at night, or choreographing complicated maneuvers and concentrating his scattered forces at the decisive point with precise timing, often left the British on the horns of a dilemma. Desert warfare favored pure mechanized war and was unlike the large horse- and mule-drawn armies that fought on the Eastern Front in Europe. Due to the high degree of mechanization on both sides, the desert campaign would provide an "ideal" testing ground for the futuristic theories and doctrines devised in the interwar period.

Infantry found great difficulty in "digging in" when they encountered rock-hard or sandy surfaces, and their attempts to fortifying defensive positions were not as effective as under European conditions. The absence of natural defensive terrain prompted both sides to make extensive use of mines to slow down and channel enemy advances. The vast expanse of the terrain and the relatively small density of soldiers, limited in number by what the stretched logistics chain was able to sustain, ensured that it was impossible to man a continuous defensive line. Therefore, it was nearly always possible to outflank an enemy defensive line. Mobile warfare forced units manning static positions to adopt all-around defenses, as the defenders could expect an enemy attack from any direction. The British attempted to construct a static defense at Gazala in May 1942, and they hoped to achieve this by laying an extensive belt of mines reaching far south into the desert. Brigade-size "boxes" adopted an all-around defense along the Gazala line that they bolstered with additional mines. The vast distances involved precluded the defensive boxes from being mutually supportive. In a final irony, the brigades sent away their transport vehicles to the rear, thereby removing an essential element of their survivability, their mobility.[95] The British kept their mobile armor brigades in the rear as a reserve for counteracting any German forays through or around the static line. This type of deployment harked back to First World War tactics—a doctrine that found more favor with the British. The Gazala line was an interesting, albeit unsuccessful, attempt by the British to impose their static way of war on the Germans.

The side that could master the art of maneuver and possessed the means of mobility to concentrate their forces, coupled with an ability to fight with combined arms, had the clear tactical advantage in desert warfare. The massive columns of immobile foot soldiers fielded by the Italians in the invasion of Egypt in 1940 quickly succumbed to the numerically inferior but highly mobile British formations. The best form of defense in a highly fluid war proved to be mobility rather than attempts to dig in and hunker down behind an all-around defense. A unit's survival depended on its ability to resist a superior force overwhelming them—not an easy task while defending a static position. In abandoning static warfare, mobility enabled a unit to remove itself from danger or add its strength to a gathering mass. In the desert, the side that managed to mass the bigger force (concentration) in the shortest possible time (tempo) at the focal point (*Schwerpunkt*) using combined arms tactics, usually managed to overwhelm the enemy by overrunning their positions, one by one, in a piecemeal fashion.[96]

Both sides evolved an art of war suited to the unique terrain and topography of North Africa. Terrain affected logistics, equipment, maintenance, vehicle recovery, communications, mobility, the art of maneuver, the defense and the offense, and many other aspects. Whereas the Germans merely adapted their highly successful doctrine, the desert war marked a period of British military unorthodoxy not seen before in

British military history.[97] These unorthodox methods attracted disastrous results and were especially expensive in human cost for the South Africans. The British had two glaring operational and tactical deficiencies which put them at a distinct disadvantage. They were incapable of combined arms tactics except at the very lowest levels and they had a tendency to disperse their forces rather than concentrate them. Some of this tendency was due to a lack of skill and some to a conscious decision in pursuit of flawed doctrine. An example of one of these conscious decisions was to form the infamous "Jock Columns," named after Lieutenant Colonel "Jock" Campbell.

These small, weak combined arms units, consisting of infantry, artillery, and antitank elements, were not able to carry out sustained fighting, but being highly mobile, they were suitable for hit-and-run raiding tactics. The British began to use these "Jock Columns" extensively, and they dispersed British fighting power and were no more than a nuisance to the Germans. The British also tended to disperse their highly effective 25-pounder artillery, arguably their strongest arm, among the "Jock Columns" and as an antitank weapon in support of the infantry. The unorthodox dispersion of the artillery denuded the British of significant fighting power where it mattered.[98] The British, lacking the prerequisite skill, were more comfortable in devolving all their fighting power down to brigade level and even down to "Jock Columns" while the Germans were able to use the division as their core fighting structure. Often a British brigade, unable to concentrate with other brigades, had to ward off a full German division alone, with disastrous results. General Fritz Beyerlein (1899–1970), one of Rommel's capable operations officers, identified the single outstanding British tactical failure as their inability to concentrate their forces, which went against all tactical principles. According to Bayerlein, the British were slow in making decisions and even slower in implementing them.[99]

In contrast to "Jock Columns," which were an exercise in dispersion, the Germans concentrated a combined arms force into a flexible battlegroup (*Kampfgruppe*).[100] Although the Germans employed a standard *Panzer* division, they were much more flexible in the field. The Germans could quickly form up an ad hoc battlegroup based on the immediate task at hand. These *Kampfgruppe*, usually named after the officer in command, varied greatly in size and composition. *Kampfgruppe* could range from a company up to battalion strength. What they all had in common was their temporary nature and that they invariably combined different arms in various combinations to tackle the task at hand. *Kampfgruppe* invariably contained armor, infantry, artillery, antiaircraft, reconnaissance elements, and engineers. This arrangement allowed the Germans to continue to be effective even when divisions had suffered heavy casualties and replacements were slow in arriving. Such was the extent of German flexibility that they could form components of the *Kampfgruppe* from other formations outside the division. At the end of the task, the Germans dissolved the battlegroup and all the elements returned to their parent divisions.[101] The Allies attempted to emulate the German *Kampfgruppe* doctrine throughout the war with varying degrees of success. The traditional British regimental system with strong regimental affiliations was uncomfortable with the concept of battlegroups of combined arms. The idea of *Kampfgruppe* required a cultural rather than a doctrinal change that the British Army, stuck to its traditions, found almost impossible to implement.[102]

The objective in the desert became the destruction of the enemy force rather than the capture of a significant landmark or mere territorial acquisition. The farther one moved away from a logistical hub the tougher it became to resupply advancing formations. Destruction of an enemy force required, as did naval warfare, the swift location of the enemy, followed by a rapid concentration of forces, so as to overwhelm and destroy the enemy. Reconnaissance and intelligence played an enormous role in operational and tactical success, especially under desert conditions, where the battle lines are particularly fluid and the tactical situation changes with startling rapidity. The South African armored cars played a significant role in the desert in a reconnaissance role and provided the Eighth Army with much-needed tactical information on many occasions. Both sides expended considerable resources on gaining intelligence. The British benefited from radio intercepts derived from their Ultra information, and Rommel owed much of his tactical surprise to the work of his Italian military intelligence.[103] Both sides, when they experienced a failure of intelligence, tended to overestimate the damage inflicted on the enemy, especially in the critical area of tank losses. This overestimation of tank casualties was more damaging to the British and played a significant role in the demise of the South African 5th Brigade at Sidi Rezegh and the ill-conceived British counterattacks on the "Cauldron" in the Gazala battles.

The British tended to believe that the German tanks substantially outclassed their tanks in hitting power and in defensive armor, whereas in reality, especially in Operation Crusader, they were quite evenly matched.[104] British tanks matched or outclassed their opponents in armor penetration and weight of armor in many instances. It is significant that most of the British manufactured tanks equipped with the 2-pounder main armament carried solid shot exclusively, which was useful only in an antitank role, and ineffective against personnel or soft-skinned targets. German tanks, on the other hand, carried equal amounts of solid shot and high-explosive ammunition, giving them a capability beyond a pure antitank role. This anomaly was a result of British doctrine that saw the tank's main role as that of destroying enemy tanks.[105] The arrival of the American Grant tank, in time for the Gazala battles, gave the British a distinct advantage over the Germans as the Grant outclassed anything on the German side. However, this temporary qualitative advantage, although costing the Germans many tanks destroyed at the hands of the superior Grant, did not translate into an operational victory for the British in those battles.[106]

Where the British suffered a distinct disadvantage was in the area of antitank weapons. Not only was the German proportion of antitank weapons to infantry considerably higher than the British, they also enjoyed a qualitative superiority in the 88mm antitank gun,[107] although these were not available in large numbers for Operation Crusader. The main German advantage came through their bold doctrine of deploying antitank weapons well forward and using them offensively. The British tended to deploy their 25-pounder artillery in an antitank role to make up for the deficit in their antitank assets, to the detriment of the substantial fighting power of their artillery.[108] That the vast majority of British tanks were lost to the German antitank guns, rather than in tank-on-tank engagements, was not initially apparent to the British, who believed, incorrectly, in the superiority of German tanks to their own.[109]

The Germans outclassed the British in another important area: the recovery of their disabled tanks. German recovery crews operated well up-front with the attacking or defending forces. They often retrieved vehicles in the firing line at great personal danger to themselves. The Germans were able to reintroduce back into the fray a significant portion of the tanks put out of action in combat the next day, due to the diligence and skill of the recovery crews. It also assisted the Germans that they were able to control and take possession of the battlefield during the night, when the recovery crews were most active, and were then able to use the cover of darkness to do their work. In contrast, the British abandoned the battlefield to the Germans on most occasions as it was their policy to retire to a safe haven to rest and repair. The German superior ability to recover and repair their vehicles was an important factor in the British overestimation of German tank losses.[110] Interestingly, Martel ascribes the superior reliability of German tanks to superior maintenance and the greater number of "fitters" available to the Germans. The German readiness to work on their tanks and plentiful supply of spares provided huge dividends for them on the battlefield.[111]

Desert warfare had a Napoleonic feel to it in certain key aspects. Napoleon enjoyed an advantage in his early career by having had the ability to move his armies in a dispersed fashion, and then to quickly concentrate his forces at the chosen point of engagement. Although not wholly conceived by Napoleon, the French military of that time was organized into divisions and corps, and like the German *Panzer* divisions were all arms balanced and self-sufficient. A division was able to hold its own against a larger enemy and pin them down for a period, allowing a larger force to concentrate and overwhelm the enemy elsewhere.[112] Desert conditions were similar to nineteenth-century warfare in some important aspects, such as the impossibility of forming a continuous linear defense, as had developed in France during the First World War.

The desert offered very little in the way of tactical concealment and even less in the way of cover. Both sides employed dust with good effect to disguise military intentions. Rommel especially made use of dust as a form of subterfuge on many occasions, either creating dust clouds or using the opportunities offered by the prolific dust storms that occurred naturally in the desert. The Germans made use of their transport vehicles to create dust and to give the illusion of the proximity of their forces. They accomplished this initially by dragging tarpaulins behind the trucks, but soon graduated in sophistication by fitting some with propellers.[113] The sudden appearance of dust was a sure sign of a significant movement of the enemy and this was true throughout the ages of desert warfare. Once battle commenced and a melee ensued, it was not long before dust shrouded the whole scene, obscuring friend from foe and adding greatly to the general confusion. Dust was a major factor in substantially reducing mechanical reliability and thus putting a further strain on an already taxed logistical system.[114]

Another method of achieving tactical surprise and concealment was the use of nighttime to move and amass forces making use of the limited visibility.[115] Both sides made use of the hours of darkness to maneuver their forces, but it was the Germans who seem to have best mastered the art of moving and amassing their forces at night. The opening move by Rommel at Gazala on May 26, 1942, occurred at night, when he skillfully maneuvered his forces in a wide outflanking movement, placing them behind the British lines at dawn. In a later phase of the battle Rommel once again used a night move when he turned his armored forces back from the Egyptian frontier in a 180-degree change of direction and assembled them for an attack on the southeast corner of Tobruk at dawn. The South Africans were reluctant to move at night and continually bemoaned the fact that they had not been afforded the time to practice their night navigation, an essential skill in terrain largely devoid of landmarks.[116]

Logistics played a prominent part in the desert war. Inhospitable conditions and a lack of infrastructure and local resources, coupled with extremely long lines of communication, played havoc with battle readiness. The very vehicles transporting the supplies to the front consumed a good portion of the supplies they were carrying in getting them to their destination. The enormous distances involved necessitated the use of forward supply depots that were difficult to defend, and in a war of high mobility they were vulnerable to attack from any direction.[117] If desert warfare was unique, then it was especially so when considering logistics in the harsh desert conditions. The desert offers little in the way of sustenance for a huge mechanized army. In Europe armies found resources locally, thereby allowing for partial sustenance. The Axis forces procured every ton of supplies via an enormously long supply route, initiated in Italy and then shipped over the Mediterranean to ports in Libya. Once there, a massive wheeled logistic chain transported essential supplies hundreds of kilometers to the front line.[118] The British were slightly better off in having their main supply depot in Cairo. The distances involved were enormous and dwarfed those that the belligerents had to contend with in Europe or even in the USSR. Harsh desert conditions hurt both man and machine, with the Germans believing that a soldier could serve no more than two years in such conditions before succumbing to permanent damage. The heat and the dust wreaked havoc on machinery designed for European conditions and the harsh conditions halved and quartered engine lives. Fuel and water consumption per mile was close to double that found in European conditions.[119] The small size of the armies deployed on both sides reflected the logistic impossibility of sustaining larger forces, given the difficulties in the supply chain.[120]

Conclusion

The desert provided an ideal testing ground for the conflict between the various military doctrines. It was a battlefield uncluttered with civilians and it possessed few built-up areas and infrastructure. It was an environment that favored mechanized warfare and a war of maneuver.

After the First World War, the British and the Germans set off on two different paths in their approaches to conducting a future war. The Germans emerged from the war reasonably satisfied with their combat doctrine, a product of evolution over centuries. The already solid foundations of German tactical thought incorporated the lessons learned and systems developed during the First World War, such as infiltration tactics and flexible defense. The Germans were satisfied that they had restored mobility through their innovative infiltration tactics, which so nearly ended the war in their favor in 1918. They looked on the development of tank doctrine by the British with a keen interest in the interwar years. However, the final result was far more pragmatic than that of the British. Unlike the British, who believed that the tank was a war-winning weapon, the Germans took the approach of integrating the tank as yet another arm in a combined arms force.

The British took an intellectual approach to formulating a new war doctrine. Led by Fuller and Liddell Hart, the tank became the centerpiece of any future armed struggle. Their intellectual vision saw very little use for the more traditional arms of infantry and artillery. This vision of an army dominated by tanks came to fruition under the leadership of Hobart and his Mobile Force just before the outbreak of the war. The desert army, which struggled against the Germans, adopted his unorthodox approach to warfare in significant part. The Germans destroyed British tanks, unsupported by infantry and artillery, in droves. The damage, unbeknown to the British, came mainly from lethal German antitank guns. The British military culture and structure were unable to deliver sufficient firepower at the critical point. They were unable to provide a combined arms force to overwhelm an often inferior and vulnerable enemy. Time and again they failed to concentrate their forces and arrived at the battlefield in dribs and drabs.

The South Africans possessed a distinct military doctrine of their own. Theirs was a culture of maneuver warfare in which they sought to pry an enemy away from prepared positions by threatening encirclement. It was a way of war that could trace its roots back centuries to the mounted infantry of the commandos. The South Africans preferred to use the inherent mobility of their motorized infantry to unbalance the enemy in the attack or get out of trouble in the defense. A pitched battle was anathema to the South African way of war. They were naturally averse to the high casualties that frontal assaults entailed. It was a system that they put to good use in defeating the numerically superior Italians in East Africa in 1940–1941. The South Africans also made good use of their armored vehicles in that war in a successful exercise of combined arms warfare. The South Africans, poised to fight a war in the Western Desert after East Africa, had some unpleasant realities foisted upon them. The British stripped them of their integral armored support and their natural tendency for mobility, with disastrous consequences.

The South Africans arrive in Egypt. These men are most probably fresh from their successful recent campaign in East Africa against the Italians.

The South Africans spent a good proportion of their time strengthening the defenses of Mersa Matruh at the expense of vital desert training in the months before the disaster of Sidi Rezegh.

Wearing their distinctive pith helmets, motorized troops of the Union Defence Force arrive in Egypt.

South Africans in Egypt!

The South African Air Force played its part in the desert air war. Here pilots and aircrew walk away from a Curtiss P-40 Kittyhawk Mk1A.

Field Marshal Jan Smuts (left), prime minister of the Union of South Africa, and Major-General George Brink (center), commander of the 1st South African Division, perform an inspection tour in North Africa.

General Pierre van Ryneveld (left), founding commander of the South African Air Force and Chief of the General Staff for the duration of World War II, with Smuts and Brink.

Major-General Frank Theron (right), the officer commanding the Union Defence Force's Administration in the Middle East, on inspection in the desert with Smuts (left).

The South Africans busied themselves on arrival in Egypt with strengthening the fortifications and defences around Mersa Matruh.

South African "Troopies" arrive by troop ship in Egypt. Some were fresh out of training camp in South Africa, while others were veterans of the East African Campaign against the Italians.

Major-General Isaac Pierre de Villiers, a veteran of World War I in Africa and the Western Front, commanded the 2nd South African Infantry Division destined to surrender en masse at Tobruk in June 1942.

The Mosque at Sidi Rezegh, the tomb of an Arab saint and his son. The South African 5th Brigade perished near this site during Operation Crusader on November 23, 1941.

Brigadier Dan Pienaar, commander of the South African 1st Brigade and later commander of the 1st Division, was a decorated veteran of World War I and the more recent campaign against the Italians in East Africa.

Thousands of Axis prisoners, under escort, march into captivity after the South Africans captured Bardia on January 2, 1942.

Delighted South African soldiers fool around for the camera after their capture of Bardia January 2, 1942.

A near miss! South Africans hug the ground as Axis artillery explodes around them.

Brigadier Dan Pienaar stays close to the radio set at the back of a command vehicle.

South Africans man an antiaircraft 40mm Bofors gun.

(Left to right) Lieutenant-General William Gott, commander of the 7th Armoured Division; Pienaar; Brink; General Neil Ritchie, commander of the Eighth Army, and unidentified officer.

Members of the Transvaal Scottish Regiment wearing their distinctive tam o' shanters.

Smuts and Theron address the troops on a podium draped with the "Oranje, Blanje, Blou" South African flag.

Troops posing with a Thompson machine gun and a "sticky" bomb, used to disable enemy armor.

Command and control using a bull horn to communicate with the troops manning the widely distributed foxholes in a defensive position.

South African 25-pounder artillery. It was a deadly weapon when used against tanks or in its proper role as an indirect fire weapon against soft targets.

A South African AA gunner and his clip of 40mm ammunition.

A South African antiaircraft gunner mans a 40mm Bofors in an attempt to protect the mobile columns from ever present air attack.

Germany made Colonel Brink (center of photo) feel welcome in 1937, and there he witnessed regimental exercises and experienced firsthand the German way of war.
DODA ARCHIVES, AANWINSTE GP1, BOX 50, FILE BRINK PRIVATE PAPERS

A confident looking Klopper (right) wearing Brigadier rank and amphigarious wings together with Field Marshal Jan Smuts.

A South African 25-pounder blasts out from its camouflage dugout. The 25-pounder artillery was the most effective weapon deployed against enemy armor and infantry.

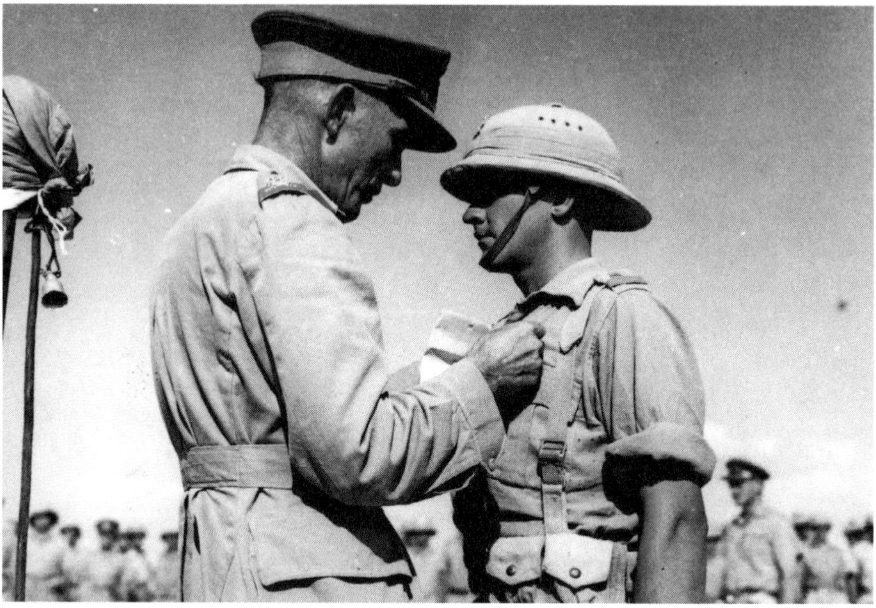

Pienaar decorates a South African soldier after the Crusader operation.

Sergeant Quinton Smythe (center), member of the Union Defence Force, recipient of the Victoria Cross. Severely wounded, he single-handedly destroyed a machine gun post, taking the crew prisoner. Then armed with rifle and bayonet, he repeated the feat with an enemy antitank gun crew.

25-pounder shell casings aplenty. The intensity of the South African artillery barrages brought the German attack outside El Alamein to a grinding halt.

Black members of the Union Defence Force (The Native Labour Corps) served mainly in the vital support services when denied a role in combat units. However, despite gross discrimination they served with honor and valor.

A chance to pose with a captured Italian flag and Italian officer's sword brings a welcome break to the intense fighting at the El Alamein perimeter.

The South African Air Force had a number of Junkers JU 52 transport planes in their fleet. This one bears a captured German shield with the ironic word "Tobruk" emblazoned on it.

Chapter 4

Operation Crusader: Buildup to North Africa's Largest Tank Battle

"This offensive," said Mr Churchill, "has been long and elaborately prepared. We have waited for nearly five months in order that the Army should be well equipped with all the weapons that have made their mark in this war. If in this case the enemy's armour is destroyed or seriously defeated and his air power dominated, the plight of his infantry and artillery, crowded in the coastal regions, will evidently become serious. The object of the British and Empire offensive is not so much to occupy this or that locality, but to destroy the army, and primarily the armoured forces, of the enemy."[1]

The retreat of the British Expeditionary Force (BEF) and its evacuation at Dunkirk in June 1940 signalled the end of major British operations in Europe until the invasion of Sicily in July 1943. For three years North Africa became the primary focus of the British landward effort. The North African campaign would become a genuinely international effort, hosting contingents from Australia, New Zealand, Poland, India, Czechoslovakia, South Africa, and finally the substantial forces of the United States. The opposing armies in North Africa were minuscule compared to the hundreds of divisions deployed on the Eastern Front and even later on the Western Front. The relatively small size of the forces in North Africa was a function of logistical limitations that precluded the deployment of larger forces.[2] However, the North African theater enjoyed an unprecedented level of mechanization that exceeded all other theaters, especially the Eastern Front, where enormous amounts of horse-drawn transport were the order of the day.

Initially, British efforts in North Africa were pitted against the poorly trained and equipped, largely immobile Italians. The large Italian desert army outnumbered the British forces but was significantly inferior in mobility, being in the large part nonmotorized infantry and totally unsuited for the fast pace of desert warfare. The small, professional, and highly mobile mechanized British forces trounced the immobile Italian infantry. They quickly captured Bardia on January 5, 1941, followed by Tobruk on January 22 and El Agheila in February. The British missed an opportunity to expel the defeated Italians completely from Africa when they transferred the best elements of the Western Desert Force to deal with the Axis's invasion of Greece. The ease and magnitude of the British victory had the unfortunate effect of validating British doctrine while masking some of its critical shortfalls. The British remained confident in their belief in the supremacy of the tank, to the exclusion of combined arms warfare.[3]

The Germans, fearful of the prospect of an Italian collapse in North Africa, sent German reinforcements commanded by Rommel, with the limited aim of halting the rampant Allied advance. Rommel had other ideas and was unwilling to adopt a passive defensive posture. He set in motion an audacious surprise attack on March 31 before the full might of his force had arrived in Africa. The British, weakened after sending the cream of their desert force to Greece, were soon in full retreat and abandoned Benghazi on April 3, 1941. The Germans captured Generals Neame and O'Conner on April 7 and surrounded Tobruk on April 11. The Germans drove the British all the way back to the Egyptian frontier and there, with both sides now exhausted, came to a halt. The isolated Tobruk garrison continued to receive supplies and support at great cost to the Royal Navy, and bravely withstood Rommel's obsessive attempts at capture.

General A. P. Wavell (1883–1950), Commander-in-Chief Middle East, tried to relieve Tobruk in mid-May 1941, undertaking a small-scale operation named Brevity. The attack was both ill-planned and premature and achieved none of its objectives.[4] The British launched Operation Battleaxe on June 15, 1941, on a much larger scale. This second attempt to relieve Tobruk achieved equally dismal results. Once again the British incorrectly attributed the defeat to the supposed qualitative superiority enjoyed by German tanks.[5] However, most British tanks were lost to skillful and bold use of the German antitank guns. The new long-barrelled 50mm PAK 38 antitank gun was undoubtedly more able than the British 2-pounders, and the German 88mm also wreaked havoc on the British tanks. The British did have an answer to the powerful German 88mm antitank gun. Their 3.7-inch antiaircraft gun was very similar to the German 88mm, and they possessed three times as many. The British lost an opportunity to redress the balance somewhat when they earmarked the 3.7-inch AA gun for exclusive use in the antiaircraft role, despite urgings in certain sectors to use this weapon as an antitank gun.[6]

Operation Crusader: Context and Historiography

Operation Crusader, with all its complexity, is a particularly intriguing campaign to study, especially from a South African perspective. It was the single most expensive military operation ever undertaken by South Africans in their military history until the tragedy of Tobruk in 1942. Approximately 3,800 men were killed, wounded, or taken prisoner in the battle, surpassing the military calamity of Delville Wood in 1916 (1,709 wounded and 763 killed). The reversals suffered by the South Africans at Sidi Rezegh and Tobruk resonated internationally and on the home fronts, causing much embarrassment and discomfort to Churchill and Smuts. The South Africans entered the North Africa fray in May 1941 after concluding a successful campaign in East Africa. The UDF was flushed with victory and new battle honors, achieved with the minimum of casualties.[7] On May 3, 1941, the 5th SAI Brigade under Armstrong, together with the 1st SAI Division Headquarters, disembarked at Suez after an eleven-day journey from Mombasa. The final destination of two South African infantry divisions was the Middle East. Churchill was the most impatient to see the South Africans transfer from Kenya to the Western Desert.[8] They arrived against the backdrop of a series of defeats inflicted on the British at the hands of Rommel.

Crusader took place in the wide open expanses of the North African desert. The battlefield was devoid of population and distinctive terrain features. These conditions, despite major logistical challenges, were ideal for mobile and maneuver warfare in its purest form. In Crusader, the armored theories of the British, the inventors of the tank, were pitted against those of the Germans, the masters of combined arms and mobile warfare. Both armies, thus far in the war, had enjoyed periods of enormous military success. The British defeated the Italians in East and North Africa using highly mobile forces, and the Germans conquered all comers in Europe. Crusader was the first large-scale British–Axis armored encounter thus far in the war. It was a unique testing ground for mobile warfare doctrine, providing insights that persist to the present day. General H. Norman Schwarzkopf Jr. (1934–2012), commander of the U.S. Forces of Desert Storm fame, read Rommel's book *Infantry Attacks*[9] as a source of inspiration before the operation. One can safely assume that he was not alone in considering the Second World War exploits in the desert to be instructive as to the conduct of Desert Storm in 1991.[10]

Crusader marked the first time in the Second World War that the British defeated the German *Wehrmacht*. It was not a clear-cut victory, but it came after a string of defeats at the hands of the Germans in Norway, France, Greece, and North Africa. El Alamein, a battle that occurred many months later, has the incorrect honor of the first victory over German-led forces.[11] It is correct to consider Crusader as a first victory for the British, because it achieved its primary objectives of relieving Tobruk and expelling the Axis from Cyrenaica. The campaign restored access to airfields, reenabling air cover to convoys from Malta. However, although Crusader was undoubtedly an Allied minor strategic victory, it did not feel like one. The Germans hopelessly outclassed the British at the operational and tactical levels of war.[12] The subsequent, more famous battles of Gazala and Alamein overshadowed Crusader, which as a result has received relatively little attention.

History has treated unfairly the crucial role played by the Italians in the campaign. Historians have tended to underplay the Italian part in unhinging the South Africans, especially in the early stages of Crusader. The Italian contribution is somewhat obscure due to the dearth of Italian publications translated into English.[13] An interesting phenomenon existed both during and after the war. Those who fought against the Axis in North Africa preferred to think they were fighting against the Germans rather than the Italians. It was especially so when they suffered defeat at the hands of the Italians.[14] This theme comes across strongly in the narrative that follows. The South Africans are guilty of identifying their adversary as German instead of Italian on some occasions. This chapter makes use of the Italian official histories to redress the lack of accessible Italian sources and obtain a more balanced picture of the events.[15]

The South African official history remains the best secondary source on the subject of the South Africans at Sidi Rezegh and is arguably the best source for Operation Crusader as a whole.[16] Besides the official histories of the participants, very few secondary sources exist that deal with Crusader exclusively. Two books dedicated to the study of Crusader are *Crusader*,[17] which seems little more than a rehash of secondary sources, and *Inside the Afrika Korps*,[18] which is an interesting account giving the German point of view by the chief of staff of one of Rommel's *Panzer* divisions. Osprey has produced a more recent book on the subject, *Operation Crusader 1941*, which is rather concise and adds little new to the existing pool of knowledge.[19] Published personal memoirs of the battle from both sides exist, which are useful in giving a first hand account of the events; two of these are *Brazen Chariots*,[20] giving the British point of view, and *With Rommel in the Desert*,[21] giving the German one. Michael Carver's interpretation of the desert war is particularly instructive, being largely a first hand account as well as an incisive analysis of the strategy and tactics employed by both sides in the conflict.[22] Many secondary sources deal with Crusader in passing; some of the better ones are *The Early Battles of the Eighth Army*,[23] and *The Desert Generals*,[24] which are both refreshingly revisionist in nature. Shelford Bidwell is indispensable in providing insight into the employment of artillery, arguably the best arm of the British desert army, with his *Gunners at War*.[25]

The unpublished narratives and primary documents residing in the files of the UWHS, housed at the DODA, contain the most rewarding source of information on Crusader. This book makes extensive use of these in reexamining and reevaluating the events leading up to and including the destruction of the 5th South African Infantry Brigade at Sidi Rezegh. Included in the collection are the important first hand accounts of Major-General G. E. "George" Brink (commander of the 1st South African Division) and Brigadier B. F. Armstrong (commander of the 5th SAI Brigade), which give a uniquely South African perspective of the battle often lacking in the secondary sources. The chapter makes copious use of the personal accounts of individuals who took part in the battle at all levels. The UWHS also contains rare translated German and Italian documents providing further insights into the operation.

The aim of this chapter is to reexamine the battle of Sidi Rezegh to gain a better understanding, from a South African perspective, of the events surrounding the battle and the actions that took place that day. The combination of varied sources gives a vivid account of the demise of the South African 5th SAI Brigade at Sidi Rezegh. The chapter will reassess the South African role in inflicting grievous casualties on the German armor at Sidi Rezegh and their significance to the overall outcome of Operation Crusader.

Operation Crusader: The Strategic Plan

Crusader was born out of the strategic necessity to relieve Tobruk, surrounded by the Axis since April 11, 1941. Lifting the siege of Tobruk would effectively remove the Axis from Cyrenaica and allow the establishment of airfields to cover the convoys between Alexandria and Malta.[26] The timing of Crusader was opportune due to Germany's preoccupation with the invasion of Russia.[27] When Tobruk was finally relieved on November 27, 1941, the stronghold had endured 240 days in isolation behind the Axis lines. It was one of the longest sieges of the war besides that of Leningrad, which endured 872 days. The British desire to lift the siege of Tobruk matched Rommel's need to capture the fortress once and for all. While the British held Tobruk, Rommel was unable to launch an effective invasion of Egypt. Rommel was in the advanced stage of planning a massive assault on Tobruk when Crusader was unleashed, rudely interrupting his offensive.

Prevailing British doctrine called for the elimination of the enemy's tank forces as the first step of an operation. British tank formations would engage enemy tank forces in a massive tank-versus-tank battle. The British believed that their superior numbers coupled with greater élan would quickly reduce the Axis tank forces, leaving British tanks and accompanying infantry to mop up the remaining Axis infantry. Accordingly, the British designed the primary objective and first phase of the operation to lure the enemy armored forces to Gabr Saleh. It was a central position on the map of no real consequence. Planners hoped to tempt the Germans into a pitched battle with the British armor. Superior numbers and concentration would defeat the Axis tanks in detail.[28] In the words of General Sir Claude Auchinleck (1884–1981), Commander-in-Chief Middle East,

> The German armoured divisions were the backbone of the enemy's army, and to destroy them was our principal object. The three

> armoured brigades were concentrated in the XXX Corps and commanded by Norrie who was instructed to use them to seek out and destroy the enemy's armour. When the *Panzer* divisions had been well and truly dealt with, the rest of our forces would carry out their parts in the operation.[29]

The British therefore aimed the first phase of Crusader at nothing less than the destruction of Rommel's armor using superior British numbers in a pitched tank-versus-tank battle.[30] However, even this intention to concentrate armor contained a tendency toward fragmentation. Cunningham, recently appointed the commander of the Eighth Army in August 1941, was overheard at a signal exercise prior to Crusader to say, "I am dispersing the armoured brigades to strike at three points to force Rommel to fight as any one of our armoured brigades is equal to his whole tank force."[31] When Cunningham uttered these words he had never witnessed a tank battle and his more experienced subordinates, who could have counseled him, chose to remain silent. The operation contained an undesirable ambiguity in British leadership at the outset. The concept of concentration of forces at the decisive point lacked clarity and decisiveness. Lieutenant-General Willoughby Norrie (1893–1977), commander of the XXX Corps, was unhappy on two counts at the outset. He did not feel that Gabr Saleh possessed the correct strategic importance to entice the enemy to attack, and he felt that the two tasks allocated to the armor of protecting the left flank of XIII Corps and of destroying the German armor were conflicting.[32] (See Map 1.)

The secondary objective and second phase of the operation involved the infantry divisions of the South Africans and New Zealanders linking up with the garrison of Tobruk, who on a given signal would break out of the fortress to meet the relieving troops.[33] The time to give the signal was once the enemy armor had been neutralized and ceased being a threat to the infantry. The initial objective for the South Africans was to man the extreme left wing of XXX Corps, so that "The first task of the 1st South African Infantry Division was to protect the western and south-western flanks of the communications of the Armoured Division."[34] On the destruction of the Axis tanks, the infantry divisions would be unleashed to relieve Tobruk and cut off the enemy forces occupying the frontier.[35] The XIII Corps reinforced with the 1st Army Tank Brigade

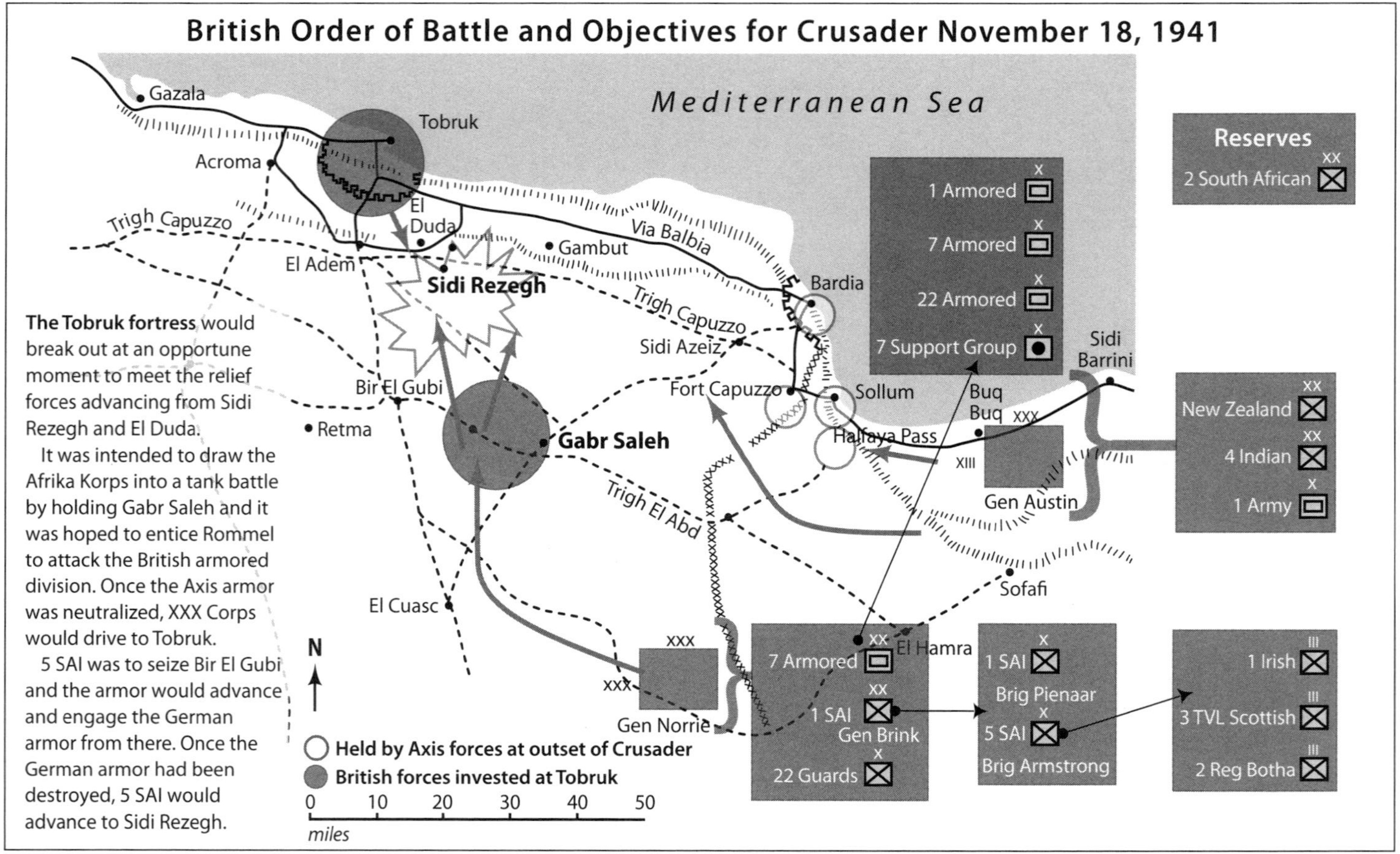

Map 1. The Planned First Phase of Crusader November 18, 1941.

and, commanded by Lieutenant-General A. R. Godwin-Austen (1889–1963), was tasked to pin down the Axis frontier positions, while flanking those same positions on the south and appearing in the rear of the enemy frontier defenses.

The XXX Corps, entrusted with destroying Rommel's tanks, contained the bulk of Eighth Army tank assets in the form of the 7th Armoured Division, commanded by Major-General William H. E. "Strafer" Gott (1897–1942), consisting of the 7th, 22nd, and 4th Armoured Brigade and the 7th Support Group.[36] Norrie also had under his command the 1st South African Infantry Division, commanded by Brink and consisting of the 1st (commanded by Pienaar) and 5th (commanded by Armstrong) Infantry Brigades. The two SAI brigades' objective was to advance and capture Bir El Gubi and mask the 132a Divisione Corazzata "*Ariete*" (*Ariete*), commanded by General Mario Balotta, the Italian armored division occupying defensive positions in the area. The British reinforced Tobruk, manned by the 70th Division and commanded by Major-General Ronald Scobie (1893–1969), with the 32nd Army Tank Brigade. They tasked Scobie to break out of the fortress when ordered, to meet the relief force once the enemy armored force had been defeated.[37] The plan envisioned the destruction of the Axis armor by superior numbers of British tanks, followed by a simultaneous infantry attack toward and from Tobruk to relieve the garrison with a further simultaneous infantry aimed at surrounding and destroying the Axis forces manning the Egyptian border.

Operation Crusader: Operational and Tactical Assessment

The strategic plan seemed sound, given the overall superiority the British enjoyed in manpower and material. However, the plan contained serious flaws at the operational level. These flaws undermined the prospects for a decisive victory and contained the seeds of the destruction of the South African 5th Brigade. The success of the whole operation depended on the neutralization of the Axis tank forces in a preliminary tank-versus-tank battle. British armored military doctrine dictated that this initial clash of armor would be a pure tank battle, and relegated the infantry and support groups to a secondary role. The supporting arms were nothing more than spectators awaiting the outcome of the titanic tank struggle that was to take place. The British failure to deploy their fighting formations using combined arms left the infantry formations unsupported by tanks and vulnerable to attacks by Axis armor. In a signal to Churchill, Auchinleck, two days after assuming command, eloquently summed up his feelings as to the role of the infantry brigades in the coming battle.

> It is quite clear to me that infantry divisions, however well trained and equipped, are no good for offensive operations in this terrain against enemy armoured forces. Infantry divisions are and will be needed to hold defended localities after enemy armoured forces have been neutralised and destroyed, but the main offensive must be carried out by armoured formations and supported by motorised formations.[38]

The lack of combined arms doctrine had an equally negative flip side and the resulting unbalanced fighting formation meant that British armored formations lacked an integral infantry and artillery component. The Armoured Division concentrated its artillery and infantry assets in a separate support brigade, in this case, the 7th Support Group under the command of Brigadier J. C. "Jock" Campbell, which often found itself acting independently of the armor. Commanders came under constant pressure to assign precious armor resources to vulnerable infantry to ensure their safety and on occasion even their rescue. Liddell Hart quotes Carver in saying,

> The Crusader operation was fought to an unending accompaniment of screams from one infantry division headquarters, or field maintenance centre, after another for tanks to come and protect them against the presence or threat of enemy tanks.[39]

The armor's dual function of destroying enemy tanks and protecting the infantry was not conducive to concentration but rather led to fragmentation of the British armored forces.[40] The 4th Armoured Brigade's task was keeping watch of the XIII Corps left flank as it swung around the Axis defensive line at the Egyptian frontier. This dual role ensured the separation of 4th and 7th Armoured Brigades by up to 20 km, instead of their concentration as a single force in the drive to Gabr Saleh.[41] Similarly, the 22nd Armoured Brigade had the task of screening the South Africans from *Ariete*, and they too would find themselves many kilometers from Gabr Saleh. The concentration of armor via the three armored brigades was essential if the British were to avoid arriving at the battle in a piecemeal fashion. Fragmentation allowed the concentrated Axis armor to engage each brigade separately in time instead of being presented with an overwhelming concentrated force.[42]

Another flaw in the operational plan was the choice of a point on the map of no real consequence, Gabr Saleh, as the focal point to lure the German armor into a destructive tank battle on British terms.[43] Gabr Saleh proved to be so inconsequential that Rommel failed to take the bait.[44] Had the British chosen a more strategic objective, such as Sidi Rezegh or even Tobruk, and seized the initiative, it would have forced Rommel to take decisive action. Norrie had identified this problem early in the planning phase and expressed his preference for aiming at a more decisive target to force the Germans to react. He preferred to aim for Sidi Rezegh or Tobruk itself and concentrate the three tank brigades against these objectives. The choice of Gabr Saleh was a compromise, as Lieutenant-General Bernard Cyril Freyberg (1889–1963), commander of the New Zealand 2nd Division, was concerned that his division would be vulnerable to the German tanks when he executed his flanking attack on the Axis frontier positions. The 4th Armoured Brigade was earmarked to guard his flank, and Gabr Saleh, being closer than Sidi Rezegh, was more suitable to this dual purpose.[45]

Crusader called for great secrecy and the British went to great lengths to ensure that it came as a complete surprise to the Axis.[46] However, the success of subterfuge militated against the objective of luring Rommel into attacking the superior British armor at Gabr Saleh. Rommel was preoccupied with his preparations for an assault on Tobruk, which he had scheduled for November 23, 1941. He was so intent on Tobruk to the point of fixation that the British offensive failed to distract him for days. Torrential rain swamped the Axis airfields on November 18, and therefore the *Luftwaffe* undertook no reconnaissance. Rommel was unaware of the scale of the British offensive or its intention to relieve Tobruk, and contrary to what the British intended, he neglected to attack the British armor at the time and place of their choosing. A more strategic target than Gabr Saleh would have spurred the Germans on to attack the gathering British armor.[47]

Operation Crusader: South African Preparations

The first formations of South Africans to arrive in Egypt were the headquarters of the 1st Division on May 4, 1941. The South Africans took over the fortress of Mersa Matruh, eventually manning it with the 5th Brigade, which arrived on June 14, followed by the 2nd Brigade on June 30, both of which had seen active service in East Africa.[48] The 1st Division then proceeded to busy themselves with the repair and enhancement of the Mersa Matruh fortifications while acclimatizing themselves to the harsh desert conditions and the military atmosphere of the British command system. The divisional report, authored by Brink, refers bitterly to the fact that the South Africans spent more time building the defenses of Matruh than embarking on essential desert training.[49] Early signs of South African unpreparedness for the harsh conditions of desert combat began to emerge. Brink highlighted a lack of trained South African staff officers. He called for an ample supply to be appointed to serve, including with the frontline units. South Africa's lack of trained staff officers was not a new phenomenon; it had hampered operations in East Africa, and would again in Crusader.[50]

Brink received the role and objectives of the South Africans in Crusader at a conference held on October 6. In the first phase of the operation, the South Africans' role was to guard the left flank of XXX Corps. Once the British neutralized the Axis armor, the South Africans would complete the second phase, which was to advance on to Tobruk and meet the forces simultaneously breaking out there. At a further conference on October 15, Brink requested tank support for his division, and the British agreed to provide "some cruisers" from Tobruk once 1st Division linked up with the garrison. Smuts, ever the visionary, had told Cunningham weeks before Crusader that he wanted the South African units to be "infused" with "armored weapons" so as to achieve a balanced formation of all arms.[51] Furthermore, the British gave assurances at that conference that they would not bring up the 1st Division until either the tank battle was over or the enemy armored forces were effectively hemmed in. Brink received assurances at the same conference that every effort would be made to prevent the enemy armored force from attacking the 1st Division, although if the situation demanded, "the Div(ision) would have to be prepared to fight tanks if necessary." They would place an additional antitank regiment under command for this purpose. The British never fulfilled this promise, according to Brink, with Cunningham going back on his word and allotting the antitank regiment to XXX Corps.[52] Brink was not overly concerned with the threat of tanks, as he felt that the main tank concentration and resulting tank battles would take place away from the 1st Division locality due to the enemy having to respond to the threat caused by "the concentration of 7 Armoured Division."[53] The tanks of the Italian *Ariete* Division, holding defensive positions at Bir El Gubi, which would prove later in Crusader to be one of the leading causes of anxiety to the British 22nd Armoured Brigade and South Africans, did not seem to bother Brink at this stage.[54]

What was of major concern to Brink was the diminution of the fighting power of the division. Brink, to his dismay, learned that he would field only two brigades instead of the normal three called for in the order of battle. The Eighth Army left his third brigade languishing in Matruh as a reserve, as it apparently did not have the resources to support a larger force that far west. The absence of a third brigade in the division would curtail the full fighting and defensive power of the formation. It was Freyberg who identified that the South African relieving force sent to Tobruk was not strong enough and would have to face five Italian divisions and a strong German division.[55] Brink's request for a third brigade to fill his ranks and additional artillery in the form of two batteries fell on deaf ears, and was supposedly denied for administrative and infrastructure reasons. Brink went on to say,

> This decision had to be accepted as inevitable but left me with the uncomfortable feeling that I would have to engage in serious operations with a weak Division and that I would be faced with the same problems that faced me in Abyssinia of having little in hand with which to influence a battle or cope with any unexpected situation that might arise.[56]

Brink had for a period harbored concerns that the South Africans would not be able to maintain two fully fledged divisions in the field due to the existing inadequate rate of recruitment. Van Ryneveld would not accept Brink's concerns. He sought solutions via an increase in the recruitment rate and the availability of 6,000 men in South Africa's 3rd Division for reinforcement. Brink, at this stage, touted the idea of converting the motorized infantry to an armored division, or even two armored divisions requiring less manpower. He had taken the step of sending a memorandum in June 1941 to Lieutenant-General Arthur Smith, CGS Middle East. It contained proposals to convert the South African divisions to armored formations. The armored cars, so effective in East Africa, had become obsolete and hopelessly outclassed by the enemy.[57]

Brink was growing increasingly concerned with the slow rate of arrival of desert-worthy motorized transport meant to replace the worn-out transport brought with the division from the East African campaign. Adding to the transport woes were the substantial amount of drivers on loan to the forward dumping program. The British assigned a significant portion of the South African drivers to carry supplies ahead of the offensive to dumps along the proposed path of attack. At first, "native" drivers replaced the European drivers, and they trained in tactical formations, visual signals, and general operating conditions in the desert. No sooner had the native contingent completed their training than they, in turn, were replaced by relatively untrained Coloured Corps drivers.[58] The shortage of transport and trained drivers seriously impinged on the required desert training of the division.[59]

On November 2, Brink was not yet in possession of his transport despite assurances from the Divisional Quarter Master General in Cairo that he would receive them by the end of October. Brink placed his position in writing, stating that due to the delays in receiving adequate transport, he was unable to undertake the required desert training and would therefore not be ready for any deployment until November 21.[60] The British, in the face of increasing impatience from Churchill, laid the blame for the delay in launching Crusader firmly at the door of the South Africans. A bitter antagonism was growing between the British and South African generals.[61] Cunningham threatened to reassign the South Africans to a semi-defensive role, and Auchinleck in words contained in a signal to Churchill, said,

> I became aware of General Brink's doubts as to the readiness of his Division . . . His fears were based on what he considered to be the insufficient training of the Division, and one of its brigades in particular, in mechanised movement in open formation in the desert. This insufficiency of training was said to be due to the fact that the

> full scale of vehicles for the Division had not been issued to it by the date on which they had been promised . . . The first question I asked myself was why this lack of confidence was not disclosed before, and the only answer I can find is that General Brink, in common with so many of his countrymen, is secretive and reserved by nature. They are magnificent men but they have their own peculiar traits.[62]

Brink felt forced to relent and he reluctantly moved the date to November 18. He was clearly unhappy with the situation and succumbed to the ultimatum offered to him to save honor and maintain the reputation of the South African contingent.[63] Brink's diary reflects his discomfort with the role assigned to his inexperienced Division.

> There was no time to ponder or argue. The army commander was applying the acid test. I was not happy about the state of training of my division and in my heart I felt it was not in a fit state, tactically, and did not possess the hitting power to engage in serious operations.[64]

During the period November 3–13, the 1st and 5th Brigades carried out training exercises although petrol rationing limited the scope of these. The brigades made a night move on the evening of November 16 despite representations from Brink that these would prove to be "expensive in vehicles, water, petrol and efficiency and that the brigades should rather undertake a day move." One cannot overemphasise the importance of the ability to move at night. The South Africans showed a great reluctance to do so throughout Crusader, and thus disposed of the best method of concealment in desert warfare conditions.[65] An astounding fact is that when the 1st Division began to move toward their jump-off point for Crusader on November 14, it was the division's first experience of desert movement as a complete unit. The final arrangements for the operation inundated the staff and precluded the division HQ in partaking in the exercises prior to Crusader.[66]

It is interesting to contrast these belated brigade exercises with those conducted by the New Zealanders, who launched a full-scale brigade exercise on October 8, a month earlier. By early October, all battalions had exercised with their attached antitank and Vickers guns. The New Zealanders busied themselves with navigation skills, especially at night, and improvement in marksmanship with small arms and mortars. Significantly, night marches and patrols were part of an extensive curriculum.[67] The New Zealand 2nd Division, in contrast to their South African counterparts, seemed to have received adequate training, despite the British assigning similar duties in strengthening the Baggush defenses. The New Zealand official history stresses that unlike the South Africans, training came first, due to the resolve of the division's energetic commander, who would have put up stern opposition should the British have insisted otherwise. Due to the increasing anxiety of their senior officers, the South Africans were unable to conduct even a battalion-size exercise for the five months leading up to October 11, being preoccupied with the defenses of Matruh.[68]

Brink's report brings to our attention the considerable problems that B Echelon posed when the formation found itself in a combat situation. B Echelon consisted of thousands of soft-skinned vehicles needed to transport and supply the division.[69] The South Africans struggled to find suitable doctrine for dispersing and protecting motorized transport during movement phases and for their disposition when hastily attacking or defending a position. It was through the soft underbelly of B Echelon that the Germans would strike and destroy the 5th Brigade.[70] In his after battle report, Brink suggested the disallowance of transport formations from accompanying the fighting formations into battle. The presence of thousands of vehicles from B Echelon on the southern front of the 5th Brigade had unnecessarily complicated the formulation of an all-around defense and was instrumental in the ultimate demise of the brigade. Brink went on to recommend as essential the concept of all-around defense in mobile warfare, combined with mutually supporting antitank weapons. It was clearly lacking in the defenses of 5th Brigade, whose southern flank was largely bereft of infantry, but filled with the elements of B Echelon.[71]

Operation Crusader: Order of Battle

In the aftermath of Battleaxe, Churchill sacked Wavell and replaced him with Auchinleck on June 21, 1941. The Eighth Army[72] consisted of two corps and a garrison of approximately a division in the Tobruk Fortress. Auchinleck appointed Cunningham to command the Eighth Army. The Eighth Army, besides the handicap of outmoded doctrine, lacked experience in modern warfare. Auchinleck, Cunningham, and the two corps commanders, Godwin-Austen and Norrie, were devoid of desert war experience and none had ever fought with armored formations. The Axis commanders, on the other hand, shared a wealth of experience, most having fought in tough desert conditions for many months after acquiring extensive armored warfare experience from the campaigns in Europe. Rommel was a masterful tactician and since arriving in Africa had inflicted successive defeats on the British, chasing them all the way back to the Egyptian frontier. Rommel led the Axis forces well and they were flushed with victory and supreme confidence in the superiority of their fighting ability.[73]

The British significantly outnumbered the Germans in the crucial area of tank numbers at the outset of Crusader (see Table 1). British tank superiority approached a 2-to-1 ratio, and despite many texts that offer the opposite view, the Germans did not enjoy a significant qualitative superiority. In most areas, including armor and armament, British tanks were on an equal, if not superior, footing to their German counterparts.[74] Underestimation of Italian fighting power was to cost the British grievously in the opening days of Crusader, when the Italian *Ariete* Division decimated the green 22nd Armoured Brigade. An insight into this mindset appears in Auchinleck's dispatch, where he states, "To give a reasonable chance of our offensive succeeding, we should have about 50 percent, numerical superiority over the German armored forces, though we can accept equality with the Italians."[75]

The British also enjoyed the luxury of a vast number of tank reserves, unlike the Germans, who had few.[76] Liddell Hart estimates that the British had 259 tanks in reserve with a further 96 in shipment, together with a further 231 tanks with armored divisions not deployed for the operation. The Germans had 50 tanks in total held in reserve or under repair. The Axis did enjoy a significant advantage in antitank weapons both numerically and qualitatively and in their tactical superiority. The British fell back on their 25-pounder artillery and made extensive use of them in the antitank role in an attempt to redress their deficiencies in this area. On the occasions that they were able to bring this powerful and versatile weapon to bear, they extracted a grievous tally on the Axis armor. However, the use of the 25-pounder artillery weapon in the antitank role detracted from their intended purpose of providing the infantry with all necessary artillery cover.[77] The 1st Brigade after battle report also drew

Comparison of Armored Forces at the Inception of Operation Crusader November 18, 1941

EIGHTH ARMY					
	30th Corps	**13th Corps**	**Tobruk**	**Total**	**% Total**
TANK TYPE					
Light Tanks			25	25	3%
Early Cruisers	32	3	32	67	9%
Cruiser A13	62			62	8%
Cruiser A15	210			210	28%
Stuarts	173			173	23%
I tanks		132	69	201	27%
	477	135	126	738	
AXIS					
	15 Panzer Div	**21 Panzer Div**	**Ariete**	**Total**	
Pzkw II	38	32		70	18%
Pzkw III	75	64		139	36%
Pzkw IV	20	15		35	9%
M13/40			146	146	37%
	133	111	146	390	

A ratio of 1.89 to 1 (738 to 390)

1. Removing the light tanks from both sides, as they were relatively ineffectual due to obsolescence, renders a ratio of 2.2 to 1 in favor of the British. The British enjoyed a significant numerical advantage in any event.
2. The German *Panzer* divisions had approximately the same number of tanks compared to a British armored brigade. However, the German *Panzer* division was a balanced formation in comparison, having a strong motorized infantry and artillery component that was proficient in the art of combined arms warfare.
3. Most authors incorrectly discount the Italian tanks when comparing force strengths of the opposing armies. To do so is misleading as the Italian *Ariete* division played a fundamental role throughout Crusader, including singlehandedly defeating the 22nd Armoured Brigade on November 19, 1941.

Table 1. Comparison of British and Axis armored forces at the beginning of Operation Crusader November 18, 1941.[78]

attention to the lack of sufficient antitanks available to the brigade and suggested an increase to three or four troops (12–16 guns) per battalion. Recommendations asked that these convert to infantry weapons, as the expertise to operate direct-fire weapons was at a lower level than artillery, which had a far more complicated indirect fire capability. The increase in antitank weapons would free up the artillery from antitank duties and thereby restore their designed role of indirect fire. The brigade also called for heavy armored cars armed with 2-pounder or 6-pounder guns to allow the infantry to act independently of the armored units, giving them the capability of flanking enemy units and engaging enemy armor.[79]

Conclusion

Operation Crusader provided an ideal setting to test the efficacy of the military doctrines adopted by the British and German armies. The British believed in the supremacy of the tank on the battlefield and they aimed their tank formations toward the elimination of the enemy armored forces in a tank-versus-tank battle. The Germans believed in a balanced combined arms formation where each arm had a role in supporting the other in combat. The British doctrine found little role for the infantry in a tank-versus-tank scenario. The British command and divisional structure were conducive to fragmentation rather than concentration of forces. The British conducted their operations at a brigade rather than a divisional level, while the more experienced Germans and Italians built their operations around a divisional structure. German experience, military doctrine, and force structure ensured that they were able to concentrate faster and react more quickly to a developing situation, while the British command structure was cumbersome in comparison. These factors heavily impinged on the British advantage in numerical strength.

The British plan also contained the seeds that led to the destruction of much of their armor and the 5th Brigade. They gave their tanks the dual role of protecting the infantry and of seeking out and destroying the enemy armor formations. This dual role fragmented the British armored formations and separated the brigades by many kilometers in their attempt to safeguard the infantry brigades on the flanks of their main objective, Gabr Saleh. The initial objective of Gabr Saleh, chosen to lure Rommel into a destructive tank battle, was a poor one. The British would have done far better to concentrate their armored formations on Sidi Rezegh or head straight for Tobruk, creating an operational statement that Rommel could not have ignored.

The South Africans were ill prepared to partake in Operation Crusader. They were short of a brigade and delays in providing transport curtailed essential training. Brink harbored severe reservations in committing the South Africans to a battle in which they were unprepared. He may have been wiser to withhold his troops from frontline action until they had received the necessary training and enough transport for the third brigade. Brink would have preferred to support his advance with tanks under his command and failing that, more antitank weapons. He neglected to secure either. He succumbed to political pressure, and against his better judgment he sent the South Africans forward into what proved to be a disastrous situation.

Chapter 5

Operation Crusader: The Destruction of the 5th South African Infantry Brigade at Sidi Rezegh

I have it in command from the King to express to all ranks of the Army and RAF in the Western Desert and to the Med. Fleet, that His Majesty is confident that they will do their duty with exemplary devotion in the supremely important battle which lies before them. For the first time, British and Empire troops will meet Germans with an ample equipment in modern weapons of all kinds. The battle itself will affect the whole course of the War. Now is the time to strike the hardest blow yet for final Victory, Home and Freedom. The Desert Army may add a page to history which will rank with Blenheim and with Waterloo. The eyes of all nations are upon you.[1]

The Battle Begins: The Launch of Crusader November 18 and 19, 1941

Crusader coincided with a massive thunderstorm and torrential rain, making for heightened levels of discomfort among the troops, and rendering all air operations on both sides nearly impossible. The soggy conditions impeded non-tracked vehicle movement for days to come, and the low cloud conditions, which persisted until the end of the month, severely hampered air reconnaissance.[2] Ironically, the Allied efforts at subterfuge, aided by foul weather and coupled with Rommel's preoccupation with his imminent attack on Tobruk, adversely affected the plan to entice the German armor into a tank battle. The British had achieved complete surprise, which although desirable at the strategic level, was less welcome at the tactical level. The Germans were unaware of the armored threat developing at Gabr Saleh and failed to comply with the British plan. This left the British armored brigades gathering there, to languish.

The non-appearance of the German armored forces was a clear indication that the choice of Gabr Saleh as a point on the map in which to entice the Germans was a mistaken one.

Cunningham's plan rested on the premise that the enemy would react quickly and attack the gathering armor at Gabr Saleh. The failure to draw the German armor placed the British in a quandary as to the next step in the plan. The entire Eighth Army was in motion and it was difficult to constrain the momentum, especially the breakout from Tobruk and the encirclement of the frontier positions. There was now a subtle change in plan that required 7th Armoured Brigade to proceed to Sidi Rezegh, thus threatening the opening of a corridor to Tobruk. This they would have to accomplish alone as Gott decided to dislodge *Ariete* at Bir El Gubi with the 22nd Brigade. Gott made his disastrous decision to use the 22nd Armoured Brigade to attack *Ariete* without consulting his corps commander, Norrie. The 4th Armoured Brigade's allotted task of guarding the flank of XIII Corps split the British armored forces in three in a single stroke.[3] In the background was Auchinleck's keenness to unleash the sortie from Tobruk as soon as it was possible. Norrie did not issue the order to break out of Tobruk, as the South Africans were not yet in striking distance of El Duda and the bulk of the enemy armor remained intact.[4]

Despite the poor weather conditions, the 1st SAI Division together with the remainder of XXX Corps, led by elements of the 4th South African Armoured Car Regiment, made real progress over the flat terrain. There was no sign of the enemy except for a few German reconnaissance units. By the evening of November 18, the 1st SAI Brigade had advanced 144 km, covering the west flank of XXX Corps and reaching its objective at El Cuasc with the 5th SAI Brigade just 32 km to the south.[5] It is there that they received their orders for the next day, which entailed the occupation of Bir El Gubi by 1st Brigade and Gueret Hamza 16 km to the south by 5th Brigade. Gott gave the task of dislodging *Ariete*, based at Bir El Gubi, to the 22nd Armoured Brigade.[6] The South African official history identifies the attack on Bir El Gubi by the 22nd Armoured Brigade as the first in a series of events that deviated from the original plan and had the effect of breaking the cohesion of the 7th Armoured Division. The original plan did not anticipate the attack by one of the three armored brigades on *Ariete*, which, in fact, discouraged pursuit of *Ariete* and earmarked the German armor as the main target.[7]

The Germans were preoccupied with their preparations for the scheduled attack on Tobruk and were unwilling to be distracted with what they believed to be a British reconnaissance in force rather than a full-blown attack with the entire Eighth Army. *Generalleutnant* Ludwig Crüwell (1892–1958), commander of the Afrika Korps, was rather more concerned, but at *Panzer* Group Headquarters, Major-General Gause believed that an enemy offensive was out of the question. Rommel's arrival at headquarters and his appeal for all present not to lose their nerves swung opinion firmly toward the belief that the British mission was merely an attempt at delaying the attack on Tobruk. *Generalmajor* Max Sümmermann, poised to attack Tobruk with the 90th Light Division, took a different view. During the night, he took the precaution of ordering Colonel Mickl of the 155th Infantry Regiment to take up defensive positions facing south and southwest between Sidi Rezegh and El Adem so as to guard against a stab in the back.[8]

The second day of Crusader started uneventfully for the South Africans, who grabbed the opportunity to take care of administrative and logistical matters. At noon, Brink received orders to move his 1st Brigade to Gueret Hamza and 5th Brigade to El Cuasc, and there to await news and developments of the armored attack by the 22nd Armoured Brigade on *Ariete* at Bir El Gubi. Heavy air strikes fell on both brigades during their advance that afternoon, resulting in 1st Brigade suffering nineteen casualties.[9] At 1600 hours Brink received orders from XXX Corps to occupy Bir El Gubi by 1800 hours, and on his inquiry as to the situation there, he received confirmation that 22nd Armoured Brigade had destroyed 45 tanks and captured 200 enemy personnel.[10] The British believed that *Ariete* had suffered a decisive blow and that the South Africans would have little trouble in occupying Bir El Gubi in the face of weakened Italian opposition.[11]

At 1715 hours Brink received an immediate halt order based on the fact that the position at Bir El Gubi was unknown. It was the first indication that the attack may not have been as successful as first hoped. A while later, a liaison officer from 22nd Armoured Brigade confirmed the fact that *Ariete* held the position in strength. Brink received information at 2045 that 22nd Armoured Brigade would proceed to Sidi Rezegh in the morning and that he must make plans to occupy the position and be prepared later in the day to send a brigade to Sidi Rezegh to support

7th Armoured Division. The occupation of Bir El Gubi by 1st Brigade was later watered down to the "masking" of *Ariete*, a more prudent task given that 22nd Brigade with its tanks had already failed against the Italians.[12] The necessity for the South Africans to mask Bir El Gubi and relieve 22nd Armoured Brigade came about due to a steady change in the original plan of concentrating armored forces at Gabr Saleh and awaiting a German reaction. The German failure to rise to the bait, and the fact that 7th Armoured Brigade had seized the vital airfield of Sidi Rezegh earlier that day, moved the British to opt for a much bolder plan. The new area of concentration was Sidi Rezegh.[13]

Two factors conspired to infuse this new scheme with complications. These would erode the ultimate intention to concentrate all available armored forces and engage in a decisive battle with the German tanks. The first complication arose from an unlikely source, the Italian armored division, *Ariete*, holding defensive positions at Bir El Gubi. The inexperienced but well-equipped 22nd Armoured Brigade failed to dislodge the Italians from their strongly held positions earlier that day. The armored brigade, unsupported by infantry and lacking adequate artillery, charged headlong into the well-prepared Italian defenses and suffered accordingly.[14] The Italian official history describes the British tank attack as being similar to a cavalry charge. The British ventured into prepared Italian defensive positions protected by antitank guns of varying caliber. The Italian guns extracted a fearful toll.[15] At one stage some members of the Bersaglieri were overwhelmed by the weight of the British attack and attempted to surrender, but they soon realized that the British tanks were unaccompanied by infantry and were able to pick up their weapons and re-man the defenses.[16] The bitter fighting culminated in an armored battle when 100 tanks of *Ariete* counterattacked the heavily engaged British thrust, and the British then withdrew at 1630 in considerable disarray, according to the Italian official history.[17]

Sources vary as to the exact casualty figures but the inexperienced British suffered a severe and unexpected reversal at the hands of a supposedly inept enemy.[18] The losses sustained by the 22nd Armoured Brigade would have been more acceptable if a German formation had caused them, but instead, the fighting power of the 22nd Brigade depreciated against a foe that was largely discounted in the original calculations of enemy strength. Brink's divisional after battle report strikingly demonstrates the disbelief in Italian ability to "put up a decent fight." In his report, he incorrectly attributes the surprisingly good Italian performance in Crusader to the fact that the Italian tanks were partially crewed and hence stiffened by German personnel.[19] This failure to defeat the Italians ensured that they remained a constant threat to the British flank in succeeding days. Their presence intimidated the SAI brigades to the extent of inhibiting their ability to maneuver decisively in the forthcoming battles.[20]

The second factor that worked against the British ability to concentrate their armor for a powerful knockout blow was the constant need to protect the vulnerable infantry brigades from Axis tanks. The 4th Armoured Brigade had the dual purpose of guarding the New Zealand Infantry Division and providing a component of the concentrated armor at Gabr Saleh. When the new concentration point moved farther north to Sidi Rezegh, the distance increased between the armor and infantry brigades. The conflicting objectives of infantry protection and concentration for an attack against the Axis tanks had the effect of fragmenting British efforts. The dual role of the armored brigades worked against the intention to consolidate all available armor for a massive attack against the German armor.[21]

The British 7th Armoured Brigade's success in capturing the airfield at Sidi Rezegh threatened the Axis forces holding the corridor between Tobruk and Sidi Rezegh (Map 2). Up to this point in the battle, Rommel had been in denial that the British advance was anything more than a diversion to distract his forces from their main objective of attacking Tobruk. The British arrival at Sidi Rezegh forced Rommel to reconsider their true intentions and he authorized an attack by *Kampfgruppe* Stephan on 4th Brigade near Gabr Saleh.[22] In what was the first large-scale clash of armor in desert warfare, the two sides crashed into each other in an increasingly complex battle. The battle ended at dusk with the British forces, unsupported by artillery, unable to harass the Germans, who were resupplying their tanks on the battlefield behind an antitank screen. Importantly, the British retired from the battlefield to laager [23] as was their practice, leaving the Germans to recover and repair their damaged tanks and denying the same opportunity to the British. The toll for the day's battle amounted to twenty-four British tanks destroyed against three destroyed and three damaged for the Germans. British claims to have knocked out twenty-four enemy tanks were disastrously optimistic. It marked the beginning of a cycle of gross overestimation of

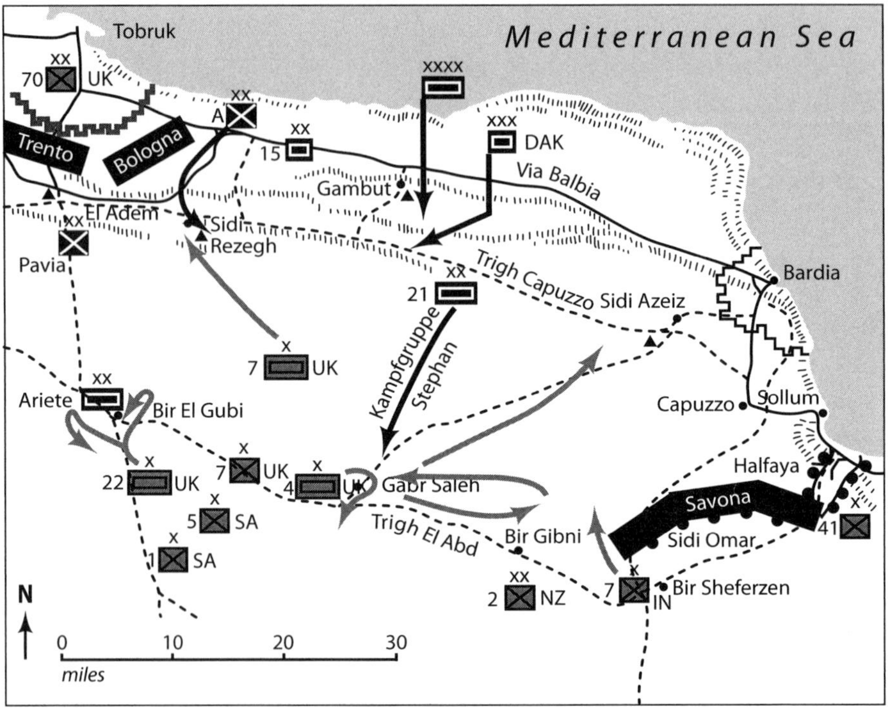

Map 2. Movements and events on November 19, depicting the rebuff of the 22nd Armoured Brigade by *Ariete*, and the spread of the British armored brigades with the 22nd and 4th "looking after the infantry."

enemy losses which would influence British decisions over the next few days of the campaign.[24]

Rommel Realizes That Crusader Is Not a Diversion: November 20, 1941

The Germans scheduled their attack on Tobruk for the morning of November 21. The British capture of Sidi Rezegh airfield convinced Rommel of the seriousness of British intentions. He quickly realized that Crusader was more than a diversion intended to distract his planned attack on Tobruk. Rommel ordered Crüwell to seek and destroy the British armor in a last-ditch attempt to keep the attack on Tobruk on track. Crüwell ordered his two scattered tank divisions to advance and concentrate on Gabr Saleh and attack the British 4th Armoured Division using overwhelming force. Fortunately for the British, intelligence intercepts revealed the German plan. It prompted Norrie to order 22nd Brigade to disengage with *Ariete* and move across from Bir El Gubi to Gabr Saleh to support 4th Brigade.[25] The 22nd Brigade was dispatched from Bir El Gubi before it had managed to dislodge the Italians. Their hasty departure left the South Africans with the onerous job of dealing with *Ariete,* thereby leaving the South African infantry to battle against Italian tanks where the British armor had failed dismally.

The British had at last achieved their desire for a tank-on-tank battle at Gabr Saleh, but due to fragmentation, they had to be satisfied with pitting two armored brigades (the 22nd and the 4th) against the two German *Panzer* divisions. It fell short of the full concentration of British armored forces pictured in the original plan because the drive by 7th Armoured Brigade and the Support Group on Sidi Rezegh was premature. As a result, when the clash did occur at 1630 hours, it took place between 4th Armoured Brigade and 15 *Panzer*-Division as 22nd Armoured Brigade and 21 *Panzer*-Division had not yet arrived on the battlefield. The British, who had assumed a strong defensive position, steadily retreated, once again leaving control of the battlefield to the Germans at dusk. Once again, the retention of the battlefield enabled the Germans to recover and repair their damaged vehicles, while the British permanently lost damaged tanks. The German war diary for the 15 *Panzer*-Division shows no losses in tanks for the day, while the 4th Armoured Brigade had suffered a total of sixty-eight tanks lost in three days.[26]

During the day, the 7th Armoured Brigade, inadequately supported with only a company of infantry, defended Sidi Rezegh. The defense of the area was a task better suited to an infantry division and the British tanks soon came under attack by the German 90th Light Division reinforced with heavy artillery. Despite a concerted effort, the British retained their positions and the Germans were unable to dislodge them. Gott decided to replace the 7th Armoured Brigade with the Support Group, commanded by Major-General J. C. "Jock" Campbell (1894–1942), which due to its infantry and artillery component, was better suited to defend and exploit the gains made thus far at Sidi Rezegh. At the same time, he ordered the 5th South African Infantry Brigade to advance up to Sidi Rezegh, and he expected them to arrive by late afternoon. Their arrival would aid the defense and add much-needed infantry support there.[27] Pienaar's 1st SAI Brigade, which should have joined the 5th Brigade, continued with the somewhat vague task of "masking" the Italians firmly ensconced at Bir El Gubi. The Italians had succeeded in splitting the South Africans and fragmenting their fighting power.

At this stage of the battle, the British did not hold the rim of the escarpment and had no real foothold in the area surrounding the Sidi Rezegh airfield. Gott, in the meantime, had gained the impression that the enemy forces manning the escarpment in front of 7th Armoured Brigade were weak.[28] The British left the capture of the escarpment area to the South Africans and the Support Group.[29] They suggested that the Support Group, together with 5th Brigade, clear the escarpment overlooking Sidi Rezegh at 0700 on November 21. The 7th Armoured Brigade was then to make contact with the Tobruk garrison at dawn on November 21, by meeting elements of the 70th Division ordered to break out of the encirclement.[30] Cunningham agreed that Major-General R. M. Scobie (1893–1969), commander of the 70th Division ensconced in Tobruk, would attack out of the Tobruk perimeter toward El Duda at dawn on November 21, while the Support Group assisted by the 5th Brigade would drive northwest, simultaneously joining up with it.[31] The 1st Brigade would remain at Bir El Gubi screening *Ariete*. The proposed linking up with Tobruk marked yet another important departure point from the original plan, which called for the destruction or neutralization of the enemy armor before any attempted breakout from Tobruk.[32] The confidence displayed by the British in invoking the linkup with Tobruk before they decisively defeated the German tanks was ill founded. Poor intelligence fuelled British misconception of the enemy tank losses inflicted thus far in the battle, and this they incorrectly extrapolated to what they hoped would be gained in the impending tank battle.[33]

That morning the South Africans received orders to move 1st Brigade up to Bir El Gubi and either capture the area if the Italians did not defend it too vigorously or mask it if Pienaar felt that an attack would draw unnecessary casualties. The British obviously felt that the 22nd Armoured Brigade had dealt *Ariete* a sharp blow and that the South Africans would be able to dislodge the supposedly weakened Italians from Bir El Gubi with ease. The 5th Brigade was to move up to the vicinity of Sidi Rezegh in support of 7th Armoured Brigade and meet the sortie sallying forth from Tobruk. The South Africans were to provide 7th Armoured Brigade with valuable infantry support by seizing and holding the raised rim of the escarpment to the north, thereby allowing observation to as far as El Duda.[34]

On the morning of November 20, reconnaissance units of the 1st Brigade made contact with elements of *Ariete*. The British ordered an attack on *Ariete* in conjunction with the 22nd Armoured Brigade at 1400. The 22nd Armoured Brigade would ward off the armored elements of *Ariete*. However, a change of plan saw the 22nd Armoured Brigade rushing off to Gabr Saleh, to bolster the 4th Armoured Brigade for the much anticipated tank clash. Their sudden departure exposed the South Africans to the Italian armored formation at Bir El Gubi, leaving them decidedly edgy at the prospect of fighting alone against a tank division, albeit an Italian one.[35] Pienaar was hesitant and lacked precise information as to the strength and disposition of *Ariete*. At 0900, while cautiously advancing, the lead elements of 1st Brigade came under Italian artillery fire and the South Africans halted and entered into an artillery duel with *Ariete* which persisted the whole day.[36]

The 5th Brigade received information at 1138 that the 7th Armoured Brigade had captured Sidi Rezegh and that they must advance up to Sidi Rezegh and make ready to move forward the next day to El Duda, linking up with the Australians breaking out of Tobruk.[37] At 1400 Brink received a message from Brigadier Dan Pienaar, the commander of 1st Brigade, that 22nd Armoured Brigade had departed and that he felt that an attack on *Ariete* at Bir El Gubi by infantry would be a useless waste of lives.[38] The 1st Brigade history indicates that the intended attack on the Italian positions at Bir El Gubi was to be a combined arms operation by both the 1st Brigade and the 22nd Armoured Brigade. Once Pienaar received notification that the 22nd Armoured Brigade was proceeding on its own to the north of Bir El Gubi, he called off the attack. Pienaar intimated that an attack on a heavily defended position, unsupported by armor, particularly when the actual enemy dispositions and strength were unknown, would lead to unnecessary and probably heavy loss of life without the possibility of real success.[39] Brink concurred with Pienaar and instructed him to take up defensive positions effectively masking *Ariete*.

At 1600 XXX Corps confirmed that Armstrong, commander of 5th Brigade, was to advance on Sidi Rezegh, and in response, at 1630, 5th Brigade made a somewhat cautious move toward their objective. Brink was concerned that a night move might have to take place, and he received permission from Gott to halt 5th Brigade as soon as night fell and then resume the advance at dawn. The South Africans were reluctant to move at night, having had an adverse experience on their approach march at the beginning of Crusader. Night moves were essential in desert warfare, being one of only a few methods available for concealment in a desert bereft of foliage and terrain features. The South Africans placed themselves at an acute disadvantage compared with the enemy, who made good use of darkness to maneuver their forces.[40] Armstrong eventually halted at 1805, a mere 20 km short of Sidi Rezegh, after three low-flying attacks delayed his brigade and resulted in some casualties.[41] The Italian presence on the flank of the South Africans greatly contributed to the nervousness and caution of the brigade's advance.

At the close of day, the British managed to concentrate two of their armored brigades, the 4th and 22nd, at Gabr Saleh, both of which had suffered grievous losses while inflicting insignificant damage on the core of the Axis armored formations. The 7th Armoured Brigade held the prominent landmark of Sidi Rezegh, which left the British confident that the forces in front of them were weak and buoyed them in the belief that they had destroyed approximately one hundred Axis tanks to date, which supposedly amounted to a substantial percentage of the forces facing them. In fact, the Axis had suffered relatively little, managing to inflict substantially more damage than they had received. (See Table 2 and Table 3.) It was due to the inaccurate assessment of the damage inflicted on the Axis armored forces that the British ordered the 70th Division, holding Tobruk, to undertake their breakout the next day. Originally, the breakout from Tobruk was dependent on the neutralization of the Axis armored forces. The British earmarked the 5th Brigade and the 7th Support Group to link up with elements of the 70th Division breaking out of Tobruk.

The Approach of the South Africans to Sidi Rezegh, the Attempted Breakout of Tobruk, and the Near Annihilation of 7th Armoured Brigade—November 21

Rommel soon realized that the British forces gathering at Sidi Rezegh were poised to relieve Tobruk. During the evening of November 20–21, he encouraged Crüwell to mobilise the *DAK* in the vicinity of Sidi Rezegh and to neutralize the threat. After breaking contact at Gabr Saleh,

Rommel ordered 15 *Panzer* and 21 *Panzer* to advance northwestwards through Sidi Rezegh to Belhamed at 0630 on November 21. Rommel calculated that this risky maneuver would end all chance of a junction between the invaders and the garrison of Tobruk. He left a small screen of antitank and field gunners with sapper infantry to cover the rear and hold off the British forces, namely the 4th and 22nd Armoured Brigades, south of Gabr Saleh. It is noteworthy that Rommel was confident that his small screening force would be able to hold off a much larger force long enough for him to execute his maneuver.[42]

At this stage, the British harbored high hopes that Crusader was at last gathering momentum. The Tobruk garrison was poised to break out of the Italian encirclement and seize El Duda with its two brigades of infantry supported by strong artillery and a substantial tank force. Once the die was cast, the 7th Armoured Brigade would pass through the Support Group at Sidi Rezegh and make contact with the Tobruk garrison. The South Africans were advancing and well on their way to consolidating the

TANK LOSSES PER DAY NOVEMBER 18–22, 1941

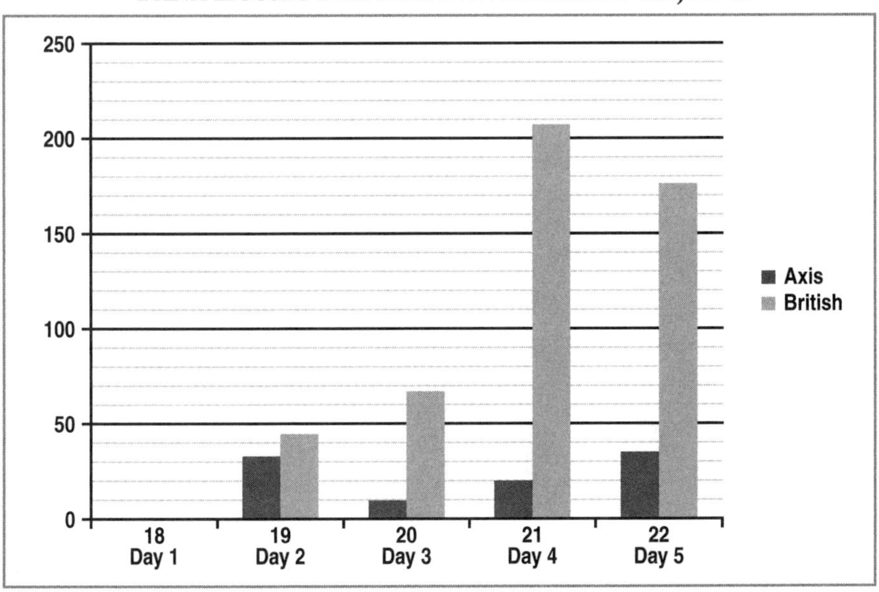

Table 2. British tank losses per day far outnumbered those of the Axis. By the end of November 22, the British had lost 498 tanks in total compared to 100 Axis tanks.

British positions at Sidi Rezegh. The 4th and 22nd Armoured Brigades would pin down and take care of the German armor facing them at Gabr Saleh. At dawn, after much preparation, the 70th Division besieged in Tobruk launched an attack toward Sidi Rezegh, a mere 18 km away, and after some hard fighting against resilient Italians and Germans from the 90th Light division, belatedly inserted by Rommel at the last minute, managed to penetrate within 6 km of El Duda. In grinding their way to their objective, the 70th Division suffered a loss of 60 of their compliment of 109 tanks. It was a testimony to the tough defense put up by the Italians and Germans.[43] (See Table 2 and Table 3.)

The southern pincer was to be formed by 7th Armoured Brigade, but instead of launching an attack to meet the forces breaking out from Tobruk, it instead found itself fighting for its life when, a half hour before the assault was to be launched, news came of the arrival of both German *Panzer* divisions. The Germans crashed into the British armor at Sidi Rezegh and all but annihilated the 7th Armoured Brigade, reducing it to 28 tanks out of an original strength of 141 tanks at the start of the day.[44] The obvious question is why the British left 7th Armoured Brigade alone to fend off the entire German armor force. Due to overconfidence and an overestimation of losses inflicted, Norrie had read the German armor disengagement from the 4th and 22nd Brigades incorrectly as a retreat. Although the British followed in hot pursuit, they were no match for the German pace nor the actions of the small German rearguard. Norrie mentions that both the 22nd and the 4th Armoured Brigades had a "hitch in petrol supply" and needed to call a halt to refuel.[45] The fuel stop and the skillful German rearguard delayed the British in closing the gap and they were never able to regain contact, leaving 7th Brigade to its own devices.[47] Furthermore, Norrie had misinterpreted the relocation of the two *Panzer* divisions to Sidi Rezegh as a general retreat by all the Axis forces from the frontier positions, and in response unleashed the relatively idle XIII Corps.[48] The British directed the corps to encircle the Axis positions on the frontier and cut off the "retreat." By nightfall XIII Corps had succeeded in isolating the Axis forces holding the border at Halfaya, Sidi Omar, and Bardia, although at a cost of thirty-five tanks lost in a hard fought series of battles.[49]

British tank losses thus far in the campaign had outstripped the German losses by a factor of five. The New Zealand official history

Tank Strengths Per Day November 18–22, 1941

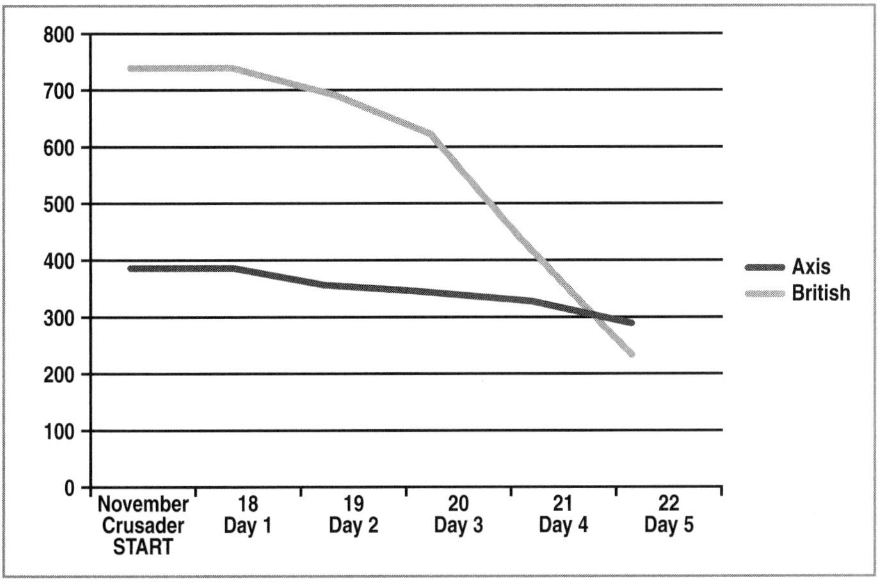

Table 3. By the end of the fifth day of combat, the Germans had managed to destroy the larger part of the British tank force and reverse the British overwhelming numerical superiority. The British had 240 tanks remaining, including 126 "I" tanks against a total of 290 Axis tanks.[46]

states, "in four days Eighth Army had lost some 530 tanks while the enemy lost about 100. Of 500 cruisers 7 Armoured Division retained fewer than 90, whereas the three enemy armored divisions still had 250 tanks (170 of them German) of the 356 with which they had started the battle." (See Table 2 and Table 3.) The official history explains the disparity in losses as, "against the *Panzer* divisions the British tank units were outclassed in a way that defies explanation in terms of personalities or of relative armor and armament, the terms chiefly considered in the Middle East at the time." The official history offers up as an explanation, "The essential difference was not of equipment, but of method. The Germans were favored by a tactical doctrine, inspired by British prophets unhonoured in their own country, which had been refined by years of close study and experiment."[50] Unbeknown to the British, their numerical armor superiority had all but disappeared, leaving the Eighth Army in great danger.

While mayhem descended on Sidi Rezegh, farther to the north, the 1st SAI Brigade maintained its screening duties of *Ariete* in the Bir El Gubi area. There the South Africans endured an extended artillery duel with the Italians for the better part of the day.[51] The South Africans were also subject to two heavy air attacks that fortunately caused little damage. The operational report describes the situation in front of 1st Brigade as "obscure," as no prisoners were captured and no information was received from XXX Corps.[52] The South Africans received messages throughout the day alluding to the large numbers of enemy tanks "knocked out" by the 7th Armoured Division, coupled with the encouraging news that the German *Panzer* seemed to be withdrawing. The 5th Brigade had reached a point 22 km south of Sidi Rezegh the previous day before stopping as night approached. In his dispatch, Auchinleck, although treading carefully, throws some light on the excruciating slowness of the South African efforts to close up on Sidi Rezegh. It boiled down to two words: inexperience and Italians.

> The 5th South African Infantry Brigade, which was expected to reach the scene before the development of the enemy attack, failed to do so, partly owing to the opposition of the *Ariete* Armoured Division and partly because of inexperience in handling the very large number of vehicles with which it took the field.[53]

The revised orders from the previous day had instructed the 5th Brigade to arrive in Sidi Rezegh by 0815 on November 21. However, the 5th Brigade set out later than required the next morning and had only covered 7 km toward their objective when Gott stopped them. He instructed them to halt and form a defensive posture until the tank battles raging to the north had been resolved.[54] Brink had instructed Armstrong to leave all his nonessential B Echelon vehicles behind in the staging area before departing to Sidi Rezegh. In fact, contrary to the instruction given by Brink, the entire B Echelon accompanied the brigade.[55]

The 5th Brigade registered its first clash with the tanks of *Ariete*, the event, no doubt, adding to the general unease in the South African camp. At about midday reports began to come in of unidentified enemy vehicles advancing from the west and southwest. The Italians attacked the 5th Brigade at 1300 in the flank with tanks and they were rebuffed with a mix of South African artillery and antitank weapons. The South Africans reported eight tanks destroyed, but this was impossible to confirm. The Italians turned back a South African patrol with heavy fire. The South Africans took twenty Italian prisoners for the loss of five killed and eleven wounded. Sightings of enemy armor to the west at 1400 met with an artillery barrage at a range of 3,000 m. The South Africans reinforced their left flank to meet the Italian threat to the west of their positions.[56] The Italians, discounted as ineffective at the outset of the operation, were proving to be a thorn in the side (literally and figuratively) of the South Africans.

The British plan was to get both SAI brigades, if possible, to link up with the 70th Division breaking out of Tobruk the next day. The planners were, of course, ignorant of the fact that the numerical armor balance had tipped decisively in favor of the Germans. The British ordered the 22nd Guards Brigade to relieve the 1st Brigade from its masking duties of *Ariete* at Bir El Gubi so that the South Africans could join the 5th Brigade at Sidi Rezegh. According to the British, there was good reason for optimism, and a corps situation report issued at 2010 estimated that the Axis had lost 170 tanks, many vehicles and guns had been disabled or captured, and the Italians were rapidly withdrawing "true to form."[57] The reality was different; the British had lost close to 180 tanks for the day while managing to inflict a relatively paltry 12 tank casualties on the Germans, with the South Africans knocking out a further 8 Italian tanks. (See Table 2 and Table 3.) The vast overestimation of the damage inflicted on German armor would adversely influence British decision making throughout Crusader. British intentions to destroy the Axis armor in detail had not materialized and their overwhelming superiority in tanks had evaporated. Failure to concentrate their armor and overwhelm the numerically inferior Axis had cost the British dearly.

Fortunately for the British, the Germans were equally in the dark as to the extent of damage inflicted on the British armor formations. Rommel was anxious to maintain the siege of Tobruk and eventually, through economy of his resources and a more defensive posture, he hoped to launch an attack to breach its defenses. Crüwell, on the other hand, was intent on reducing the British armor through a battle of maneuver using superior German battle skills. The 21 *Panzer*-Division took up defensive positions near Belhamed and the 15 *Panzer*-Division headed south for

Gasr el Arid in a bid to outflank the British forces gathering at Sidi Rezegh. The consequence of German indecision as to the *Schwerpunkt* was a compromise between Rommel and Crüwell that had the result of dividing the *Panzer* divisions instead of concentrating them. A brief window of opportunity once again presented itself for the British to concentrate their resources against the weaker of the two *Panzer* divisions.[58]

THE 5TH BRIGADE ATTACKS AND IS REPULSED BY THE GERMANS HOLDING POINT 178 ON THE SIDI REZEGH ESCARPMENT—NOVEMBER 22

Dawn began with the tactical withdrawal of the two victorious *Panzer* divisions, the 21st assembling at Belhamed and assuming a blocking role on any further British advance to Tobruk, and the 15th driving back east and assembling at Gasr el Arid to allow room to maneuver and maintain a flanking threat to the British positions at Sidi Rezegh.[59] The de-concentration and withdrawal of the *Panzer* divisions presented a fleeting opportunity to concentrate the remnants of 7th Armoured Division against the 21 *Panzer*-Division and push through to Tobruk. The British misconstrued the German disengagement as the retreat of a defeated enemy. The British still had the advantage of superior numbers and of holding better ground. It was a chance to smash through the German forces and join up with the Tobruk garrison. That the British did not avail themselves of the opportunity is due in large part to the ruinous tank losses suffered the previous day. The startling fact was that the 7th Armoured Division possessed a mere 204 tanks in working order. The result of unsupported and fragmented attacks littered the desert with the burned-out hulks of British tanks. The devastation wrought on the armored brigades invited a note of caution despite the gross overestimates of tank losses inflicted on the Germans.[60]

The resultant lull afforded by the German withdrawal from the battlefield encouraged Gott to order the South African 1st Brigade to move up to Sidi Rezegh at 1330 to seize the high ground at point 178 and establish a firm base for the intended thrust toward Tobruk earmarked for the next morning.[61] In response, Brink ordered Pienaar to move up to Sidi Rezegh, as the 22nd Guards Brigade would be taking over the masking duties of *Ariete* from the 1st Brigade. Pienaar replied that he would not be able to comply immediately but would begin the maneuver at 1630. Until fully relieved by the 22nd Guards Brigade, Pienaar remained reluctant to move. Pienaar signalled to Brink just before the designated time to begin his move to Sidi Rezegh that his motorized transport remained dispersed and his artillery was deployed on a wide front and in-depth. Due to his dispersed dispositions, he was unable to undertake operation before 1730. The menacing presence of the Italians on the South African flank invoked hesitancy in Armstrong and especially Pienaar, who continued to cast a wary eye toward *Ariete*.[62]

The South African 5th Brigade, although only a few kilometers from where the epic tank battles had taken place, maneuvered up to the edge of the southern escarpment. Gott ordered them to attack point 178 and occupy the positions held by the German 155th Infantry Regiment. At 1330 Armstrong sent in the 3 Transvaal Scottish supported by eight 25-pounder guns. Due to the lack of effective reconnaissance, the South Africans knew little of the German dispositions that occupied positions on the reverse slope. As a result, the artillery was not able to identify targets and effectively engage the enemy.[63] The Transvaal Scottish attack was quickly pinned down by accurate and heavy enemy defensive firepower supported by artillery and airpower. One of the 5th Brigade staff describes the brave futility of the Transvaal Scottish attack, in the face of well-prepared German positions and subject to withering fire.

> At 1330 hours, casually, with their rifles with fixed bayonets slung on their backs, a thin line of men advances. In the middle, in front, is their colonel. Fire is opened on them, bullets are whizzing and shells are bursting. They advance slowly and surely. Then, as if it were manoeuvres, they drop to the ground and take cover—but not their Colonel. Then on again—short, sharp rushes, then drop and up again.[64]

Lack of adequate reconnaissance and too little artillery support resulted in the loss of Lieutenant-Colonel Kirby, the commanding officer, and the second-in-command, Major J. D. F. Gartly, together with twenty-three men killed and ninety-two wounded or missing. The South Africans incurred unacceptably high casualties without making an impression on the enemy.[65] (See Map 3.)

Norrie hoped that the South Africans would combine both of their brigades on the southern escarpment after the 1st Brigade was relieved

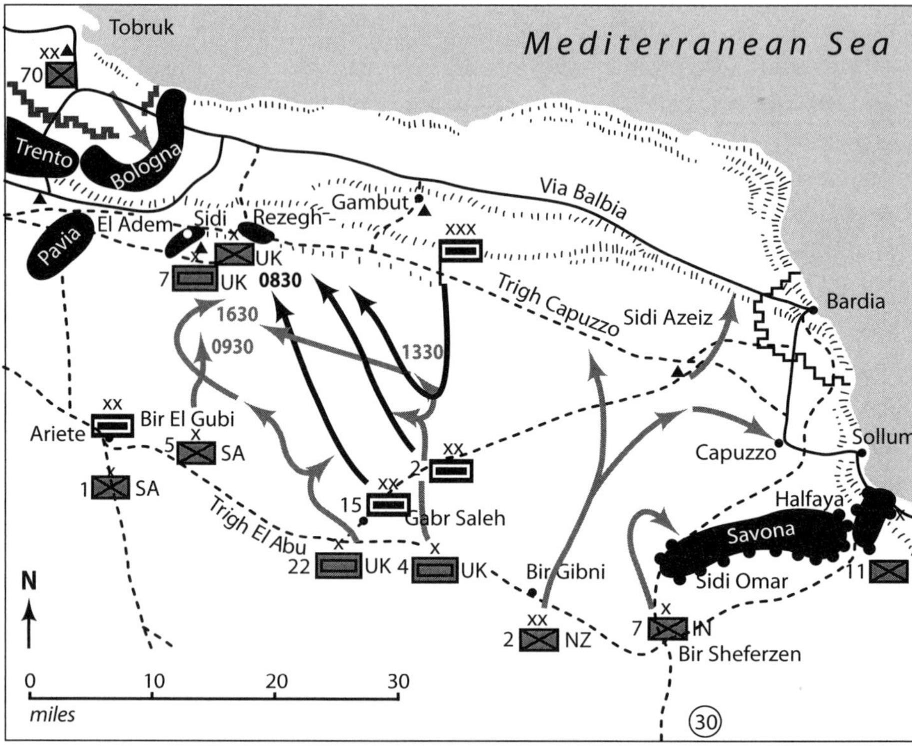

Map 3. November 22. The 5th Brigade began its hesitant move up to Sidi Rezegh. One can see the threat of *Ariete* to the South African flank. The South Africans moved forward with one eye cast to the left flank at all times. The Tobruk garrison begins its breakout!

from its masking duties at Bir El Gubi by the 22nd Guards Brigade. However, after numerous delays by Pienaar this was not to be. Brink fully supported the strenuous objections lodged by Pienaar to undertaking a night march. In the face of the South African objections, it was decided that Pienaar would instead consolidate his position at Bir El Gubi, and then make ready to move up to Sidi Rezegh at first light.[66] The New Zealand official history finds no reason for the failure of this vital linkup intended by Norrie. Pienaar proved a short while later that he was fully capable of undertaking a night move under much more precarious conditions. This occurred when the brigade, under Pienaar, managed to retreat 29 km with precision on the night of November 25. Movement at night was an essential part of desert warfare, and certainly the Germans had no qualms about using the concealment offered by darkness to maneuver their forces to best advantage.[67]

It was Pienaar's tardiness that led to the brigade only starting to move at 1730, despite the British request to do so many hours beforehand and after their warning, early in the afternoon, of the possibility that a delay would necessitate a night move. This hesitancy, or what has been better described as obduracy, in the Transvaal Scottish Regimental History has led some critics to believe that Pienaar, due to his excessive caution, had abandoned the 5th Brigade to its fate. British unit staffs and the New Zealanders expressed bitterness at Pienaar's "insubordination" and "dereliction of duty." According to *The Saga of the Transvaal Scottish*, Pienaar's excuse was that his brigade would have made no difference, in the absence of armored support, in avoiding the destruction of 5th Brigade. He felt his first duty was to preserve his brigade.[68]

Unaware of the hesitancy in the South African camp, Rommel and Crüwell were more concerned with the British concentration of forces developing to the south of Sidi Rezegh. They independently ordered the 21 and 15 *Panzer*-Divisions to attack the concentration. Rommel intended the attack by the 21 *Panzer*-Division, the weaker of the two, to be merely in support of the 15 *Panzer*-Division. But the battlefield ensures the early demise of the best of intentions and plans after the first shot fired. The 21 *Panzer*-Division, commanded by Generalmajor Walter Neumann-Silkow, attacked soon after at 1420 in what amounted to a lone effort without the support of 15 *Panzer*-Division. Nevertheless, despite Rommel not intending for this to be a solo effort, Generalmajor Johann von Ravenstein's 21 *Panzer*-Division managed to inflict a resounding defeat on the British forces in general and the armor in particular. The victorious Germans managed to capture the airfield at Sidi Rezegh and surrounding positions. The crushing defeat delivered by 57 German tanks, part of a combined arms team, reduced the 7th Armoured Division to 149 tanks. The 22nd, 7th, and 4th Armoured Brigades had 34, 15, and 100 tanks remaining, respectively. The Germans, who suffered a fraction of the casualties that they inflicted, had lost 19 tanks from 15 *Panzer*-Division and 17 tanks from 21 *Panzer*-Division.[69] It was an unqualified vindication of the German way of war and an exercise in the superiority of combined arms warfare. The British fought with great courage but their lack of coordination with all arms was no match for the expertise of the Germans. (See Table 2 and Table 3.)

The British received yet a further blow at the closing stages of the day's battle. The 15 *Panzer*-Division attack, when it eventually got under way, occurred at nightfall and resulted in the capture of the 4th Armoured Brigade headquarters, consisting of 17 officers and 150 others together with 35 tanks. Importantly, it effectively rendered the 4th Brigade inoperative for at least twenty-four hours due to the paralysis inflicted with the loss of its headquarters.[70] The Germans' triumphant defeat of the British armor effectively signalled the end of the 7th Armoured Division's contribution to the campaign. It was the infantry and gunners of the two army tank brigades, with their infantry tanks, which would have to bear the brunt in reducing the German armor over the remaining days and then eventually wrest victory from a very close run battle.[71]

The British, at this stage, had little prospect of forcing a corridor to Tobruk. The combined effect of the comprehensive defeats in the preceding day's battles resulted in them forfeiting their initial numerical advantage in tanks. The British found themselves outnumbered by the Axis forces for the first time in Crusader and they lost the airfield at Sidi Rezegh to boot. Brink remained optimistic that the situation remained well in hand, despite receiving a report at 2330 that Sidi Rezegh airfield had fallen and many German tanks were in the vicinity.[72] His optimism was no doubt fed by his ignorance that the Axis armor had roundly defeated the British tank brigades. The advance of the New Zealand Brigade toward Tobruk further buoyed his unfounded confidence. Brink was not alone in harboring baseless optimism, which was rife in the British camp. Overinflated German and Italian tank losses, reported since the beginning of the campaign, concealed the great danger about to descend on the hapless South Africans.

Brink, of course, had little reason for optimism, as in truth, the disastrous day's events meant doom for the 5th SAI Brigade. The Germans maintained the fighting power of their armor formations by convincingly winning the first phase of the operation, while that of the British had all but evaporated. The 5th Brigade was left isolated and vulnerable due to the tardiness of its sister unit, the 1st Brigade, and the destruction of the tanks that were supposedly there to defend the infantry. Pienaar was unwilling to close up with Armstrong and his brigade remained languishing kilometers to the south. There was also no effective communication or command mechanism in place that would allow the South Africans to coordinate their defense with the little that remained of the British tanks in the vicinity or the 7th Support Group. Little time or inclination was left to correct an outmoded doctrine that did not envisage combined arms operations. The South Africans were about to face the full might of the entire German and Italian armored divisions.

The Annihilation of 5th Brigade at Sidi Rezegh—November 23

The scene was set for the disaster that was to befall the 5th SAI Brigade. The Axis had taken advantage of the British failure to concentrate their forces, with the result that the British advantage in tank numbers of some 738 to 390 (see Table 1) had been whittled away to 240 opposing 290 German tanks by the end of the November 22. (See Table 2 and 3.) The Axis, for the first time in the battle, not only enjoyed a slight numerical superiority in armor but had achieved a measure of concentration, unlike the British, whose tanks were scattered among the various brigades. The remaining British tanks consisted of 126 infantry tanks and 114 Cruiser tanks with the armored divisions, of which the vast majority belonged to the 4th Brigade, which was effectively out of operation due to the loss of their headquarters the previous day. Rommel sought nothing less than the elimination of the entire 7th Armoured Division together with the 1st South African Division, and he set about concentrating his tank divisions to execute a deadly assault.[73]

Norrie possessed few options in what was rapidly amounting to a bleak situation. He commanded a dissipated and scattered armored force, and he faced a rampant, skilled, and victorious enemy that now significantly outgunned him in tanks. His intention was to build a strong infantry position around the 5th Brigade and use the remaining British armor to hold off attacks by the "depleted" enemy armor. The remnants of 22nd Armoured Brigade, with thirty tanks, held positions to the west of 5th Brigade, and the remains of the 7th Support Group manned positions to the east. The British again urged Brink to expedite the joining of his reluctant 1st Brigade with the 5th Brigade. Brink and the South Africans had little sense of the impending danger gathering against them and incorrectly evaluated that the "situation was in hand."[74] He assumed incorrectly that 7th Armoured Division had emerged from the recent tank battles victorious and largely intact. In reality, it fielded only a fraction of its original tank strength and his reliance on the belief that 7th Armoured Division was able to deal with the enemy tank threat was to cost the South Africans dearly. Brink's unfounded optimism was bolstered further by the expectation of the imminent arrival of the New Zealand Division, which would add its "I" tanks to the armored strength of the British forces south of Sidi Rezegh.[75]

The South African 5th Brigade stationed itself some 3 km short of point 178. It was a position that they had unsuccessfully attacked the previous day in an attempt to dislodge the Germans from the escarpment. Armstrong arranged the brigade in a 3 km defensive box with the 3 Transvaal Scottish facing north and the 1st South African Irish Regiment and Regiment Botha manning the west and east side of the box, respectively. The southern portion of the box consisted mainly of the B Echelon elements dispersed at the required 100 m apart, stretching many kilometers into the desert. The 22nd Armoured Brigade deployed 1.6 km to the west of the 5th Brigade. To the east lay the Support Group together with a small remnant of the 7th Armoured Brigade, both having borne the brunt of the German attack on the Sidi Rezegh airfield the previous day. The largely intact 4th Armoured Brigade would play no role on the day, incapacitated due to the capture of its headquarters the previous day.[76] The British dispositions around Sidi Rezegh were not concentrated and formed three distinct formations, a situation not conducive to meeting the impending Axis onslaught. Furthermore, there were no means of direct communication between Armstrong's headquarters and the British forces to the east and west of the South African laager.[77] The South African inability to communicate effectively with other units nearby, especially those of the armored formations, put them at a severe disadvantage in coordinating a common defense.[78]

Rommel and Crüwell intended crushing the British in an overwhelming attack but differed in their method of implementation. Rommel favored a northerly attack with the *Panzer* divisions first driving south to meet up with *Ariete* and then attacking back toward the north and destroying everything in between. Crüwell had other ideas—doubting *Ariete*'s capability of holding the south against a British retreat, he decided that he would rather send his 15 *Panzer*-Division with a tank regiment of 21 *Panzer* around the eastern flank of the 5th Brigade to link up with *Ariete*. He then intended to launch an attack northwards with the Italians toward Sidi Rezegh. The *Panzer* divisions in the south would constitute the hammer that drove toward the German infantry anvil manning the escarpment in front of the South Africans.[79] Crüwell's plan was not without merit, but it entailed splitting off half his infantry and artillery to man the northern escarpment, and then sending the remainder, with all his tanks, to join *Ariete*. The Germans had no idea that their drive south would place them between the 5th and the 1st Brigades—as it was their intention to be south of the entire XXX Corps.[80] Despite some riskiness, the success or otherwise of Crüwell's bold outflanking maneuver would be largely determined by whether an attack from the south would catch the British by surprise, and whether Gott was able to coordinate and reorient the defenders to face the new threat from the south as opposed to the north.[81]

Pienaar and his 1st Brigade declined to undertake a night march and close the southern flank of the 5th Brigade. The failure to marry up with the 5th Brigade left its southern flank exposed and relatively undefended, manned with little more than the entire B Echelon. Pienaar's unwillingness to undertake a night march meant that an opportunity was lost to combine the strength of the two SAI brigades under the concealment of dark. The fact that some support echelons of the 1st Brigade went ahead at night and effectively linked up with the 5th Brigade indicated the ease with which Pienaar could have completed this maneuver.[82] In any event, all chances of linking up had begun to disappear by daybreak as the Axis armor gathered in the south and effectively drove a wedge between the two brigades. It was ironic that Pienaar's B Echelon, field company, and ambulances had in fact outstripped the fighting units of 1st Division in the night approach march and were now ahead of them. However, this mass of transport found in front of Pienaar at daybreak further slowed his snail-paced progress north.

The Germans disturbed Pienaar's belated attempts to advance north and link up with 5th Brigade as Crüwell drove his *Panzer* regiments southwards toward *Ariete* at Bir el Gubi. He accomplished the link up with the Italians at 1235.[83] The 1st Brigade made contact with the enemy shortly after 0700 and in the ensuing contact reported destruction of three enemy tanks by the brigade's artillery.[84] Pienaar's prospects of joining with the 5th Brigade steadily diminished with the growing armor threat directly in his path to the north. Despite the receding possibility of 1st Brigade linking up with 5th Brigade, Brink felt confident enough to signal Armstrong at 1230, "*Ons is naby en ons kom. Ander mense kom ook van ander kant hou vas.*" (We are nearby, other people are coming from another direction—hold on.)[85]

The German move southward surprised the British. Their first indication that something was afoot was when German forces brushed against the eastern outposts of the South African defensive box. The Germans crashed through the tail of B Echelon as they wheeled west en route to *Ariete*. Panic gripped the B Echelon, which was strung out for kilometers at the undefended south side of the defensive box, and they put to flight in all directions. By 1430 the Germans, together with *Ariete,* completed their assembly and reoriented to face north against the weak southern flank of 5th Brigade. Crüwell's intention that his route would take him south of all the elements of XXX Corps had misfired, and he had no idea that he occupied the narrow gap between Brink's two SAI brigades.[86]

Gott spent the night with the 5th Brigade leaguer and advised Armstrong to strengthen the southern flank of his position. After regrouping and shuffling the artillery and antitank weapons, the brigade considerably strengthened the southern flank of the defensive box.[87] (See Table 4.) Gott's timely intervention ensured that the southern sector now contained 50 percent of the brigade's available artillery to meet the German attack. The German official history describes the positions of

Artillery Dispositions 5th Brigade per Defensive Sector November 23

	25 Pounder	18 Pounder	2 Pounder	Total
Northern Sector	8			8
Western Sector	10		2	12
Eastern Sector	16		1	17
Southern Sector	12	2	21	35
Total	46	2	24	72

Table 4. Artillery dispositions of 5th Brigade per defensive sector November 23, after Gott's timely intervention.Over 50 percent of the 5th Brigade antitank assets faced south and caused havoc among the German armor.[88]

the 5th Brigade as "thoroughly prepared," 10 km wide and 8 km deep, and defended by over one hundred artillery pieces and numerous antitank guns.[89] Gott did remark that the South African 2-pounder antitank guns remained on their portees and that they should rather have been taken off the trucks and dug in, as many were lost immediately, contributing to the eventual German success. The official history offers that the situation was fluid, with Gott himself warning the South Africans of an attack from the north. Rommel had favored a northern attack, and the South Africans may have seen Crüwell's outflanking maneuver as a feint. The feasibility of digging in on the rock-hard terrain is moot.[90] The fog of war was thick and it blanketed the battlefield, obscuring the vision of both sides equally.

The dispositions around the Sidi Rezegh battlefield were among the most complex to be found in the history of warfare, and demonstrate the complicated nature of mobile warfare. The British and German dispositions resembled a layer cake. The British forces in Tobruk faced mainly Italian forces, who were back-to-back with mainly German forces, who in turn faced the British who occupied Sidi Rezegh. In turn, those defending Sidi Rezegh, including the South Africans, faced in two directions to meet the threat both to the north and south of their positions. The German armor that had gathered to the south of the 5th Brigade had the South Africans to their north and the South African 1st Brigade to their south. The battlefield, therefore, consisted of no less than seven "lines" facing in different directions.[91]

The South Africans, who could have used artillery fire, had done little to disrupt the concentration of enemy forces taking place to the southeast corner of the defensive box. There is a case for the conservation of ammunition, due to the fact that the Axis forces effectively cut off the brigade and they did not have an excess of ammunition on hand. A further reason for the lack of interdicting artillery fire was the uncertainty as to the status of the forces gathering to the south, given that the 5th Brigade expected the imminent arrival of the 1st Brigade from that direction throughout the day.[92] A further reason was that once the 25-pounder artillery had been deployed in a dispersed antitank role, its effectiveness in the proper role of concentrated artillery was somewhat negated.[93] On the other side of the hill, the Germans described their efforts to deploy their forces as hindered by the South African artillery, which far outnumbered their weak artillery resources.[94] It is disappointing that South African reconnaissance units, who accurately reported on the composition of the gathering enemy forces to brigade headquarters, were dismissed with an attitude bordering on contempt.[95] However, the antitank dispositions, which the brigade concentrated in the south, do seem to indicate that they accurately assessed the direction of the most imminent danger.

This was despite German efforts to distract the defenses of the 5th Brigade and lure the defenders into thinking that an attack from the north was imminent. The Germans brought down a concentrated artillery barrage from the north and southwest at 1130 on the Irish positions. At 1300 the barrage intensified and the South African guns attempted to return fire, but this was largely ineffective due to enemy positions not being located. The intense barrage, coupled with intense machine-gun fire, gave all the signs that an infantry attack to the north of the brigade box was imminent. The South Africans began to draw reinforcements, amounting to two companies, from the west and east defenses and send them up to the Transvaal Scottish lines defending the north. Bren gun carriers from the Support Group soon joined them. At 1545 the German attack on this sector subsided and this coincided with reports that B Echelon was under a major attack by tanks on the southwest corner of the 5th Brigade box. It now became apparent that the German attack to the northwest was merely a diversion designed to draw in the tanks of the 22nd Armoured Brigade, leaving the South Africans in the south without tank support.[96]

The German demonstrations in the northern sector that encouraged a strengthening of the line also drew off two antitank weapons from the southern sector. At approximately 1400 hours the South African reconnaissance of 4th South African Armoured Cars confirmed that a concentration of Germans had formed up almost in line abreast and facing north. Gott greeted this news with a surprising comment: "Your South African Brigade seems stuck down with gum—they won't move and they won't turn their artillery round and they are not dug in—I am sorry for them." The comment seemed out of place given the artillery dispositions concentrated in the south to meet the German attack. It seems more likely to have referred to the inertia displayed by Pienaar and his 1st Brigade.[97] At 1555 wireless contact between 1st Division and 5th Brigade suddenly broke off with the last word, "wait," uttered by the brigade radio operator.[98] At 1700 Brink decided that the obscurity of the situation in front of 1st Brigade obviated the possibility of it moving up to offer assistance to 5th Brigade.[99]

Having assembled all their armored forces, the Axis began their attack at 1600 hours in what has been described by the New Zealand official history as "a radical departure not only from accepted *Panzer* tactics but from the fundamentals of their trade."[100] The German attack faced an extremely deep position, and under normal circumstances, would have required the Germans to deploy their forces in depth rather than the 16 km breadth in which their three armored formations now found themselves.[101] Crüwell's decision to leave half his infantry and artillery to man the northern escarpment meant that the remaining infantry and artillery component of the *Panzer* divisions were covering double the usual frontage. Furthermore, once the attack got under way, only the central portion of the assault formation managed to engage the 5th Brigade solidly. The two wings, *Ariete* on the left and 5 *Panzer*-Regiment and the 200th Infantry Regiment on the right flank, only brushed past the 5th Brigade's flanks initially. The Germans failed to concentrate their forces effectively, and this was to cost them dearly.[102]

The Germans offered some reasons for their decision to attack a broad rather than narrow front. For strategic reasons, the Germans launched the attack on a wide front to prevent the enemy from escaping east. There was also no time to arrange a deliberate infantry attack using tried and tested infantry tactics, and therefore they decided on the riskier venture of remaining in their vehicles and charging at the enemy in the wake of the tanks. Lastly, a nonnegotiable swamp that lay to the south of the German formations inhibited their concentration of forces. Also, according to the Germans, the South Africans raked the area with the artillery fire from Pienaar's and Armstrong's brigades, which effectively sandwiched the Germans in a narrow corridor.[103] (See Map 4.)

The Germans charged at the South Africans with 110 tanks of the 8 *Panzer*-Regiment followed closely by two infantry battalions of the 115th Infantry Regiment who were carried forward in their vulnerable lorries. One of the largest tank attacks of the desert war met with a hail of fire by the South African gunners lurking among the transport vehicles of the B Echelon. The German infantry following the tanks tried to stay in their vehicles for as long as possible but met with a withering

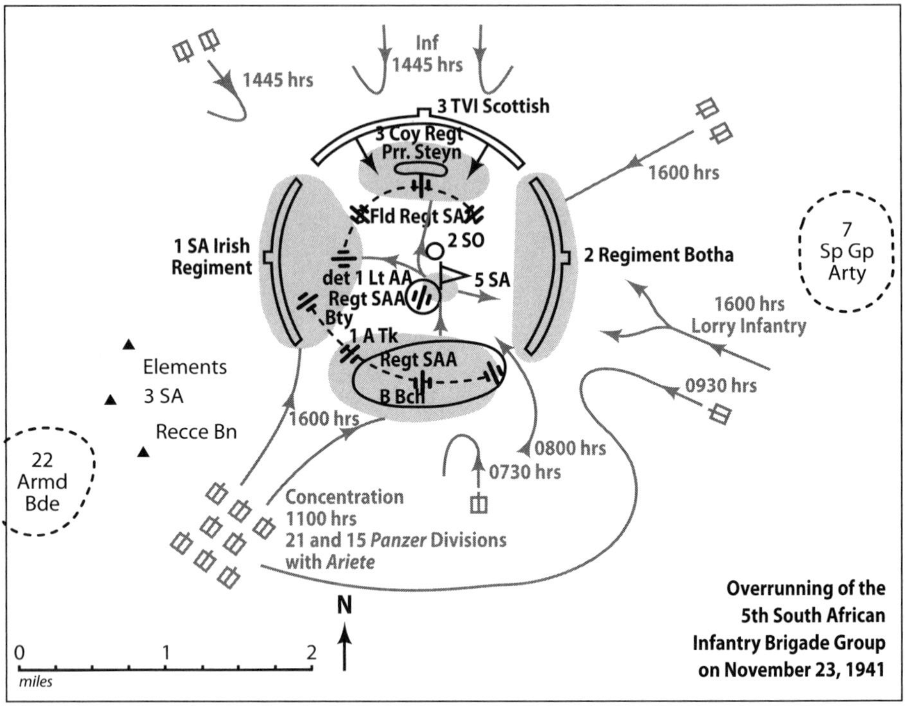

Map 4. The end of the 5th Brigade at Sidi Rezegh on November 23, 1941. Known as Totensontag by the Germans.[104]

fire that claimed many killed and wounded. Lieutenant Heinz Schmidt, aide-de-camp to Rommel, graphically describes the resulting carnage inflicted on the Germans in the battle. He requested Rommel transfer him to active service, shortly before the battle, and he found himself in the thick of things with the 115 Rifle Regiment lining up to attack the South Africans' southern flank.

> Attack! The order was passed swiftly. The regimental commander led, standing erect in his open car. The Major's cars followed, with me right behind him. We headed straight for the enemy tanks. I glanced back. Behind me was a fan of our vehicles—a curious assortment of all types—spread out as far as the eye could see. They were armoured troop-carriers, cars of various kinds, caterpillars hauling mobile guns, heavy trucks with infantry, motorised anti-aircraft units. Thus, we roared on toward the enemy 'barricade.'

> I stared to the front fascinated. Right ahead was the erect figure of the colonel commanding the regiment. On the left close by and slightly in the rear of him was the Major's car. Tank shells were whizzing through the air. The defenders were firing from every muzzle of their 25-pounders and their little 2-pounder antitank guns. We raced on at a suicidal pace.
>
> The battalion commander's car lurched and stopped suddenly—a direct hit. I had just time to notice the Colonel steadying himself. He turned sideways and dropped from the car like a felled tree. Then I had flashed past him. The Major was still ahead. I recognised infantry positions in front of me. There was a tall, thin fellow out in the open, running backwards as if impelled by a jet from a hose. I heard bursts behind me and followed the tracer as it whipped past me into the distance ahead. How slowly tracer seems to travel! The tall fellow dropped.
>
> We had almost reached the screen of antitank guns and the tanks. A cold shiver ran down my spine. I saw small round holes forming in the windscreen of my car—just as though some invisible mechanic were drilling them there. Machine-gun fire! My driver huddled lower and lower over the wheel. The Major's car lurched and went over on its side. I was alone out ahead of this inferno now. In front, I saw nothing but belching guns. Then suddenly there was a violent jolt, a screeching and a hiss, and my car stopped dead. I saw a trench immediately ahead, leaped from the car, and plunged towards the slit. My driver leaped out even as I did. But before he could dive on his face, he suddenly stiffened up erect, spun on his axis, and then dropped limp.[105]

The South Africans continued to fight in small pockets and opposed the German infantry vigorously.[106] Assistance for the South Africans came in the form of a counterattack by the remnants of the 22nd Armoured Brigade, who fought a "solid and skilful" action falling back by degrees through the huge South African laager.[107] The South Africans extracted a fearsome toll on the advancing Germans. Despite enormous losses, the Germans steadily overran the South African positions and made Armstrong a prisoner, together with his headquarters. They were seen carrying them off into captivity on top of a German tank. The battlefield was rapidly becoming confused. Staff-Sergeant B. F. Hesselbarth, in the thick of the fighting, gives an indication of the chaos and confusion as the German tanks infiltrated behind the 5th Brigade lines.

> The Germans appeared to veer round to our rear and to the left. Our vehicles started moving about apparently trying to disperse. . . . British artillery kept rushing from one side of our lines to the other. Pandemonium appeared to have broken loose. We fired with rifles and Tommy-guns at German tanks which were not far distant. . . . Shells flew over our heads and burst all round us. We lay flat behind our mounds for approximately two hours (Owing to the rocky nature of the ground it was impossible to dig shell slits) . . . Later on we saw two lines of German tanks approaching us. They were covered by their own artillery fire. It was literally raining heavy fire above and around us. We saw shells burst among the trucks and saw trucks fly into the air in pieces, bundles of kit and equipment being thrown into the sky.[108]

Major W. D. Pretorius was eyewitness to the destruction of the 5th Brigade when the German tanks overran their positions, causing chaos, confusion, and eventually, panic.

> Enemy tanks had broken through our lines somewhere in the rear and I found myself being fired on from three different sides, machine-gun and mortar fire from my front and machine-gun and anti-tank fire from my left and rear. By this time men from the Irish (South African Irish Regiment) and T.S. (Transvaal Scottish) swarmed through my lines causing panic. I heard several voices shout "Retire, retire." I tried to stop them and get them down again without success. I gave the order to withdraw under cover of darkness. I had no idea where to withdraw to as communication with Battalion HQ had broken down and the enemy were all around us.[109]

Lieutenant-Colonel Mason, the Officer commanding 2 Regiment Botha on the east flank of the 5th Brigade box, gave his testimony as to the ferocity of the battle now unfolding around him.

> At approximately 1530 hours I noticed an enemy tank column moving towards me line ahead. It was evident they proposed to encircle my Battalion and dispose of it piecemeal. I waited until the tanks were approximately 800 yards to my south-east and ordered the guns to open fire. Eight tanks were immediately put out of action and the remainder veered off and made for the east-southeast. Simultaneously with the tank attack in the rear, enemy infantry attacked from the northwest, this was successfully beaten off with machine-gun and mortar fire. Following the beating off of the tanks, the enemy put down a heavy barrage on my Battalion inflicting a large number of casualties. I was hit at about 1630 hours, and was for a short time unconscious.[110]

Scattered remnants of 5th Brigade that escaped death or captivity made their way east to the British lines, one of whom was Major Cochran, the acting commanding officer of the South African Irish, who fled with four 25-pounders and some men.[111]

At 1930 Brink received a message that tanks were heavily attacking "Armstrong's boys" on both sides and that they were in a very delicate position, having suffered heavy casualties. At 1945 Brink received a final indication that Armstrong had been overrun by "over one hundred tanks" and that a significant number of 5th Brigade were prisoners. The realization finally dawned on Brink that the British had indeed lost the tank battle, leaving his brigade to the mercy of the German tanks.[112] In the process the 5th Brigade was annihilated, suffering 224 killed, 379 wounded, and approximately 2,800 captured. The Germans, suffering grievously, lost 72 out of 162 tanks deployed in the attack, as well as severe casualties among their commissioned and noncommissioned officers.[113] The 15 *Panzer*-Division had lost both its battalion commanders, five of its six company commanders, and the majority of troop carriers.[114] By all accounts, the South Africans had fought bravely, inflicting significant losses in the face of overwhelming German superiority. The 5th Brigade had "cut the heart out" of Crüwell's command.[115] The South Africans gunners had played a decisive role in inflicting German tank casualties, and one source describes their efforts as "magnificent."[116] An American correspondent and eyewitness described the day's events, stating in his letter,

> The South African Brigade (I forget its numeral but its Brigadier was Armstrong) fought with the utmost bravery and devotion and willing sacrifice of its own lives, but was simply overwhelmed. Infantry of course is as helpless as a troop of boy scouts against tanks in the open desert.[117]

General Auchinleck was unstinting in his praise in a personal letter to Smuts and expressed his regret that "Union troops should have suffered so heavily in their first major engagement in Libya." He described the South Africans as "gallant," and said they had fought to the last round against a tank and truck-borne infantry.[118]

The last words giving testimony to the ferocity of the battle belong to the party allocated the grim task of burying the dead after the guns fell silent:

> Work started on the 3rd January and was completed on the 14th January. Work was rather slow at first as we struck a layer of rock just below the surface, and a considerable amount of blasting was necessary. Holes were drilled by hand and took a long time. There was however any quantity of explosives still lying about the battlefield which we used. An average of 17 men a day were buried which was quite good going considering the bad weather experienced during the whole period. We only saw the sun for one day. A total of 206 men were buried and of these 51 were unidentified as they had no disks, and many others were only identified through articles found on the bodies. The graveyard is situated about 4 miles south of the Sidi Rezegh aerodrome, and is almost in the centre of the battle area.
>
> The area was still littered with burnt out vehicles and tanks of all descriptions, rifles and ammunition in good condition. In one of the Irish lines there were seven or eight German heavy tanks in the space of 25 square yards, which had been put out of action by 2-pounders. The tanks [were] full of marks where the shells had glanced off, but when a shell did penetrate it was sufficient to put them out of action. Two antitank bullets that had struck square had penetrated about an inch into the armour plating. Some of the shell slits were no(t) deep enough, as some of the men were actually crushed to death by the tanks.[119]

In the Aftermath of Sidi Rezegh

Those opposed to the war effort back home may have felt vindicated at the needless sacrifice of South Africans at Sidi Rezegh due to British incompetence in the conduct of Operation Crusader. The reaction of the New Zealanders, who suffered similarly in the campaign, is insightful. The New Zealand official history describes the New Zealand Division as; "injured, puzzled, and to some extent ill-used" in the aftermath of Crusader. Experience with the British in previous campaigns had influenced Lieutenant-General Bernard Freyberg, who commanded the 2nd New Zealand Division in North Africa. The less than brilliant British conduct of the Crusader operation convinced Freyberg that it was in New Zealand's best interest to get its forces out of the desert campaign altogether.[120] Freyberg was not alone in disagreeing with British methods of dividing divisions into brigade groups, a view shared by Brink, whom he describes as "in despair over dissipation of his forces and manner in which his brigades are employed even without reference to him." As a result of British "faulty" ideas, Freyberg had his division transferred to Syria to "safeguard the interests of New Zealand and of the Division."[121] The South Africans, without the luxury of the New Zealand Charter, reserving the right of the government of New Zealand to decide on the use of the division, had no option but to remain under the desert command.

It was unfair to lay the entire blame for the disaster at Britain's door. Brink's conduct in Crusader also came under some scrutiny. There was an impression in Pretoria at that time of moves afoot to recall him, or even demote him. General Sir Pierre van Ryneveld (1891–1972), the South African Chief of the General Staff, may have lost confidence in Brink as a divisional commander.[122] Criticism of Brink after the war took the form of whether he was right to have committed his division to the battle, despite their unpreparedness and lack of training. In the face of such criticism, he was unwavering in his answer that South Africa's honor was at stake, and stated, "It was the hardest decision of my life but I agreed to the division playing an important offensive role. Even knowing as I do now what followed, I would make the same decision today."[123] Undoubtedly Brink felt that the South African forces would have lost face within the Union and with the Eighth Army, should he have decided not to take the main role in Operation Crusader.[124]

The occasion of this debate was the release of the second in a series of books, produced by the UWHS in 1957, appropriately titled *The Sidi Rezegh Battles 1941*.[125] It was, in fact, a prelude to the first release by the UWHS, which dealt with the surrender of Tobruk.[126] The release of the book caused a minor stir in the local South African press with references to a "blunderbuss" campaign in which the core lesson learned is that "no troops should be committed to battle before they are properly trained from the commander-in-chief to the lowest formation."[127] The UWHS produced a monumental work on Operation Crusader in general, and a detailed account of the demise of the 5th Brigade at Sidi Rezegh. Their careful research had, in fact, revealed that the 5th Brigade had extracted a fearful toll on the German armor in succumbing to the might of the German attack, perhaps signalling a tipping point in Operation Crusader.[128] The South Africans had certainly put up a brave fight by all accounts, in what Colonel Rainer Kriebel, the operations staff officer of 15 *Panzer*-Division, describes as "the most difficult [attack] which tanks and rifleman were called upon to carry out in the course of this campaign."[129]

The regimental historian of the Transvaal Scottish described the destruction of the 5th Brigade as inevitable, once the Germans had destroyed the protective British armor in the days preceding the battle. Unlike the official history, the regimental history bemoans the fact that, "the heavy outlay in precious lives was not offset by a tangible return. . . ."[130] The South African Irish regimental historian describes the German triumph as a Pyrrhic victory and sees the sacrifice of the 5th Brigade as the initiator of a chain of events that would eventually lead to the Axis withdrawal from Cyrenaica within three weeks. The regimental history discusses the failure of the 1st Brigade to close up with the 5th Brigade on the Sidi Rezegh escarpment, and the general hesitancy of Pienaar in the days preceding the 5th Brigade's destruction. However, the authors do not offer a strong viewpoint, either way, citing the point as moot, highly contentious, and purely academic.[131] Given the reverence with which South Africa held Pienaar, the author's reluctance to render an opinion by interrogating and interpreting the facts is perhaps understandable. This is despite the fact that the publication of the South African Irish Regimental History took place in 1991, a half a century after the event.

Pienaar received some scathing criticism for his conduct in Operation Crusader, both from the official and the Transvaal Scottish Regimental histories. That he did is even more remarkable in light of the fact that Pienaar had achieved close to hero status in South Africa, a situation no doubt propelled by his untimely death in an airplane accident on December 19, 1942, at age forty-nine. Pienaar, at the time of his death, had become one of South Africa's most charismatic and popular military commanders. Some, including his close subordinates and even influential people in the United Kingdom High Commission in Pretoria, thought of Pienaar as a potential successor to Smuts—a victorious Afrikaner general who could have held back the reactionary forces of Afrikaner nationalism. Ironically, it was during Operation Crusader at the battle of Taib el Esem on November 25, 1941, a few short days after the loss of the 5th Brigade, that Pienaar's reputation as a gifted and courageous general began to take root.

In *Pienaar of Alamein*, Pollock describes the battle of Taib el Esem as Pienaar's greatest achievement, where he demonstrated "for the first time that infantry and guns, properly handled and disposed, were a match for the dreaded German *Panzer*s." It was at Taib el Esem that Pienaar and his 1st Brigade took on the 21 *Panzer*-Division, allowing the Eighth Army to regroup and deliver a thrust that eventually relieved the Tobruk garrison.[132] Eric Rosenthal repeats the legend of this epic battle against the German armor in his book on Pienaar, thus adding, at the time, to the myth surrounding these events.[133] The official history encases "The Battle of Taieb el Esem" in quotation marks, for in fact, for all intents and purposes, the battle as described in legend never took place. Elements of *Ariete* delivered the attack on Pienaar's 1st Brigade halfheartedly. The 21 *Panzer*-Division had no part in the action. Thus, the official history describes that a legend grew, undiscouraged by its members, that the "1st SA Brigade held off the German armor when 5th Brigade collapsed."[134] Throughout the so-called battle, Pienaar insisted that he was locked in combat with German *Panzers* and he called for immediate armored support. Brink, remembering the fate of the 5th Brigade, and believing Pienaar, pressured XXX Corps to supply armored support and even bomber support. Writing in 1954, Gatehouse said that on his arrival at the 1st Brigade positions, he could see no sign of the supposed attack, and Pienaar was in an excitable state.[135] The final indignity took the form of Pienaar rather disingenuously withdrawing from his position, against the wishes of XXX Corps and to the severe embarrassment of Brink.[136]

The brigade conducted the withdrawal at night and carried it out with some precision. It showed that the brigade was fully capable of making night marches, provoking a bitter comment in the Transvaal Scottish Regimental history referring to Pienaar's hesitancy to move swiftly by night when so required.[137]

The contribution the South Africans had made in wearing down the German fighting power through their sacrifice remained largely unknown until revealed by the UWHS through the publication of *The Sidi Rezegh Battles* in 1957. In the immediate aftermath of Sidi Rezegh, and on the occasion of Pienaar's untimely death, storytellers hailed the "non-battle" of Taib el Esem as a heroic victory, despite Pienaar's casualty list of three slightly wounded, including himself, telling a rather different tale.[138] Though it highlighted Pienaar's hesitancy and insubordination, the official history seemed to have little impact on the reputation of this "famed and fabulous" general. Despite being difficult, obstinate, and temperamental, flouting orders or just disobeying them, or being lethargic in obeying orders, his ability was not doubted by the popular press.[139] Robert Crisp, a fellow South African who served as a tank commander with the British, overheard a staff officer saying, "Uncle George [Brink] is all right, and Uncle George's boys are all right; but Uncle George's nephew [Pienaar] is just bloody awkward. We can't get him to fight a battle, or even to move to a place where he might have to fight a battle."[140]

If Pienaar's obduracy was not enough to dent his reputation with the men who served under his command, or diminish his popularity in South Africa, it certainly had a negative effect on the British who commanded him. The second battle of Sidi Rezegh on November 29 and 30 again highlighted Pienaar's hesitancy, when General Norrie took it upon himself to shake the 1st Brigade out of its "South African huddle" and "apply ginger," after repeated delays by Pienaar to advance. It allegedly took all of Norrie's patient determination and persistence to get Pienaar to move. With Norrie personally leading from the front, the South Africans reached the escarpment, but once there they would move no farther. The official history refers to Pienaar's lethargy and seeks to abrogate it by reminding the reader that Pienaar had witnessed the overrunning of the 5th Brigade a week earlier.[141] His relationship with Gott was fraught with animosity and he actively disliked his commander. His view of orders was not one of accepting them blindly—rather, in accordance with Afrikaner military culture, he saw them as the opening position in a debate.[142]

Lessons Learned by the South Africans from Sidi Rezegh

In the immediate aftermath of the battle, the South Africans, who had suffered grievously at the hands of the Axis forces, attempted to identify the reasons for the defeat and offer solutions so as to avoid the same tragedy occurring again. These recommendations or "lessons learned" formed part of the operational report constructed by Brink soon after the battle.[143]

One of Brink's first recommendations calls for the establishment of a firm base from which the infantry and armor can conduct subsequent operations. These firm bases would provide harbors for the armored formations to effect repairs and salvage. Here Brink tried to impose a static type of warfare, which was a form of warfare that conformed more to the British First World War doctrine. This kind of thinking approached that of British doctrine in the prewar period. However, what emerged from Crusader was that the infantry brigades were far from helpless against German armor, especially when the infantry were on the defensive. The 1st Brigade emerged from Crusader believing that infantry formations were well able to defend themselves from an armored attack. Brink considered brigade movement via a box formation to be proof against armored attack. The box consisted of a frontage of 2,500 m, with one battalion in front and the other two on the flanks, with components of the two flank battalions and the field engineers bringing up the rear with B Echelon. Brink conceded that this type of formation required extensive training in order to avoid confusion and mix-ups. Armored car reconnaissance 8 to 10 km ahead of the box allowed for an early warning of the presence of enemy formations. Battalions were to disperse the antitank and artillery among them so as to effect an all-around capability, which was mutually supporting in the case of the artillery. The brigade would dig in whenever it came to a halt in the same formation as when on the move.[144]

Brink suggested that when tanks forced infantry to defend themselves, all weapons should deploy against the tank threat, subordinating themselves to the antitank defense and placing themselves at the disposal of the artillery commander. Protection for the artillery units from infantry infiltration should come in the form of defending infantry sections placed among the artillery. Brink also spoke of dug in infantry tank-hunting squads that would defend the ammunition and parked fighting vehicles and deal with any tanks that had infiltrated the defenses. The New Zealanders talked of placing the antitank weapons well forward in the German fashion.[145] They proposed digging in the greater proportion of antitank weapons, which was not the case at Sidi Rezegh, while the remainder were to remain mobile to meet any infiltration.[146] This contrasts with the German doctrine of using antitank weapons in a highly mobile role, often accompanying the tanks into a fluid battle situation.[147]

The nature of the battle convinced Brink that had the 5th Brigade possessed an additional artillery regiment and a squadron of infantry tanks, they would have beaten off the attacks that finally overwhelmed them. He recommended that commanders of infantry formations have tanks under command, which would facilitate allowing the pure armored formations to deal with the enemy tanks without having to worry about protecting the infantry.[148] This reference to the detaching of infantry tanks to the infantry formations and further reference to pure tank formations is indicative of the British doctrine of the period, which contrasted with the German practice of combined arms warfare and using antitank weapons as the primary weapon against tanks.[149] Brink does make a passing reference, in identifying a need for adequate training and the necessity for training to include cooperation with other arms, particularly with armored formations. The New Zealanders correctly identify the German ability to coordinate their tanks with artillery and antitank guns with infantry as something to emulate.[150] Brink bemoans the fact that the South Africans had little time to train in desert conditions and that in the months before Crusader, they languished in a static operational role.[151]

The South Africans operated a two-brigade division for the duration of Crusader rather than the normal and optimal three brigades. This diminution was detrimental to the fighting power they were able to bring to bear on the battlefield. Brink correctly identifies that this was a major shortcoming for the South Africans in Crusader. He makes the point that it was disastrous for units and formations to reassign from one formation to another during operations as troops preferred, and fought better and more efficiently when they served under their familiar commanders.[152]

The South Africans, in a similar fashion to the British, preferred to conduct their operations at brigade level, unlike the Germans, who comfortably conducted their operations using their armored formations at a divisional level. The operation of mobile warfare at a divisional level facilitates the essential concentration of forces at the decisive point and allows the division to concentrate all the divisional assets.[153] This level of concentration is not achievable at brigade level. To his credit, Brink realized these shortcomings and called for a greater level of combined training at the divisional level.[154]

The British also conducted some research after Crusader in the form of the Martel Report authored by Lieutenant-General Giffard Le Quesne Martel (1889–1958), the General Officer Commanding the Royal Armoured Corps.[155] In his report, Martel stressed the importance of combined arms in defeating the enemy armor. "It seems that the part of the training of the armored division in the Middle East before the war, for the 'all armored' idea, for tanks to go in alone, had not been entirely eradicated." He saw a significant role for the artillery and the infantry in destroying enemy armor. He correctly attributes many of the enemy armor losses to the "unarmored" brigades and debunks the theory that unarmored forces would play only a small role in armored battles. He concluded, as did the South Africans, that an infantry formation equipped with antitank guns could successfully defend themselves against armor. Therefore, it was unnecessary to disperse armor forces to protect infantry. Well-equipped and trained infantry were more than a match, in a defensive battle, for enemy armor.

Martel favored the seizing of ground vital to the enemy to force them to attack ground that was not of their choosing. The seizing and holding of significant ground was the task of a combined force consisting of infantry, artillery, antitank guns, and armor. The report notes the reluctance of Germans to engage in a tank-versus-tank battle and their preference to take up defensive positions in a meeting engagement protected by their artillery and antitank guns. Martel notes that German armor refused battle unless the circumstances were favorable to them.[156]

When one examines these recommendations it becomes apparent that the South Africans, mirroring the British, had little inkling as to what made the Germans such a formidable enemy. The Germans perfected the crucial role of recovering damaged tanks immediately after the battle, giving them an edge in mitigating tank losses.[157] Brink's report fails to grasp the full extent of German aggressive and offensive use of antitank weapons. He correctly came to the conclusion that the utilization of the 25-pounder in an antitank role weakened the fighting power of the artillery as an indirect support weapon.[158] Most of the recommendations disregard the requirements for a mobile war based on maneuver and consist of measures designed to safeguard a pure infantry brigade in the event of a meet up with powerful armored forces. Brink hardly envisages a balanced combined arms force but rather harks back to defensive measures and seeking refuge in statically prepared defenses that were rather anachronistic in modern maneuver warfare.

Conclusion

The South Africans managed to inflict significant losses on the German armored formations before their destruction, a fact underplayed or ignored in most of the secondary sources on the subject. Norrie describes the resistance of the 5th Brigade as "gallant" and argues that it "may have been the turning point in this phase of the campaign. The loss of 50 enemy tanks was a factor of immense importance."[159] There is no single reason why the 5th Brigade was shattered at Sidi Rezegh on November 23, 1941, rather it is better to attribute the reason for its demise to a series of factors.

The British and South Africans paid dearly because of superior battle tactics employed by the Germans. They failed to adopt a combined arms approach and relied on tanks to destroy enemy tanks, and because of this skewed doctrine, the role of the supporting arms was relegated. The British had a tendency toward fragmentation where the Germans had an opposite tendency toward concentration. The British emphasis on a brigade rather than a divisional structure made the concentration of fighting power at the *Schwerpunkt* all but impossible and resulted in brigades often being committed one by one, and then destroyed piecemeal. Exacerbating their tendency toward fragmentation was the dual mission assigned to the armor formations at the outset of Crusader of destroying the German tanks and protecting the vulnerable infantry. These two tasks proved to be mutually exclusive.

The Germans made use of their antitank guns as the primary weapon against tanks and used them in an aggressive manner, often placing them up front in an attack against armor. The British tended to use their antitank weapons in a more passive and static role in support of the infantry and believed the primary weapon against tanks was another tank. Furthermore, the British tended to use their field artillery piece, the 25-pounder, as a stopgap antitank weapon. It had the undesirable effect of weakening their best arm of service, the artillery, which if concentrated and deployed in its original role would have caused considerable damage to the vulnerable German antitank guns. The British outclassed the Germans in quantity and quality of artillery but dissipated this advantage with a tendency to fragment the power of the guns through using them in "Jock Columns," or at battalion or even company level.

The seeds of the destruction of the 5th Brigade were also sown in the numerous planning problems that afflicted Crusader at the operational level. The primary objective of destroying the Axis tank force in a massive tank-on-tank battle was unsound and Gabr Saleh, a non-strategic dot on the map, was a poor choice of bait to lure forth German armor. The obscurity of Gabr Saleh and the ambiguous objective of destroying the enemy armor had the effect of surrendering the initiative to the Germans when they failed to oblige the British by taking the bait. The British plan conspired against the concentration of their tank forces by assigning the armored brigades two conflicting objectives: defeating the German armor and, at the same time, shielding the vulnerable infantry. This dilemma ensured that the British were not able to concentrate their tanks against the Germans. It allowed the Germans to deal with the British one brigade at a time instead of having to fight the entire British armor combined. The failure to concentrate the armored forces, coupled with the faulty doctrine that denied the armor of its artillery and infantry support, left the British tanks vulnerable to German antitank guns. Once the British armor had dissipated their strength, they left the South African infantry brigades exposed and vulnerable to attack by the combined forces of the Axis. British doctrine also ensured that instead of the South Africans fighting as part of a combined team, they would have to face the German armor relatively unsupported. On November 23, 1941, the SAI brigade, although flanked by the remnants of two tank brigades and a support brigade, had no way of coordinating their defense with their nearby comrades.

The dismal performance of the intelligence service grossly exaggerated the number of German tanks destroyed. Overestimation was a problem that plagued both sides and contributed mightily to the fog of war. The British overestimated German tank losses by a factor of five, leaving them in a state of complacency that nearly led to their demise. False complacency resulted in the premature movement of the South Africans to Sidi Rezegh contrary to the original plan and before the main objective of the campaign had been achieved, namely the neutralization of the German armor. In his debrief Brink stressed the need for accurate intelligence. He cited the fact that the incorrect estimates of the number of enemy tanks destroyed were a major factor responsible for the decision to move the 5th Brigade to the Sidi Rezegh area at too early a stage.[160]

Poor decision making peppered Crusader at the operational level. The decision to attack *Ariete* was born out of misguided contempt for the fighting power of the Italians. Disregard for the Italians resulted in a disastrous early loss of tanks as well as fragmentation of the armored forces. Early on, the Italian 132nd Armoured Division *Ariete* dealt a severe blow to the British 22nd Brigade, effectively diminishing its fighting power for the rest of the campaign. Early British failure to dislodge the Italians from their positions at Bir El Gubi ensured that they posed a threat to the South Africans, who as a result became increasingly reluctant and hesitant to maneuver as ordered. *Ariete*'s unexpectedly strong showing effectively split the British armored brigades and militated against British attempts to consolidate their tank force.

It is due in large part to the menacing Italian presence in the form of *Ariete* that the 1st Brigade failed to close up with the 5th Brigade, ensuring that Armstrong and his troops would face the might of the German armor alone. The importance of the Italian contribution to the battle is unfortunately poorly covered in the Italian sources and only a few have been translated into English. The Italians were a constant thorn in the side of the South Africans, and their resolute performance against the British ensured that the South Africans were always casting one eye toward them for the entire campaign. The role of the Italians in this campaign and their excellent performance in the initial stages of Crusader are also in need of a reassessment. Their German allies have almost entirely overshadowed their contribution.

The South Africans too must share responsibility for the tragic demise of the 5th Brigade. The South Africans, veterans of the East African campaign, were poorly trained in desert warfare and reluctant to conduct night maneuvers, which was an essential part of being effective against a well-trained and highly motivated enemy.[161] Their inability or unwillingness to move at night put them at a severe disadvantage and this cost them dearly when the two brigades were unable to combine to offer a common defense. The decision to field only two of the normally three divisional brigades severely hampered the South Africans' offensive and defensive strength. Brink was caught on the horns of a dilemma and had to choose between withdrawing his poorly trained forces from Crusader or risking them to maintain the good name of South Africa. He chose the latter, and his decision to deploy an undertrained and understrength division into the teeth of battle was questionable at best and reckless at worst. Once Brink committed the South Africans to Crusader, their conduct throughout the operation was tentative at best. One can level this accusation with more justification in Pienaar's case, citing his obstinate refusal to advance his 1st Brigade to close up with the 5th Brigade. His neglect in doing so severely weakened the fighting power of the South African division at the critical moment.

The South Africans adopted a static defensive posture that is often fatal in mobile warfare. The South Africans would have fared better if they had used their mobility to evade the German attack instead of meeting it head-on. It can be argued that when the Germans launched the final attack on the South African positions, the South Africans could have done more to bolster their defenses. Armstrong should have taken more heed of the reconnaissance reports, which alluded to the imminence of the German attack and its southern direction through B Echelon. As it turned out, the South Africans did indeed take measures to fortify their southern flank using half the artillery at their disposal. In so doing, they inflicted grievous damage on the Germans. It is a moot point whether Armstrong could have done more, given the very real threats on other fronts and the thick fog of war. However, there is little doubt that the presence of B Echelon, and the lack of infantry, weakened and confused the defenses on the southern front of the 5th Brigade box.

Despite all the flaws and mistakes surrounding the final disaster, it was the Germans who, mimicking the wild cavalry charges of the British, suffered their biggest tank losses of the campaign in their attack on the South Africans. The Germans failed to prepare their attack in depth, and due to their dispositions in breadth they were unable to concentrate the full might of their forces on the South Africans. The German attack amounted to a hasty charge rather than their usual careful combined arms preparation against a well-defended target. Perhaps carried away with their previous successes, they threw caution to the winds and charged onto the South African guns and suffered grievously. The South African infantry had succeeded where British tanks had failed, proving that it was concentrated artillery supported by infantry that was the actual killer of the tank.

Surprisingly, it was in the destruction of the 5th Brigade by the full might of the Axis armored forces that the Germans suffered their first grievous tank losses of the campaign. Up to that time in Crusader, it had been a one-sided affair, with the British suffering five tanks destroyed for every one of the Axis's. The British kept the supposedly vulnerable infantry brigades out of the battle, until they overwhelmed the German tank forces. In a strange turn of events, it was the relatively "helpless" infantry brigades, bolstered by artillery, which eventually broke the back of the *DAK*.

Chapter 6

The Gazala Battles 1942: Rommel on the Rampage

Yearly we've ridden the Djebel Stakes,
Yearly fought back on our course,
Yearly we've made the same silly mistakes,
Over-ridden a failing horse,
At a fence too stiff for his strength to leap,
With a rotten take-off, unfirm, too steep,
Heavily breasted the top of the bank,
Pawed, grasped and struggled, then hopelessly sank,
Shocked, hurt and surprised at the toss we took–
Rolling back adown the ditch at Tobruk.

Major General Francis Tucker[1]

The End of Operation Crusader: Rommel Retreats November 24–January 1, 1942

Rommel was in a confident mood after crushing the South African 5th Brigade and the British armored brigades. He was confident enough to order his mobile forces to advance to the Egyptian Frontier, a move famously known as the "Dash to the Wire." Part of his reasoning for this audacious thrust was to bring relief to his immobile forces at the frontier whom XIII Corps were in the process of surrounding. The boldness of Rommel's move, bordering on reckless, unnerved Cunningham, who contemplated withdrawing his entire Eighth Army back to the Egyptian border. It took Auchinleck's intervention to prevent a general withdrawal, and instead he encouraged Cunningham to ignore Rommel and concentrate on attacking the Axis in the Sidi Rezegh area. Auchinleck's intuition in this case proved correct, as Rommel was short on fuel and his piecemeal attacks in the frontier region amounted to nothing. The absence of Rommel at the Sidi Rezegh *Schwerpunkt* allowed the British to recover and build up their forces in the area. On November 26, the New Zealanders advanced on Tobruk and Cunningham was relieved of his command and replaced by Major-General Neil Ritchie (1897–1983).

November 27 marked the end of the 241-day siege of Tobruk, when elements of the 70th Division met up with the relieving forces advancing on the port. Rommel realized that his bluff had failed and he hastily recalled his advance to the frontier and directed his forces to attack the XXX Corps in the vicinity of Sidi Rezegh. The battle around Sidi Rezegh became one of attrition as Rommel's ever-diminishing *Panzer* forces fought against increasing British infantry formations. Once again, Pienaar's caution came under scrutiny when the British ordered him to bring his 1st SA Brigade up to the northern ridge at point 175 with haste to join 6th New Zealand Brigade. Caution and hesitancy ensured that his formation was far from its objective by the end of the day. It had advanced only 18 of the 35 km toward point 175 when it stopped for the night. In the process, the Germans heavily mauled the New Zealanders and they were withdrawn back to Egypt for a badly needed refit. The British enjoyed a distinct advantage by introducing new infantry formations into the battle, while Rommel struggled to replace his losses at anywhere near the same rate. He ordered a fighting withdrawal back to the Gazala line on December 7. It degenerated into a fully-fledged retreat and by December 15 the Axis lost Cyrenaica. The retreat finally came to a halt at El Agheila on January 1, 1942, the exact point of Rommel's astounding advance nine months earlier.

THE ROAD TO TOBRUK: THE 2ND SOUTH AFRICAN INFANTRY DIVISION CAPTURES BARDIA–JANUARY 2, 1942

January 1942 marked the third calendar year of the war in the North African desert. Operation Crusader was a close-run battle but the British infantry had managed to wear down Rommel's deadly armor forces in what became a battle of attrition and logistics. The British pushed Rommel all the way back from the Egyptian border to El Agheila, which was his start point of advance in March 1941. The Eighth Army removed the Axis from the Cyrenaica and more importantly relieved Tobruk from its 241-day siege. Rommel had reluctantly abandoned his static troops manning the frontier defenses when he beat a retreat to El Agheila. It fell to the 2nd South African Infantry Division, commanded by Major-General I. P. de Villiers (1891–1967), to mop up the remaining Axis forces cut off in Bardia.[2] It was a chance for the 2nd Division to see its first substantial action, after having missed the East African campaign and being held in reserve for lack of transport in the initial stages of Operation Crusader.[3]

On December 5, 1941, the 3rd Brigade advanced toward Bardia. The Axis occupied the town with approximately 8,800 troops, commanded by Major-General Artur Schmitt (1888–1972). He was a veteran of the First World War and no stranger to the South Africans, who had captured him in the German South West African campaign of 1915. The 2,200 Germans manning the Bardia defenses were mostly from the rear echelon administrative services. The remaining 6,600 troops were Italian and possessed little in the way of artillery.[4] On December 7, Rommel requested that the Italians immediately evacuate Bardia, a task that the Italians considered impossible. The South Africans proceeded with cautious mopping-up operations and by December 14 they successfully hemmed in the Germans and Italians in Bardia, Halfaya, and Sollum. The Eighth Army tasked the South African 3rd Brigade to reduce the garrison at Bardia. There was only a vague idea of the nature of the defenses or the strength of the garrison. The South Africans pitted a brigade against a force that they believed totalled no more than 4,840 men.[5] Faulty intelligence led to the attackers being outnumbered two to one. However, mere numbers were not a true reflection of the strength of the Axis garrison, as it was composed mainly of stragglers of varying fighting quality.[6] The brigade attack, which drastically underestimated enemy strength, and whose objective of capturing the port was ambiguous, was doomed to failure. The South Africans called off the ill-conceived attack on December 17.[7] The SAI Brigade suffered heavy casualties for little gain in their first ill-conceived operation. Schmitt was determined to make a stand despite the fact that the South Africans surrounded him, and he was as a result cut off from his overland supply lines.[8]

De Villiers scheduled the next attack for December 29, and he instructed that the attack must be conducted with the minimum loss of life. The attack on Bardia by the 2nd South African Division was to be a carefully prepared operation carried out in three phases, and called for close cooperation of artillery and the tanks of the 1st Army Tank Brigade.[9] The artillery support for the operation was the greatest concentration yet seen in the Middle East. The artillery arranged to conduct the barrage was made up of 150 guns, which amounted to a formidable array of weapons at this stage of the campaign.[10] The operational order and instructions for the South African contingent exceeded one hundred pages of single-spaced type and covered nearly every conceivable contingency. These orders were drawn up under the guidance of none other than Colonel H. B. Klopper (later to be the unfortunate commander at Tobruk), "who was left much to his own devices."[11] The attack was prepared using strict timetables and well-defined objectives mimicking the set piece battles that became the hallmark of trench warfare in the First World War. The South Africans undertook a full-scale rehearsal of the attack on December 29, much to the impatience of Winston Churchill, who demanded that the Eighth Army clear the remaining pockets as soon as possible. Churchill demonstrated less sensitivity than Ritchie to potential South African casualties.[12] It is tempting to draw comparisons between the labored preparations for the siege of Bardia and the later storming of Tobruk conducted by Rommel. South African offensive preparations took many weeks and they detailed the attack via extensive written orders. In stark contrast, Rommel's future attack on Tobruk would be spontaneous, being prepared in under twenty-four hours and noteworthy for the absence of written orders, barring a hastily sketched map.[13] It is an exemplary example of the difference between German and British doctrine regarding the different attitude to written orders.

The attack on Bardia eventually got under way after dark on December 30 in cold and windy conditions. The heaviest artillery barrage yet seen in Africa opened up at 0400, only eclipsed some ten months later at Alamein.[14] Following the barrage was the attack by the infantry units, who cleared paths for the tanks to follow and after some hard-fought battles began to achieve the first objectives. The garrison, possessing only two 88mm antitank weapons, exacted a heavy toll on the advancing British tanks.[15] The surprisingly tough resistance put up by Schmitt and his stragglers, coupled with the inexperience of the attacking troops, ensured that optimistic expectations of capturing Bardia that day evaporated. Priority went into consolidating the positions gained and then regrouping those forces which had penetrated the perimeter. The Germans and Italians made good use of the night hours, reoccupying four of the strong points overrun by the South Africans the previous day.[16]

A midday sandstorm on January 1 halted further operations, and the South Africans drew up new plans for phase two of the operation. They launched the attack on the night of January 1 at 2200, preceded by a heavy artillery barrage, with waves of tanks leading the infantry. Interestingly, there was no time available for the brigades to issue extensive written orders, as had been done for phase one. In contrast, commanders issued instructions verbally, thereby allowing for greater flexibility.[17] The South African attack gained ground steadily and captured the garrison's last remaining 88mm antitank weapon. The attackers penetrated into the interior of the fortress and captured ammunition dumps and provision depots. Schmitt signalled Rommel at 1300 on January 2 that the German and Italian soldiers had done their duty and he intended to surrender. Schmitt was the first German general in the Second World War to surrender to the Allies and signalled a successful end to the 2nd South African Division's first major operation.[18] The South Africans suffered 132 killed and 270 wounded, taking some 8,000 German and Italian prisoners. The liberation of Bardia led to the release of 1,150 British (including 650 New Zealander) POWs held there.[19]

It is with some irony that in a little over six months' time, Klopper, newly promoted to general commanding the 2nd Division and appointed as the garrison commander of Tobruk, would again face the Germans and Italians under similar circumstances, except for the fact that he would be the one besieged. The South African 6th Brigade soon cleared the Axis positions at Halfaya and Sollum and their capture signalled the end of the Axis presence in Cyrenaica. Nevertheless, the manner and planning of the South African attack on Bardia found favor with American official observers who concluded that "the British defeated a numerically superior Axis force in a strongly fortified position with a combined infantry and tank force." They noted, in particular, the use of a night attack and that, "success is to be achieved by careful planning, close coordination of all arms, and a correct application of the principles of war."[20]

THE DJEBEL STAKES–ALL THE WAY BACK TO GAZALA

Rommel beat a hasty retreat all the way back to El Agheila, and there he enjoyed the benefit of shortened supply lines and was able to replenish and rebuild his strength quite rapidly. On January 5, 1942, a convoy safely delivered fifty-four German tanks and twenty armored cars as well as a good number of antiaircraft and artillery pieces.[21] Rommel, ever irrepressible and boosted with these supplies, felt confident enough to launch an attack against the thinly held British outposts facing him.[22] His attack on January 21 took the British by complete surprise, coming just sixteen days after the last of Rommel's rearguard had retired behind the El Agheila defenses.[23] Within eight days Rommel reconquered Benghazi and the British only avoided complete destruction by hastily withdrawing to safety. Once again, insufficient logistics rescued the British and caused Rommel to halt after advancing 560 km in just two weeks. His pugnacious offensive led to the reconquering of much of the territory lost in the Crusader operation.[24]

The British came to rest on the partially complete Gazala line some 64 km to the west of Tobruk. The 1st South African Division, recently devastated at Sidi Rezegh when it lost the 5th Brigade, was newly reconstituted and comprised of the 1st, 2nd, and 3rd Brigades. The division occupied the far northern position on the Gazala line, directly in front of Tobruk. Pienaar now commanded the 1st Division, replacing Brink, who injured his back on March 10, 1942. Brink wrote of Pienaar, "He is to my mind the only other potential South African divisional commander we have in this theatre."[25] The 1st South African Infantry Brigade, Pienaar's previous command, had by now earned the distinction of being the most experienced SAI brigade in the desert and mobile warfare. Its casualties in Crusader were light, only 40 white and 6 black soldiers lost in action, with a further 150 white and 37 black soldiers wounded and 156 missing, believed to be prisoners of war. Of all the casualties suffered, only 51 were attributed to ground attack, the remainder being the victims of air attack. The brigade had captured 138 enemy soldiers, and claimed 12 enemy tanks and 15 aircraft destroyed.[26] The 2nd South African Division, newly commanded by Klopper (who had taken over from de Villiers) occupied Tobruk, directly behind the 1st Division. Dorman-Smith had strong views on the deployment of the South African division in a static role defending the Gazala line.

> I could not help feeling that men whose minds were so naturally attuned to the wide, open spaces could have been more fitly engaged

> in a mobile rather than as static role. I saw the magnificent service of the South African armoured car units on the southern flank of the Gazala line where they fulfilled the most difficult role to the admiration of the whole Eighth Army and I felt even more strongly that the 1st Division was wasted in the north, on the sea coast, instead of being active where there was elbow room for its natural aptitudes and high scale of mechanisation. But the British, I fear, have rigid minds: as the 1st South African was called an infantry division, an infantry division it had to be, with no regard to its capacity for mobility. The powers-that-were refused to understand that South African troops are something more than infantry—that they are, as it were, *mounted* infantry, the best in the world when they have scope for their talents.[27]

Both sides took the opportunity afforded by the temporary respite to rest, replenish, build up their forces, train their soldiers, and prepare to launch an offensive. It was a race against time to see who would build up faster and be the first to unleash a full-blown attack. It took another four months for hostilities to resume on May 26, 1942.

THE RACE TO LAUNCH AN OFFENSIVE: THE OPPOSING PLANS AND THE OPPOSING ARMIES

Ritchie replaced Cunningham on November 26, 1941, after the latter lost the confidence of Auchinleck. It came about when Cunningham suggested a curtailment of Crusader in the face of the German annihilation of the British armor and Rommel's bold "Dash to the Wire." Auchinleck would hear nothing of it and accused him of thinking defensively.[28] Auchinleck was determined to beat back the Germans, which through perseverance, the Eighth Army was eventually able to do. Ritchie, relatively junior and inexperienced compared to others in the Eighth Army, was initially intended as a temporary appointment until the Eighth Army could find a more suitable commander. Notwithstanding the temporary nature of his appointment, he ended up commanding the Eighth Army for over six months. Ritchie was under no illusion that he was the best man for the job but he accepted the position on Auchinleck's insistence. He felt obliged to inform and canvass Auchinleck on most of his decisions and he failed to seize complete control over his command of the Eighth Army during his tenure.[29]

Auchinleck, in turn, did not exercise an entirely unfettered command of his forces, in the strategic sense. He would have enjoyed more of a free hand in building up his forces and deciding the date of his next offensive. However, there was a steady and inexorable pressure emanating from Churchill to act decisively and conduct an offensive sooner rather than later. Churchill's overriding concern was over the prospects of Malta, and his apprehension brought about increasing pressure on Auchinleck to launch an attack against the Axis forces. Churchill was also suitably distressed at the British overall contribution to the general war effort, stating, "It was lamentable that the British and Imperial armies . . . should stand idle for so long a period . . . while the Russians were fighting desperately and valiantly along their whole vast front."[30] It was a view shared by Smuts, who harbored a genuine concern that the Russians were carrying the greater proportion of the Allied burden.[31]

Auchinleck was summoned to London in March 1942 to discuss the precarious Malta situation brought about by recent Axis successes both at sea and in Libya. He anticipated the inordinate pressure he would be subjected to and flatly refused to go to London. He did, however, concede under pressure to an unsatisfactory compromise to launch an attack by mid-May. He was quite aware that there was a good chance that Rommel would attack first, in the interim, and that he would have to commit to a battle in any event. Auchinleck received what amounted to an ultimatum on May 8 to launch an attack by the beginning of June at the latest, or be relieved of his command.[32] Succumbing to the pressure to act, he reluctantly agreed to launch an attack in mid-May and he put into effect preparations for an offensive.[33] The vacillations between launching an offensive and remaining on the defensive adversely affected the fighting power of the Eighth Army. The dispositions of an army preparing an offensive are significantly different from those of an army adopting a defensive posture. An army arrayed for an offensive is particularly vulnerable to an attacker just prior to it launching an attack.

Before Auchinleck was able to complete preparations for his offensive, Ultra Intelligence disclosed Rommel's own preparations to launch a major attack on May 26. This left Auchinleck little other option than to receive Rommel's offensive and place the Eighth Army on the defensive, thereby surrendering the initiative to the enemy.[34] An unfortunate result of the Eighth Army's belated preparations for an offensive was the huge buildup of stores well forward at Belhamed and at Tobruk. The fortress of Tobruk, manned by two South African infantry brigades, the 4th and 6th, and an Indian brigade, the 9th, both commanded by Klopper, formed the northeastern edge of an Allied defensive system arranged in depth.[35] Tobruk was crucial as a logistical hub as well as a center where ordnance could be repaired and units replenished. The constant need to protect these stores and deny them to Rommel significantly influenced British operational planning once the Axis offensive got under way.[36] Tobruk was a crucial forward staging point for any British offensive, but would prove to be a liability when the British were placed on the defensive. It shall be seen that when the time came, the decision to defend Tobruk was decided rather belatedly.

An inevitable consequence of switching to the defensive at the last moment was that the dispositions of the Eighth Army were more suitable to facilitate an offensive and far less than optimal for a defensive posture. The mutually exclusive desire to launch an attack at the soonest possible occasion compromised the system of defense.[37] The British placed the brigade positions well forward compared to how they would have positioned them had they been aligned for purely defensive purposes. Furthermore, the reason why the defensive line stretched so far south to Bir Hakim was the need to keep Rommel at arm's length from the supply dumps at Belhamed. Therefore, the British placement reflected a dangerous compromise between the desire to launch an offensive and the need to conduct an adequate defense in the face of a full-scale Axis attack.

Seven infantry brigades held a line stretching from the coast of Mediterranean sea at Gazala to the southern fortress of Bir Hakim, held by the Free French Brigade. The combatants knew this as the Gazala line. The British positioned the infantry brigades behind an extensive belt of mines that served to close the gaps between the brigades and also enhanced the ability of the defenders to resist attack. The infantry brigades formed up in defensive boxes, affording all-around protection.[38] Of significance was that the defensive positions were not mutually supportive, given that the distance between them was too great to facilitate any defensive overlap.[39] The survival of the infantry brigades depended on the ability of the mobile armored brigades to come swiftly to the support of the infantry boxes and destroy the attacking enemy armor. The destruction or substantial weakening of the British armor or failure of the British armor to concentrate their fighting power would leave the vulnerable infantry brigades to be knocked off one at a time by the concentrated Axis armor divisions. Furthermore, adopting a defensive posture in the form of brigade "boxes" sacrificed the brigade's mobility. The mechanized and motorized brigades sent their vulnerable transport vehicles away from the defensive box. The result was that they sacrificed their means of mobility to ensure the safety of the transport vehicles in the event of an attack.[40] The British clearly favored a static defense over a mobile defense when it came to their infantry brigades.

Auchinleck decided to fall back on a brigade structure as opposed to a divisional structure due to the "unwieldiness" of a division. He recognized that a brigade would have significantly less fighting power than a division, but he hoped the all-around defenses and minefields of the brigade boxes would offset this. It is significant that the German formations operated from a divisional structure and as such were able to concentrate their divisional assets at the *Schwerpunkt*, or decisive point. The British divided up their divisional assets among the brigades, such as the artillery and antitank guns, which were crucial to their survival against rampaging German armor. This diminution of the fighting assets under divisional command was an exercise contrary to the concentration of forces.[41] The infantry brigades became mini divisions, resulting in the fragmentation of the all-important artillery. To facilitate a static defense, the British sacrificed flexibility in the form of mobility, which amounted to an exercise of counterintuitiveness and futility.

The British formed up the bulk of the armor behind the Gazala line in six armored brigades and two motorized brigades. As discussed above, the two motorized brigades were rendered immobile due to them sending their transport to the rear. When the attack began they remained fixed in their positions. Ritchie committed a cardinal sin when he dispersed his armor along the length of the Gazala line rather than concentrate it. He exposed his forces to a piecemeal engagement in the event of a concentrated attack, allowing the enemy to plough through each scattered brigade successively. Auchinleck expressed his concerns to Ritchie on May 20, 1942:

> They (the armoured brigades) have been trained to fight as divisions, I hope, and fight as divisions they should. Norrie must handle them

> as a Corps Commander, and thus be able to take advantage of the flexibility which the fact of having two formations gives him.[42]

Part of the reason for dispersing the tank brigades was once again the necessity to protect the vulnerable infantry brigades, who would feel intense insecurity in the event of the tank brigades not being close at hand. Another conceivable reason offered for dispersing the armored brigades is that had the British concentrated their armor at any one point, it may have enticed Rommel to attack the point where concentration did not occur. However, arguing for or against concentration is a spurious exercise, because Rommel was not averse to dispersing his forces on many occasions. The test was rather one of how rapidly a dispersed force could concentrate and quickly cooperate with the other arms of service to form a combined operations force at the crucial time and critical point.[43]

As we have seen, the initial Eighth Army deployment had the dual purpose of providing a defensive position together with a springboard for a possible attack. However, it seems that a defensive mentality prevailed and mobility gave way to extensive fortifications and minefields. Ritchie received intelligence reports in May 1942 of an imminent Axis attack and abandoned any offensive plans he may have had.[44] It is interesting to compare the defensive doctrine of Ritchie to the maneuver warfare proffered by O'Conner at Mersa Matruh in 1940. Here he grasped the principles of mobile mechanized desert warfare, and when facing the Italians he held his main forces 100 km behind a line thinly manned by forward patrols, thereby removing them from the shock of a surprise action. O'Conner ensured that his units could move freely in any direction by keeping them mobile on wheels. Barnett propagates this view, but Carver does not share it. He thinks Barnett naïve and points out that if Ritchie pulled his forces back by 100 km, leaving only a thin screening force to cover Tobruk, it would have exposed it to capture without a preliminary fight behind a solid defense.[45] Nevertheless, the Gazala line amounted to a regression in tactics. It resorted to the erroneous British doctrine of separating infantry from mechanized forces and attempting to build a solid line of defense in a theater where it was impossible to secure both flanks at once.[46] The British tried to impose a static type of warfare on the Germans, which was a condition the British felt more comfortable with, rather than the cut and thrust of maneuver warfare.

The British prepared to meet two eventualities: either an attack by Rommel through the middle of the Gazala defensive positions or an outflanking maneuver around the southern flank of the Gazala line. Rommel would obviously aim both lines of attack at the ultimate capture of Tobruk. Auchinleck was inclined to believe that the German attack would punch through the center of the Gazala line, while Ritchie made the correct assumption, as it turned out, that Rommel would try and outflank the Gazala line.[47] The disagreement between Auchinleck and Ritchie as to where the Axis would deliver the attack had the effect of dispersing the efforts of the armored brigades. It should not have been the case. For no matter where they initially stationed the brigades, they had the ability, due to their mobility, to meet Rommel's forces in time, whether they arrived in the center or the south. What retarded the armored brigade's ability to react quickly and concentrate at one point (*Schwerpunkt*) was the divergent view among the corps commanders as to where the blow would fall, which mirrored that between Ritchie and Auchinleck.[48] Auchinleck's expectation of a central attack on the Gazala line permeated the depths of the Eighth Army and influenced many of the brigade commanders into believing that an outflanking maneuver from the south would most probably be a feint or subsidiary action. It led commanders to be unduly cautious about committing the armored brigades until they were certain as to where the enemy's main effort was.[49] The confusion among the brigade commanders was a direct result of Auchinleck's subtle retention of his reign of power over the Eighth Army and Ritchie's lack of seniority over the generals he commanded.

Auchinleck instituted two important changes in the organization of the Eighth Army as a result of the experiences and "lessons learned" from Operation Crusader. He attempted to facilitate greater cooperation between the various arms of service in achieving a combined arms approach. He reformed the armored divisions to consist of one armored brigade and one motorized brigade, thereby reducing the armor and increasing the infantry component. The new structure assigned both brigade types a regiment of artillery and antitank guns and other supporting arms. Auchinleck organized the infantry division around three brigades, each brigade being a self-contained unit containing artillery and antitank guns and other supporting units, thus spreading the divisional assets down to brigade level. As a result, the basic infantry formation became the brigade instead of the division in an endeavor for more flexibility, but at the cost of rendering the brigade more vulnerable.[50]

The Eighth Army was unable to extricate itself from the quagmire of fragmentation even after the lessons learned from Operation Crusader. Fragmentation was rife throughout the Eighth Army, including at the strategic, operational, and structural levels. There was no clear-cut command structure and the relationship between Auchinleck and Ritchie was ambiguous. This ambiguity permeated throughout the command structure and had the effect of confusing the leadership as to their operational objectives. The mixed objective of maintaining an offensive capacity and of building a static defensive line was a further cause of fragmentation of effort and deployment. The armored brigades suffered from a dual role of protecting the vulnerable infantry "boxes" and of meeting the Axis armored thrusts in concertation. These two tasks were often mutually exclusive and had the effect of fragmenting the British armored efforts. The British organized the Eighth Army on a brigade and divisional basis, while the Germans and Italians operated on a divisional basis and were therefore able to deliver a heavier, coordinated blow to their chosen *Schwerpunkt*.

Again, as in Crusader, the British enjoyed an overwhelming numerical advantage in tanks of almost two to one. (See Table 5.) If one discounts the German Mark II tanks, because they were worth no more than a contribution to the reconnaissance role, then the advantage to the British was even greater.[51] Some authors tend to discount the contribution of the Italian tank forces, but this is clearly a mistake, as demonstrated in the early stages of the Crusader battles and again in the initial battles of Gazala, where they managed to overrun the Indian Brigade very early in the campaign.[52] The Italians, especially their mobile forces under Rommel's guidance, proved to be a hardy and formidable foe most of the time, unlike their previous showing in the early stages of the desert campaign and East Africa.[53] The German air arm, under Field Marshal Albert Kesselring (1885–1960), enjoyed air superiority during the period January to June 1942. This air superiority, together with the suppression of Malta, resulted in an increase in the flow of supplies to Rommel that enabled him to launch an offensive of limited objectives.

Both sides fielded new, more powerful weapons as a result of the lessons learned in Crusader. The more significant on the German side was

FALL OF TOBRUK
OPPOSING TANK STRENGTH ON MAY 27, 1942, ON THE EVE OF BATTLE

	On Hand	In Reserve[1]	Total
BRITISH			
Valentines	166		166
Matildas	110		110
Grant[4]	167	75	242
Stuart	149	70	219
Crusader	257		257
	849	145	994
GERMAN			
Mark III (H)	223		
Mark III (J)[2]	19		
Mark IV	40		
Mark II	50		
Italian M13/40[3]	228		
	560[5]		

1. The 1st Armoured Brigade was on its way to join the Eighth Army.
2. The III (J) was armed with the formidable long 50mm gun.
3. The Italian tanks are seldom taken into account, a practice that is clearly erroneous considering their significant contribution to the Cauldron battles.
4. The Grant was a recent addition from the USA and arguably the best tank on the battlefield, out-gunning and out-armoring all the Axis machines.
5. The Germans had 77 tanks of all kinds in reserve.

Table 5. Comparative tank strength of the opposing forces on the eve of the battle, May 27, 1942.[54]

the *Panzer* III Special, which mounted a long 50mm gun, giving the same powerful performance as their 50mm antitank gun. Significantly, only 19 of these were available compared to the 242 new American Grant tanks armed with powerful 75mm sponson guns in the hull, capable of firing high-explosive rounds. This new welcome addition to the Eighth Army was arguably superior to any tank in the Axis desert arsenal. Its 75mm main armament was capable of lobbing powerful high-explosive shells that could easily disable enemy antitank positions. This ability filled a gap in British tank armament that they traditionally equipped with the 2-pounder, capable of only firing solid-shot antitank rounds. A powerful gun had arrived on the scene for the Eighth in the form of the new 6-pounder antitank gun, which significantly outperformed the 2-pounders and, more importantly, were superior to the German 50mm antitank gun. Unfortunately, the advantages enjoyed with the new 6-pounder antitank gun were somewhat offset by insufficient training time on the new weapon. The preeminent tank killer remained the deadly German 88mm antitank gun, of which Rommel had 48 available.[55]

Rommel possessed a number of options in attacking the Allied positions, keeping in mind that the focal point of any offensive was the capture of Tobruk. His first option was a direct attack along the coast toward Tobruk. The second option was to attack the Gazala line in the center and punch a way through the defenses using overwhelming force at the point of attack. In choosing to attack through the center of the British line, Rommel would have had to negotiate extensive minefields, which would have caused considerable delay, thus allowing the British ample time to concentrate their armored forces for a counterattack. The third option, which was the one chosen, was to outflank the Gazala line using the Axis mobile forces to move around the southern point of the line by passing Bir Hakim and installing powerful armored forces deep in the rear of the Gazala line.[56] The Germans would then engage and defeat the British armor in detail, allowing their armor to cut off the infantry brigades manning the Gazala line. Once the Germans eliminated these brigades, the way to capture Tobruk would be open.[57] The optimistic timing for the capture of Tobruk was the third day of the offensive.[58] Influencing his plan and shaping his decisions and operational planning was Rommel's gross underestimation of British tank strength, which he estimated to be

650 tanks (there were in actuality 849, see Table 5). He was also unaware of the new British firepower in the form of the Grant tank.[59]

Rommel's choice of the outflanking option required the German and Italian armor to move a great distance to envelop the British line and this would necessitate refueling at least once before they reached their objective deep behind the British lines. The long distances and need to refuel would allow a reasonable time for the British to arrange a counterattack in strength if they detected the Germans.[60] Therefore, it was important not to reveal German intentions until the very last moment, thereby retaining the element of surprise and hopefully catching the British in a dispersed state. A frontal diversionary attack by the Italian X and XXI Infantry Corps commanded by Lieutenant-General Enea Navarrini (1885–1977) against the 1st and 50th South African Divisions would accompany the outflanking maneuver. The Italians would demonstrate along the coastal road in the north to draw off as many Allied mobile forces as possible.[61] Vehicles would be driven around to raise dust and simulate tank concentrations in this area.[62] Toppe describes Rommel's attack with comparatively weak forces into the heart of the Allied defenses, after an enveloping march of some 200km, as "an enterprise of unprecedented daring." This type of maneuver was not possible except in the vast expanse offered under desert conditions. In Europe it would be impossible to move such a large mass of troops in such a short space of time because of the necessity to move in columns along the road networks. In the desert, Rommel would move the way he fought, in a wide attack formation.[63]

Rommel Attacks: Operation Venezia, May 26–29, 1942

The Axis offensive began at 1400 on May 26, 1942, with the Italian diversionary attack in the north of the Gazala line against the South Africans. Crüwell, commanding the Italians, was able to report that he had seized most of the day's objectives by 2000. The British seemed to attach no importance to this diversionary attack.[64] Over 10,000 Axis vehicles comprising the encircling forces launched their attack on a front of 50 km at 2100, after a night march. The massive enveloping force comprised the 15 and 21 *Panzer*-Divisions together with the 90th Light Division. The Italian component, the XX Corps commanded by Lieutenant-General Gastone Gambara, consisted of *Ariete* and the 101st Motorized Division

Trieste. By taking the indirect approach and making a giant flanking movement, they rapidly headed for an assembly area to the south of Bir Hakim. The German official history describes the night move, on this unprecedented scale, as being something unique in the history of warfare.[65] Rommel led from the front and the huge Axis mechanized formation reached the assembly point with the "smoothness of a well-oiled machine" at 0300 on May 27. After refueling, the massive mechanized ensemble turned north in an enormous encircling maneuver. At 0700 the 15 *Panzer*-Division encountered its first opposition when it bumped into fifty to sixty tanks of the 4th Armoured Brigade.[66] (See Map 5.)

The British intention of building a formidable line of defense based on infantry brigades in all-around defensive boxes depended for its success on their ability to rapidly concentrate their mobile armored forces and

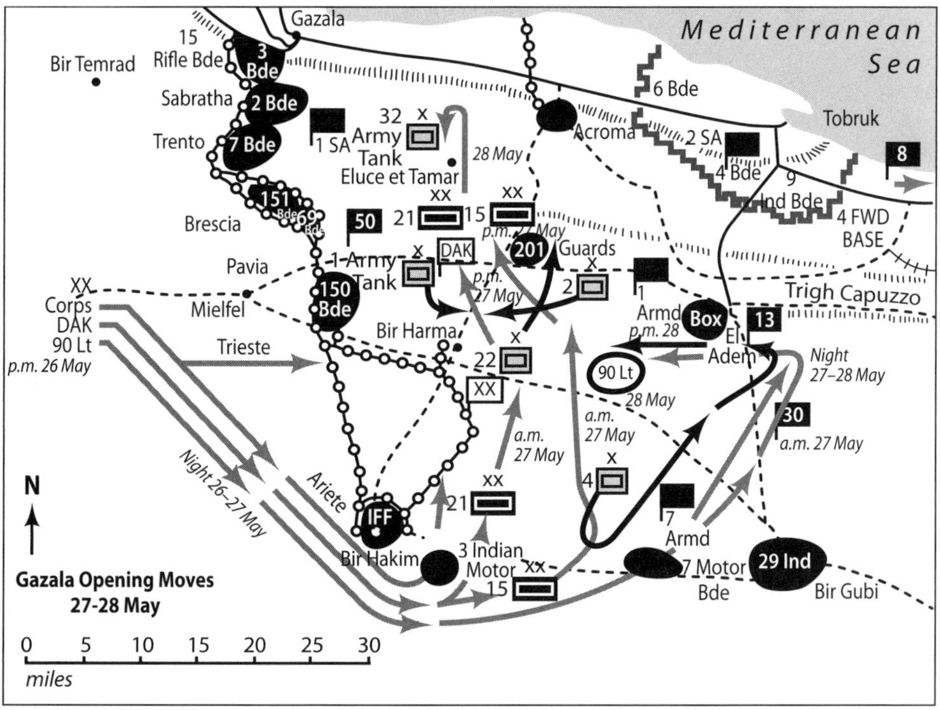

Map 5. Rommel's opening moves and outflanking attack on the Gazala line. The British were startled by *Ariete*'s overrunning of the 3rd Indian Brigade as well as the *DAK*'s overrunning of the 7th Motorised Brigade. Rommel followed this with an attack on the isolated 4th Armoured Brigade.

meet Rommel's attack head-on with a clear numerical advantage. Failure to identify the main axis of attack, and after that to concentrate fighting power on time, would doom the infantry brigades, and the *Panzer* divisions would overwhelm them one at a time. The armored brigades would suffer the same fate as the infantry brigade boxes if the British fed them into the battle in a similar piecemeal fashion.[67] At the outset, the German night attack took the British by surprise and opinion among the commanders was devoid of consensus as to the direction of the final assault. The British hesitated when they should have reacted and concentrated their forces for an immediate counterattack.

It was not until May 27 at 0600 that air reconnaissance confirmed the presence of significant Axis forces to the south of Bir Hakim and substantially convinced the British that this was the main attack.[68] The confirmation of the German intent came too late as Rommel's concentrated mechanized force swept away two hapless British motorized brigades, the 3rd Indian and the 7th, which were in their path. It fell to *Ariete* to overrun the 3rd Indian Brigade, inflicting casualties of 41 officers and 453 men killed with 600 prisoners. In turn, the Italians suffered 76 casualties and the loss of 25 tanks. The short and sharp battle registered a considerable victory early on.[69] The Germans then surprise attacked the unprepared 4th Armoured Brigade, who even at this late stage had doubts as to the true intentions of the enemy.[70] However, it was by no means a one-sided engagement. The new Grant tanks outgunned the Axis tanks they encountered and extracted a high toll before the Germans managed to put them out of action and put flight to the brigade. The 4th Brigade eventually retreated to El Adam.[71] It was not the first time in the desert war that the Germans managed to pit a concentrated force of armor against scattered British formations, offered up in a piecemeal fashion in the vain hope of slowing down a determined Axis advance. Rommel found the British tendency of splitting up their armored brigades and introducing them one at a time into the battle incomprehensible.[72]

The 21 *Panzer*-Division ran into the 22nd Armoured Brigade at 0900. Although ordered into the fray to assist the 4th Armoured Brigade, the 22nd Brigade had not yet conformed to that instruction. Unbeknown to the British, the Germans had dealt roughly with the 4th Armoured Brigade, and as a result they suffered heavy casualties, with the commander of the 7th Armoured Division, Major General Frank Messervy, made a prisoner of war in the confused melee. The 22nd Brigade met the full brunt of the Axis attack and it too retreated in some disorder, for the loss of thirty tanks, all the way back to the Knightsbridge box, although it managed to put up a feisty performance that began to slow the impetus of Rommel's rampant forces.[73] Finally, at 0945, the British ordered the 2nd Armoured Brigade to attack south. It was only at 1400, after a false start, that they were able to launch a coordinated assault on the Germans. The attack launched by 2nd Armoured Brigade ran into the exposed flank of the Axis and managed to extract a high price, forcing the Axis armored divisions to a halt short of their objectives. Earlier in the day *Ariete* failed to storm the defenses of Bir Hakim, losing thirty-two of their tanks when the Free French rebuffed them.[74]

The British had suffered grievous losses, including much of their defensive system in the south, with two brigades overrun and failure of their mobile forces to launch a concentrated attack against the German armor. Notwithstanding this early success, Rommel had underestimated the strength of the British forces. The Germans had lost over a third of their tanks and their forces straddled the coast all the way around the Gazala line, reaching deep behind the enemy line. It left the Axis supply route exposed and in a precarious position. The 15 *Panzer*-Division was short of fuel and ammunition and the 90th Light Division had failed to reach its objective and became detached from the corps, leaving it isolated and vulnerable.[75] According to Rommel, his plan to overrun the British forces behind the Gazala line had not succeeded. The principal cause of this failure was the underestimation of the numerical strength of the British armored divisions. The introduction of the Grant tank, with its 75mm gun, unnerved Rommel to a certain extent. "Our entire force now stood in heavy and destructive combat with a superior force."[76] German dispersion and frail logistics presented an opportunity for the British to launch a consolidated armored strike.

Some in the German camp suggested withdrawal in the face of what was an almost complete failure. The plan to overrun the British forces behind the Gazala line never materialized and Rommel failed to advance to the coast and cut off the 1st and 50th South African Divisions.[77] However, although "very worried," Rommel saw a defensive opportunity to allow the British to go over to the attack and thereby weaken themselves against the German defenses. A factor undoubtedly strengthening his resolve was his acute awareness of the piecemeal fashion in which the British armor had launched their uncoordinated attacks during the day.

> However, in spite of the precarious situation and the difficult problems with which it faced us, I looked forward that evening full of hope to what the battle might bring. For Ritchie had thrown his armour into the battle piecemeal and had thus given us the chance of engaging them on each separate occasion with just about enough of our own tanks. This dispersal of the British armour brigades was incomprehensible. The principal aim of the British should have been to have brought all the armour they had into action at one and the same time. They should never have allowed themselves to be duped into dividing their forces before the battle or during our feint attack against the Gazala line.[78]

He was confident that the British would continue in this vein, and he would renew the attack once he had extracted a heavy toll from their inevitable and futile counterattacks.[79]

Rommel's advance behind the Gazala line opened up a direct threat to Tobruk with German forces now only a few kilometers from the defenses. The occupation of the fortified port remained the primary objective of any Axis offensive. One is tempted to ask which event should have triggered the Tobruk garrison to prepare its defensives to meet a direct Axis thrust. The proximity of powerful enemy forces a mere 20 km away should have acted as a powerful incentive for that purpose. The opposite was true, for during the Gazala fighting the defenses of Tobruk were concentrated along the inner perimeter or the line of the inner minefields. Klopper made the decision to man the defenses on the outer perimeter only twenty-four to thirty-six hours before the Axis cut off Tobruk.[80] In preparing their brigade positions for all-around defensive boxes, the British should naturally have afforded the Tobruk enclave the opportunity to construct the same type of all-around defense. The desert war had already demonstrated that fixed positions and continuous lines were unworkable against a doctrine calling for mobility and agility. A large proportion of the historiography suggests that the first indication the defenders of Tobruk had of a requirement to offer an all-around defense was when the Axis forces surrounded and isolated them on June 18, 1942.

The sun rose on May 28, throwing light over a confused battlefield. Rommel's forces lay scattered over a wide area behind the Gazala line, short of essential supplies and looking, for all intents and purposes, decidedly vulnerable and isolated from their front lines. Rommel had dealt a severe blow to the British, but in turn had suffered grievous losses and fell short of his objectives.[81] The Germans and Italians and were strung out from the coast and isolated behind enemy positions. Their supply lines were long and precarious, snaking around Bir Hakim and leaving them vulnerable to roving British columns. There was no better opportunity for a concentrated British force to launch a decisive counterattack against a weakened and disorganized enemy.[82] Unfortunately, the British missed the opportunity, as their disorganization and lack of initiative saw the fleeting advantage offered by the vulnerability of the scattered, immobile Axis forces go by. Rommel's immediate need to regroup and consolidate his fragmented encircling forces, especially the isolated 90th Light Division, eclipsed his objective of capturing Tobruk. His plan of action for the day was to push his forces farther north toward the coast road to establish a shorter supply route by breaking through the northern sector of the Gazala line. Despite a clear opportunity, the British forces remained on the defensive and it was already midday when they managed to gain a clearer picture. When they finally acted, it came in the form of a pincer movement, to cut off the Germans by attacking *Ariete*, who were holding Bir Harmat. The Italian 88mm and 90mm antitank fire extracted a fearful toll on the British, who had little to show for it in return.[83] Once again, the Italians beat off the uncoordinated British attacks using superior defensive tactics. (See Map 6.)

Rommel too had not fulfilled his intentions by the end of the day. The 21 *Panzer*-Division advanced without the support of the 15 *Panzer*-Division, who were short of supplies. They fell short of their intended target of the coastal road. *Ariete* and 90th Light Division remained on the defensive at Bir El Harmat, where the British continually harassed them. Rommel drove back that evening to meet the supply columns and guide them back to their destination. He narrowly evaded capture in the process of this daring mission. This is but one example of Rommel placing himself at the head of the lowest levels of a command chain in order to

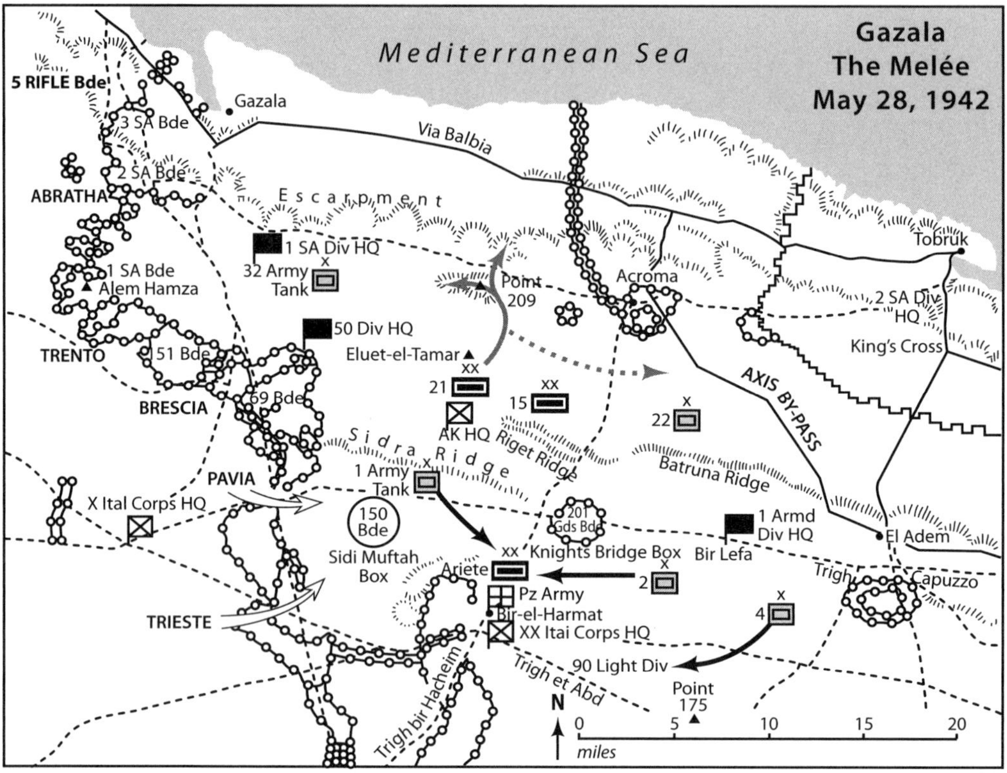

Map 6. Rommel intended to consolidate his scattered forces behind the Gazala line and re-establish a supply line through the northern sector of the line by using the coastal road.

achieve the desired result. His efforts ensured that the 15 and 21 *Panzer-Divisions* received fuel and ammunition on the morning of May 29, once again restoring mobility and striking power to the cutting edge of the *DAK*. On that morning the Germans could field 150 tanks together with a further 90 Italian tanks against the British, who could still muster 420 tanks.[84] Not for the first time, the odds were heavily stacked against the Germans on a purely numerical basis.

May 29 brought a change of pace to the Axis offensive when Rommel made a decision to break off his drive to the coast and assume a temporary defensive position. His objective was to consolidate his forces behind the Gazala line in the vicinity of Knightsbridge, using the British minefields to protect his western flank and throwing up a powerful antitank screen on the eastern front. Adding impetus to the strength of this defensive position was the successful action by the Italian *Trieste* Division in opening up an alternative line of supply by clearing a narrow path through the minefields south of the 150th Brigade position.[85] Rommel, safely ensconced between British mines and German antitank weapons and resupplied through cleared paths through the British minefields, hoped to consolidate his forces for a further attack. At the same time, he provided enticing bait for further British attacks.

> I foresaw that the British mechanised brigades would continue to run their heads against our well organised defensive front and use up their strength in the process. The defence was to be conducted with the maximum of elasticity and mobility.[86]

At first glance, Rommel's resorting to a defensive stance may seem to fly in the face of a German doctrine that encourages offensive action above all else. However, German doctrine makes provision for defensive action as long as it is combined with offensive action. "Any position is of value, only when it forces the enemy to attack and, during the enemy's attempt at envelopment procures for the defender the necessary time or favorable conditions for his offensive action."[87] More often than not, Rommel was a product of a rigorous German culture and training. His actions conformed closely with German doctrine, although it may be said he applied it with extraordinary vigor and élan. The British were unable to seize the advantage of Rommel's precarious situation while he consolidated his forces. Norrie, commanding the XXX Corps,[88] launched what was supposed to have been a concentrated attack of all of his armor against an encircled and immobile enemy. However, this show of force soon degenerated into an uncoordinated piecemeal attack resulting in heavy casualties among the precious British armor. Once again the British missed a fleeting opportunity to do real damage to the wounded *DAK*.[89]

Rommel Defends—"The Cauldron" and the Destruction of the Gazala Line: May 30–June 10, 1942

The German switch to the defensive marked the end of the first phase of the Gazala battles. In the second twelve-day phase, Rommel was devoted to solving his supply issues, consolidating his forces, securing the German positions, and dismantling the British defensive boxes manning the Gazala line. He was also able to draw the British tanks onto his defenses and steadily erode the British numerical advantage. The British defensive box held by the 150th Brigade now became the center of German efforts over the next few days in an area dubbed "the Cauldron" by the British. The 150th Brigade, situated to the rear of the German "hedgehog" and straddling the two logistical paths back to the Axis lines, constituted a thorn in Rommel's side. Rommel fended off the British mechanized attacks on his eastern flank with his antitank screen while concentrating his forces against the 150th Brigade. The brigade stood little chance against overwhelming odds and finally succumbed on June 1 after a spirited defense and the death of its commander Brigadier C. W. Haydon. The Germans bagged 3,000 prisoners, including a brigadier, and destroyed an estimated 101 tanks and armored cars in the two days of fighting.[90] Rommel took personal control of one of the leading platoons in the final attack against the 150th Brigade, once again demonstrating his hands-on approach to warfare. Rommel conceded that an infantry brigade could be effective against tanks if its members prepared its defenses properly.[91]

The elimination of the 150th Brigade now opened up a clear and uninterrupted route for the Axis supply columns to resupply Rommel's armored forces in the Cauldron. It is worthwhile pausing to reflect on how remarkable the conduct of the German operation was up to this point in the battle. After undertaking a risky night move to outflank the Gazala line, the Germans duly inserted themselves between the British static and mobile forces. There they assumed the defensive and made use of enemy minefields to defend their western flank and their antitank screen to defend their eastern flank. They then fought backwards toward the German lines to reestablish their supply route. This bold maneuver is a first in military history and exemplifies the German art of *Bewegungskrieg* at its zenith, as practiced by one of its most capable proponents in the desert of North Africa.[92] The Germans, in an astounding feat of arms, extricated themselves from a precarious position and now commanded a strongly concentrated position, easily supplied and defended, from whence they could sally forth at will by threatening multiple targets deep in the Allied rear. This threat included the biggest prize of all—Tobruk.

The next defensive box to receive Rommel's attention was manned by 3,000 to 4,000 Free French at Bir Hakim, commanded by General Marie-Pierre Koenig (1898–1970). Bir Hakim marked the southernmost position of the Gazala line. On the evening of June 1, Rommel ordered the 90th Light and *Trieste* Divisions to destroy the Free French outpost that to date had offered stubborn resistance. The destruction of the French position was the key to unlocking the Gazala line and make the British positions north of the line untenable. The French had carved out a defensive system in the featureless desert using ingenuity and largely obsolete armaments and they defended their position with tenacity. Up to this stage in the battle, the Italian attacks on the French position showed little success and incurred heavy casualties. The 90th Light Division launched another attack on June 6 that came within 700 m of the inner redoubt of the fort before failing.[93] The Germans launched yet another failed attack on June 8, this time led by Rommel himself.

> I frequently took over command of the assault forces myself and seldom in Africa was I given such a hard fought struggle. The French fought in a skilfully planned system of field positions and small defence works—slit trenches, small pillboxes, machine gun and anti-tank gun nests—all surrounded by dense minefields. Attack after attack came to a halt in the excellent British defence system.[94]

In all the time that the French garrison held off against the combined Italian and German onslaughts, the British were strangely absent from the battle. They had made the decision, one that was evident to the Germans and the French, to leave Bir Hakim to its own devices and instead ensure the safety of their supply lines.[95] The garrison held on bravely through June 8 and 9 despite repeated air and ground assaults by vastly superior forces. The position inside the box became critical and the French decided to withdraw on the evening of June 10. Only 2,600 men out of an original garrison of 3,700 eventually made it back to British lines.[96]

While the French at Bir Hakim occupied Rommel's attention, the British vacillated on a course of action. Auchinleck never took his eye off receiving a possible attack in the northern sector, even when Rommel was deep in the rear of the Gazala line. As a consequence, the South Africans and the 50th Division together with the 32nd Army Tank Brigade prepared for an action that never happened. A further distraction was a plan hatched by Auchinleck, code-named Operation Limerick, whose implementation he pushed as late as June 3. It proposed an assault by the South Africans and the 50th Brigade in a westerly direction toward Temrad in a pinning maneuver. A flanking maneuver would take place to the south of Bir Hakim and aim for Segnali to cut off the Axis supply lines. Auchinleck urged this course of action rather than an assault on the Cauldron. Pienaar felt that any penetration of the Axis lines in front of him would be a "sore finger stuck into enemy territory, very vulnerable to attack from the flank." He flatly refused to make a brigade attack without tank support. In the absence of any tank support, Gott eventually persuaded Pienaar to send some small parties forward. Pienaar refused to have too many casualties coming from any one formation and believed in spreading any losses.[97] Indecision caused consternation among the Eighth Army commanders as they argued over the best course of action. Pienaar and Ramsden, doubtful of the success of such an operation, dragged their feet at its implementation. One is tempted to compare the plodding, often ramshackle British command structure to the nimble way Rommel operated. He placed himself, in person, more often than not, at the decisive spot, and his subordinates followed his orders efficiently and executed them expeditiously without argument.[98]

Ritchie eventually found a measure of decisiveness on June 3 when he decided to abandon Limerick and launch a full offensive against the Cauldron. He certainly had a distinct advantage with over 400 tanks against 130 German and some Italian tanks.[99] The plan for Operation Aberdeen seemed a good one on paper; its weakness lay in its execution. It called for cooperation between the tanks and the infantry and the plan directed the main attack at Rommel's eastern front at the Cauldron. The RAF would support the assault by supplying appropriate airpower. Operation Aberdeen degenerated into disaster as the British tanks fell victim to the Italian and German antitank guns. The British attempts to use infantry and artillery in a combined arms fashion against the German guns did not yield high dividends. Combining different weapons in a coordinated attack takes practice and the Cauldron was not an appropriate place to learn. The Eighth Army's introduction of new tactics was causing them great difficulty. Their use of combined arms tactics on such a large scale for the first time was problematic, as their experience in using it in battle on this magnitude was nil.[100]

The attack launched on the Cauldron on June 5, 1942, first used infantry and artillery to penetrate the minefields and then armor to exploit the gains. Unfortunately, the artillery barrages fell on the empty desert as the *DAK* had withdrawn the front slightly. The largely uncoordinated British attack suffered heavily before Rommel's antitank screen and lost up to 70 tanks by the end of the day in fruitless attempts to dislodge the *DAK* from their positions in the Cauldron. Estimates of British losses in the Cauldron battles approach 100 to 170 tanks, leaving only 132 of the original 424 medium tanks remaining by June 7.[101] Rommel then launched a limited counterattack that inflicted yet more losses and sowed more confusion on the retreating British forces. With the British licking their wounds Rommel was free to concentrate on eliminating the troublesome Free French box at Bir Hakim.[102]

The fall of Bir Hakim on June 10 signalled the end of the Gazala line and left the British manning positions that ran lengthwise along the coast from the original position at Gazala in the west to Tobruk in the east. However, the British still enjoyed a numerical advantage of 330 to the 230 Axis tanks and a clear numerical superiority in men.[103] Rommel positioned himself to the south of the British, having concentrated all his armor and now having the ability to strike in any direction. The time bought at Bir Hakim by the stubborn French resistance had not been used efficiently and the British were content to withdraw behind their defensive boxes and hand the initiative over to the Axis. On June 11 Rommel struck out at Tobruk and the supply center of Belhamed in a two-pronged attack. A hasty British counterattack on June 12 and 13 suffered from a lack of coordination between the British divisional and brigade commanders and endured more crippling losses of tanks. The British lost some 138 tanks in one afternoon alone.

The advantage had now swung decisively over to Rommel and he enjoyed tank superiority for the first time since May 27. The British abandoned their position at the Knightsbridge box in the face of the defeat of their mechanized forces. With that, the last positions on the Gazala line became untenable and faced encirclement and subsequent annihilation. Rommel was once again free to resume a war of movement, having secured his supply lines and eliminated the southern strong points of the

Gazala line.[104] At this stage, Pienaar was becoming intensely uncomfortable and he felt his position on the north of the Gazala line to be vulnerable. On June 13, he contacted Ramsden, who commanded the adjacent 50th Division. Ramsden told Pienaar that he felt their positions were secure and that they would be in Benghazi within the week. Pienaar sarcastically agreed, saying, "Christ yes, as blooming prisoners."[105] Pienaar was on the verge of insisting on his division's pulling out when Ritchie ordered the 1st South African and 50th Divisions to withdraw from the Gazala line on June 14.[106] Rommel's way to Tobruk was open!

Chapter 7

Tobruk 1942: The Surrender of the 2nd South African Division

Defeat is one thing; disgrace is another.[1]

The loss of the 3rd Indian and 7th Motorised Brigades at the outset of the German attack and the subsequent loss of the 150th Brigade and then the southernmost position of Bir Hakim had unhinged the British positions along the Gazala line. This was especially true after the Germans defeated the British mobile formations in the battles of the Cauldron. The remaining positions on the Gazala line held by the 1st South African and 50th Divisions were in a precarious position and in imminent danger of Rommel's victorious *Panzers* cutting them off. The Germans threatened Tobruk itself, held by the 2nd South African Division, with imminent investment. However, there was a plan in existence should this highly likely scenario be visited upon the British. Many months before the impending disaster, the British decided that should the Eighth Army find itself in this predicament, the Gazala line and Tobruk must be abandoned and all British forces should withdraw to the Egyptian frontier. There they would regroup, consolidate, and rebuild. It was a sound plan, because the British could afford to trade space for time; however, it was not to be.

Tobruk Is Not to Be Invested Again!

The decision to defend Tobruk, once the Gazala line became untenable, was not one forced on the British. Tobruk could have, and perhaps should have, been evacuated before being encircled, had the British in fact chosen this course of action. The British made the decision to hold Tobruk at the eleventh hour and went against British policy of not allowing the Axis to invest Tobruk for the second time. The decision to defend Tobruk even took some of the troops by surprise.

> An hour before sunset, came the order for the column to withdraw towards Tobruk. We could sense that something was wrong. My officer came back from an order group. He asked me how would I like to stay in Tobruk for a long time. This was the first time that we had heard mention of Tobruk being held again.[2]

Operation Freeborn contained details for the evacuation of Tobruk under these circumstances and the British had made the plan many months prior to the Gazala debacle. Auchinleck made it clear on more than one occasion that should the Eighth Army be defeated at Gazala, Tobruk would not be defended a second time and the Eighth Army would withdraw to the Egyptian frontier. He again confirmed this clearly to Ritchie in writing on June 13.[3] It seems that the theory of withdrawal was easier to promulgate than the actual implementation of abandoning Tobruk once reality descended. Once again political considerations overpowered good military practice.

Smuts was not averse to the British holding onto Tobruk. On June 18, on learning that Tobruk was isolated, he suggested to Auchinleck that Tobruk must be held "both to save it and to bring (the) enemy to (a) decisive battle."[4] The resolute defense offered by the Australians in the first siege, lasting 242 days, was a major hindrance to Rommel's drive into Egypt, due to its position astride a major artery of Axis supply and the denial of its port facilities to the Axis. Rommel was preoccupied with the siege of Tobruk and this distraction precluded a drive into the heart of Egypt. However, the Royal Navy, which ensured the survival of the fortress of Tobruk, achieved this at a great price and they were reluctant to suffer such losses again. Consequently, in February 1942, the British decided not to defend Tobruk, but rather to abandon it, if the Axis threatened it again with a siege. In February 1942 Auchinleck had informed London that in the event of an enemy offensive "I was determined not to allow Tobruk to be besieged for a second time. . . . I did not consider that I could afford to lock up one and a half divisions in a fortress." Admiral Cunningham agreed, particularly since the siege had proved so costly in ships, and so did Air Chief Marshal Tedder, who doubted that he had sufficient aircraft to provide air cover.[5] Auchinleck made it quite clear:

> If, for any reason, we should be forced at some future date to withdraw from our present forward positions, every effort will still be made to prevent Tobruk being lost to the enemy; but it is not my intention to continue to hold it once the enemy is in a position to invest it effectively. Should this appear inevitable, the place will be evacuated, and the maximum amount of destruction carried out in it, so as to make it useless to the enemy as a supply base. In this eventuality the enemy's advance will be stopped on the general line Sollum-Maddalena-Giarabub, as laid down in Operation Instruction No. 110. 19 January 1942.[6]

The withdrawal to the Egyptian border ordered by Ritchie was not some hasty, ill-conceived plan thought up on the spur of the moment in the face of a relentless enemy. He executed it in terms of an operational order to XIII Corps dated May 10, 1942, which clearly stated that if the defense of the Gazala line became untenable, then the defenders must demolish and abandon the facilities at Tobruk and the entire corps should withdraw to the Egyptian frontier.[7]

Muddled command had already cost the British dearly in the battles around the Cauldron. It was to fail the Eighth Army again when Auchinleck decided to intervene at the operational level. Once the defense of the Gazala line became untenable after the costly tank battles of June 13, Auchinleck proposed that the withdrawal of the Eighth Army would be to the line Acroma–El Adem and southwards.[8] It was a clear change of plan and not in accordance with Operation Freeborn. Auchinleck perceived that the circumstances surrounding the triggering of the implementation of Operation Freeborn were different from what he originally anticipated. He felt that the Eighth Army was not yet beaten and that the infantry divisions were largely intact. Auchinleck reasoned that

> The Eighth Army was . . . still strong enough to provide an adequate garrison for Tobruk and to maintain a mobile field force to the east and south capable of preventing the fortress being permanently besieged.[9]

An unfortunate difference of understanding between Auchinleck and Ritchie arose at the time of withdrawing the 1st South African and 50th Divisions from the Gazala line. Auchinleck believed that the British would defend the line Acroma–El Adem–Bir Gubi with the two retreating divisions taking up positions on that line. Ritchie, on the other hand, followed the directives of Operation Freeborn and ordered the two divisions to the Egyptian frontier. Ritchie failed to inform Auchinleck of his true intentions. They were to withdraw to the Egyptian frontier notwithstanding whether the South Africans held Tobruk in isolation or abandoned it. When corresponding with Auchinleck, Ritchie couched his intentions in less definite terms and spoke of the possibility of the Germans cutting off Tobruk for a time. Adding grist to the mill of confusion, Churchill and Smuts sought assurances from Auchinleck that he would not abandon Tobruk to the Axis.[10] Ritchie, pressed by Auchinleck to hold Tobruk, decided to allow the Germans to temporarily besiege the garrison, with the knowledge that there were enough provisions to withstand encirclement for three months. In the meantime, he would rebuild the Eighth Army behind the infantry divisions manning prepared positions on the Egyptian frontier. Ritchie was prone to be guided by Gott, commander of XIII Corps, and he was influenced by the latter's confidence that Tobruk was capable of withstanding a siege for at least two months. Gott was also in favor of withdrawing behind the frontier and rebuilding the Eighth Army in relative safety.[11] Ritchie secured an agreement from Auchinleck that the Axis could temporarily invest Tobruk but he failed to inform him that he had ordered the withdrawal of the 1st South African and 50th divisions to the Egyptian frontier. Auchinleck now envisaged that Ritchie would hold Tobruk as part of a defensive line manned by relatively unscathed troops. He was not aware that all that remained of the Tobruk–Acroma–El Adem–Bir Gubi line was but a thin veneer; the relatively unscathed divisions had withdrawn to the Egyptian frontier.[12]

On June 14 the 1st South African and 50th Divisions successfully withdrew from the Gazala line and made for the Egyptian border. Pienaar's South Africans retreated eastwards through Tobruk, and while the 1st Division made its way through the fortress, he paid a visit to Klopper. After seeing Pienaar, it is impossible to imagine that Klopper had illusions that Pienaar's division was to play any part in a defensive line with

Tobruk. Klopper recalled, according to Hartshorn, that Pienaar and his staff paid a visit to his headquarters and in their discussions on the dire situation facing Tobruk, Pienaar was heard to say, "Kloppie, you've had it."[13] The 50th Division took a far more hazardous route in their retreat to the Egyptian frontier. The division had to fight its way westward through the surrounding Italian forces and make a large detour through the desert behind enemy lines as far south as Bir Hakim. German proximity to the coastal road created a bottleneck and constricted the retreat of the 1st Division, forcing the 50th Division to retreat "forwards" through the Axis lines. They reached the frontier virtually intact despite the multiple hazards they had to face deep behind enemy lines. It was another example, the other being Bir Hakim, of a successful evacuation from encirclement. It was most difficult if not impossible to effect a watertight encirclement under desert conditions, and one should keep this in mind when assessing the fate of the South Africans at Tobruk. The 1st and 50th Divisions condemned Tobruk to early encirclement by not taking up defensive positions on the line Acroma–El Adem–Bir el Gubi. A thin screening force made up of infantry brigade remnants and a much-weakened 4th Armoured Brigade, recently mauled in the Cauldron battles, was all the British left in place to hold the rampant *DAK* at bay.

Rommel ordered his *Panzer* divisions forward to attack Belhamed and El Adem on June 15. These positions effectively screened the vulnerable southeast corner of the Tobruk perimeter. The British repulsed the initial German attacks but success was short-lived and Rommel, not accepting the rebuff, forced the defenders of El Adem to abandon their position on June 16/17. Inexplicably, the British did not inform Klopper of the abandonment of El Adem and he only became aware of the grave situation once his reconnaissance units of the Umvoti Mounted Rifles discovered it to be in enemy hands on June 17. The British officially informed Klopper on June 18 of El Adem's abandonment, which can be considered extremely tardy, as the retention of the position was key to the conduct of Tobruk's defenses.[14] Adding to the precarious situation was the capture of the forward British airstrips, effectively precluding future air support for the Tobruk garrison. Rommel was able to report triumphantly to Berlin on June 18 that he had surrounded the port of Tobruk and the nearest enemy force of any consequence, besides those invested in Tobruk, were 64 km away on the Egyptian frontier.[15]

Introducing Major-General Hendrik Balsazer Klopper

If a commander can exercise a decisive influence on the outcome of a battle, then the battle for Tobruk was an example of a gross mismatch in command ability. Rommel was a capable and gifted commander and needs little introduction. His reputation as a fierce proponent of maneuver warfare and audacious tactics, sometimes bordering on the reckless, are the subject matter of multiple books and he has deservedly or undeservedly become a legend. Rommel's reputation as a gifted general remains largely intact even after a great passage of time and even when one strips away some of the myth. Other able commanders' reputations have succumbed to a plethora of inevitable revisionist material. The reputations of men such as Field-Marshal Bernard Montgomery, General George Patton, and General Douglas MacArthur have certainly not endured as well.[16] Rommel was one of the more competent German generals, but only one of many German officers who were the product of superior German doctrine that found its roots a century and a half prior to the Second World War.

This disparity between Allied and German doctrine was to cost the British, and later the United States, dearly in North Africa. Unlike Rommel, historians know little about Klopper and his career before the Second World War. This unfortunate historiographical lacuna applies to all but a few of South Africa's generals in both World Wars.[17] One has to be cautious, when evaluating Klopper, not to allow the stigma of his surrendering Tobruk, nor the popular perception that his attempts at defense were especially poor, to obliterate the facts. Despite this stigma, Klopper went on to enjoy a successful army career, serving as Army Chief of Staff (1951–1953), as Inspector-General (1953–1956), and as Commandant-General, head of the Union Defence Forces (1956–1958). However, the Tobruk fiasco continued to haunt him and he was never fully successful in reversing this blight on his career. The subsequent resuscitation of his career owed more to the ascendancy of the Nationalists after their 1948 election victory than to any of his efforts to get history reviewed. Like Rommel, Major-General Hendrik Balsazer Klopper (1902–1978) was a product of his nation's military schooling, which relied on a ponderous and underdeveloped British way of war. According to Van der Waag,

> Smuts's generals on the eve of the Second World War had little education, little real training, and no experience beyond minor pacification operations. Moreover, an emphasis on management and the good execution of clerical and desk tasks induced intellectual stagnation.[18]

One sees his first efforts to regain his reputation in a letter addressed to Major-General Beyers on April 17, 1944. After his escape from captivity in 1943, he requested that the UDF put him back on active service as he felt he was subject to "severe criticism in staying in the Union when other ex P.O.W.'s are being sent on active service."[19] His postwar efforts to clear his name took the form of a series of articles in the 1950 *Huisgenoot* magazine,[20] various interviews with the Union War Histories Section giving his version of events, and a behind the scenes attempt, backed by the South African Government, to alter a 1942 dispatch authored by Field-Marshal Auchinleck.[21]

Klopper was born on September 25, 1902, in Somerset West, South Africa. Once he had finished his studies and a short stint as a primary school teacher, he joined the UDF on August 5, 1924.[22] To gain access to the permanent force, he was obliged to undergo a program of amphigarious training, which attracted a high failure rate due to its rigorous nature.[23] Receiving a commission and his pilot wings in September 1926, Klopper seemed to struggle with the most theoretical aspects of his course, failing some of his subjects in Military Law and Staff Duties.[24] He was married on December 22, 1928, and had a son. Notwithstanding a somewhat mediocre academic career in the UDF, his immediate superiors described him as a person having a strong personality and outstanding ability and tact, whom they could rely upon in all circumstances and possessing a higher sense of honor and devotion. Klopper was found to be hardworking, able and conscientious, a good disciplinarian, and a man popular with all ranks.[25] These accolades are more an indicator of what the UDF considered necessary in peacetime, rather than a practical assessment of the capabilities demanded of Klopper when placed in a difficult wartime situation.

One of the few reports containing anything negative about Klopper indicated a need to develop his personality. Klopper was "a little too inclined to find excuses for things done and left undone." The report describes Klopper as about average for his newly acquired rank of captain in 1933.[26] In that same year, Klopper remained attached to the College Staff of the S.A. Military College. The UDF promoted him to a substantive major in June 1934 and he moved from the Staff of Officer Commanding Orange Free State (OFS) Command and assumed command of the Pioneer Battalion in February 1935. Klopper was appointed Officer Commanding OFS Command Training Depot in June 1937. Lieutenant-Colonel Klopper relinquished his post as commander of 1 Special Services Battalion and took up his position as the Deputy Director of Infantry Training in October 1939. He was appointed to act as Officer in Command S.A. Instructional Corps as a vice to Major-General G. E. Brink in November 1940. Klopper then assumed the duties of General Staff Officer for the 2nd SAI Division, a post he retained until he was made commander of 3rd SAI Brigade and promoted to brigadier in January 1942. Klopper's wife took ill and passed away in October 1941, leaving his brother-in-law and his wife to care for his son. Personal bereavement may have adversely impacted Klopper's performance some eight months later at Tobruk in June 1942.[27]

A newly promoted Major-General Klopper took over command of the 2nd SAI Division on May 15, 1942, from Major-General I. P. de Villiers, who was then eleven years his senior and had seen service in the First World War, in South West Africa and France. Klopper experienced a somewhat meteoric rise to become a divisional commander some fifteen years after his attestation and a general before his fortieth birthday. It was his first combat command, as he never commanded a regiment or a brigade in the heat of war and was too young to have seen any First World War service. His short duty as brigade commander of 3rd Brigade from January to May 1942 took place in a relatively quiet period of the desert war. His command, the 2nd SAI Division, was equally inexperienced, having seen little action since it arrived in Egypt on June 6, 1941. During the Operation Crusader, the British held 2nd SAI Division in reserve due to a lack of transport. Newly promoted officers filled the command structures of 2nd Division, the most seasoned ones having departed with General de Villiers. Klopper's inexperience matched that of his chief of staff, Lieutenant-Colonel Kriek, who lacked operational experience and high-grade staff training.[28]

We have a picture of a very young, inexperienced commander, assisted by an inexperienced staff and commanding a division that had seen very little action, facing an enormous and complicated task. Brigadier L. F. Thompson, a veteran of the first siege, was appointed as Klopper's second-in-command, and he provided some much-needed combat experience. However, his influence on the battle, if any, is obscure. According to a witness in the HQ, Thompson did not make one constructive suggestion to Klopper during the entire battle.[29] The British left behind Colonel Bastin, the quartermaster general of XIII Corps, to assist coordination between the rear area and garrison headquarters.[30] The battle-hardened commanders of the 32nd Army Tank Brigade and the 201st Mechanised Brigade may have been able to add considerable experience to the defense, had Klopper been able to provide leadership and seize control over his seasoned brigade commanders. The question remains as to why the British left so complicated and onerous a task as defending Tobruk, in the face of difficult circumstances, in the hands of a relatively inexperienced leader group. There was talk of giving the position to the previous siege commander, Lieutenant-General L. J. Morshead (1889–1959), and even Gott considered taking the position, giving some indication that Ritchie may have had concerns about Klopper's leadership.[31]

Rommel spoke of the qualities that made for a dynamic commander. He saw superb leadership as a function of having a driving desire to achieve a goal against insurmountable odds rather than an intellectual pursuit, where one's intellectualism might hinder the achievement of results. In the final analysis, there is a huge divergence between the more academic and organizational approach of a staff officer, such as Klopper, and the dynamic, calculated risk-taking personality of a leader of men who takes his division into combat. Rommel said, "It has frequently happened in the past that a General of high intellectual powers has been defeated by a less intelligent but stronger willed adversary."[32] As the events around Tobruk unfolded it would become apparent that Klopper was out of his depth and his reactions were ponderous and miscalculated. It stands in stark contrast to the nimble and intuitive (*Fingerspitzengefühl*, literally "finger tips feeling") generalship of Rommel, who seemed in tune with an ever-changing situation and was able to take advantage of fleeting opportunities as they presented themselves on the battlefield.

Tobruk Besieged—June 18, 1942

Secondary sources are in agreement that the defenses of Tobruk, in June 1942, were in a poor state of repair compared to their condition in the first siege of 1941. Back then, Morshead had commanded Tobruk defenses, and he withstood two serious attacks and many more minor ones, in what military historians recognize as a brilliantly coordinated defense. What is also beyond dispute is that the defenders of Tobruk in 1941 did not have to face as concentrated or as powerful an offensive as that delivered by Rommel on June 20, 1942. No matter the state of the physical defenses, it is debatable whether Morshead would have prevailed against so concerted an attack as was delivered on Klopper. However, although it is interesting to make the inevitable comparisons, they serve no real analytical purpose. History, especially military history, rather than teaching lessons in a didactic manner, is far more useful in showing what is possible and perhaps highlighting some of the mistakes that one could have avoided in similar circumstances.

The Tobruk fortress consisted of a double line of prepared strong points comprising concrete dugouts and wire defenses along a 33 mile (52.8 km) perimeter enclosed by a double line of wire, antitank ditch, and perimeter minefields. The inner defenses, much strengthened by Morshead, consisted of strongpoints at strategic positions and internal minefields coordinated into an interior line of defense known as the blue line.[33] The South African official history describes the deterioration in the Tobruk defenses. It claims that the antitank ditch, long neglected, had begun to silt up, and was deliberately filled in at points X and Y on the southeast perimeter to facilitate an easy evacuation. The composition and layout of minefields on the southeastern corner of the fortress, sown by successive defenders of varying nationality over the previous two years, is vague.[34] The most vulnerable sector of the fortress remained the southeast corner, where large quantities of mines had supposedly been lifted "and were never replaced" during the Crusader operations in November 1941. The British lifted the mines during Crusader to facilitate the planned breakout from Tobruk.[35] More than a few sources mention that the British denuded the perimeter defenses of wire and mines in an effort to strengthen the Gazala positions.[36] Most secondary sources paint a picture of neglect, lamenting the cannibalization of large sections of the defenses stripped to reinforce the Gazala positions. What remained of the defenses was supposedly poorly maintained due to the general understanding that in the event the British failed to hold the Gazala position, they would evacuate Tobruk.[37]

However, this dismal picture of neglect flies in the face of the evidence presented at the Court of Enquiry by Brigadier C. de L. Gaussen. He was the chief engineer of XIII Corps and stated that "it was not the policy to touch any of the perimeter defences at all" and that very little dismantling was undertaken.[38] Brigadier F. H. Kisch, the chief engineer of the Eighth Army, in giving evidence at the same inquiry, felt that the defenses of Tobruk had deteriorated and that the Gazala defenses had made extensive use of mines and wire taken from Tobruk. However, in discussions reported by Kisch with the South African chief engineer of 2nd Division, Colonel Henderson, the South African engineer felt that he had made good any deficiencies in the defenses by laying new mines to close the gaps.[39] Klopper confirmed that there were whole minefields lifted for use at Gazala and Knightsbridge, but stated that he had replaced them. He flatly denied that the minefields were in a poor condition at the outset of the siege.[40] Auchinleck, obviously basing his evidence on the Court of Enquiry, states in his dispatch that,

> The defences are believed to be in a better state than when Tobruk was first invested. A certain amount of wire had been removed from inside the perimeter but not to the extent of weakening the defences.

He goes on to concede that there may have been a deterioration in the minefields in certain areas, but draws attention to the fact that there were 40,000 antitank mines readily available within the fortress.[41] The witness reports as to the state of the defenses on the eve of the siege, especially concerning the state of the minefields, are conflicting at best and do not warrant the certainty modern authors have adopted as to their state of disrepair.

The morale of the troops manning the defenses of Tobruk is also an important factor, and it is no exaggeration that the morale of the Australians under Morshead in the first siege greatly aided its ultimately successful defense. Despite the relative inexperience of the leader group commanding 2nd South Africa Infantry Division and the inexperience of the division itself, the morale of the commander at Tobruk seems to have been high. Theron found both Pienaar and Klopper determined and in good spirits when he visited Tobruk on May 30.[42] Klopper clearly stated his confidence and described a "general feeling of optimism" in Tobruk in a letter to Major-General F. H. Theron dated June 16, 1942. Pienaar reported that the fighting spirit and morale were high, following a visit to Klopper on his retreat through Tobruk eastwards toward the Egyptian frontier.[43] However, at the time of writing the letter, Klopper believed that Tobruk was part of a defensive line and the British would leave him isolated. He based his optimism on assurances by the Eighth Army that they would hold El Adem and Belhamed, both key to the Tobruk defenses on the southeastern front. Theron stresses that Klopper was optimistic, but he qualified his optimism by writing, "We are all looking forward to a good stand and *we are supported by the very best of British troops*." (Author's emphasis.)[44]

The general feeling of optimism was again confirmed in a meeting held in Tobruk on June 16 and attended by Ritchie, Gott, and Klopper. There Klopper agreed that he was able to hold the fortress for at least ninety days.[45] It is not the only reference to Klopper's enthusiasm for the task. The UWHS describes Klopper and his divisional staff as being most enthusiastic about holding Tobruk, and states that Klopper's optimism and assurances may have influenced Auchinleck's final decision to hold the fortress.[46] Pienaar was not as confident as Klopper and urged Ritchie that they should not hold Tobruk.[47] Whether the same confidence permeated down to the lower command structures is less certain. The series of unbroken reversals suffered by the Eighth Army and experienced firsthand by a significant number of the troops now manning the Tobruk defenses must have impacted negatively on their general morale. A good proportion of the garrison consisted of disparate units, some of whom experienced rough treatment at the hands of the *DAK* in the Cauldron battles. Others were stragglers from retreating units passing through the fortress on their way to the Egyptian frontier. It was a difficult task for a staff used to handling a division of 9,000 to 12,000 men to be responsible for a garrison of 33,000 made up of "bits and pieces" from different units.[48] Klopper remained an unknown entity to most of those in Tobruk, including his own South African division, and this fact, combined with the inevitable confusion due to a rapidly developing situation, was not conducive to a state of high morale.[49]

The South African contingent at Tobruk consisted of two SAI brigades, the 4th and 6th Brigades, together with a battalion from 1st Division left behind by Pienaar as he retreated through Tobruk. The South Africans manned the perimeter defenses from the coast to the southwest corner of the fortress. The 11th Indian Brigade, under the command of the experienced Brigadier A. Anderson, manned the vulnerable southeast corner of the remaining 21 km perimeter together with a composite South African battalion called the Beer group. The mobile element of the defenses included the 32nd Army Tank Brigade under the command of the experienced Brigadier A. C. Willison. However, the tank brigade had seen extensive action and suffered heavy casualties in the Gazala battles. The last of the defenders was the 201st Guards Brigade, which was, in fact, a hastily put together composite unit commanded by newly appointed Brigadier H. F. Johnson. The mobile forces possessed fifty-four operational infantry tanks and a number of the newly issued, highly effective 6-pounder antitank guns. The mobile forces took up positions in the Fort Pilistrano area, which was almost central in the Tobruk fortress. The critical crossroads of Kings Cross were devoid of manned permanent positions and the only force covering the area were an artillery regiment and the reaction force of 201st Guards Battalion.[50] The Tobruk Court of Enquiry gives comparative strength analysis of the Tobruk garrison as at May 1, 1941, and June 18, 1942.[51] (See Table 6.)

According to Willison, there were twice as many armored cars in Tobruk in June 1942 than in the previous siege (making more than 60) and these were contained in 7th S.A. Reconnaissance Battalion and distributed within the perimeter.[52] The *DAK* Tank State for June 18, 1942, shows the number of German medium tanks deployed in the assault of Tobruk at 94. It was not an overwhelming advantage in purely numerical terms, especially when the antitank weapons available for the defense were added. General Fritz Bayerlein (1899–1970), Rommel's chief of staff, admits that there were 125 tanks available for the attack on Tobruk in the corps area on the morning of June 20. However, the Germans deployed no more than half of these.[53] The German force multiplier came in the form of superior operational ability rather than any numerical or qualitative superiority.

Comparison to the previous siege is inevitable, and it is apparent that the defenders of Tobruk in June 1942 enjoyed a numerical advantage over their predecessor in nearly every area. Klopper commanded a far superior armored component with access to heavy infantry tanks rather than the

Fall of Tobruk Comparative Strength Between the First and Second Siege		
INFANTRY		
	May 1, 1941	**June 18, 1942**
Infantry Battalions	11	14
Motorized Battalions	1	2
MG Battalions	1	1
	13	17
ARMORED FIGHTING VEHICLES		
Infantry	16	77
Cruiser	28	
Light	33	
Armored Cars	31	N/A
	108	77
ARTILLERY		
Field	72	72
Medium		29
	72	101
ANTITANK GUNS		
Antitank 2-pounder	16	41
Antitank 6-pounder		23
Antitank 3.7mm	25	
	41	64
AA ARTILLERY		
Heavy	16	16
Light	53	60
	69	76

Table 6. Comparative strength analysis of the Tobruk garrison as of May 1, 1941, and June 18, 1942.[54]

obsolete and lighter cruiser tanks. He also had a good number of armored cars at his disposal. Klopper enjoyed advantages over his predecessor in the all-important area of antitank guns. Significantly, twenty-three of the antitank guns consisted of the new, powerful 6-pounder, which had the potential to wreak havoc on any enemy armored attack on the perimeter defenses if the defenders deployed them correctly. There was no reason for Klopper to be embarrassed when it came to artillery or antiaircraft guns, for here too, his strengths compared favorably with those of his predecessor. There seems to have been an ample supply of ammunition for all weapons, which is not surprising given that Tobruk was a designated supply base for the Gazala positions. By all accounts, the defenders of Tobruk enjoyed stores and provisions in abundance. The British provided for adequate transport in the form of three Royal Armoured Service Corps companies left in the fortress to facilitate withdrawing the garrison should that eventuality arise.[55]

The South African official history describes the field artillery as being formidable in quantity and well-provided with ammunition. Some of the batteries suffered a lack of sufficient ammunition due to some strange policy decisions. In the words of Major A. J. Morris of the 2nd Battery SAA, who asked for ammunition to be placed nearer his gun positions,

> [I] was told that it was not the policy to dump ammunition in view of the closeness of the fortress dumps—only about 4–5 miles away. Despite this refusal, I managed to "acquire" odd lots of ammunition which proved most valuable. In the battle of Tobruk we were badly handicapped in having to conserve ammunition as we couldn't bring up supplies quickly enough and suffered a lot of casualties in men, vehicles and very precious ammunition in having to bring up ammunition over open country in the middle of a battle, till eventually further supply was completely impossible.[56]

Furthermore, Klopper fragmented the artillery fighting power because, unlike the previous siege, it was scattered among the entire defense and not placed under the centralized command and thereby concentrated. Although similar in quantity and quality in comparison to the first siege, it was uncoordinated and unable to bring down concentrated "fire on any spot within the perimeter . . . at a moment's notice," which was the case under Morshead. Artillery fire plans, as well as the communication systems, were inferior, and taken together with a poor chain of command this poor organization negated an essential element in repelling the Axis penetration of the perimeter defenses.[57] The antitank defenses of Tobruk, consisting of approximately sixty-nine guns, were similarly dispersed among the various battalions with little coordination or concentration. The antiaircraft defenses had eighteen 3.7 inch guns, roughly equivalent to the deadly German 88mm, and there was an authorization to use these in an antitank role if necessary.[58]

The Organization of the Defense and Counterattack Force of Tobruk

Lieutenant-Colonel Max Gooler, the official United States Military Observer, reported early indicators of a dysfunctional command structure in Tobruk. Gooler took note that there appeared to be a decided lack of cooperation between Klopper, his chief of staff, and the heads of the various staff sections, in particular, operations and intelligence.

> The staff openly complained that General Klopper did not have the correct picture of the enemy situation or realize its serious potentialities. And what was more serious, apparently did not trust his chiefs of sections. In my opinion, he was not in touch with the situation, and during the major portion of the afternoon of the 19th, to the best of my knowledge, neither he nor his Chief of Staff visited the Staff Sections referred to above, although they were set up only a short distance from the Divisional Commander's CP.[59]

On June 15 at 1400, Klopper called a meeting of his brigade commanders and explained that they were to hold Tobruk for a minimum of three months. Apparently, no tactical questions were discussed at this conference, which is surprising given the gravity of the situation and the much-altered role that the garrison was expected to perform in holding as opposed to evacuating the fortress.[60] It was only after the meeting that Willison, a veteran of the previous siege, approached Klopper and expressed his concern as to the placement of the forces defending Tobruk. Willison made a sound and reasonable request that Klopper centralize all armored cars and tanks under his command and give him responsibility for any enemy attacks on the coastal area. All the brigades would be freed up to man the perimeter of Tobruk as had been the case in the previous siege. Under Klopper's direction, the 6th Brigade manned the coast as a measure to prevent a seaward attack. The British considered this a real threat throughout the battle, whereas in the previous siege a small screening force manned the area. Willison criticized Klopper for positioning the gun emplacements too far forward and too far back and suggested that they instead occupy a central and concentrated position on the Pilastrino Ridge. Klopper listened politely to Willison's sound views but made little effort to define or clarify Willison's role or his sphere of command. What may have lain behind Klopper's lack of urgency was his belief that Rommel would invest Tobruk and then chase after the Eighth Army. Klopper was confident that the Germans would bypass Tobruk despite an appreciation by his intelligence staff that Rommel would make a determined effort to capture the town. Klopper got annoyed with his intelligence staff's continuous insistence on the imminent danger Tobruk faced.[61]

An administrative conference held the same day confirmed that the supply situation appeared to be adequate; however, according to the official history, there was an alarming shortage of medium ammunition, at only 450 rounds per gun. The defenders dealt with this shortage by applying a strict ration of 5 rounds per day based on a three-month siege. This arithmetical approach reveals something of the bureaucratic nature of the Tobruk leadership and is incomprehensible in the face of the reality facing the defenders. The defenders should have expended ammunition in accordance with enemy activity and threat levels, rather than on an arbitrary arithmetic formula. Klopper, in an interview after the war, confirmed the shortage of artillery ammunition, saying it was far below requirements and that on June 20, 1942, E-Boats were bringing in additional artillery ammunition. On the other hand, Captain Fannin stated during an interview in 1946 that "there was plenty of ammunition in Tobruk, the only acute shortage was in shells for the medium artillery." Major N. Wessels, commander of the 6th South African Light Anti-Aircraft Battery, supported this view and said in his interview in 1946 that the ammunition supply was adequate. Colonel H. Richards, commander of the Divisional Artillery, told of one officer who was responsible for issuing ammunition that insisted he had authority to do so from headquarters, even though the German tanks were already visible and rapidly approaching at the time.[62]

On June 16 Ritchie paid a visit to the fortress, flying into Tobruk using a captured Fiesler-Störch.[63] There he held a conference with Gott and Klopper. Participants described the conference as hitting an optimistic note, with Klopper confidently undertaking to hold the fort for three months.[64] Klopper and his staff made this undertaking despite some misgivings. It seems that he was confident insofar as the British held El Adem and Belhamed, protecting the southeastern perimeter of the fortress.[65] On the same day, Klopper gave his agreement to a provisional plan drawn up by Johnson to coordinate the artillery, armored force, and infantry as a reaction and counterattack force using a combined battle headquarters. Unfortunately, neither the commander nor his representative of the Army Tank Brigade, nor the commander of the Royal Artillery, bothered to attend the conference earmarked to implement the plans.[66] In an interview conducted by the UWHS after the war, Klopper stated that he was always in favor of a mobile defense rather than a static defense. He suggested to the commanders of the two brigades in the counterattack force—General William H. E. "Strafer" Gott and Major-General Neil Ritchie—that they attack beyond the perimeter while the enemy was forming up so as to disrupt them. Both brigadiers said their troops were quite incapable of making such an attack.[67] It seems Ritchie dissuaded Klopper from conducting a mobile defense as he would have preferred and insisted that he not fight outside the perimeter.[68]

The defenders attended to the physical defenses of the fortress on June 17, which consisted of digging, wiring, mine laying, and reconnoitring in certain areas. Another precious day had passed before they attempted to attend to the vital task of coordinating the reserves to form a mobile combined arms counterattack force. Klopper held another conference on June 18, where he decided that the 32nd Army Tank Brigade and 201st Guards Battalion would form the reserve of the garrison. Klopper agreed to send Colonel Richards, the commander of the artillery, to see Willison about artillery support. It was an arrangement decisively different from that of the first siege. There Morshead placed the counterattack force, consisting of all the armored vehicles, a full infantry brigade, and a regiment of guns with a troop of antitank guns, under the command of Willison. Therefore, rather than create a reserve of combined arms under the orders of one man, Klopper had chosen Johnson's proposal to establish a combined battle headquarters when the need arose.

Klopper and his staff neglected to produce a detailed counterattack plan or organize the defenses on any dynamic basis. The result was a static defense spread evenly along the perimeter, instead of a highly mobile counterattack force that would meet head-on any breach in the perimeter. The arrangements to organize the artillery, infantry, and armor reserve into a combined dynamic counterattack force were inadequate at best and resulted in a piecemeal and uncoordinated application of the reserves to the breach. The counterattack force was fundamental to the effective defense of the fortress. The perimeter defenses, rather than providing an impregnable wall against attack, should have fulfilled the role of an early warning system. They would have revealed the direction of an enemy attack and after that delayed its progress long enough to assemble and unleash a counterattack to reseal the defense. The minefields acted act as a mechanism to delay and then channel the enemy onto the waiting counter-attack forces. The failure to strike back at a penetration with all the forces at hand, promptly, would almost certainly spell the doom of the fortress.

Rommel Attacks Tobruk—June 20, 1942

When it became apparent that the noose was steadily tightening around Tobruk on June 18 and 19, Johnson proposed launching a bold preemptive counterattack against the enemy threat forming up in the El Adem area. This was soon reconsidered and the less bold measure of a concentrated artillery barrage, designed to disperse the enemy gathering in the area, was suggested. The official South African history has singled out this event as the reason for the ammunition rationing, as the artillery exceeded its daily allowance and had difficulty in securing more ammunition. Further conflicting evidence about the situation in the garrison came to light when Morshead passed through Tobruk on June 17 and reported an abundance of ammunition. Sergeant A. N. Goldman of the 2nd Royal Durban Light Infantry talked of vast ammunition dumps.[69] In the end, the artillery barrage seemed to have little effect in diverting the efforts of the *DAK*, who were hell-bent on launching a massive offensive on the fortress of Tobruk.

It is debatable whether the German offensive launched on the morning of June 20 came as a complete surprise to the Eighth Army, or indeed the Tobruk garrison. Right up to the last moment, Klopper believed that Rommel would attack the western sector. This belief differed from the opinion of Willison and Thompson, both of whom were veterans of the first siege.[70] Klopper placed his two best brigades in the western sector and directed his main attention to this point. Klopper gained the impression that the Eighth Army would take care of his southeastern corner and Ritchie instructed him to make certain to hold the western sector.[71] Auchinleck says in his dispatch that once the Axis forces invested Tobruk, an expected attack would closely follow the original and elaborate German plan of the previous November. It called for an attack on Tobruk in the southeast. Ritchie, on realizing this, apparently sent details of this plan by wireless to General Klopper's headquarters. The UWHS considers that Auchinleck's comments are most unfair to Klopper and give a misleading impression, as there was no evidence of when Ritchie signalled this plan to Klopper.[72]

What is certain is that the German maneuver of bypassing the garrison in an eastward drive to the Egyptian border and then leaving a screening force to deal with Eighth Army, while turning the *DAK* 180 degrees to drive westwards to the southeastern perimeter of Tobruk, was a remarkable achievement.[73] This movement took place at night on June 19/20 and required a massive effort of coordination to ensure the assault troops and artillery were ready in their exact jump-off points before the assault. It goes a long way to demonstrate how far ahead the Germans were at this stage in the art of mobile warfare.[74] Rommel's complicated attempt at subterfuge may not have fooled Ritchie. He signalled to Auchinleck on the night of June 19 his belief that the Germans were going to attack Tobruk rather than the frontier. Neither was Auchinleck fooled, and he sent a signal to Eighth Army: "Enemy movement yesterday showed intention launch early attack Tobruk from the East." However, according to German sources, the deception had worked and they took the Tobruk defenders by surprise.[75] The 11th Indian Brigade, manning the specific sector the Germans were to attack, realized after sending out patrols that an attack was imminent. Gooler reported that during the afternoon of June 19 a South African armored car unit commander informed the intelligence section of a concentration of German armor and artillery in the southeast of Tobruk. He pointed out on the maps the exact location where Rommel proposed the final German assault in the previous siege. One of the staff had a copy of a captured German map from that operation and Gooler reported that they could reasonably expect an attack along similar lines.[76]

Dawn broke and the German forces preparing for the attack came into full view of the defenders. The South African Battery commenced fire on the German concentration, and the Germans soon replied in kind with artillery and air attacks, mainly concentrated on strongpoint 63. When the staff informed Klopper of the dawn attack he responded nonchalantly, "The party is on."[77] The German official history describes the attack on June 20 as "a prime example of coordination between the air force and army formations." One can only contrast this feat of combined arms with the unsuccessful counterattack launched a few hours later by the defenders.[78] Eyewitness accounts, including Rommel's, describe how effective the massive air and artillery assault was on the defenses and the morale of the defenders. The air attack consisted of "every single Stuka Kesselring had." Bayerlein describes the air strike as "crushing" both "morally and materially."[79] When the preparatory bombardment finally lifted, the infantry assault troops moved up to the defenses through the lanes cleared in the minefields the night before. Klopper described how the preparatory German aerial and artillery bombardment detonated a good percentage of the defender's mines. The UWHS dismissed this possibility as highly unlikely, yet the Transvaal Scottish Regimental history described the same incident: "The bombs that did not burst harmlessly in the sand thundered in doubled and redoubled explosions as whole chains of mines erupted."[80]

It took the Germans a further two hours to drive a wedge into the defenses, and by 0800 they bridged the antitank ditch, making it possible for the armor to penetrate into the heart of the garrison. When Major Pope, of the 25th Field Regiment, asked the commander of the artillery for support, he received the reply that headquarters were by no means certain that this was the main attack. It was only at 0800 that the defenders allocated reinforcements to this sector.[81] The defenders had put up little resistance to the offensive so far and the Germans were surprised at how weak the initial resistance was, with perimeter strongpoints R58 to R69 falling into German hands in quick succession in the zone of attack. The poor defensive efforts cannot be put down to the element of surprise, as Anderson of the 11th Indian Brigade had anticipated the German attack and promptly threw his reserve company and platoon into the fray.[82]

In the meantime, Johnson of the 201st Guards Brigade had not been idle. He attempted to set up a combined headquarters at Kings Cross in accordance with the arrangements agreed to for a counterattack. At this crucial moment, Willison declined to leave his headquarters, while Johnson busied himself with setting up headquarters and the appropriate communications. The South African official history suggests Willison's hesitancy in leaving his headquarters was because Klopper wanted his senior tank officer to be close to him. It spelled doom for any chance of a combined operation before it had even started.[83] Klopper described Willison at this point in the battle as a defeated man, although Klopper did not realize this at the time.[84] He now intervened and issued orders for Willison to take command of a combined force and launch a counterattack in cooperation with the Indian Brigade. Klopper's belated decision was a fatally flawed one, as the formation under Willison was not part of the plan agreed to at the conference beforehand. All had agreed to set up a joint headquarters, after which the brigade commanders would decide the composition and delivery of the counterattack.[85] Anderson sent a liaison officer to the combined headquarters at Kings Cross at 0700 in anticipation of the arrival of Willison and the 32nd Army Tank Brigade. At 0745 the artillery of the 25th Field Regiment opened fire, holding out until then so as not to disclose their position, which would have compromised their antitank role if revealed too early.[86] Speed, at this point, was of the essence. The defenders needed to throw the tanks into the fray before the Germans had a chance to set up their antitank defenses. The crucial objective should have been to seal off the attack and immediately throw the German offensive back to its start lines. It was up to the defenders to muster a significant amount of the heavy armored infantry tanks to meet the attack on almost equal numerical terms.[87]

Willison ordered Lieutenant-Colonel B. Reeves of the 4th Royal Tank Regiment, the closest tank regiment near the action, to send his battalion against the German penetration at 0800. In an inexplicable display of sluggishness, the two squadrons of tanks of the 4th Royal Tank Regiment arrived at Kings Cross at 0930. The UWHS draft narrative identifies the failure of 32nd Tank Brigade to arrive on time as being the fundamental cause of the failure of the counterattack and the single most important cause of the fall of Tobruk. The narrative uses strong language such as "since Longstreet marked time at Gettysburg, no such inexplicable delay has occurred in military history."[88] An opportunity to marry up with the infantry component of the counterattack force was lost when Reeves, on receiving a party of officers from the Coldstream Guards, denied all knowledge of, or responsibility for, cooperation with any infantry force. The Coldstream Guards received no instructions from headquarters, and as a result stayed put while the group of liaison officers made their way to Kings Cross and languished there.[89] At the insistence of Anderson, who was growing more desperate as his situation deteriorated, the Coldstream Guards were ordered forward to Kings Cross to join their officers at 1000. Upon arrival they remained there, never forming part of an essential combined arms counterattack reserve. They failed to leave the Kings Cross area and counterattack on the insistence of their commander Johnson, who would only commit them to exploit the successes gained or to make good any ground recovered by the tanks. The tanks failing in this impossible endeavor ensured that the infantry never ventured forth.[90]

Two and a half hours had now elapsed since Klopper ordered Willison to send his tanks into the fray. Adding to the general tardiness of the operation thus far, Reeves proceeded to commit his tanks to the battle without bothering to either liaise with the headquarters of the Indian Brigade or with the combined headquarters. According to an eyewitness report by Major Morris, the commander of 2nd SA Field Battery, they did not even see the tanks fire as they moved within 500 yards of the enemy tanks. The Germans put them out of action one at a time, the whole affair being over in less than fifteen minutes.[91] The artillery neglected to come in at the crucial early stage of the attack and the *DAK* reported that the fire of the Allied artillery, which up to then had been essentially weak and ineffective, noticeably increased after 0850.[92]

The picture on the German side looked decidedly different, with Rommel leading the penetrating forces from the front and General Walther Nehring (1892–1983) not far behind in the advance headquarters of the 15 *Panzer*-Division.[93] The Germans overran the Mahrattas headquarters and eliminated a troop of South African artillery at 1000. At the same time, the 4th Royal Tank Regiment made slow progress along the Bardia road and arrived in the inner minefield gap. The 7th Royal Tank Regiment was ordered to form up to the west of Kings Cross. Their commander, Lieutenant-Colonel Foote, decided to deploy his regiment to the right of 4th Royal Tank Regiment at L Gap after conferring with

Reeves, thereby forming a defensive line behind the inner minefield. It is here that the two tank regiments, unsupported by infantry and anti-tank weapons, began to take steady losses. With the greater part of their strength destroyed for little profit, the survivors had little choice but to withdraw to Kings Cross. Their commander, Reeves, bumped into the immobile Coldstream Guards at 1300 and reported that the enemy had all but destroyed his command and all that remained were six tanks.[94] It is worth keeping in mind that the Germans received thirty British tanks in good operating condition when the headquarters of the 32nd Tank Brigade surrendered the following morning.[95]

Information was slow to reach Fortress Command and they lacked an understanding of the extent of the perimeter breach. Klopper was dependent on 11th Indian Brigade for all his information and they, in turn, were reliant on the Mahrattas. Unfortunately, the 11th Indian Brigade was struggling to gain a clear picture of what was happening on the ground, as the initial German bombardment had wrecked communications in the sector. The sole remaining source of information, after the Mahrattas destroyed the brigade's wireless sets at 1000 before the Germans overran them, fell on the Forward Observation Officer of the 2nd South African Field Battery. A further cloud in the descending fog of war was that the intermittent communication system lagged substantially behind the rapidly developing events at the front. The lack of real-time knowledge lulled the garrison headquarters into a false sense of security. As far as Klopper was concerned, he ordered the counterattack in good time and the Indian Brigade reported that the situation was in hand. Furthermore, headquarters took Willison's noncommunication as an indicator that all was well.[96]

At 1100, in a reversal of mood and now clearly perplexed, Klopper complained that he "was completely in the dark" as to what the situation was, and he proposed that he proceed personally to Kings Cross to assess the situation for himself. He allowed Bastin and his chief of staff, Lieutenant-Colonel Kriek, to dissuade him from this wise course of action. They advised him that his correct place was at headquarters.[97] Between 1300 and 1400, Major Wessel's AA position was overrun, and he was captured and taken to King's Cross, where he saw Rommel standing on the edge of the escarpment watching the battle. He had a Mercedes staff car and an armored car with him.[98] At 1300, as Klopper was finishing lunch, the last vestiges of complacency were shattered as news of the impending disaster reached Fortress Headquarters. Willison reported the destruction of 4th Tank Regiment to Klopper, and at 1440 reports came in that the enemy had penetrated the inner minefield. At 1525 the defenders reported that sixty enemy tanks had penetrated the inner defenses and were approaching Kings Cross, which had become effectively indefensible. Rommel reached Kings Cross at about this time in his Mercedes with field glasses in hand, before most of his army had arrived, and busied himself coordinating the attack while cajoling his forces to greater efforts.[99] The contrast could not be starker between Rommel, at the head of his troops and in the thick of battle, and Klopper, safely ensconced some miles away in his headquarters. Willison reported in detail the destruction of his command, consisting of 7th and 4th Royal Tank Regiments, somewhere between 1500 and 1600, thereby signalling the demise of the entire armored reserve force. The Germans, after a lightning assault, had defeated the British armor, overrun the Indian Brigade as well as the 25th Field Regiment, and were in possession of Kings Cross. Rommel was in an excellent position to deliver the final blow to the fortress.

Klopper, after he learned of the proximity of the German offensive to Kings Cross and the destruction of 4th Royal Tank Regiment together with the greater part of his reserve force, was spurred on to organize a new defensive line to protect the crossroads at Pilastrino, running roughly along the El Adem road. He ordered a company each to detach from the 4th and 6th SAI Brigades to form a counterattack force near the new line.[100] Once Kings Cross fell to the Germans, the defenses of the Tobruk Fortress became fragmented and uncoordinated, with units fighting where they stood and constituting individual actions, uncoordinated and without central direction from Fortress Headquarters. It was a simple matter for the Germans to proceed from Kings Cross virtually unopposed and enter the harbor of Tobruk at nightfall. The Fortress Headquarters, in the meantime, destroyed wireless sets and moved office to the headquarters of 6th SAI Brigade. The destruction of the headquarter's equipment at 1600 was premature and unfortunate, as the Germans bypassed the position and chose to instead move on supply dumps in the vicinity. The destruction of the signals equipment left most formations unaware that the headquarters had relocated to 6th Brigade.[101]

A pall of smoke rose into the sky from Tobruk harbor, signalling the partial and unofficial demolition of the huge stockpile of supplies and vehicles. The capture of Tobruk was achieved with such speed that it left very little time for official orders to be given to destroy supplies and prevent them falling into German hands. All the dumps had been prepared for demolition should the unlikely eventuality arise, and Major Grant, in charge of the demolition team, felt the pressure of the Germans, who were only 200 yards away from his supply dump. He and his staff sat in his office for the entire night waiting vainly for an instruction that never came. He decided not destroy the dumps on his own responsibility as he realized there would be many prisoners who would require provisions.[102]

The Breakout That Never Happened

By nightfall the German forces were in possession of Tobruk and a considerable salient in the eastern half of the fortress. The two SAI brigades remained unscathed and unaffected by the day's events. Klopper was able to reestablish contact with the Eighth Army at 2000, and he reported the desperate plight of his forces and requested permission to break out that night. He sought clarity as to whether the promised relieving force was about to counterattack the enemy. Brigadier Whiteley, standing in for Ritchie who was away with XXX Corps, gave his permission for a breakout by signalling: "Come out tomorrow night preferably if not tonight." He repeated at the end of his transmission "Tomorrow night preferred." One knows not whether Whiteley appreciated the extent of the German successes or the dire straits the remaining garrison found itself in in the aftermath of a decisive German victory. Klopper was dissatisfied with the inconclusive conversation with Whiteley and requested his signaller to maintain contact with Eighth Army and try to locate General Ritchie. Auchinleck, in a telegram to Smuts, stressed that Klopper received immediate permission from Ritchie for a breakout. Auchinleck repeated this in his dispatch, and after the war this became a point of major contention for Klopper.[103]

One has to view the possibilities of a successful breakout against the near impossibility of complete encirclement under desert conditions. The Free French were able to break out of Bir Hakim despite vastly superior forces encircling them. The 50th Division was able to break out successfully although encircled from the west by the Italians and to the east by the Germans. They did this by concentrating their forces at the breakthrough point, and they then gained the freedom of the open desert. The victorious Germans within the Tobruk perimeter were exhausted, having been on the offensive since May 26, and they were in no condition to stop a concerted effort by the South Africans. The defenders at Tobruk, being mobile unlike their British counterparts, could have quickly mustered numerical superiority at any point of the encirclement had they chosen to do so. The reason that they were unable to do so can be put down to poor leadership and poor planning, and a paralysis in the face of an enemy that had demoralized the numerically superior defenders.[104] The will to escape had gone up in the smoke that now engulfed Tobruk.

Klopper issued a warning order for a breakout at 2200 in the aftermath of a series of informal discussions with several battalion commanders. An opposing plan, mainly propagated by Brigadier Hayton and the group leader of 4th Brigade, suggested forming a redoubt in the southwest corner of the fortress. Hayton reasoned that the brigade had lost most of its transport, which precluded a breakout.[105] General Klopper seemed to be impressed with Hayton's proposal for a last stand, and he cried out, "My God Alec, we'll fight."[106] The UWHS describes this as *pis aller* (last resort), with there being little hope of the defenders being able to hold out for longer than a day. At least this final act of defiance would satisfy some quarters by doing something to save honor.[107] In a letter to Captain Fennin, Agar-Hamilton gives a rare insight into his understanding of the effects the 4th Brigade proposal had on Klopper. The 4th Brigade effectively challenged the accepted policy to break out and this threw Klopper off balance, leading him to a course of action he did not wholly trust.[108] Within one hour of Klopper accepting the 4th Brigade proposal, they then told him that it was impractical to resist. Klopper, not being able to get ahold of Ritchie and seemingly swayed by the promise of a relieving force, together with what seemed to be a request by Whiteley to hold on for one more day, countermanded the breakout order. Preparations began for a last stand based on the 4th Brigade proposal. Klopper's last words on the conference breaking up were, "All right gentlemen, go and fight on the lines suggested by Brigadier Hayton."[109]

The proponents of the breakout group put forward a reasonable argument that a last-minute stand would achieve far less than bringing out vital equipment and personnel that the Eighth Army could use in battles to come. Captain D. G. Fannin, intelligence officer of the 4th SA Brigade, provides further insight in a letter he sent to the UWHS on

October 18, 1949. On his arrival at 6th Brigade Headquarters that night there was no accepted policy, but rather a collection of "harassed individuals" who had before them a message from Commander Eighth Army saying "Break out preferably tomorrow night." According to Fannin, no one present had any "stomach for a fight" except for Brigadier Hayton of 4th South African Infantry Brigade. Hayton, according to Fannin, believed that the garrison had not yet dispensed of its burden to stand and fight. Fannin believes that Hayton converted Klopper to his point of view, only to be persuaded to surrender by his Chief of Staff and Signals Officer once Hayton had departed.[110]

In the meantime, Ritchie, who had returned to his headquarters at 0330, signalled detailed instructions approving a breakout. There is considerable debate as to whether Klopper received permission to break out from Ritchie. On Ritchie's evidence, in his statement to Auchinleck read into evidence at the Court of Enquiry, he did give permission. The UWHS found conclusive proof that Ritchie granted permission for a breakout. The evidence is a signal sent by Ritchie to Auchinleck at 2200 on June 20, 1942, stating that "He (Klopper) requests authority to fight his way out as apparently he feels he cannot hold out. I have authorised him to do so." It is uncertain in what form and couched in what terms Klopper finally received permission to break out. On Klopper's evidence, given to the UWHS on October 22, 1945, he states, "It was quite apparent to me that there were no relief troops within striking distance of the forces [*sic*; he meant *fortress*]." He goes on to say, "I asked permission to try and fight my way out. The reply was to the effect that it was not advisable or desirable that I should withdraw at that stage but I had to wait until the following evening."[111]

In a curious twist, Hayton returned to his headquarters at 0330 and met with Lieutenant-Colonel Blake of the Blake group, who vigorously denounced the absurdity of the defensive plan proposed by Hayton. Hayton then telephoned Klopper to tell him that his battalion commanders did not wish to fight. They also cited as a further reason that there was not enough time to set up effective defenses because the conference at Kloppers HQ had gone on until the early hours of the morning.[112] Klopper insisted that this change of heart would put him in "a hell of a jam" and convinced the commanders once again to resist. However, soon after speaking to Hayton again Klopper had yet another change of heart, believing that a stand was futile in that the Eighth Army would gain no advantage while incurring many casualties.[113] The endless vacillations at the various levels of command had robbed the defenders of formulating any decisive gesture.

At 0630, after Klopper famously signalled Ritchie that he was "doing the worst," he sent a *parlementaire* to the Germans to offer capitulation. An anxious Ritchie inquired as to whether he managed to destroy the petrol and water installations. Klopper answered in the affirmative, which was partly true in the current positions held but not the case in the areas already under German control. At 0745 the German officers tasked with receiving the surrender arrived at headquarters, and with the last wireless set destroyed 10,722 South Africans of a garrison totalling 33,000 marched into captivity. Lieutenant Goldman described the ordeal, and the confusion and disbelief on receiving the news of surrender.

> My own feelings when I heard the news were very indicative of what everyone else felt. When the battalion HQ heard of the surrender the orderly room sergeant called me into his dugout and, not looking particularly glum, said: "They have surrendered." My first feeling was one of elation, but then I thought, why should they (the Germans) surrender when they have got three-quarters of Tobruk? The true position then dawned on me. "They" referred to our command. I was astounded and flabbergasted. I had not for a moment thought that we would surrender. It seems fantastic. We had not fired a shot.[114]

Those captured included one general and seven brigadiers, as well as what the UWHS describes as large deposits of arms, munitions, materials, and foodstuffs. Klopper said that his orders were for the troops to surrender on fronts where the Germans were attacking, but every facility should be given to those men who wished to escape. He said it was a great shock to him that so few men attempted to escape.[115] On the other hand, in a volte-face, he deplored the conduct of the Coldstream Guards in passing out of the perimeter of Tobruk at 1600 on June 20, without orders and authority, taking with them some of the precious antitank guns.[116] A great bounty fell into German hands consisting of fuel, foodstuffs, clothing, ammunition, and arms, including thirty undamaged tanks.[117]

The Surrender of Tobruk—An Avoidable Blunder or an Inevitable Disaster?

The seeds of incompetence leading to the surrender of Tobruk on June 20, 1942, were sown at the strategic, operational, and tactical levels of war. The British made a firm strategic decision, many months prior to Gazala, that it was not in the Eighth Army's best strategic interests to hold the fortress for the second time, if it were once again threatened with encirclement. They felt that the price paid for the successful defense of Tobruk in 1941 was too high in regard to precious naval and air assets. Auchinleck reversed this firm and sound strategic decision at the eleventh hour. There were two reasons for his sudden change of heart. First, he succumbed to immense political pressure brought to bear upon him. He allowed Churchill's persistent and unwavering insistence that the Eighth Army defend Tobruk to sway him from his sound military assessment. The political repercussions of abandoning Tobruk could never approximate attempting to hold onto it and then surrendering. There was a failure to measure the enormous ramifications the surrender would have on the South Africans and Smuts's difficult tenure in the face of Afrikaner nationalism. Second, Auchinleck did not grasp the extent of the Eighth Army's defeat at Gazala and incorrectly believed that there was enough residual strength remaining to man a defensive line incorporating Tobruk, thereby avoiding encirclement. Just as Auchinleck seemed to grasp the gravity of the situation, the political considerations took precedence over sound military sense.

The final verdict of the Court of Enquiry into the fall of Tobruk exonerates Klopper, stating "It is questionable whether even the most experienced commander with a highly trained staff could have grappled with the problems in the time available." It goes on to say, "The fact that Tobruk fell must undoubtedly be attributed to the eleventh-hour reversal of policy leading to the decision to hold the fortress."[118] One can safely discard the question of whether the fortress could have been successfully defended by a more experienced leader group in the face of a rampant *DAK*, which had all but destroyed the Eighth Army. One can accept the verdict of the court at face value. On the strategic level, Tobruk was destined to fall in the face of overwhelming odds.

The inevitability of Tobruk's swift capture was far less certain when viewed from the operational and tactical level of war. Here, the Court of Enquiry has less to say. Klopper could have done more at the operational and tactical level. Through vigorous and forceful leadership, he could have made better use of the considerable manpower and equipment available to the defenders of Tobruk. The defenders could have extracted a far higher price from the Germans, whose final casualties were light by all accounts.[119] The relatively small number of South Africans killed in action on June 20/21 reflects the low intensity of the defense.[120] Much has been made of the appalling state of the perimeter defenses at Tobruk, especially in comparison to the first siege. Their poor state of repair, a fact disputed by some of the witnesses, was not fundamental to the successful defense of Tobruk. The survival of the fortress depended on the defenders mounting a quick and effective mobile counterattack with all available reserves. It had to be in a coordinated and combined manner, delivered once the Germans breached the perimeter and the direction of their attack was determined. The fixed defenses on the perimeter were not strong enough in the first or second siege to withstand a determined assault. The South Africans planted the seeds of tactical failure during the conferences before the German offensive. They neglected to develop an adequate plan of action. Nor was a command structure, conducive to combined operations, set in place. Arguments exist that, although the garrison possessed formidable artillery assets, these were not homogenous and came from a number of different units. Klopper failed to centralize command of the artillery, which resulted in spreading the guns among the brigades. The same applied to the antitank weapons, of which there were a significant amount. Considerable numbers included the new powerful 6-pounders and some 3.5 inch antiaircraft guns, both devastating in the antitank role. A proactive leader would have been able to concentrate these instead of fragment them, and bring them to bear in a powerful capability to counterattack.

Klopper was the master of fragmentation rather than concentration at the tactical level. When he finally ordered a counterattack it differed substantially from that agreed on at the conference and subordinates delivered it piecemeal and without support. Failure to use a combined arms approach, whereby powerful artillery, tank, and infantry reserves cooperated in a mutually supporting combined force, compromised the effectiveness of the counterattack. Klopper failed to concentrate his reserves by placing them under the command of one person, which was at variance with accepted practices of sound command. The counterattack broke down almost immediately, with the armor attacking unsupported and in piecemeal fashion—by now an unfortunate trademark of the Eighth Army. The defenders delivered the counterattack hopelessly late and it only developed some two and a half hours after Klopper ordered it. Tardiness and lack of preparation allowed the Germans a good deal of time to establish themselves in the territory they had occupied. There was a reasonable chance, given the near parity of the forces, that the defenders could have survived longer and been able to extract much higher casualties from the Germans. An effective counterattack might have slowed the pace and tempo of Rommel's assault sufficiently to allow time for a relieving force from the east to bring relief.

Once the German offensive had developed and the situation on the ground appeared confused at divisional headquarters, it was incumbent on Klopper to go to Kings Cross to assess the situation and perhaps temporarily take command of the counterforce to ensure coordination and effectiveness. He too readily allowed those at headquarters to persuade him to stay put. It is perhaps unfair to compare Klopper to his famous adversary, who made a habit of leading from the front, but there comes a time in a battle when the commander must descend and deal with the crisis hands-on. On this point, it would seem that Klopper would concur, and in a postwar interview, he expressed regret that he did not go to Kings Cross himself to organize the counterattack, having been "prevented" from doing so by Colonel Bastin.[121] If ever a situation called for personal intervention, it was when Klopper felt the urge to "go and see for himself," and he should have given into that urge.

There is little doubt that the top leadership of the garrison was inexperienced and unsuited for the task at hand. Klopper had very little combat experience in a leadership role, having spent the major part of his active service in a staff and administrative position. His chief of staff was in a similar situation, being new on the job and hopelessly out of his depth. When one looks at the brigade commanders, especially those involved in the fighting on June 20, there was no lack of experience, some of the commanders having been present in the previous siege. The problem was that Klopper was unable or incapable to stamp his authority and take charge of those subordinate to him and act in a decisive manner. Klopper complained bitterly that orders from higher command were never definite, and that in this ambiguous situation he never fully grasped what he was supposed to do, or what troops were under his command, and that as a result, he and his staff never got any rest.[122] It was a similar situation to that faced by Ritchie, who was also inexperienced compared to those he commanded.

Lack of leadership and indecisiveness resulted in the bulk of the vehicles, ammunition, and stores falling into German hands when it was vital the defenders destroy them. A competent plan of action would have triggered the demolition and destruction of equipment and stores so as to deny them to the Germans, who were operating on a logistic shoestring. This windfall provided Rommel with the logistic impetus to thrust his *DAK* well beyond the Egyptian border right up to the approaches of El Alamein.

The strategic fait accompli placed Klopper in an unfortunate position not entirely of his making, but faced with this, he had a number of areas where he was obliged to perform. When he decided to defend the fortress of Tobruk, a task that he accepted with some confidence, he failed to set about the task, neither taking command effectively nor developing a sound defensive plan. He neglected to create a mobile reaction force, and when the Germans launched their offensive he failed to launch an effective counterattack. Once the Axis breached the perimeter the battle was lost. Once his counterattack force lay in tatters and a successful defense vanished, he failed to demolish and destroy the abundance of material stockpiled and coveted by the Germans. Having failed to deny vital supplies to the Germans, he then vacillated once more and failed to evacuate the garrison on the evening of June 20, allowing his entire force to walk into humiliating captivity. There was a shortage of transport due to the Germans capturing a good deal of it during the day. Klopper blamed this situation on the lack of initiative of those in charge of the corps transport who destroyed or allowed the Germans to capture the vehicles instead of driving them off to a safer place.[123] However, even in this circumstance, a good proportion of the garrison could have gotten away, while the remainder with no transport could have fought a rearguard action. Agar-Hamilton offers his opinion in one of his letters:

> All troops who could possibly be moved should have been taken out of the perimeter, with every scrap of artillery and equipment they

> could take with them. At least one third would have had a reasonable chance of getting through. The experience of 50th Division, the Free French, 29 Indian Brigade and Mersa Matruh shows it might well have been more. The remainder should have been thrown suddenly and vigorously in a night attack against the German leaguers inside the fortress. We know now that the Germans were so exhausted that they might quite easily have been thrown off their balance and driven out in confusion. In that case 2nd South African Division would have made an immense reputation.[124]

In mitigation, there is evidence that Klopper believed that the Eighth Army was sending a fighting column to relieve Tobruk. There is evidence of his repeated request for information on the progress of the relief column during June 20. His belief that the British would rescue him via a counterattack was in terms of XIII Corps Operational Order No. 36, dated June 16, 1942, in which it was stated that if Belhamed fell a combined operation would be undertaken to reopen the line of communication with Tobruk.[125] The possibility of the arrival of a relieving force may have influenced Klopper's decision not to break out on the night of June 20, 1942. It is interesting that Klopper does not mention the relieving force in his interview with Turner. He confirms receiving permission to break out at midnight on June 20, and he conferred with his brigadiers until 0100. He proposed a breakout directly through the enemy lines through the eastern sector as he considered that the day's battle must have exhausted them and the darkness would aid the confusion. The brigade commanders, however, were opposed to any attempt to break out. He finally accepted the view that there was insufficient transport to make the attempt.[126]

History found Klopper lacking when the final moments dawned and fate presented him with the last opportunity to redeem himself from what was becoming a massive military disaster. He lost precious time, in a demonstration of weak leadership, when he argued with his subordinates over the best course of action to take. The bleak situation left Klopper with two desperate choices: to stay put and fight to the last to save honor, or to break out so as to prevent the Germans from capturing the entire compliment of the garrison. In a final failure, due to endless vacillation and changing of heart, he found a third option that resulted in the ignominious surrender of the entire garrison.

Chapter 8

El Alamein: South Africa's Swan Song in Africa

We were told that Eighth Army would stand and fight on the Alamein line, which ran from the sea to where the Taqa plateau overlooked the impassable Qattara depression, a distance of only twenty miles. There was no fear of being outflanked. We heard that 1 South African Division under Dan Pienaar was holding the Alamein Box in the north and that an Indian brigade was in the Deir el Shein Box with 50 Division Group in a near position. Then came 2 N. Z. Division and south of us on the Taqa plateau was another Indian brigade. The armour was in support and the leading Australian brigade from Syria had arrived at Amiriya. In addition there were a number of "Jock" columns, at this time called "Monthly" columns, between us and the plateau. We made contact with "June," "July," and "August." They were each composed of a battery of 25-pounders and a company of motorized infantry and, acting independently as they usually did, had little fighting and no stopping value whatever. Nor could we ever find out where they were, which would have been annoying if they had been serious fighting troops. The whole position looked weak but it was reasonable to suppose that the enemy was getting weary and he was certainly at the end of a terrific line of supply.[1]

It was the President of the United States, Franklin Delano Roosevelt (1882–1945) who broke the news of the surrender of Tobruk to an incredulous Winston Churchill. Field-Marshal Lord Alanbrooke (1883–1963), Chief of the Imperial General Staff, who accompanied Churchill on their visit to the United States, stated in his diary that neither he nor Churchill contemplated such an eventuality. He described it as a staggering blow.[2] In his memoirs, Churchill, perhaps expressing his true feelings about this grievous moment, described the surrender as a disgrace.[3] Back in London dissatisfaction as to the conduct of the war was growing in the House of Commons and Churchill faced a motion of no confidence. The daily press was vociferous in its criticism of the surrender of Tobruk, calling for an inquiry into the conduct of operations in the Middle East, describing events there as a major and humiliating disaster, and drawing parallels to the first successful defense of Tobruk.[4] The fall of Tobruk was also a serious matter in South Africa and the loss of so many South Africans was a serious political blow to Smuts. Lord Harlech (1885–1964), the High Commissioner to South Africa from 1941 to 1944, offered his impressions on the impact of the surrender of Tobruk after a visit to Smuts. He described the fall of Tobruk and the surrender of the South African 2nd Division as "a grievous blow" to the South African leader, who anticipated as a result "widespread political repercussions" in the Union.[5]

Reverberations of the ignominious defeat caused acute embarrassment to the prime ministers of South Africa and the United Kingdom. The disaster was grist for the mill to those South Africans growing increasingly disaffected with the war effort, and news such as this placed further strain on an already tense home front. Churchill fended off a motion of no confidence put forward by disgruntled MPs who had no faith in the central direction of the war, after the reverses in Greece and the fall of Singapore. The loss of Tobruk, greeted with general disbelief bordering on outrage, placed the Allied positions in North Africa in a perilous situation. On the other side of the hill, Germany presented the conqueror of Tobruk, *Generaloberst* Erwin Rommel, with his Field Marshal's baton. The fall of Tobruk was a grievous blow, earning its place in history as the largest military reversal suffered by South Africa. The magnitude of the disaster surpassed the annihilation of the 5th Brigade at Sidi Rezegh and even the surrender at Paardeburg in 1900, where Boer General Piet Cronjé capitulated with some 4,019 men. Even Delville Wood in the First World War, where the South African 1st Brigade suffered huge casualties in what historians describe as the bloodiest battle of 1916, could not match the scale of the catastrophe.[6]

The South Africans smarted under an undercurrent that existed in some quarters that Klopper had given up too early without putting up a real fight. Everyone made the inevitable comparisons to the first siege, during which the Australians held out against huge odds for 244 days by employing a skilled and resourceful defense. Accusations against Klopper even went so far as to accuse him unfairly of being a traitor and an enemy sympathizer. Other accusations were even more bizarre and lacked any substance.

> There were rumours of high-ranking officers on Klopper's staff surrendering to Rommel blind drunk, of native African troops pillaging the rum stores and being shot out of hand by their captors, and of Company commanders deserting their men. . . .[7]

Klopper felt the wrath of the men he surrendered with and many felt that he had an obligation to break out of the siege instead of meekly offering the whole division up for surrender. Bitterness was rife among the troops who had surrendered with Klopper, and many believed that he had betrayed them. Their hostility was manifest when, shortly after arriving at the Derna POW camp, Klopper attempted to address the prisoners but they greeted him with "boos and hisses." Klopper retreated without saying one word.[8]

> To their everlasting indignation, the flower of South Africa's volunteer army, many of whom had distinguished themselves in action in Abyssinia during the capture of Addis Ababa from the Italians and, more recently, at the capture of Bardia and in the Gazala line in the Libyan desert, now found themselves inexplicably ordered to lay down their arms at Tobruk without, in most cases, being allowed to fire a shot. Their previous good record made this a particularly bitter pill for them to swallow—the taste of which was bound to linger, despite the subsequent distinction with which their more fortunate compatriots fought at El Alamein and then in the battles of the fierce and protracted campaign in Italy.[9]

While there was an undercurrent of wariness in certain quarters regarding South Africa's military ability, the reverse was certainly also true. Certain South African sectors, among whom the most outspoken was Dan Pienaar, believed that an inept and callous British High Command had needlessly sacrificed the South Africans at Sidi Rezegh and Tobruk. After suffering a sequence of setbacks, Pienaar had little faith left in British generalship. His trepidation for British military skills was not without foundation, and in particular, Dorman-Smith backed up his opinion that the British had misused the South Africans. The Eighth Army often confined the South Africans to a static role when the British tank brigades could have better utilized their inherent abilities at mobile warfare in their support.[10] One must consider South Africa's conduct in the battles of Alamein against the backdrop of the general mutual distrust between Pienaar and the British commanders and the disastrous loss of the South African 5th Brigade and 2nd Division.

What becomes apparent in the desert war narrative is that as inept as the British seemed to be at the operational level of war, so too were the Germans at the strategic level. What one may construe as a sweeping statement is that the British managed to get the strategic decisions right most of the time and the Germans, on the flip side, got them wrong. Soon after the fall of Tobruk, Rommel pressed his superiors to allow him to pursue what he felt was a beaten Eighth Army. The original plan, of sounder strategic thought, was to halt the Axis forces on the frontier after the fall of Tobruk and launch an airborne and seaborne operation to seize the strategic island of Malta. Rommel, who had the ear of Hitler, was able to persuade his superiors to delay the invasion of Malta and instead pursue a further advance into Africa with the final aim of capturing Cairo and the entire Middle East. It was a major strategic blunder that had little hope of success as the Eighth Army fell back on unlimited resources while the Axis stretched their supply lines beyond their limits. Every mile that Rommel drove closer to Cairo with his exhausted and depleted army meant subjecting his forces to increased Allied air superiority and fresh troops arriving from the Middle East and Cape Town. Although his daring escapades against a superior but demoralized opponent met with initial success and his brilliance carried his waning army into the heart of Egypt, the Eighth Army stopped him well short of his target, the Nile.

The German official history offers another enlightening line of thought on the driving force behind Rommel's inexorable penchant for pushing forward, rather than adopting a defensive posture, even when his armies were hopelessly depleted and faced overwhelming numerical odds. Rommel was merely employing the universal military precept, bolstered by traditional German doctrine, that the numerically weaker army can offset its disadvantage using "surprise, skillful handling, well-coordinated and flexible leadership, good intelligence, and superior equipment." A skillfully conducted offensive offers a greater prospect of success than a static defense, which makes a greater demand on manpower, is subject to heavier losses, and forgoes the initiative. Rommel had found in the British and the desert terrain an ideal adversary and idyllic battlefield conditions, respectively. British inability to conduct combined arms warfare at a concentrated level and the suitability of the desert to mobile operations gave Rommel enough advantage to overcome his numerical and eventual qualitative inferiority. However, Rommel's reliance on aggressive maneuver warfare to overcome his weakness placed him in a trap of always having to attack, and attack with success or face certain destruction. His success in operating with the minimum against all odds proved to be his undoing, as the German high command became convinced that he could manage with the minimum.[11]

Pienaar's Long Retreat from the Gazala Line, June 14–21

Pienaar was decidedly jittery and on the verge of insisting on retreat when Ritchie ordered the 1st South African and 50th Divisions to withdraw from the Gazala line on June 14.[12] At first, there was uncertainty as to where the 1st Division would retreat. The British initially expected that Pienaar and his men would man a new line proposed by Auchinleck running through Acroma, El Adem, and Bir El Gubi. However, this did not transpire, as the South African 1st Division and the 50th Division were well to the east of Tobruk by June 15. Auchinleck envisaged that the two divisions would be available to hold the new line that he proposed. He intended to make only a limited withdrawal from Gazala and then fight a battle with the entire Eighth Army on the El Adem line, while building up his strength some eighty miles back on the Egyptian frontier.[13] It was not to be, as the South Africans and other British formations made their way to the Egyptian frontier in accordance with Ritchie's and not Auchinleck's plan.

Pienaar joined the "Gazala Gallop" and executed a skillful withdrawal from the Gazala vicinity under conditions that were fraught with danger. Pienaar had escaped Rommel's clutches by the narrowest of margins. The Germans reached the sea just after daylight and cut off part of the South African rearguard. Pienaar laid the blame squarely on the 4th and 8th Royal Tank Regiments, who were supposed to have stayed on the escarpment and cover the South African's withdrawal. However, they arrived in Tobruk a full two hours before the South Africans. Pienaar claimed that the 1st Armoured Division had deserted him.[14] Ritchie issued a signal congratulating Pienaar on "a magnificent achievement of a most difficult operation."[15] The coastal town of Sollum in the north anchored the new line of defense on the frontier, which stretched southward into the desert together as a series of defensive boxes linked by a chain of minefields. Situated at the southernmost point of the defensive line was the "Kennels" defensive box. The defensive setup was not unlike the system adopted at Gazala, and like Bir Hakim, the Kennels "protected nothing but sand and it too hung like a rather less ripe pear on a rather longer stalk."[16] The frontier defensive system depended on a strong mobile armored force with the ability to counterattack enemy advances and lend support to the defensive boxes. Mobile forces were also essential to protect the open left flank of the frontier position, which bordered miles of empty desert and was vulnerable to an enemy outflanking maneuver. The problem at hand was that the British did not possess a cohesive mobile force after Rommel viciously mauled their tank brigades in the preceding weeks.

Pienaar was beginning to show signs of strain, and he voiced his objection and frustration with the British and their handling of the retreat with more frequency. It was in this atmosphere of discontent that the British informed Pienaar that they were placing the command of his 1st and 2nd Brigades under the 10th Indian Division. It effectively stripped Pienaar of his command and he saw it as nothing less than a spiteful move by Norrie calculated to destroy the morale and fighting unity of the South African Division. Pienaar sought and gained a reversal of this decision when Norrie capitulated in the face of his threats to go to the highest echelon of command. This incident was not the first or the last in a series of internecine battles that plagued the British–South African operational relationship.[17]

On June 17, the 1st South African Division occupied the Kennels and Pienaar flew off to meet Ritchie, who tasked him, together with Ramsden and his 50th Division, to form a mobile striking element. The striking element would consist of four brigades and artillery that would operate in the El Adem area with the object of harassing the enemy investing Tobruk. Ritchie cancelled this adventure the next day in the wake of the drubbing received by the 4th Armoured Brigade at Sidi Rezegh and the ambush of the 20th Indian Division at Belhamed on June 17. Pienaar continued to demonstrate his spirit of sullen uncooperativeness. He flatly refused a British request on June 18 to provide a company of troops and light antiaircraft guns to man a nearby airfield essential in the defense of Tobruk. He only reversed this refusal on the insistence by the XXX Corps commander. Ritchie's objective of harassing the enemy between the frontier and Tobruk while rebuilding his forces was proving to be near impossible, and after consultation with Auchinleck, it was decided to hand over the frontier duties to XIII Corps while XXX Corps took over the mobile strike element. On June 18, Ritchie assigned Pienaar and his 1st Division the tasks of holding the Kennels, observing the enemy up to 90 miles west of the Kennels, and guarding the two gaps in the frontier wire 20 miles from the Kennels.[18]

Pienaar sent out a signal to XIII Corps that effectively stated that he was unable to secure the Kennels position with his existing resources. One cannot construe this signal, from a divisional commander to his corps, as anything less than deliberate insubordination. Before Corps Headquarters registered the full impact of the signal, the situation at Tobruk became irretrievable, making the defense of the frontier, without a strong mobile force, untenable. Ritchie issued orders on June 21 for the 1st South African Division to evacuate the Kennels and make for El Alamein. The Eighth Army took up a new line at Matruh, from which the South Africans would be conspicuous in their absence. The New Zealand Division coming up from Syria, as well as the 50th Division, the 10th Indian Division, and a brigade from the 5th Indian Division, manned the new line. In Ritchie's and Gott's opinion the South Africans "were not in high fighting trim for the moment and need[ed] [a] period for reorganisation."[19] It was not a surprising conclusion given the signal Pienaar sent to the Corps Headquarters.

Defeat at Matruh June 26–29

The Matruh line was subject to the same defensive foibles as the Sollum line. Auchinleck noted his reservations in his dispatch.

> The argument that an armoured reserve was essential to the successful defence of the Frontier positions applied with equal force to

> the Matruh position, which owing to the configuration of the coast, could easily be isolated by movement past the southern flank. . . . I warned him [Ritchie] that I did not consider Matruh to be more easily defensible.[20]

The original intention of holding the frontier position was to gain time to build up the armored reserves. The sudden fall of Tobruk, and Rommel's rapid advance after that, put paid to that plan. If Ritchie hoped to gain time by holding Matruh, he would be subject to the same disability of not being able to field a strong mobile reserve. In any event, the South Africans were safely ensconced in the El Alamein positions by June 25. On the evening of the same day, spurred on by the precariousness of the situation, Auchinleck relieved Ritchie and assumed command of the Eighth Army.

> I decided on the 25th June that the position of the Eighth Army was so critical and the danger to Egypt so great, that I must assume command myself. I took this step with great reluctance as I knew well that one man could not carry out the duties of Commander-in-Chief and Commander of the Eighth Army with full efficiency. Moreover, I had grave doubts as to the wisdom of changing commanders at so critical a time.[21]

The German advance gave no respite and Rommel followed closely on the heels of the Eighth Army as it evacuated the frontier and made for Matruh. It is evident that the Eighth Army did very little to slow Rommel down in the retreat to Matruh and thus was not able to gain any significant time to build a strong mobile reserve. South African morale and confidence in the British ability to reverse the situation had fallen to an all-time low. In a letter to Smuts, Theron expressed his grave misgivings.

> I do feel that this crisis is indeed grave, and I fight against the feeling which will not be stifled, that the forces available cannot hold Egypt; I have not been able to see General Auchinleck since my return, despite repeated requests, but you can understand how sorely pressed he is, and as soon as I do see him, I hope I shall have more reassuring information to send you.[22]

Matruh was a critical point for the defense of Egypt, and was also of high strategic importance in the days before Wavell's offensive against the Italians and again in the first siege of Tobruk in 1941. It formed an important base for Operation Crusader in 1941, but its defenses were neglected once the front line had shifted away from the Egyptian frontier after Crusader. The South Africans were intimately familiar with Matruh, as the British had tasked them with providing its garrison and improving its defenses on their arrival in Egypt in 1941. At Matruh the Eighth Army was far stronger than the pursuing *Afrika Korps*, however, their fighting power was substantially diminished by the conflicting objectives among the Allied units and their commanders. Rommel had 60 tanks, but 15 of them were *Panzer* II's. His infantry strength was a mere 2,500 men. The Italians had 14 tanks and 2,000 infantry belonging to *Ariete* and *Trieste*, with a further 4,000 infantry being brought forward in trucks. They were no match for the 159 British tanks available (60 Grants) and the many more infantry at hand.[23] The ambiguous strategy the British adopted with regards to Matruh is best summed up in the Italian official history.

> The battle of Matruh was rather anomalous. On the one hand, there is an attacker who, without a clear idea of the position and the intentions of the enemy that he intends to destroy, drafts a plan based on little information about the enemy's defensive positions to break through and cares little about them. On the other, there is a defender that accepts to fight only because he was not able to leave in time, but that intends to disengage as soon as a favorable opportunity presents itself.[24]

Auchinleck was determined not to allow his Eighth Army to be surrounded and defeated in detail by the enemy. The reasons for not holding Matruh were similar to the reasons for not holding the frontier positions. The Eighth Army was unable to prevent a German envelopment of the southern flank or a thrust through the weak center of the line, due to the British weakness in tanks and artillery. Auchinleck wanted to keep his forces intact, mobile, and not pinned down at Matruh. Therefore, the loss of Matruh, which would hurt Egyptian morale, was a small disadvantage compared to the danger of being defeated in a piecemeal fashion.[25]

Another factor contributing to a weak defense was the disorganization of the units manning the defenses due to the haste with which the defeated and retreating Eighth Army flung together various components to form battlegroups. The formation of ad hoc battlegroups was a practice exercised with success by the Germans on many occasions and was central to their battle doctrine. However, when the British tried the same tactic it was without the essential element of specific training in combined arms warfare, and the results would prove to be disastrous.[26] The Matruh operation is a case in point of an inferior opponent being able to overwhelm a superior one. As Liddell Hart succinctly offers, "battles are decided more often by the impression made on the higher commanders than by the actual state of their troops." By placing his forces in the rear of the British and threatening their lines of retreat, as he had done previously, Rommel was able to exert an influence on the battle far greater than his theoretical fighting power. It was the pinnacle of maneuver warfare and a clear demonstration of its multiplied power in the fog of war.[27]

The defensive positions at Matruh were taken up by X Corps (commanded by Lieutenant-General William Holmes [1892–1969]), which had two infantry divisions consisting of the 10th Indian Infantry Division positioned in Mersa Matruh proper and the relics of the 50th Infantry Division east of the town protecting the eastern approach. The South Africans were not alone in questioning the efficacy of some of the orders passed down by the Eighth Army High Command. Initially, the defense of Matruh was assigned to the New Zealanders, but this met with strong opposition from General Freyberg, who objected to being bottled up in a static role. His threats of appealing to his government resulted in the 10th Indian Division taking over his position. These two divisions would take up the static role. To the south, XIII Corps was earmarked to take up the mobile role, and included the 5th Indian Infantry Division (comprising only the 29th Indian Infantry Brigade) and the newly arrived 2nd New Zealand Infantry Division together with the 1st Armoured Division. The armored division, recently decimated at Gazala, had received replacements, bringing their numbers up to 159 tanks (including 60 American Grant tanks).[28] The Eighth Army at the Matruh line consisted of two strong wings, held by the X and XIII Corps, with a thinly held, weak center. As luck would have it, when Rommel launched his attack it was through the weak British center.[29] Both corps commanders were directed by Auchinleck to offer the strongest possible resistance, and if either corps suffered attack the other was to take the opportunity to attack the Axis flank.[30] However, Auchinleck's intentions were subtly different from Ritchie's and he reversed the decision to make his final stand at Matruh.

> Realising our weakness in armour and field artillery and that the divisions which had fought round Tobruk had inevitably been disorganised I reversed the decision to make a final stand at Matruh. Instead, I decided to keep the Eighth Army fully mobile and to bring the enemy's advance to a halt in the area between Matruh, El Alamein and the Qattara Depression. Under no circumstances was any part of the Eighth Army to be allowed to be shut up in Matruh, even if this involved abandoning the position entirely.[31]

Auchinleck tried to implement a more mobile type of warfare against the Germans, and he encouraged his commanders to attain the utmost mobility and to practice the highest degree of cooperation and coordination. He exhorted his commanders to up the pace of decision making and move rapidly toward any enemy breakthrough to overwhelm the attacker. It was perhaps too much to expect the British to adopt a new way of war in the middle of a desperate battle.[32] The highly mobile mixed arms (as opposed to combined arms) battlegroups proposed by Auchinleck were in many ways a bigger version of the infamous "Jock Columns" and had the tendency to disperse instead of concentrating the artillery component. Shelford Bidwell is highly critical of this battlegroup concept, calling it an exercise in fragmenting rather than concentrating the artillery. It was an idea given birth by Dorman-Smith, who believed that infantry, not fully mobile with their own transport, were more of a hindrance than an asset. He meant for his recommendations to go toward the restructuring and reorganization of the division. In the interests of maintaining mobility, the formation would contain no more infantry than could be mounted in motor transport. Dorman-Smith's battlegroup would include an armored brigade and an artillery group over and above the artillery already integral to the formation. The formation of battlegroups as artillery batteries, with infantry as mere escorts, was an interim measure misunderstood by most, including modern-day authors.[33]

The German plan was a simple one—they intended to cut off the infantry divisions manning Matruh using the 90th Light Division, while their armor dealt a crushing blow to the British armor to the south. The Italians, who were lagging behind substantially, were to come up and join the Germans by containing the west flank of the Matruh fortress. Rommel intended to repeat his performance as executed at Tobruk, albeit on a somewhat smaller scale. The forces Rommel had at his disposal were wholly inadequate for the hazardous operation he was about to undertake. He had approximately sixty tanks between the 21 and 15 *Panzer*-Divisions with no more than 1,500 infantry. The infantry strength the 90th Light could muster was 1,000 men. Lack of transport ensured that the Italians contributed only seventy tanks and 6,000 men to the fray. Rommel's exhausted soldiers were up against well-rested Eighth Army formations. The British also enjoyed significant air superiority over the Axis forces.[34]

German reconnaissance units reached the outskirts of Mersa Matruh on the evening of June 25. Rommel planned to attack the next day, but on the morning of June 26 bombers destroyed an Axis supply column, causing a fuel shortage and delaying the attack till the afternoon. British air power was extracting a significant toll on the vulnerable supply columns.[35] Rommel's information on Allied dispositions at Matruh was sketchy at best, partly due to a lack of reconnaissance flights and partly to the loss of his wireless interception unit, the 621st Signals Battalion, which the British had become aware of and made a point of overrunning and destroying at the battle of Gazala. Nevertheless, Rommel pushed his divisions forward and by June 27 the 90th Light had cut the coastal road east of Mersa Matruh and the 21 *Panzer*-Division was threatening to outflank the New Zealanders. The British failed to implement Auchinleck's new policy of rapid concentration and mutual support when attacked. Instead, each formation largely acted on its own.[36]

The problem facing Rommel was that his formations were so understrength that a concerted attack by the British would have destroyed them in detail. At various times, the 90th Light and the 21 *Panzer*-Division, operating with only fifteen tanks, became dangerously isolated. However, the 1st Armoured Division, believing incorrectly that the Germans had overrun the New Zealanders, withdrew to Fuka instead of counterattacking, leaving the New Zealanders surrounded and cut off. Auchinleck's new directive on mobility and insistence on not allowing the Germans to encircle formations had undermined the resolve and added to the confusion of the commanders.[37] The New Zealanders gathered their resources and broke out of the German encirclement on the night of June 27/28, inflicting heavy losses on their opponents in the process.[38] The departure of the New Zealanders and the 1st Armoured Brigade left the X Corps in an awkward position. The message for a general withdrawal did not reach Holmes and his X Corps until 0430 on June 28.[39] Holmes instituted a breakout on the evening of the 28/29 and had a difficult time fighting through the 90th Light, recently reinforced by the belated arrival of the Italians. Holmes lost some 6,000 men and numerous supplies in the process. Rommel had won another stunning victory against overwhelming odds and a numerically superior foe. Rommel did not allow the Eighth Army any space to regroup or rebuild, and the victorious Axis forces rushed onwards, reaching the outskirts of El Alamein on July 1.

The Buildup to the First Battle of Alamein, June 27–30

By the end of June Rommel's forces were reaching the end of their tether. The remaining strength of the Axis forces expected to breach and envelope the Alamein line were astoundingly few. The number of tanks available to the two *Panzer* divisions was no more than 55 together with 500 infantry. The 90th Light Division could muster 1,100 infantry. Their artillery force was in better shape, totalling 330 guns of all types, including 39 captured British 25-pounders and 29 of the deadly 88mm antitank guns. The Italians could count on 30 tanks, 5,500 infantry, and 200 artillery pieces.[40] The Eighth Army in comparison could field 150 tanks, 100 armored cars, 400 guns, and 15,000 infantrymen, thus enjoying a significant numerical advantage over the Axis combined with increasing air superiority over the battlefield.[41] What was even more astonishing was the ambition of the German plan to break the Alamein line. The plan that Rommel proposed to his senior commanders followed the same general lines of the plan implemented at Matruh on June 26. The German forces were too weak for any hard combat but they were still able to maneuver, and their hope was to penetrate the defenses and arrive in the rear of the Eighth Army and once again persuade them to abandon their defenses and retreat.[42]

Rommel entrusted the 90th Light Division to perform the same role as it had done at Matruh, and in a similar fashion, to bypass Alamein from the south and go on to cut the coastal road and communications to the east.[43] The two *Panzer* divisions, accompanied by the XX Corps, *Ariete* and *Trieste*, would drive through the center of the Alamein line and then turn south to appear in the rear of the XIII Corps. *Ariete* and *Trieste* would then attack the New Zealanders thought to be holding Deir El Abed. Rommel was convinced, following what had happened at Matruh, that once his forces appeared in the British rear they would abandon their positions and retreat. The plan gave the Italians the holding role whereby the XXI Corps would attack Alamein and *Littorio*, reinforced with two batteries of 88mm antitank guns, would contain the 1st Armoured Division.[44] The Italian XX Corps was a corps in name only, as it could only muster, together with *Littorio*, some 30 M14 tanks, 45 artillery pieces, and 3,000 infantry.[45] In a final flush of optimism bordering on delusion, Rommel expected the Axis forces to assemble at 0300 on July 1 and then breach the Alamein line in the dark. There they would proceed for 56 km through unknown, difficult territory and appear behind XIII Corps at dawn ready to launch an attack in its rear.[46]

The defenders of the Alamein "line," although much stronger in numbers than the attackers, did not form a continuous and well-fortified line. The defenses consisted of four "boxes" laid out in the 60 km stretch between the sea and the Qattara Depression. The Eighth Army constructed these boxes at the railway station at Alamein, the Bab el Qattara box 13 km southwest of the Ruweisat Ridge, and the Naqb Abu Dweis box on the edge of the Qattara Depression. The South Africans at Alamein held the largest box and 10 km to the south was Deir El Shein, occupied by the 18th Indian Brigade. Then, 11 km to the south of Deir El Shein came the Bab el Qattara box held by the New Zealanders. Finally, 24 km beyond that was the Naqb Abu Dweis box held by a brigade of the 5th Indian Division. It was the job of the armored and mobile units of the Eighth Army to cover the significant gaps between the boxes. However, there were few in the way of mobile units on the first day due to the exhaustion and disorganization of the Eighth Army. Due to lack of intelligence, Rommel's plan did not take full advantage of British weaknesses. The British mobile columns barely made it onto the battlefield on July 1 until later in the day, and even then, they had a significant deterrent influence.[47]

Alamein was an insignificant railway station on the coast of Egypt. The Ruweisat Ridge was 16 km to the south of Alamein, and it gave an excellent view for many kilometers over the surrounding desert. The impassable Qattara Depression lay a farther 32 km to the south. The coast and the Qattara Depression formed the two hard shoulders of the 60 km British defensive system, and for the first time in the desert war the British were not subject to an open southern flank. It was the only place in the desert that one could construct a defensive line with two closed flanks. It was an unforgiving terrain that alternated between loose sand and pebbles and areas that were impossible to dig in. The extreme differences between night and day temperatures, coupled with swarms of flies, lack of water, and endless stretches of unvarying scenery made this one of the most terrifying battlefields of both world wars.[48]

Auchinleck pursued his new tactics with increased vigor despite the beating the Eighth Army had taken at Matruh. He was determined to fight the battle at Alamein with a concentrated force. He placed the artillery under centralized control so as to facilitate its concentration, rather than distribute it in small groups among the brigades or battlegroups. The Eighth Army would carefully husband and not squander the armor, especially the superior Grant tanks, in futile uncoordinated attacks. "Box" tactics would cease; instead Auchinleck expected the full use of mobility, together with the concentrated firepower of the artillery, to stop and turn back any enemy offensive. He broke down the divisional organization and made use of more flexible battlegroups that consisted of truck-borne infantry surrounding a nucleus of 25-pounders. The special target of the Eighth Army would be the weaker Italian component, who the Germans, due to manpower and equipment shortages, would have to bring into play in a greater role.[49]

In certain quarters, there is a belief that Norrie and none other than Pienaar overrode Auchinleck's directive for a more mobile defense. Adrian Stewart describes the salvation of the Eighth Army at Alamein as "an extraordinary irony" where the disaster was averted by "one of the Eighth Armies greatest faults—indiscipline at the top." Norrie, who was to receive the main blow delivered by Rommel, had made a decision to stand fast, which overrode Auchinleck's decision to be more flexible and withdraw if necessary to save the Eighth Army. Pienaar surprisingly backed Norrie's attitude, although he was known previously to be much in favor of retreat[50] and was more concerned with salvaging the honor of the South Africans after their humiliation at Tobruk. Both men were determined that the Eighth Army would remain static and anchor their operations on the fixed defenses of Alamein, ignoring Auchinleck's concept of moving artillery around. Norrie made the crucial decision to place the 18th Indian Brigade in a static defensive box at Deir El Shein, which was contrary to the mobile nature of Auchinleck's new vision.[51] Auchinleck's insistence that the Eighth Army be kept mobile and not allow itself to be encircled or immobilized, coupled with his contingency plan to withdraw to the Nile Delta if necessary, sent mixed messages. There was a real risk that the Eighth Army would abandon the Alamein position as had happened at Mersa Matruh, where an opportunity to stand firm was missed. Norrie's attitude to make Alamein the last stand strengthened the resolve of the Eighth Army to resist and stand and fight.[52]

The South Africans had been preparing their positions at El Alamein since their arrival on June 25, and they busied themselves with improving the defenses by sowing minefields and raising wire along the perimeter. The 1st South African Division, although not fully involved in the latest fighting, had suffered substantial casualties. Battle casualties for June stood at 1,197 in addition to the loss of "Beergroup" and "Blakegroup" at Tobruk. Although the South Africans had made good some of these losses with the addition of 2nd Regiment Botha and Regiment President Steyn, the division was not up to full strength. But what was more concerning was the pessimistic outlook of Pienaar. He did not believe that the Eighth Army was up to the task of stopping the Germans. Theron and Van Ryneveld believed that Pienaar was overtired, overwrought, and highly strung. There were concerns that Pienaar might not be able to stand up to the strain of command as he had been in continuous action since June 1940.[53] Pienaar's gloomy attitude had come to the attention of the British high command. Auchinleck was said to comment, after giving Pienaar instructions to hold the Alamein position, "and, Pienaar, if you run away from here you will have the honor of knowing you have lost the war for the British Empire." Relations between Auchinleck and the South Africans, who found him to be rude, humorless, arrogant, and most of all incompetent, were at an all-time low.[54]

A further indicator of Pienaar's general mistrust of the eventual outcome of the impending battle was his arrangement to have some of the men of the 1st Division sent back to safety. The opportunity arose on the formation of "Scrubbforce," which was a gathering of all the nonessential 1st SA Division personnel not required for the immediate defense of El Alamein. "Scrubbforce" went off to defend Alexandria with the 9th Australian Division. Pienaar took Brigadier "Scrubbs" Hartshorn into his confidence and asked him for his assistance.

> There's a pretty fair chance that this old Division will stand here forever. I don't want all of these splendid men to get wiped out. I want some to go back to South Africa and raise families. I want you to help me in this. I want you to take out tonight the worst of our soft-skinned vehicles, with a certain number of men whom the battalion commanders are at this moment selecting. They will be formed into small units, each from a battalion, and you will take the least worthwhile of our weapons. You should be able to collect more as you go. Officially, you are taking back sick men and useless vehicles to collect South African rear installations and any men available to help form a defensive line this side of Amiriya. Unofficially—and this, my old friend, is just between you and me—if we get wiped out here, which is more than likely, I want you to use all your ingenuity to collect what South Africans you can and take them back with you. I will arrange with the Oubaas (Smuts) that no matter what direction the British Army retreats if this line is wiped out, you are to go south. With your knowledge of the country you should be able to find somewhere where you will be able to withstand Jerry and at least get a few men back home from this Division.[55]

After discussion with Auchinleck at the South African headquarters on June 29, it was agreed, regarding Auchinleck's vision of a more mobile force, that they would hold the El Alamein box with the least amount of forces possible. Pienaar was reluctant to "be shut up" in the El Alamein box in particular, but this reluctance also extended to holding any fixed position at all.[56] Only one brigade, the 3rd Brigade reduced to 1,000 men, would hold an 11 km line within the Alamein box,[57] while two brigades stripped down to essential fighting components would fight outside the perimeter in a mobile fashion.[58] The 1st SAI Brigade battle-group made for the Ruweisat Ridge some 7 km from Alamein and the

2nd SAI Brigade battlegroup was positioned 3 km to the southwest of the Alamein perimeter. The 18th Indian Brigade took up positions farther to the west of the Ruweisat Ridge at the Deir El Shein box. Arriving fresh from Iraq, two of the three Indian brigade battalions were yet to receive their baptism of fire. The brigade received reinforcement of twenty-three 25-pounders and an antitank company and nine Matilda tanks.[59]

The placement of the Indian brigade proved to be crucial to the events on the battlefield on July 1, as Rommel had misplaced their whereabouts by 5 km. German intelligence was crucially faulty. The Germans placed the remnants of the 50th Division, which were actually in reserve, at Alamein instead of the relatively well-rested South African 1st Division.[60] The faulty intelligence was partly due to inferior reconnaissance that led to a false picture of the British order of battle. On the other side of the hill "Ultra" intercepts fed the British with swift and accurate intelligence, giving them a good knowledge of German intentions and force strengths.[61] The Germans incorrectly located the 1st Armoured Division well forward of the New Zealanders instead of their actual position well to the rear of the junction of the XXX and XIII Corps. The 1st Armoured Division was able to guard the flanks and the rear of the South Africans as well as cover any approach south of the Ruweisat Ridge. The 6th New Zealand Brigade held an area known as Bab el Qattara some 15 km to the south of Ruweisat Ridge.

Misfortune accompanied the Axis preliminary deployment. German intelligence failed to identify the British gaps in the Alamein line, resulting in a charge headlong into the British positions rather than an infiltration past them. A violent sandstorm restricted visibility, and combined with the intense heat caused delays in reaching the assembly points on June 30. The 21 *Panzer*-Division bumped into British tanks, which they repulsed with difficulty. Both *Panzer* divisions had to use the same routes to get to their starting points and this led to immense confusion and traffic jams. Both divisions had to make use of the moonlight to make their way to the assembly area and this they achieved a full three hours late, arriving at 0600 and launching the attack on the move. At 0615, to add to the German woes, 21 *Panzer*-Division was subject to a "colossal" bombing attack by the British.[62] The 90th Light Division set off at 1000 on June 30, suffering the effects of a strong bombing attack the previous day in which it lost nine vehicles. The division proceeded slowly due to the sandy terrain. It received light artillery fire from the South Africans at 1230. A strong sandstorm descended on the battlefield and obscured the vision of both sides. Further air attacks plagued the divisions' move to the assembly area, resulting in the loss of more vehicles and men.[63] Rommel's gamble to take the last obstacle before the Nile Delta was about to begin.

The Battle Begins: First Battle of Alamein July 1

The Italians made the first move against the Alamein box. The Trento Division and the 7 Bersaglieri advanced toward the wire but soon withdrew after coming under heavy machine-gun fire. Men of the 3rd Brigade reported the Italian advance.

> A rude shock awaited a number of Italians racing along the tarmacadam road in their lorries singing and waving their arms in joyous anticipation of the delights they were promised in Alexandria. Alas! 70 miles from their objective, astride the main road, Sergeant Wood of the Rand Light Infantry had a section of men manning Vickers machine-guns. Sergeant Wood waited for the lorries to come within shooting distance and then opened up with all his weapons. The guitars and the singing stopped. Altogether nine trucks were shot up. The Italians had passes for Alexandria![64]

British bombing attacks persisted with little effect through the night. The 90th Light made ready to proceed with the attack against the South Africans at 0320, with the troops mounted and in desert formation. Concealed by the darkness of night and the sandstorm, the division made progress toward the east without encountering the enemy. The first artillery barrage at 0510 steadily increased in intensity and rudely interrupted the relatively easy going the division experienced thus far. The 90th Light took a route too far to the north in the darkness, and instead of encircling the South Africans it crashed into the Alamein defenses, only to be pinned down by the heavy defensive fire of the South African artillery.[65]

An exhausted *DAK* left its assembly area at 0630, nearly four hours later than it planned, after a muddled and arduous approach to the assembly area and all the while being subject to a heavy air bombardment. At

0900 the 15 *Panzer*-Division unexpectedly met up with the 18th Indian Brigade at Deir El Shein. The 21 *Panzer*-Division bypassed Deir El Shein on the northeast, halting there to reconnoiter and refuel. At 1200 the 90th Light Division was able to extricate itself from the Alamein defenses under cover of a sandstorm and it once again commenced its encircling move.[66] The procession was able to advance a further 7 km to the east; however, heavy artillery, mortar and machine-gun fire forced it to stop once again. The War Diary of the 90th Light reflects the weight of the bombardment and the resulting consternation.

> The advance progresses very favorably at first but is brought to a halt about 7 km further to the north by violent artillery fire. The enemy, with some seven batteries, of which two are medium, opens his fire first from the north and the south and later on also from the southeast and a northeast direction, and finally from the east, firing into the division, with every gun he has. It seems impossible to break through in any direction.[67]

The South Africans' fire threw the Germans into confusion "not far removed from panic." Rommel went up to the 90th Light to try and get the division to move forward, but he was pinned down for up to two hours by the South African bombardment.[68] On the British side, the 1st Armoured Division had failed to come up to its appointed place near the Ruweisat Ridge. Therefore, the British fought the main action of July 1 without the intervention of their armor.[69]

The most crucial action of the entire day took place at Deir El Shein, where the 18th Indian Brigade took on the might of the *DAK*. Rommel never expected to bump into opposition and he had planned to bypass the very place that he now found himself embroiled. The 21 *Panzer*-Division soon discovered the defense in depth offered by the 1st and 2nd South African Infantry Brigade when they encountered strong resistance from the former. The presence of the South Africans dissuaded the 21 *Panzer*-Division from maneuvering past their positions and exposing their flank. Nehring made a decision to eliminate the 18th Indian Division before attempting to maneuver past the South Africans. At 1130 the German artillery opened fire and the Germans launched their attack against the Deir El Shein box. After fierce fighting, the Germans were able to breach the wire at 1300, aided by a dust storm which obscured the attackers. Once past the wire they cautiously engaged the Matilda tanks. At 1730 elements of the brigade began to surrender and at 1930 the fighting ceased, with almost 1,000 of the brigade making good their escape.[70]

The destruction of 18th Indian Brigade was not in vain and although its removal from Deir El Shein broke the link between El Alamein and the Bab el Qattara boxes, it had come at a steep price for the Germans. The *DAK* had a net loss of eighteen tanks and were down to thirty-seven runners after receiving replacements. The time wasted in capturing Deir El Shein allowed the 1st Armoured Division to reorganize and regroup. It was while the *DAK* busied itself with the 18th Indian Brigade, that the 90th Light Division was able to extricate itself from the Alamein defenses at noon under cover of a sandstorm. The division made its way east for 7 km, with the ultimate objective of cutting off the South Africans, when heavy artillery stopped them. The 90th Light had run into a firestorm of artillery emanating from the 1st, 2nd, and 3rd SAI Brigades as well as the artillery of the 1st Armoured Division. Von Mellenthin felt that the battle had blunted the cutting edge of the *Panzer* divisions and the prospects of victory were hopelessly prejudiced. What should have been a battle of maneuver had turned out to be one of attrition.[71] The War Diary of the 90th Light describes the turmoil brought about by the South African artillery.

> A panic breaks out in the Division (1530 hours) which is stopped just in time by the energetic action of the Divisional Commander and Chief of Staff. Supply columns and even parts of fighting units rush back under the ever increasing enemy artillery fire. The Commanders of Battle Groups, however, succeed in keeping the majority of their units facing the enemy and bring back the troops which have taken to flight. The Division digs itself in. It is, however, impossible to resume the advance without strong artillery support. The Chief of Staff assembles the remainder of the Division, who have been streaming back, and returns them to their respective units, the operation being successful apart from a few exceptions. The situation has been clarified and a rout prevented, but the advance has broken down under the concentrated fire.[72]

Neither the South Africans nor the British command had any idea of the devastating effect the concentrated artillery was having on the Germans of the 90th Light. Later in the afternoon Rommel attempted to reinforce and renew the 90th Light attack. This attack too was subject to a heavy bombardment that broke it up, forcing Rommel and Bayerlein to take cover for two hours. The 7 Bersaglieri renewed their attack on the western El Alamein perimeter but South African artillery fire stymied them. The British defenses remained intact and they had checked the Germans. After the day's battle the British were marginally stronger, despite the loss of a brigade, and the Germans were marginally weaker.

Pienaar was in a foul mood despite successfully holding off the Italo-German attack during the day. That night two journalists were witness to a tirade by Pienaar. He screamed into the telephone,

> Your damned bombers, tormented my 2nd Battalion of the Royal Durban Light Infantry for hours on end, which suffered unnecessary losses, although they made every possible signal. Truly shameful. You should now know, dear Sir, that my father fought furiously for 42 years in Transvaal against you damned English people, and that the feelings of my family have not changed at all since then. I can therefore understand perfectly that, in the same spirit, the plan of the Royal Air Force includes the annihilation of South African forces. I wish to have precise ideas here immediately. I want to know which side I am on. I want to know if Rommel is my friend or my enemy, if I need to shoot at him or if I need to put my anti-air into action when your planes appear, something I would do with indescribable enthusiasm. Please Sir, respond in written form. Good night![73]

The Battle Proceeds: First Battle of Alamein July 2

Rommel's solution for the next day contained some subtle differences from the first day's plan. Instead of a double envelopment developing north and south, Rommel concentrated on the northern sector of Alamein where he felt the bulk of the Eighth Army resided. The Italians would secure the southern sector to protect the flank of the northern operation.[74] He was determined to isolate and eliminate the El Alamein box by pushing the

90th Light to cut the coastal road. The rear of the Alamein box remained undefended by the South Africans. At 2136 on July 1, Rommel ordered the 90th Light to push forward by moonlight and cut the coastal road to the east. The Italians would support the 90th Light by again attacking the El Alamein box in the west. The 90th Light only set out at 0400 on July 2, without any artillery support, and as soon as they took off concentrated artillery fire halted them.[75] The Alamein defenses held up the Italians, who met with the same fate as the Germans. It became apparent to Rommel that the 90th Light would not be able to make progress without reinforcements, and given the stubborn South African defense, he issued new orders. Rommel ordered the renewal of the attack eastward, but this time with the entire *DAK* and the Italian XXI Corps supporting the 90th Light. Therefore, Rommel directed all the German forces at his disposal against the 1st South African Division. The Germans massed their troops around Deir el Shein while the 1st Armoured Division gathered to the east of the Ruweisat Ridge.

Simultaneously, Auchinleck felt that the time for a counterattack on a large scale had come. He was confident to use the South African division in a static role to ward off any direct attack, especially after they proved their fighting power on the previous day. Auchinleck planned to use 1st Armoured Division and XIII Corps as the strike force and they were to be unleashed once the Germans, with their dwindling armored forces, had made an easterly thrust. He felt that the time for a turning movement into the rear areas of the German lines was ripe even if the Germans decided not to attack.[76]

The Germans resumed their advance at 1530 after an artillery preparation of half an hour, but almost immediately the 90th Light were subject once again to the concentrated fire of the three SAI brigades.[77] In the face of withering machine-gun, artillery, and mortar fire the 90th Light halted. Once again, the South Africans had little idea of the devastating effect their fire was having on the Germans and they make little mention of it in their war diaries. The 90th Light casualties of ten killed and twelve wounded do not reflect the intensity of the artillery fire and by now an element of exhaustion and low morale may have played a part in the Germans not pressing home the attack with full vigor.[78] The Italians fared no better against the South Africans and the attacks of Trento and 7 Bersaglieri ground to a halt under the heavy artillery fire. Farther south at 1500, the *Afrika Korps* began to advance along the Ruweisat Ridge. At 1623 the *Afrika Korps* and the 1st Armoured Division collided in a classic meeting engagement. It was unintentional, as Rommel meant for the *Afrika Korps* to sweep over the South Africans and the British, in turn, were supposed to have swept around the Germans into their rear. The result was that the intended German attack eastwards never developed.[79]

The 1st SAI Brigade, which occupied positions on the northwest of the Ruweisat Ridge, came in for some particular attention from the Germans on the afternoon of July 2. The preliminary bombardment of 21 *Panzer*-Division fell heavily on the brigade positions. It was also, unfortunately, subject to two hours of friendly bombardment by the New Zealanders. In two days the brigade positions, occupying an area of 600 to 800 m, received artillery bombardments amounting to between 15,000 and 20,000 shells.[80] The bombardment was so heavy that no movement was possible within the box until after dark. The fall of Deir El Shein was a warning to the South Africans of the fate that could befall an isolated infantry brigade against tanks. With all this in mind Brigadier Furstenburg, the brigade commander, requested armor support on his left flank early on July 2. It was not possible, as Auchinleck desired the armor to make a 24 km sweep to the west. An intense bombardment bracketed the brigade at 1600 on July 2 while tanks of 21 *Panzer*-Division gathered at Deir El Shein. At 1630 the German assault moved in under cover of a smoke screen and, not for the first time that day, the concentrated artillery fire and machine-gun fire halted the attack. The division renewed the attack at 1800 and again at 1920, and met the same fate as the first assault. The 90th Light launched infantry attacks against the brigade at the same time, and the New Zealanders also beat these back. Furstenburg and his brigade major were wounded in the attacks and they were evacuated after dark. The replacement commander signalled to Pienaar that the situation was intolerable.[81]

Pienaar informed Norrie that the brigade would not be able to resist a tank attack unless he protected their left flank with armor and placed some tanks under the brigade command. Norrie was adamant that he would not split his tank force into "penny packets" (small units) to support the South Africans, and he was unable to provide armor support on the left flank because of Auchinleck's intention to sweep into the Axis rear with the 1st Armoured Division. In light of Norrie's inability or unwillingness to reinforce the 1st SAI Brigade, Pienaar requested that he allow the South Africans to withdraw the brigade 5 km to the east to Alam el Onsol so as to reduce the exposure on its flanks by lining up with the 2nd SAI Brigade.[82] Norrie's reply was an indication of the animosity that had built up between the British command and the South Africans.

> So—the South Africans want to run away again, do they? Very well, I will withdraw your Brigade into reserve and replace it with a British formation.

Pienaar protested that Norrie's attitude in threatening to replace the South Africans would show a lack of confidence in his judgment. His reply contained even more bitterness.

> Look, Norrie, let me get this straight. Am I fighting you or Rommel? If it's you say so and I will guarantee to take Alexandria in the next 24 hours and—what's more—I'll bring Rommel with me.

The result of this surreal exchange was that Norrie relented and told Pienaar to use his discretion, to which Pienaar obliged and drew the brigade back to line up with the 2nd Brigade. However, Norrie was unconvinced as to the precariousness of the position and he hastily reoccupied the position with a British column. Pienaar's anger with the 1st Brigade staff for requesting a withdrawal abated when an intense German artillery barrage flung the British column out of these same positions the next day.[83] The 1st South African Infantry Brigade had suffered six killed, twenty-seven wounded, and four missing in two days of action. According to Dorman-Smith, Pienaar's demands to withdraw the 1st Brigade shook Auchinleck's confidence in the morale of the South Africans. Auchinleck, Norrie, and Dorman-Smith were of the opinion that they could not expose the 1st South African Division to "undue operational strain." They would have to handle the South African division very carefully in the wake of the disaster of Tobruk, in order to minimize any further political repercussions. The British were of the opinion that they could not give the South Africans any serious or difficult operational tasks, and the 9th Australian Division would reinforce them to stiffen their flagging resolve.[84]

For the second day, the Germans had again failed to achieve their objective of cutting off Alamein. The 21 *Panzer*-Division was down to twenty tanks and the 15 *Panzer*-Division had only six serviceable tanks.[85] The 90th Light Division had failed in its task and its war diary painted a picture of an exhausted and depleted unit unable to take this "last English fortress before the Nile delta with the forces available." The war diary complains bitterly about the British air superiority: "every 20 or 30 minutes 15, 18, and sometimes even 20 bombers with adequate fighter protection launch their attacks." In the face of superior British airpower, the Germans had little of their own to offer back. Their last hope lay with their Italian allies and as the war diary explains, it amounted to little hope.

> The last hope that remains is the Italian Divisions which have seen but little action so far and are, therefore, more fit. However, from such comrades there is but little to be hoped. Trento Division had declined to open fire in support of the German attack excusing their inaction with the words that they did not want to bring down the enemy fire upon themselves. [We] are no longer able, with the forces and equipment still available, to achieve the objective as instructed, and therefore dig in for defense.[86]

The Axis Falters: First Battle of Alamein July 3

July 3 brought signs that the German efforts in "bouncing out" the British from the El Alamein "line" were crumbling. Rommel, in his memoirs, exaggerated the strength of the defenses that he was up against and also the rate of reinforcements available to Auchinleck. The fact was that he was trying to do the impossible with a depleted and exhausted army, against an army that was growing in strength and confidence on a daily basis. Rommel, with his divisions down to 1,200 to 1,500 men, was realistic enough to order the 90th Light to dig in and leave the offensive to the two *Panzer* divisions.[87] Rommel once again instructed the Italians XXI Corps to assault the western face of the Alamein box. The X Corps was to hold the flank at El Mreir, and he instructed XX Corps to advance to Alam Nayil and cut off the New Zealand division. On the other side of the hill, Auchinleck was content to hold the Axis with his XXX Corps and use his XIII Corps to counterattack in the south.[88]

The Axis offensive commenced at 0900, but it was a lackluster affair launched with little enthusiasm and it made little headway against a resolute opponent. The Italians proceeded with their objective of cutting off the New Zealanders; however, as *Ariete* moved southeast it was unaccompanied by *Trieste*, as the motorized division became pinned down by incessant air attacks. *Ariete*, with fifteen tanks remaining, encountered the 4th Armoured Brigade and suffered more casualties in the encounter. As *Ariete* approached the New Zealanders at a range of 2 to 4 km, an intense artillery barrage descended on them. The Italians had no time to dig in and fared worse in the subsequent gun duel, and the intense fire soon drove them from their guns. At 0940 the New Zealanders launched a bayonet charge and for the loss of two killed and twenty wounded they virtually destroyed the whole of *Ariete*'s artillery. By midday, five tanks and two guns were all that remained to *Ariete*.[89] The disintegration of *Ariete* took Rommel by surprise, as the Italian division had fought with some distinction at Gazala and had withstood numerous attacks by the British around Knightsbridge, although suffering heavy casualties. It was patently clear to Rommel that the Italians were no longer up to the heavy tasks demanded of them.[90] The decimation of *Ariete* severely weakened Axis prospects of advancing in the north. The near demise of the Italians left the southern flank open to strong British counterattack and it had taken the vigor out of Rommel's offensive.[91]

Despite his waning strength, Rommel renewed the attack at 1250 by demanding an energetic attack by the whole of the *DAK*. Not for the first time Rommel took the helm, but even he was unable to make much of a difference against such heavy odds. The attack by the 90th Light and *Littorio* ground to a halt in the face of the South African artillery fire. The main assault came in against the Ruweisat Ridge, and pressed by Rommel, the German *Panzers* advanced with the support of intense artillery fire at 1600 and succeeded in occupying most of the ridge by 1745. *Littorio* advanced with the Germans with twenty-four M14 tanks and ran into the British.

> We're lined up facing east, with the sun blinding us and making out tank armor shine. In the distance in front of us, I can make out

> the silhouettes of the enemy tanks backed up against a large mound of earth. This is it—the moment of our first combat has come, the moment for which we've been training since August of last year with so much mental and physical preparation. Major dell'Uva gives the last orders, the battalion advances to get in range, then the exchange of fire starts and tank platoon started moving. At the same time we are bombarded with enemy artillery fire, which gets more and more frequent and well aimed. In the distance in front of me I make out an enemy tank flying a pennant from its radio antenna; it must be a command tank. . . . "Halt!" I cry to Rammazzotti, "Aim 600, fire!" Following the trail of the tracer, I see the shell hit the enemy armor, but I wait in vain for the usual black smoke of burning fuel to pour out of the tank, or to see the crew throw themselves out of the vehicle. Our armor-piercing shell must have misfired—it is probably an American Grant tank, a beast with too thick a skin. I try again with another armor-piercing shell, but almost simultaneously I feel a blow on our right flank and hear the screams of the radio operator who seems to be going mad and whom Visentini, the gunner, is trying to calm down. The tank has taken a hit, fortunately not a direct hit, but on its right side, on the track, which is now hanging uselessly while the exchange of fire is getting more intense and other tanks are being destroyed. Captain Giuponni is killed, and Lieutenant Marotta seriously wounded. It seems that they are firing on the 12 battalion from all around.[92]

Despite the German's local success, the grand sweep to the sea to cut off El Alamein had failed. After consulting with Nehring and determining that no further advance was possible, Rommel ordered the *DAK* to dig in and await the inevitable British counterattack.[93]

The South Africans had played no small part in blunting and then stopping the seemingly inexorable Axis advance since the fall of Tobruk. The firepower of their overlapping artillery battered the weary Germans and Italians in what nearly became a rout. They stood and fought and did what was required of them, against an enemy at the end of its resources. They did not blink in playing what amounted to a massive game of bluff. They stood fast and fought back despite poor leadership at the highest levels and a string of demoralizing defeats against Rommel. The South

African stand was resolute, and with the all-important sacrifice of the 18th Indian Brigade, coupled with the interlocking concentrated artillery fire of the British brigades, they managed to halt Rommel. It was a rare exercise in teamwork in a campaign that had so far suffered from a distinct lack of it. However, Stewart argues that it was not a decisive victory because the British were unable to destroy the *DAK*. Nor were they able to prevent Rommel from launching further assaults in a bid to reach the Nile.[94] But though the consequences of the British failing at Alamein would certainly have had adverse strategic implications, the battle was a decisive event in so far as it denied Rommel a significant strategic victory.

Postscript

Alam el Halfa Ridge and the Second Alamein

The First Alamein was one of three battles in which the British were able to wrest the initiative decisively away from the Germans for the rest of the desert war. First Alamein was a battle between two exhausted opponents, one looking for the knockout blow that would take them all the way to Cairo, and the other fighting to survive and rebuild its fighting power. The South Africans, equally war weary, played a major role in First Alamein by stemming the Axis tide. It was not a glorious last stand in the traditional military sense, but the South Africans held their frayed nerves and stood fast, and in doing so they called Rommel's bluff. Despite the deep reservations of Pienaar, who wanted the British to abandon Alamein and retreat farther into Egypt, he gathered his resolve and drew a line in the sand. The trust between the British and South Africans had long since disappeared. Pienaar feared that the British were needlessly sacrificing his South Africans through their callous ineptitude, and they, in turn, felt that Pienaar had lost his nerve and no longer wished to do battle. The hard-won success of the First Alamein did little to repair strained relations.

After First Alamein Auchinleck busied himself with building up the Eighth Army and the defensive positions along the Alamein "line." He reinforced his northern sector and made use of extensive minefields in that area in an attempt to persuade Rommel to consider an attack to the south, past Alam el Halfa Ridge. This ridge was the key to the next battle. Rommel would have to maneuver past this ridge in any future offensive. Once again, Churchill urged Auchinleck to assume the offensive, which he was reluctant to do, preferring to rebuild his forces. Churchill demanded decisive action, and having lost patience, replaced Auchinleck with Lieutenant-General Bernard Montgomery (1887–1976). He made his decision to replace Auchinleck in consultation with Smuts and Alanbrooke on August 3, 1942.[1] Montgomery, who assumed command of the Eighth Army on August 13, decided to wait on the defensive and beat off Rommel's next offensive, much to Churchill's frustration.

Montgomery's plan was similar to Auchinleck's, and he intended to force Rommel to attack in the south by strengthening the northern sector and then to meet the Axis offensive with massed armor and artillery.

Pienaar harbored mixed impressions of Montgomery and found him too pedantic and all too ready to lay down the law before he had learned anything about the desert.[2] However, on meeting Montgomery in person, Hartshorn describes Pienaar as "a new man." An ebullient Pienaar burst forth, "Man we've just had a soldier here. There's a General for us. We've never had anyone like this before—I'll follow that man—I'll follow him anywhere." Montgomery also immediately made a favorable impression on Hartshorn.[3]

> I saluted him. "Hartshorn, 1st South African Brigade, Sir." The man smiled, greeted me with a warm handshake. "Good show I'm Montgomery." He spent an hour with my Brigade, talking with the officers and men and asking penetrating questions which left me in no doubt as to his military alertness and intelligence. The realisation that we had, in him, a really true leader had me so engrossed in our conversation that when we got back into my truck to his staff car I found I had my arm around his shoulders and was telling him earnestly, "You've arrived just in time, Sir. You're finding an army that is recovering from being a defeated rabble. . . . under your leadership it will become a victorious army. . . ."[4]

New equipment in the form of 6-pounder antitank guns and American M4 Sherman tanks added to the obvious boost in morale that Montgomery's appointment was having on the South Africans in particular, and the Eighth Army in general. General H. R. Alexander (1891–1969), who replaced Auchinleck as Commander-in-Chief of Middle East Command, immediately cleared up any confusion as to whether the Eighth Army would stand and fight. He laid down the firm principle that he did not contemplate any further withdrawal and that the Eighth Army would fight the coming battle on the ground where it then stood.[5] Montgomery reinforced the strategic Alam el Halfa Ridge with the British 44th Division, and the Eighth Army got down to business, injected with a new determination. Reinforcements poured into the line and the old expedients of "Jock columns" and independent brigade groups gave way to divisional structures, with strict orders from Montgomery that the Eighth Army would field and fight these formations as divisions.

However, despite the South Africans' newfound respect for the fresh leadership within the Eighth Army, deep divisions in doctrine persisted. The misunderstanding as to how South African mobility was to be best used manifested in a fracas between "Chuck-em-in" Ramsden and Pienaar. The argument centered on the mobility of the 1st South African Division. Ramsden felt that the South Africans had assumed a static role and they did not require their extensive transport beyond some vehicles for essential maintenance. According to Ramsden, the Eighth Army could better use the South African transport assets for training purposes, and after that it could be made available for general use in future operations. It was a clear demonstration of willful ignorance of the fact that the South African 1st Division was motorized and that the Eighth Army would have been better advised to have used them as such. When Ramsden discussed the matter with Theron at the latter's request, he intimated that the South African's were developing a complex of looking over their shoulders. He suggested that Pienaar's outlook on transport was one of getting out of the firing line if things got too hot, whereas Montgomery was determined not to retreat. Theron assured Ramsden that the South Africans, including Smuts, fully backed Montgomery's vision. Nevertheless, Theron took the opportunity to have a heart-to-heart talk with Pienaar, and he stressed that the 1st Division must resist any German advance to the utmost.[6]

Rommel launched his much-anticipated attack on the night of August 30/31. The Germans confronted belts of mines that the British had placed in such great depth that they severely slowed the German advance, almost halting it. The British subjected the Germans to intense artillery fire and relays of air strikes. They were able to stage a controlled withdrawal in the face of the German assault, and by dawn they were able to track the exact direction of the German offensive. Rommel hoped to penetrate 45 km into the British line by dawn and thereafter swing for the coast.[7] He had to modify his plans in the face of the Eighth Army's stiff resistance. The momentum of Rommel's thrust brought the Germans to the west of Alam el Halfa Ridge, straight into the teeth of Montgomery's waiting, hull-down tanks and antitank guns. There, the defenders were content to remain put, and they extracted a fearful toll among the German tanks.

Rommel failed to entice the British out of their prepared positions. The British air strikes on the regrouping Germans persisted throughout the night, allowing the Axis troops no respite.[8]

Rommel renewed the attack at dawn, but again it met with little success in the face of a determined and well-prepared defense. He had little option but to place his army on the defensive and prepare for another night of incessant bombing. Now, it was Montgomery's chance to take action. He reinforced the Alam el Halfa Ridge, confident in the fact that the enemy had committed the bulk of his forces. The South African 2nd Brigade was ordered farther south to take up positions just north of the ridge. The time had come to strike back at Rommel with everything the Eighth Army had. However, the massive counterattack never materialized, and Montgomery proceeded with the utmost caution. He husbanded his tanks and was content to squeeze the Germans back by continuously harassing them. The battle of Alam el Halfa ended with the German withdrawal of their *Panzers* to the west of the British minefields. The South Africans only played an indirect role in this battle, as the action occurred to the south of their positions. The desert had witnessed Rommel's last offensive. More importantly, this defensive victory marked the first time that the British had successfully defended a position against a large-scale Axis offensive in the war.[9] The extreme exertions over many months left Rommel a sick man and he returned to Europe for much overdue convalescence on September 22.[10]

Montgomery was more than happy with the results of the battle for Alam el Halfa Ridge, and no sooner had the guns fell silent than he began preparations for a massive offensive using the Eighth Army's overwhelming numerical superiority. Montgomery replaced Ramsden with Lieutenant-General Oliver Leese as commander of the XXX Corps. The replacement of Ramsden came much to the relief of the South Africans, who harbored a particular dislike of the man. Churchill, as he had done on so many other occasions, began to apply pressure for an early offensive before the scheduled Anglo-American landings in French North Africa took place.[11] The Eighth Army had more than doubled its firepower in the weeks leading up to the proposed offensive. The picture for the Axis forces defending on the other side of the minefields was not as rosy. Cruel attrition suffered in fighting too many battles had reduced the once proud and highly mobile *Panzerarmee Afrika* to a static role. Demoralized

Italians and battle-weary Germans ensconced themselves behind extensive minefields, which were laid out in immense depth in the vain hope of stopping an overwhelming British assault. The Axis forces were short of supplies, men, and equipment and their dynamic leader was recuperating many miles from the battlefield.[12]

Montgomery, in Operation Lightfoot, planned his main attack to take place north of the line and a secondary attack to occur in the south. X Corps, which held most of the armor and mobile assets of the Eighth Army, was to exploit the successful completion of these attacks. He intended to cut two corridors through the Axis minefields in the north. One corridor was to run in a southwesterly direction through the New Zealand division's sector toward the center of Miteriya Ridge, while the second would proceed in a westerly direction, passing two miles north of the western end of Miteriya Ridge and straddling the 9th Australian and 51st (Highland) Division sectors. The British armor would then pass through the cleared corridors and go on to defeat the German armor. The British armor, positioning itself astride the Axis supply routes, would force the German armor to attack the numerically and qualitatively superior British force and in the process be defeated in detail.[13] On the first night of the offensive, four infantry divisions (of which the South African 1st Division was one) were to advance on a 26 km front to an objective code-named the Oxalic Line, thus overrunning the forward Axis defenses. The process of opening the attack with infantry and aiming to destroy the enemy infantry first was a reversal of normal British practice, which always sought to eliminate the enemy tanks as the initial priority. Montgomery hoped that by first attacking the Axis infantry the Eighth Army would lure the Axis armor forth to come to the infantry's assistance and thereby blunt their armor-fighting edge.[14]

Montgomery handed the 1st South African Division and the New Zealanders the task of attacking and securing the southern end of Miteriya Ridge using two brigades. The offensive was significant for the South Africans in that it marked their final assault on the Axis forces in North Africa. Brigadier W. H. E. Poole (1902–1969) commanded the 2nd SAI Brigade and he would go on to command the 6th South African Armoured Division in Italy in 1944. Brigadier R. J. Palmer commanded the 3rd SAI Brigade and he would also go on to fight in Italy in command of a motorized brigade. The 1st SAI Brigade was deployed farther south and was responsible for creating an antitank screen to protect the left flank of the South African attack. The brigade was well armed with armored cars, machine guns, and antitank guns for their task of guarding the division's left flank as they advanced. The Australians and Highlanders were to force a northern corridor through the Axis minefields in a similar fashion to the South Africans and New Zealanders. The infantry would clear a path through the minefields for the tanks to pass through on a 16 km front.[15]

Operation Lightfoot burst upon the Axis defenders at 2140 on October 23 with a five-hour artillery barrage. It was the greatest concentrated barrage since the First World War, and for the first time in the desert war the British deployed their artillery in its true role under a centralized command.[16] The Desert Air Force added its considerable weight to the bombardment by picking out known enemy targets. All four divisions made reasonable progress against stiffening resistance and mounting casualties. The South Africans captured Miteriya Ridge at 0800 on the following morning. However, the 1st and 10th Armoured Divisions had not broken through into the open areas west of the line as originally planned, and they were unable to exploit the infantry's penetration. Montgomery resorted to attritional tactics or, as he called them, "crumbling," where he would grind down the Axis infantry and lure the enemy tanks forward into the battle. Despite Montgomery's orders resorting to threats against his armored commanders, there was an unwillingness by the armor to break out into the open. Freyberg and his New Zealanders were rapidly losing faith in the British armor. They had failed to seize the opportunities presented during the first day of operations.[17]

However, the crumbling tactics were wearing the Axis down, and Rommel, who had returned to the front, had little option but to commit his tanks in small numbers to bolster his defenses. The situation for the Axis was dire and the attritional battles were steadily grinding away at their fighting power. The success of the crumbling tactics had come at significant cost to the infantry divisions involved, and the South Africans had suffered 600 casualties by October 26. Frustration at the slow rate of progress was manifest everywhere, and Montgomery decided that over the next two days, while continuing the process of attrition, he would thin out his front line to create a reserve with which to restore his momentum. The thinning out of the line involved a complicated set of maneuvers by the infantry divisions. In the meantime, while Montgomery regrouped his forces, the infantry divisions, accompanied by ceaseless air strikes, continued to grind down the Axis forces.[18]

On October 26, Leese issued orders for the 1st SA Division to "sidestep" north in conjunction with a similar move by the 4th Indian. This maneuver was in response to Montgomery wishing to create a new reserve. Pienaar immediately voiced his objections and was once again less than cooperative. He claimed that he had insufficient transport to make the move in the required time. On hearing Pienaar's objections, Freyberg commented to those around him, "Then I will spike his guns; he doesn't like accepting help." Then, turning to Pienaar, he asked whether transport was his only problem. Pienaar answered "yes," and Freyberg grabbed the opportunity to offer him transport from the New Zealand division. That marked the end of Pienaar's objections, and he executed the redeployment without further ado.[19] It also marked the end of the South Africans' direct role in offensive action in the desert war.

Faced with an impossible situation, Rommel began to withdraw the Axis forces from Alamein on November 2. Montgomery ordered Operation Supercharge to proceed. The South African 1st Division played little role in this phase of the operation. The South African contribution to the pursuit of the rapidly retreating Axis forces fell to their armored cars.[20] For the 1st South African Division, the war was finally over. The South Africans were keen to withdraw the 1st Division, which had seen non-stop action since the campaign in East Africa. The division was due to reequip and become an armored division that was more suited to South Africa's style of warfare.

The military disasters in North Africa, coupled with failure of confidence in Britain's tactical ability, had done much to unnerve Smuts. South Africa's sensitivity to losses, coupled with an unstable home front, once again influenced war policy. Smuts cast a nervous eye toward the impending 1943 general election and carefully considered that any further needless battlefield losses risked his chances of reelection. He was answerable to a war-weary and divided nation.[21] He was determined to create a "good atmosphere" for the election and was prepared to wait for "the heavenly and war omens."[22] Besides troublesome nationalists revelling in South African military setbacks, there was increasing black labor unrest due to wage and political grievances. In December 1942, lethal riots occurred in Pretoria, resulting in 15 dead and 111 wounded. Strikes and shooting incidents were becoming common.[23] In Smuts's mind, this all pointed to the necessity of repatriating the 1st Divison back to South Africa as soon as possible.

On his way back from London in November 1942, Smuts took the opportunity to review his troops in North Africa, and he told them that they would be going home to train and reequip as an armored division.[24] This surprising announcement, at the height of the battle of Alamein, was unwelcome to some senior British officers.[25] Churchill expressed his surprise and displeasure that the Eighth Army would be "woefully reduced" as a result of the South African withdrawal of the 1st Division.[26] But Smuts had made up his mind and on January 1, 1943, the 1st SAI Division embarked for home, with troops returning to their parent units in South Africa. The UDF dissolved the 1st Division and the new 6th South African Armoured Division absorbed many of its former units and personnel.

Epilogue

The 6th South African Armoured Division was established February 1, 1943, and was formed around a nucleus of men from the 1st South African Division, including its new commander, a veteran of the desert war, Major-General W. H. E. Poole. The division saw distinguished service in Italy during 1944 and 1945. It initially served with the British Eighth Army in Italy and was then transferred to the US Fifth Army, commanded by Lieutenant General Mark W. Clark (1896–1984) until the end of the campaign. The armored division was the culmination of years of the South Africans cajoling the British to allow them to form a tank and mechanized formation. There seemed to be a reluctance on the part of the British because they preferred their dominions to provide infantry formations, while the armor was strictly a British preserve. It is ironic that the South Africans managed to fulfill their ambition only for the British to deploy them to Italy, where the mountainous terrain was totally unsuited for an armored division. The South African penchant for mobile warfare found itself once again stifled, and their tanks were often reduced to an infantry support role.

There is no doubt that the 6th Division would have been commanded by Dan Pienaar if it were not for a tragic air crash in Kenya on December 19, 1942. The accident killed him and all of the other occupants of the plane that was ferrying them back to South Africa. The men that served him in combat revered him, and back home in South Africa he was a hero to many. He was a veteran of two world wars and his death was a significant loss to South Africa and the UDF. Some quarters viewed him as a natural successor to Smuts and there was a reasonable chance that he may have succeeded him and become the premier of South Africa. His premature death robbed South Africa of a person who, if given the chance, may have changed the course of history in South Africa.

B. F. Armstrong was one of the first casualties at Sidi Rezegh, when German tanks overran his headquarters during the height of the battle.

His men last saw him carried into German captivity on top of a German tank. He escaped from an Italian prisoner of war camp in Italy in 1944. On his return to South Africa, he served as the commanding officer of Witwatersrand Command as a major-general. He retired in 1950 after becoming Acting Chief of the General Staff in 1949.[1]

H. B. Klopper was taken into captivity together with the men of his 1st Division and spent the next year and a half in a prisoner of war camp in Italy. In a bizarre turn of fate, he was rescued by Lieutenant-Colonel Vladimir Peniakoff, more famously known as "Popski, " the commander of Popski's Private Army.[2] When Klopper introduced himself as the former garrison commander of Tobruk, Popski retorted, "I have heard a lot of gossip, mostly malicious. You will soon realize that most uninformed people like me are under the impression that you surrendered too easily." Klopper replied that he knew there was an adverse stain on his record and he was keen to get back to South Africa to clear his name in a court of inquiry.[3] Klopper was not able to avail himself of that chance as the British had already convened a Court of Inquiry in his absence in 1942 and it found him to be largely blameless for the surrender.

On his return to South Africa, Klopper spent the remainder of the war years trying to get an active command, to vindicate, it seems, his ignominious capitulation at Tobruk. He nearly achieved this when Smuts touted him to command a Cape Coloured Brigade that was to deploy to Italy. However, Smuts scrapped the idea of an armed Cape Coloured Brigade, due to the political backlash of arming "non-whites." Klopper's chances to see combat vanished at the last minute.[4] He continued to battle to clear his name after the war and even resorted to publishing his version of events in a popular Afrikaans periodical.[5] He became embroiled in a scuffle over the way Auchinleck portrayed him in his dispatch. Unfortunately, the political ramifications reached far beyond his personal honor and Klopper had to accept minor modifications to Auchinleck's dispatch, which were less than satisfactory to him. He felt strongly that he was let down by the British and that Auchinleck did not give him a fair hearing in his postwar recollections.[6] However, Klopper's somewhat dubious Second World War military career proved no obstacle to his next meteoric rise under a Nationalist government. He became Director General of Land Forces 1950–1952, Chief of Staff of the Army 1952–1953, and in the same year of 1953, he became Inspector General.

Klopper reached the height of his career when he became Commandant-General of the Union Defence Force from 1956–1958.[7]

George Brink hurt his back in February 1942 during a rugby match and the UDF invalided him back home to South Africa. He became the GOC of the Inland Area of South Africa. South Africa's most senior veteran field commander then became Director General of Demobilisation. It is a role that he threw himself into with great vigor and one that he performed admirably. He retired in 1946 and retained a keen interest in recording South Africa's Second World War military history. He was instrumental in continuing the work of the UWHS and formed the South African War Histories Committee in 1961, when political reasons led to the premature closure of the UWHS. Through his efforts, the semi-official South African Forces World War II series was published, partially fulfilling the work of the UWHS.

Smuts, who was worried about the internal situation in South Africa, went on to win a resounding election victory in 1943. The Afrikaner nationalist tide had receded in the face of the rising military prospects of the Allies. Whether the repatriation of the 1st Division helped boost Smuts at the polls is moot, but the result was that the South Africans were not present in numbers when the Eighth Army managed to eliminate Rommel once and for all from Africa in 1943. It seems a shame that the South Africans were present at some of the Eighth Army's greatest defeats but not at the final victory in Africa. Smuts realized his greatest fear when the resurgent Nationalists beat him and his party at the polls in the 1948 election. Many of those who had openly backed the Nazis in the war and even committed acts of treason now held seats of power. Smuts's dream of a Greater South Africa within the British Empire had amounted to naught. The Nationalists spent the next few decades steadily dismantling their links with the United Kingdom. Smuts suffered a heart attack on May 29, 1950, a week after the public celebration of his eightieth birthday. He passed away at Doornkloof, his family farm in Irene, near Pretoria, on September 11, 1950.

Abbreviations

AA	Antiaircraft
ACF	Active Citizen Force
AFVs	Armored Fighting Vehicles
AP	Armor piercing or Anti-personnel
APC	Armor Personnel Carrier
AT	Antitank
ATM	Antitank mine
Bde	Brigade
Brig	Brigadier
Brig-Gen	Brigadier General
Bty	Battery
Capt	Captain
CGS	Chief of the General Staff
CO	Commanding Officer
Col	Colonel
Coy	Company
DAK	Deutches Afrika Korps
DCM	Distinguished Conduct Medal
DG	Director General
DHQ	Divisional Headquarters
DHQ	Defence Headquarters
Div	Division
DODA	SANDF Documentation Centre (Military Archives)
DOD	Department of Defence
DRA	Defence Rifle Association
DSM	Distinguished Service Medal
DSO	Distinguished Service Order
FDL	Forward defense location
Gen	General
GOC	General Officer in Command

HCT	High Commission Territories
HQ	Headquarters
JSP	Jan Smuts Papers
KIA	Killed in Action
LMG	Light machine gun
Lt	Lieutenant
Lt-Col	Lieutenant-colonel
Maj-Gen	Major-general
MIA	Missing in Action
NAAFI	Navy Army and Air Force Institute
NAP	National Archives Pretoria
TNA	National Archives United Kingdom
NCO	Non-commissioned officer
OB	Ossewa Brandwag
OOB	Order of battle
PF	Permanent Force
Pl	Platoon
POW	Prisoner of War
QMG	Quarter Master General
RAF	Royal Air Force
RB	Regiment Botha
Rgt	Regiment
RSM	Regimental Sergeant Major
SAI	South African Infantry
SAIR	South African Irish Regiment
SANDF	South African National Defence Force
SSB	Special Service Battalion
THA	Transvaal Horse Artillery
TS	Transvaal Scottish
UDF	Union Defence Force
UWHS	Union War Histories Section

Sources

1. Books

Addington, L. H. *The Blitzkrieg Era.* New Brunswick: Rutgers University Press, 1971.
Axelson, E. A. *Year in Italy.* Port Elizabeth, n.d.
Baily, J. *The First World War and the Birth of the Modern Style of Warfare.* Camberley, UK: Strategic and Combat Studies Institute, 1996.
Barnett, C. *The Desert Generals.* New York: Viking Press, 1961.
Barr, N. *Pendulum of War: The Three Battles of El Alamein.* London: Jonathan Cape, 2004.
Battistelli, P. P. *Rommel's Afrika Korps Tobruk to El Alamein.* London: Osprey Publishing, 2006.
Beevor, A. *Ardennes 1944: Hitler's Last Gamble.* London: Penguin, 2015.
Bidwell, S. *Gunners at War.* London: Arms and Armour Press, 1970.
Bidwell, S., and G. Dominick. *Fire-Power: The British Army Weapons & Theories of War 1904–1945.* Barnsley: Pen and Sword Books, 2004.
Bimberg, E. *Tricolor Over the Sahara: The Desert Battles of the Free French 1940–1942.* Westport: Greenwood, 2002.
Birkby, C. *It's a Long Way to Addis.* London: Frederick Muller, 1943.
Black, J. *Rethinking Military History.* New York: Routledge, 2004.
Blanckenberg, P. B. *The Thoughts of General Smuts.* Cape Town: Juta and Co, 1951.
Bosworth, R. J. B. *Explaining Auschwitz and Hiroshima: History Writing and the Second World War 1945–1990.* London and New York: Routledge, 1994.
Bourhill, J. *Come back to Portofino.* Johannesburg: 30 Degrees South, 2011.
Bradford, J. C. *A Companion to American Military History.* Vol. II. Boston: Wiley-Blackwell, 2009.
Bunting, B. *The Rise of the South African Reich.* London: Penguin Books, 1969.
Carver, M. *Dilemmas of the Desert War: A New Look at the Libyan Campaign 1940–1942.* London: B. T. Batsford, 1986.
Carver, M. *Out of Step: The Memoirs of Field Marshal Lord Carver.* London: Hutchinson, 1989.
Carver, M. *Tobruk.* London: B. T. Batsford, 1964.
Churchill, W. *The Second World War: The Hinge of Fate.* Vol. IV. Middlesex: Penguin, 1985.
Citino, R. M. *Death of the Wehrmacht: The German Campaigns of 1942.* Kansas: University Press of Kansas, 2007.
Citino, R. M. *The Path to Blitzkrieg: Doctrine and Training in the German Army, 1920–39.* Mechanicsburg, PA: Stackpole, 1999.
Collins, J. M. *Military Geography.* Dulles: Potomac Books, 2006.
Condell, B., and D. Zabecki. *On the German Art of War Truppenfuhrung: German Army Manual for Unit Command in World War II.* Mechanicsburg, PA: Stackpole, 2009.

Crisp, R. *Brazen Chariots.* London: Frederick Muller, 1959.
Danchev, A., and D. Todman (eds). *War Diaries 1939–1945 Field Marshal Lord Alanbrooke.* Los Angeles: University of California, 2001.
Deighton, L. *Blitzkrieg.* London: Triad/Granada, 1980.
Dinardo, R. L. *Germany's Panzer Arm in WWII.* Mechanicsburg, PA: Stackpole, 1997.
Dubow, S. "Introduction." In *South Africa's 1940s: World of Possibilities*, edited by A. Jeeves and S. Dubow. Cape Town: Double Storey Books, 2005.
Dugard, J. (ed). *The South West Africa / Namibia Dispute: Documents and Scholarly Writings on the Controversy Between South Africa and the United Nations.* Los Angeles: University of California, 1973.
Fage, J. D., and R. A. Oliver (eds). *The Cambridge History of Africa 1905–1940.* Vol. VII. Cambridge: Cambridge University, 2001.
Fitz-Gibbon, S. *Not Mentioned in Despatches: The History and Mythology of the Battle of Goose Green.* Cambridge: Lutterworth Press, 1995.
FM 90-3: Desert Operations. Washington: US Marine Corps, 1993.
Ford, K. *Gazala 1942: Rommel's Greatest Victory.* Oxford: Osprey, 2009.
Ford, K. *Operation Crusader 1941: Rommel in Retreat.* Oxford: Osprey, 2010.
Fox, J. *The Life and Art of François Krige.* Vlaeberg: Fernwood Press, 2000.
Frieser, K. H. *The Blitzkrieg Legend: The 1940 Campaign in the West.* Annapolis: Naval Institute Press, 2005.
Fuller, J. F. C. *Lectures on FSR III.* London: Sifton Praed & Co., 1932.
Fuller, J. F. C. *Memoirs of an Unconventional Soldier.* London: Ivor Nicholson and Watson, 1936.
Fuller, J. F. C. *On Future Warfare.* London: Sifton Praed, 1928.
Fuller, J. F. C. *The Foundations of the Science of War.* Kansas: U.S. Army Command and General Staff College Press, 1993.
Fuller, J. F. C. *A Military History of the Western World: From the American Civil War to the End of World War II.* Vol. III. New York: Da Capo, 1957.
Fuller, J. F. C. *The Reformation of War.* London: Hutchinson, 1923.
Furlong, P. J. *Between Crown and Swastika: The Impact of the Radical Right on the Afrikaner Movement in the Fascist Era.* Johannesburg: Witwatersrand University Press, 1991.
Gat, A. *British Armour Theory and the Rise of the Panzer Arm: Revising the Revisionists.* London: MacMillan Press, 2000.
Giliomee, H. *The Afrikaners: Biography of a People.* Cape Town: Tafelberg, 2003.
Goerlitz, W. *The German General Staff 1657–1945.* New York: Praeger, 1959.
Griess, T. E. (ed). *The West Point Military History Series: Atlas for the Second World War.* New Jersey: Avery, n.d.
Griffith, P. *World War II Desert Tactics.* Oxford: Osprey, 2008.
Grundlingh, A. M. "South Africa and the Second World War." In *South Africa in the 20th Century*, edited by S. B. Spies and B. J. Liebenberg. Pretoria: J. L. van Schaik Academic, 1993.
Hammond, B. *El Alamein: The Battle that Turned the Tide of the Second World War.* Oxford: Osprey, 2012.
Harris, J. *Men, Ideas and Tanks: British Military Thought and Armoured F orces 1903–1939.* Manchester: Manchester University Press, 1995.
Hart, B. Liddell. *The North African Campaign 1940–43.* Dehradun: Natraj, 1983.
Hartshorn, E. P. *Avenge Tobruk.* Cape Town: Purnell, 1960.

Hattersley A. F. *Carbineer: The History of the Royal Natal Carbineers.* Aldershot: Gale and Polden, 1950.

Heckstall-Smith, A. *Tobruk: The Story of a Siege.* London: Anthony Blond, 1959.

Heywood, C. *A History of South African Literature.* Cambridge: Cambridge University Press, 2004.

Hillegas, H. C. *With The Boer Forces.* London: Methuen and Co., 1900.

House, J. *Toward Combined Arms Warfare: A Survey of 20th-Century Tactics, Doctrine, and Organization.* Honolulu: University Press of the Pacific, 1984.

Humble, R. *Crusader: The Eighth Army's Forgotten Victory November 1941–January 1942.* London: Leo Cooper, 1987.

Hyam, R., and P. Henshaw. *The Lion and the Springbok: Britain and South Africa since the Boer War.* Cambridge: Cambridge University Press, 2003.

Hyam, R. *The Failure of South African Expansion, 1908–1948.* London: Macmillan, 1972.

Hyam, R. *Understanding the British Empire.* Cambridge: Cambridge University Press, 2010.

Jackson, A. *The British Empire and the Second World War.* London: Hambledon Continuum, 2006.

Jackson, W. *The Battle for North Africa 1940–1943.* New York: Mason/Charter, 1975.

Jarymowycz, R. *Tank Tactics from Normandy to Lorraine.* Mechanicsburg, PA: Stackpole, 2009.

Jones, S. *From Boer War to World War: Tactical Reform of the British Army 1902–1914.* Norman: University of Oklahoma Press, 2012.

Katzenellenbogen, S. *South Africa and Southern Mozambique: Labour, Railways, and Trade in the Making of a Relationship.* Manchester: Manchester University Press, 1982.

Keegan, J. *The Face of Battle.* London: Pimilco, 1995.

Klein, H. *Springboks in Armour.* Cape Town: Purnell, 1965.

Knox, M. *Military Effectiveness: The Second World War.* Edited by A. R. Millet and M. Williamson. Vol. III. New York: Cambridge, 2010.

Kriebel, R. *Inside the Afrika Korps.* Edited by B. I. Gudmundsson. London: Greenhill, 1999.

Kros, J. *War in Italy: With the South Africans from Taranto to the Alps.* Johannesburg: Ashanti, 1992.

Kruger, D. W. *The Making of a Nation.* Johannesburg: Macmillan, 1977.

Liddell Hart, B. H. *History of The Second World War.* London: Pan Books Ltd, 1974.

Macleod, J. "Introduction." In *Defeat and Memory: Cultural Histories of Military Defeat in the Modern Era.* Edited by J. Macleod. Hampshire: Pallgrave MacMillan, 2008.

Macleod, J. *Reconsidering Gallipoli.* Manchester: Manchester University Press, 2004.

Malherbe, E. G. *Never a Dull Moment.* Cape Town: Howard Timmins, 1981.

Martin, H. J., and N. Orpen. *South African Forces World War II—South Africa at War: Preparations and Operations on the Home Front, 1939/45.* Vol. VII. Cape Town: Purnell, 1979.

Mearsheimer, J. *Liddell Hart and the Weight of History.* London: Cornell University, 1988.

Mitcham Jr., S. *Rommel's Greatest Victory: The Desert Fox and the Fall of Tobruk, Spring 1942.* Novato: Presidio, 2001.

Mitcham Jr., S. *Rommel's Desert Commanders: The Men Who Served the Desert Fox, North Africa, 1941–42.* Mechanicsburg, PA: Stackpole, 2007.

Mitcham, S. W. *Rommel's Desert War: The Life and Death of the Afrika Korps.* Mechanicsburg, PA: Stackpole, 2007.
Moreman, Tim. *Desert Rats: British 8th Army in North Africa 1941–1943.* London: Osprey Publishing, 2007.
Murphy, W. *The Relief of Tobruk.* Edited by M. Fairbrother. Wellington: Historical Publications Branch, 1961.
Murray, W., and A. R. Millet. *Military Innovation in the Interwar Period.* New York: Cambridge University, 2008.
Nasson, B. *South Africa at War 1939–1945.* Johannesburg: Jacana Media, 2012.
Pakenham, T. *The Scramble for Africa.* Johannesburg: Jonathan Ball, 1997.
Preston, R. A., A. Roland, and S. F. Wise. *Men in Arms: A History of Warfare and Its Interrelationships with Western Society.* Orlando, FL: Harcourt Brace Jovanovich, Inc, 1991.
Roberts, M., and A. E. G. Trollip. *The South African Opposition 1939–1945.* London: Longmans Green & Co., 1947.
Rommel, E. *Infantry Attacks.* Brattleboro: Echo Point Books & Media, 2015.
Roos, N. *Ordinary Springboks: White Servicemen and Social Justice in South Africa, 1939–1961.* Aldershot: Ashgate, 2005.
Samson, A. *Britain, South Africa and the East Africa Campaign, 1914–1918.* London: Tauris, 2006.
Samson, A. *World War I in Africa.* London: Tauris, 2013.
Simpson, J. S. M. *South Africa Fights.* London: Hodder and Stoughton, 1941.
Smith, W. *Power of the Sword.* London: Heinemann, 1986.
Smuts, J. C. *Greater South Africa: Plans for a Better World.* Edited by E. B. Robertson and T. C. Dawson. Johannesburg: Truth Legion, 1940.
Spies, S. B. "South Africa and the First World War." In *South Africa in the 20th Century*, edited by B. J. Liebenberg and S. B. Spies. Pretoria: Van Schaik, 1993.
Stacey, C. P. *Arms, Men and Governments: The War Policies of Canada 1939–1945.* Ottawa: Minister of National Defence, 1970.
Stapleton, T. J. *A Military History of South Africa: From the Dutch-Khoi Wars to the End of Apartheid.* Santa Barbara, CA: Praeger, 2010.
Stewart, A. *Empire Lost: Britain, the Dominions and the Second World War.* London: Continuum, 2008.
Stewart, A. *The Early Battles of the Eighth Army: Crusader to the Alamein Line, 1941–42.* Mechanicsburg, PA: Stackpole, 2002.
Stone, G. "No way to treat an ancient ally: Britain and the Portuguese connection, 1919–1933." In *Peacemaking, Peacemakers and Diplomacy, 1880–1939: Essays in Honour of Professor Alan Sharp.* Edited by K. Hamilton and P. Salmon. Newcastle upon Tyne: Cambridge Scholars Publications, 2010.
Strachan, H. *The First World War in Africa.* Oxford: Oxford University Press, 2004.
Stultz, N. M. *The Nationalists in Opposition 1934–1948.* Pretoria: Human & Rousseau, 1974.
Toppe, A. *Desert Warfare: German Experiences in World War II.* Report Paper, Combat Studies Institute, U.S. Army Command and General Staff College. Kansas: Fort Leavenworth, 1952.
Van Creveld, M. *Supplying War: Logistics from Wallenstein to Patton.* New York: Cambridge University, 2009.

Van der Waag, I. "Contested histories: Official history and the South African military in the 20th century." In *The Last Word? Essays on Official History, in the United States and British Commonwealth*. Edited by J. Grey. Westport, CT, and London: Praeger, 2003.
Van der Waag, I. *A Military History of Modern South Africa*. Cape Town: Jonathan Ball, 2015.
Verwy, E. J. *New Dictionary of South African Biography*. Pretoria: HSRC, 1995.
Von Clausewitz, C. *On War*. Edited by M. Howard and P. Paret. Princeton, NJ: Princeton University Press, 1976.
Von Mellenthin, F. *Panzer Battles*. London: Futura, 1979.
Von Seeckt, H. *Command and Combat Use of Combined Arms (German Field Service Regulations)*. Translated by Capt. P. B. Harm. Germany: United States of America Army War College, 1921.
Von Seeckt, H. *Command and Combat Use of Combined Arms*. Edited by P. B. Harm. U.S.A.: Army War College, 1925.
Walker, I. *Iron Hulls Iron Hearts: Mussolini's Elite Armoured Divisions in North Africa*. Ramsbury: Crowood Press, 2006.
Warhurst, P. R. *Anglo-Portuguese Relations in South-Central Africa 1890–1900*. London: Longmans, 1962.
Webster, R. *The Illustrated at the Fireside: True Southern African Stories*. Cape Town: New Africa Books, 2012.
Willmott, H. *The Second World War in the East*. Edited by J. Keegan. London: Cassel, 1999.
Willmuth, T. J. *The Study of Military History through Commercial War Games: A Look at Operation Crusader with the Operational Art of War*. Kansas: Fort Leavenworth, 2001.
Winters, H. A. *Battling the Elements: Weather and Terrain in the Conduct of War*. Baltimore: Johns Hopkins, 1998.

2. Official And Semi-Official Histories

Agar-Hamilton, J. A. I., and L. C. F. Turner. *The Sidi Rezegh Battles, 1941*. Cape Town: Oxford University Press, 1957.
Agar-Hamilton, J. A. I., and L. C. F. Turner. *Crisis in the Desert: May–July 1942*. London: Oxford, 1952.
Birkby, C. *The Saga of the Transvaal Scottish Regiment 1932–1950*. Cape Town: Hodder and Stoughton, 1950.
Boog H., W. Rahn, R. Stumpf, and B. Wegner. *Germany and the Second World War: The Global War*. Edited by Militargeschichtliches Forschungsamt. Vol. VI. Oxford: Claredon Press, 2001.
Brown, J. A. *A Gathering of Eagles*. Cape Town: Purnell, 1970.
Brown, J. A. *Eagles Strike*. Cape Town: Purnell, 1974.
Brown, J. A. *Retreat to Victory: A Springbok's Diary in North Africa*. Johannesburg: Ashanti, 1991.
Brown, J. A. *The War of a Hundred Days: Springboks in Somalia and Abyssinia 1940–1941*. Johannesburg: Ashanti, 1990.
Collyer, J. J. *The South Africans with General Smuts in German East Africa 1916*. London: Imperial War Museum and Battery Press, 2004.
Crwys-Williams, J. *A Country at War 1939–1945: The Mood of a Nation*. Johannesburg: Ashanti, 1992.

Gleeson, I. *The Unknown Force: Black, Indian and Coloured Soldiers Through Two World Wars.* Johannesburg: Ashanti, 1994.

Leigh, M. *Captives Courageous.* Johannesburg: Ashanti, 1992.

Liddell Hart, B. H. *The Tanks: The History of the Royal Tank Regiment.* London: Cassel, 1959.

Loughnan, R. J. M. *The Official History of New Zealand in the Second World War 1939–1945: Divisional Cavalry.* Wellington: Historical Publications Branch, 1963.

MacDonald, J. F. *The War History of Southern Rhodesia.* Vol. II. Salisbury: Rhodesian Government Printers, 1950.

Mackenzie, C. *Eastern Epic: September 1939–March 1943.* Vol. I. London: Chatto & Windus, 1951.

McKenzie, A. G. *The Dukes: A History of the Duke of Edinburgh's Own Rifles 1855–1956.* Cape Town: Regimental Council, 1956.

Monick, S., and O. E. F. Baker. *Clear the Way ("Faugh-A-Ballag"). The Military Heritage of the South African Irish 1880–1990.* Johannesburg: South African Irish Regimental Association, 1991.

Montanari, M. *Le Operazioni In Africa Settentrionale (Marzo 1941–Gennaio 1942).* Vol. II. Rome: Ufficio Storico, 1993.

Montanari, M. *The Three Battles of Alamein (June –November 1942).* Rome: Stato Maggiore Esercito, 2007.

Orpen, N., and H. J. Martin. *Salute the Sappers: The Operations of the SAEC in East Africa and the Middle East.* Sappers Association, 1981.

Orpen, N. *South African Forces World War II: East African and Abyssinian Campaigns.* Vol. I. Cape Town: Purnell, 1968.

Orpen, N. *South African Forces World War II: Victory in Italy.* Vol. V. Cape Town: Purnell, 1975.

Orpen, N. *South African Forces World War II: War in the Desert.* Vol. III. Cape Town: Purnell, 1971.

Playfair, I. S. O. *A History of the Second World War: The Mediterranean and Middle East.* Edited by J. R. M. Butler. Vol. I. Uckfield: Naval and Military Press, 2004.

Playfair, I. S. O. *A History of the Second World War: The Mediterranean and Middle East.* Edited by J. Butler. Vol. III. Uckfield: Naval & Military Press, 2004.

Scoullar, J. L. *Battle for Egypt: The Summer of 1942.* Edited by H. Kippenberger. Wellington: Historical Publications Branch, 1955.

Stegemann, B., G. Schreiber, and D. Vogel. *Germany and the Second World War: The Mediterranean, South-east Europe, and North Africa 1939–1941.* Vol. III. Oxford: Oxford, 1995.

Tungay, R. W. *The Fighting Third.* Cape Town: Unie-Volkspers, 1947.

3. Biographies

Armstrong, H. C. *Grey Steel.* London: Methuen, 1941.

Beyers, C. J., and J. L. Basson (eds). *Dictionary of South African Biography Volume V.* Pretoria: Human Sciences Research Council, 1987.

Birkby, C. *Uncle George: The Boer Boyhood, Letters and Battles of Lieutenant-General George Edwin Brink.* Johannesburg: Jonathan Ball, 1987.

Hancock, W. K. *Smuts: The Fields of Force 1919–1950.* Vol. II. London: Cambridge University Press, 1968.

Hancock, W. K. *Smuts: The Sanguine Years 1870–1919.* London: Cambridge University Press, 1962.
Hastings, M. *Finest Years: Churchill as Warlord 1940–45.* London: Harper Press, 2009.
Kippenburger H. *Infantry Brigadier.* London: Geoffrey Cumberlege, 1949.
Liddell Hart, B. H. *The Rommel Papers.* New York: De Capo Press, 1953.
Peniakoff, V. *Private Army.* London: Jonathan Cape, 1950.
Pirow, O. *James Barry Munnik Hertzog.* Cape Town: Howard Timmins, 1958.
Pollock, A. *Pienaar of Alamein.* Cape Town: Cape Times, 1943.
Reitz, D. *Adrift on the Open Veld: The Anglo-Boer War and its Aftermath 1899–1943.* Cape Town: Stormberg, 2011.
Rosenthal, E. *General Dan Pienaar: His Life and His Battles.* Cape Town: Unie-Volkspers, 1943.
Rosmarin, I. *Inside Story.* Cape Town: W. J. Flesch & Partners, 1990.
Schmidt, H. W. *With Rommel in the Desert.* Durban: Albatross, 1950.
Smuts, J. C. (Japie). *Jan Christian Smuts.* London: Cassell, 1952.

4. Theses

Boulter, R. S. "F. C. Erasmus and the Politics of South African Defence 1948–1959." Doctoral Thesis, Philosophy, Rhodes University, 1997.
Du Plessis, T. A. P. "Die Geskiedenis van Regiment Botha 1934–1946." Master's Thesis, Arts/Humanities, University of Pretoria, 1983.
Garcia, A. "Manoeuvre Warfare in the South African Campaign in German South West Africa During the First World War." Master's Thesis, Humanities, University of South Africa, 2015.
Garson, G. "The Swaziland Question and a Road to the Sea 1887–1895." Master's Thesis, Master of Arts, University of Witwatersrand, 1955.
Groenewald, A. J. " 'n Krtitiese ontleding van die faktore wat gelei het tot die oorgawe van die Suid-Afrikaanse magte by die slag van Tobruk." Doctoral Thesis, Arts/Humanities, University of the Orange Free State, 1991.
Grundlingh, L. "The Participation of South African Blacks in the Second World War." Doctoral Thesis, Arts/Humanities, Rand Afrikaans University, 1986.
Jacobs, C. J. " 'n Evaluering van die rol van die Eerste Suid-Afrikaanse Infanteriedivisie tydens die eerste slag van El Alamein 1–10 July 1942." Master's Thesis, Arts/Humanities, Stellenbosch University, 1988.
Kleynhans, E. "Armoured Warfare: The South African Experience in East Africa, 1940–1941." Master's thesis, Military Science, University of Stellenbosch, 2014.
Vardi, Gil-li. "The Enigma of German Operational Theory: The Evolution of Military Thought in Germany, 1919–1938." Doctoral Thesis, Philosophy, The London School of Economies, London, 2008.
Visser, G. E. "Die Geskiedenis van die Middelandse Regiment 1934–1943." Master's Thesis, Arts/Humanities, University of South Africa, 1983.
Winslett, M. "The Nadir of Alliance: The British Ultimatum of 1890 and its Place in Anglo-Portuguese Relations, 1147–1945." Master's Thesis, Master of Arts in History, University of Texas at Arlington, 2008.

5. Journal Articles and Book Chapters

Baker, O. E. F. "The South African Irish Regiment: An Exemplar of the Military Traditions of the Irish in South Africa." The South African Military History Society, Johannesburg: *Military History Journal* 6, no. 1 (n.d.).

Beckett, I. "The Boer War: Army, Nation and Empire: The 1999 Chief of Army/Australian War Memorial Military History Conference," ed. by P. Dennis and J. Grey. Canberra: Australia Department of Defence Army History Unit, 2000.

Bentz, G. "From El Wak to Sidi Rezegh: The Union Defence Force's First Experience of Battle in East and North Africa, 1940–1941." *Scientia Militaria* 40, no. 3 (2012).

Bidwell, S. "Indirect Fire Artillery as a Battle Winner/Loser." In *Old Battles and New Defences*. Oxford: Brassey's Defence Publisher, 1986.

Citino, R. M. "Military Histories Old and New: A Reintroduction." *American Historical Review* (2007).

Dedering, T. "South Africa and the Italo-Ethiopian War, 1935–6." *The International History Review* (2013).

Echols, E. "Military Dust." *The Classical Journal* 47.7, no. 7 (1952).

Ellis, J. "Oswald Pirow's Five-Year Plan for the Reorganisation of the Union Defence Force, 1933–1939." *Scientia Militaria* 30, no. 2 (2000).

Fennel, J. "Steel my soldier's hearts: El Alamein Reappraised." *Journal of Military and Strategic Studies* (2011).

Garson, N. G. "South Africa and World War I." *The Journal of Imperial and Commonwealth History* 8, no. 1 (1979).

Grey, J. "Standing Humbly in the Ante-Chambers of Clio: The Rise and Fall of Union War Histories." *Scientia Militaria* 30 (2000).

Grundlingh, A. "The King's Afrikaners? Enlistment and Ethnic Identity in the Union of South Africa's Defence Force during the Second World War, 1939–45." *The Journal of African History* 40, no. 3 (1999).

Henshaw, P. "South African Territorial Expansion and the International Reaction to South African Racial Polices, 1939 to 1948." *South African Historical Journal* 50, no.1 (2009).

Henshaw, P. "The Key to South Africa in the 1890's: Delagoa Bay and the Origins of the South African War." *Journal of Southern African Studies* 24, no. 3 (1988).

Horn, K. "Narratives from North Africa: South African Prisoner-of-War Experience Following the Fall of Tobruk, June 1942." *Historia* 56.2 (2011).

Jacobs, F. J., and R. Bouch. "6 Armoured Division Italy." *Militaria* 4, nos.2 and 3 (1974).

Judd, B. C. "Major General Sir Henry Timson Lukin, KCB, CMG, DSO." *The South African Military History Society Military History Journal* 7.3 (1987).

Katz, D. B., and K. Horn, "The Surrender of Tobruk in 1942: Press Reports and Soldiers' Memories." *Scientia Militaria* 44.1 (2016): 190–208.

Katz, D. B. "A Case of Arrested Development: The Historiography Relating to South Africa's Participation in the Second World War." *Scientia Militaria* 40, no. 3 (2012): 280–317.

Katz, D. B. "The Greatest Military Reversal of South African Arms: The Fall of Tobruk 1942, an Avoidable Blunder or an Inevitable Disaster?" *Journal for Contemporary History* 37, no. 2 (2012): 71–104.

Keogh, E. G. "Allied Strategy in World War II —A Rejoinder." *The Australian Quarterly* 21, no. 1 (1949): 12–18.

Kleynhans, E. "The First South African Armoured Battle in Italy during the Second World War: The Battle of Celleno—10 June 1944." *Scientia Militaria* 40, no. 3 (2012).

Langhorne, R. "Anglo-German Negotiations Concerning the Future of the Portuguese Colonies, 1911–1914." *The Historical Journal* 16, no. 2 (1973).

Lillie, A. C. "The Origin and Development of the South African Army." *Scientia Militaria* 12, no. 2 (1982).

Mather, D. C. M. "A Journey Through the Qattara Depression." *The Geographical Journal* 103, no. 4 (n.d.): 152–60.

McCormack, R. L. "Man with a Mission: Oswald Pirow and South African Airways, 1933–1939." *The Journal of African History* 20, no. 4 (1979).

Miller, S. "Lord Methuen and the British Advance to the Modder River." *The South African Military History Society Military History Journal* 10.4 (1996).

Miller, W. A. "The 9th Australian Division Versus the Africa Corps: An Infantry Division Against Tanks—Tobruk, Libya, 1941." Paper, U.S. Army Command and General Staff College, Fort Leavenworth, Kansas, 1986.

Monama, F. L. "The Second World War and South African Society." In *Reflections on War*, edited by I. Liebenberg T. Potgieter. Stellenbosch: Sun Media, 2012.

Monick S. "A Man Who Knew Men: The Memoirs of Major M. G. Ind." *Scientia Militaria* 20, no. 1 (1990).

Monick, S., and O. E. F. Baker. "Mega, February 1941: The Role of the 1st South African Irish Regiment." *Scientia Militaria* 20.4 (1990).

Nasson, B. "War Opinion in South Africa, 1914." *The Journal of Imperial and Commonwealth History* 23 (1995).

North, J. W. "South African Army Postal Services, 1940–1946." *Scientia Militaria* 2, no. 6 (1970).

Olick, J. "Collective Memory: The Two Cultures." *Sociological Theory* 17, no. 3 (1999).

Pan, C. L. "The Population of Libya." *Population Studies* 3, no. 1 (1949): 100-125.

Pirow, O. "How Far Is the Union Interested in the Continent of Africa?" *Journal of the Royal African Society* 36, no. 144 (1937).

Pugsley, C. "We Have Been Here Before: The Evolution of the Doctrine of Decentralised Command in the British Army 1905–1989." *Sandhurst Occasional Papers*, 2011.

Romjue, J. L. "The Origins of Contemporary Doctrine." In *The Occasional (30)*, ed. by J. Gooch. Camberley, UK: Strategic and Combat Studies Institute, 1997.

Sadkovich, J. J. "Of Myths and Men: Rommel and the Italians in North Africa, 1940–1942." *The International History Review* 13, no. 2 (1991): 248-313.

Sadkovich, J. J. "Understanding Defeat: Reappraising Italy's Role in World War II." *Journal of Contemporary History* 24, no. 1 (1989).

Sandford, K. S. "Libyan Frontiers." *The Geographical Journal* 96, no. 6 (Dec. 1940): 377–88.

Schanzer, C. "Italian Colonial Policy in Northern Africa." *Foreign Affairs* 2, no. 3 (1924): 446–56.

Sinclair, A. "Geoffrey Long's Artistic Impressions of South Africa's Industrialisation Process during the Second World War." *Military History Journal* (2000).

Southey, N., and F. A. Mouton. "A Volksvreemde Historian: J. A. I. Agar-Hamilton and the Production of History in an Alien Environment." *South African Historical Journal* 44 (2001).

Spies, S. B. "The Outbreak of the First World War and the Botha Government." *South African Historical Journal* I (1969).

Stewart, A. "The 'Atomic' Despatch: Field Marshal Auchinleck, the Fall of the Tobruk Garrison and Post-War Anglo-South African Relations." *Scientia Militaria* 36, no. 1 (2008).

Stewart, A. "The British Government and the South African Neutrality Crisis, 1938–39." *English Historical Review* 123 (2008): 947-72.

Stewart, A. "The Klopper Affair: Anglo-South African Relations and the Surrender of the Tobruk Garrison." *Twentieth Century British History* 17, no. 4 (2006).

Swart, S. "Desperate Men: The 1914 Rebellion and the Politics of Poverty." *South African Historical Journal* 42.1 (2000): 161–75.

Theunissen, A. B. "Major-General W. H. Evered Poole, CB, CBE, DSO: 1902–1969 Personal Retrospects." *Military History Journal* 9 (June 1994).

Van der Waag, I. "All splendid, but Horrible: The Politics of South Africa's Second 'Little Bit' and the War on the Western Front, 1915–1918." *Scientia Militaria* 40, no. 3 (2012).

Van der Waag, I. "Boer Generalship and the Politics of Command." *War in History* 12, no. 1 (2005).

Van der Waag, I. "Major J. G. W. Leipoldt, D.S.O.: A Portrait of a South African Surveyor and Intelligence Officer, 1912–1923." *Scientia Militaria* 25, no. 1 (1995): 12-34.

Van der Waag, I. "Smuts's Generals: Towards a First Portrait of the South African High Command,1912–1948." *War in History* 18, no. 1 (2011): 33-61.

Van der Waag, I. "The Thin Edge of the Wedge: Anglo-South African Relations, Dominion Nationalism and the Formation of a Seaward Defence Force in 1939–1940." *Contemporary British History* 24, no. 4 (2010).

Van der Waag, I. "The Union Defence Force Between the Two World Wars, 1919–1940." *Scientia Militaria* 30, no. 2 (2000).

Van der Waag, I., and D. Visser. "Between History, Amnesia and Selective Memory: The South African Armed Forces, a Century's Perspective." *Scientia Militaria* 40, no. 3 (2012).

Van der Waag, I. A., and D Visser. *The South African Armed Forces 2012: A Century's Perspective.* 3. Vol. 40. Saldanha: Stellenbosch University, 2013.

Visser, D. "Accolades and Albatrosses: The South African National Defence Force's Centenary and the Commemoration of Milestones in South African Military History." *Scientia Militaria* 40, no. 3 (2013).

Visser, D. "Anglo-South African Relations and the Erebus Scheme, 1936–1939." *Scientia Militaria* 35, no.1 (2007): 68-98.

Warhurst, P. R. "Smuts and Africa: A Study in Sub-Imperialism." *South African Historical Journal* 16.1, no. 1 (1984).

Weddell, J. M. "Surgery In Tunisia: November, 1942, to May, 1943." *The British Medical Journal* 2, no. 4370 (1944): 459–62.

Wessels, A. "The First Two Years of War: The Development of the Union Defence Forces (UDF), September 1939 to September 1941." *Military History Journal*, June 2000 (11/5).

Williams, R. "Historical Parallel or Historical Amnesia? The Formation of the Union Defence Force." *South African Defence Review No. 2*, 1992.

Yearwood, P. J. "Great Britain and the Repartition of Africa, 1914–19." *The Journal of Imperial and Commonwealth History* 18, no. 3 (1990).

6. NEWSPAPERS AND MEDIA

Greater South Africa: Plans for a Better World. Johannesburg: Truth Legion, 1940.

Ice Cold in Alex. Directed by J. L. Thompson, 1958.

Klopper, H. B. "Voorsmaak van die Stryd!" *Huisgenoot,* June 1950.

Long, G. *Field of Sidi Rezegh.* South African Military History Museum, Saxonwold Johannesburg.

Seven Against the Sun. Directed by D. Millin, 1964.

South African Military History Society Newsletter. November 2001.

Sunday Express. "War History says Gen. Pienaar flouted orders." November 11, 1957.

Sunday Times. "Gen. Brink on Sidi Rezegh." November 10, 1957.

The Natal Daily News. "The Sidi Rezegh Battles—An official history." November 8, 1957.

7. INTERNET RESOURCES

Ariete's Contribution to Sidi Rezegh. n.d. http://crusaderproject.wordpress.com/2013/08/10/Arietes-contribution-to-sidi-rezegh-di-nisio-column/ (accessed August 18, 2013).

Bennet, C. "Corporal Masego." *Go South Online.* n.d. http://gosouthonline.co.za/corporal-masego-replied-oh-i-sank-a-steamer/ (accessed November 11, 2013).

Carro Veloce CV-35. n.d. http://en.wikipedia.org/wiki/L3/35 (accessed February 10, 2013).

Euroreferendum.com. n.d. http://eureferendum.blogspot.com/2011/12/it-must-be-true.html (accessed March 10, 2013).

Forsyth, D. "About the South African Military History Society." *The South African.* n.d. http://samilitaryhistory.org/archive1.html (accessed June 14, 2013).

Gigaba, M. *South African Government Information.* n.d. http://www.info.gov.za/speech/DynamicAction?pageid=461&sid=11015&tid=11032 (accessed May 8, 2013).

Le Petit Journal. n.d. http://gallica.bnf.fr/ark:/12148/bpt6k717516r.image (accessed May 25, 2013).

Leroux, C. *Chicago Tribune.* February 1991. http://articles.chicagotribune.com/1991-02-19/news/9101160457_1_desert-warfare-military-history-petrol (accessed March 19, 2013).

Low, David. *Guardian Unlimited.* n.d. http://www.guardian.co.uk/pictures/image/0,8543,-10904410005,00.html (accessed March 10, 2013).

Macmillan Dictionary. n.d. http://www.macmillandictionary.com/dictionary/british/the-Dunkirk-spirit (accessed July 4, 2013).

Millar, J. *Sounding Taps: Why Military History is Being Retired.* 2006. http://www.nationalreview.com/nrd/article/?q=YTdiMDkzZDJjYTYwOWM4YmIyMmE4N2IwODFlNWU0MjE= (accessed September 10, 2012).

Motlanthe, K. *Address by the Deputy President Kgalema Motlanthe, at the Parliamentary debate on the centenary of the union of South Africa.* n.d. http://www.info.gov.za/speech/DynamicAction?pageid=461&sid=12785&tid=17442 (accessed May 8, 2013).

Motlanthe, K. *SA: Motlanthe: Address by the Deputy President of South Africa, during the 1860 Legacy Foundation Gala Dinner, Cape Town (15/11/2010).* November 15, 2010. http://www.polity.org.za/article/sa-motlanthe-address-by-the-deputy-president-of-south-africa-during-the-1860-legacy-foundation-gala-dinner-cape-town-15112010-2010-11-15 (accessed May 6, 2013).

Nathan Bedford Forrest. n.d. http://en.wikipedia.org/wiki/Nathan_Bedford_Forrest (accessed August 11, 2013).

"Oswald Pirow." *Wikipedia.* n.d. http://en.wikipedia.org/wiki/Oswald_Pirow (accessed January 6, 2013).

PIENAAR Daniel Hermanus 1893–1942. n.d. http://www.eggsa.org/library/main.php?g2_itemId=1375638 (accessed July 2, 2013).

Pirow Bush Cart. n.d. http://www.flickr.com/photos/dvdmerwe/5991743884/in/set-72157627317108244 (accessed March 15, 2013).

Skriletz, Michael. *Welcom to militarysunhelmets.com.* n.d. http://www.militarysunhelmets.com/2012/the-south-african-soldier-circa-1940-recreated (accessed July 7, 2013).

Stanley, P. *Why does Gallipoli mean so much?* n.d. http://www.abc.net.au/news/2008-04-25/why-does-gallipoli-mean-so-much/2416166 (accessed July 4, 2013).

"Torch Commando." *Wikipedia.* n.d. http://af.wikipedia.org/wiki/Torch_Commando (accessed June 30, 2013).

TVSA. n.d. http://www.tvsa.co.za/showinfo.asp?showid=1947 (accessed December 20, 2013).

Warwick, R. "Dan Pienaar and El Alamein." *Politicsweb.* October 23, 2012. http://www.politicsweb.co.za/politicsweb/view/politicsweb/en/page71639?oid=334732&sn=Detail (accessed October 31, 2013).

Warwick, R. "SA's forgotten fight against fascism." *Politicsweb.* n.d. http://www.politicsweb.co.za/politicsweb/view/politicsweb/en/page71639?oid=273680&sn=Detail&pid=71639 (accessed November 25, 2013).

Warwick, R. *The Witness.* n.d. http://www.witness.co.za/index.php?showcontent&global%5B_id%5D=72466 (accessed November 11, 2013).

Wikipedia. n.d. http://en.wikipedia.org/wiki/File:Vereeniging2.jpg (accessed May 7, 2013).

8. Government Publications

Churchill, W. "Agreement with Portugal." Hansard. Vol. 392, cc716, 1943.

9. Published Primary Sources

Hancock, W. K., and J. van der Poel. *Selections from the Smuts Papers June 1902 - May 1910.* Vol. II. Cambridge: Cambridge University Press, 1966.

Hancock, W. K., and J. van der Poel. *Selections from the Smuts Papers June 1910 - November 1918.* Vol. III. London: Cambridge, 1966.

Hancock, W. K., and J. van der Poel, *Selections from the Smuts Papers November 1918 - August 1919.* Vol. IV. London: Cambridge, 1966.

Lewsen, P., ed. *Selections from the Correspondence of John X. Merriman 1905–1924.* Vol. 50. Cape Town: Van Riebeck Society, 1969.

Van der Poel, J., ed. *Selections from the Smuts Papers September 1919 - November 1934.* Vol. V. Cambridge: Cambridge University Press, 1973.

Van der Poel, J., *Selections from the Smuts Papers December 1934 - August 1945.* Vol. VI. London: Cambridge University, 1973.

10. Archival Sources

10.1 Archive Repository For The South African National Defence Force (DODA)

10.1.1 Personal Records

Record of Service, H. B. Klopper 1933–1944

10.1.2 Union War Histories Section–Civil (UWHS–Civil)

Box 321, Narrative prepared for UK Cabinet	General Auchinleck's Offensive and the Relief Of Tobruch	June–November 1941
Box 363, Tobruk Correspondence 1948–1950	Agar-Hamilton on Klopper. Letter Agar-Hamilton to Capt. Fannin.	18 November 1948
Box 363, PMH62C Reports of South African Officers	Interview with Brigadier H. B. Klopper. Notes on Major Turner's Interview.	6 May 1946
Box 363, PMH62C Reports of South African Officers	Written Comments of Lieutenant-Colonel Thompson 2nd Battalion TVL Scottish	4 December 1945
Box 363, Tobruk Correspondence 1948–1950	Letter Captain Fannin to Agar-Hamilton on Klopper.	11 December 1948
Box 366 Tobruk Studies	Tobruk Artillery Narrative.	
Box 366, File PMH62N/1 Tobruk Studies	Narrative on the Decision to hold Tobruk.	
Box 366, File PMH62N/2 Tobruk Studies	Narrative on the Fall of El Adem.	
Box 366, File PMH62N/3 Tobruk Studies	Narrative on the Crisis at Tobruk.	
Box 366, File PMH62N/4 Tobruk Studies	Narrative on The Eighth Army and the Surrender of Tobruk.	
Box 371, File Operations in the Western Desert	Tobruk Court of Enquiry	25 September 1942

10.1.3 Chief of General Staff War (CGS War)

Box 6, File 2/8 SAAC	Armoured Corps Conference.	25 March 1943
Box 47, File 10/11 Tobruk Enquiry	Casualties South African Forces.	19 November 1942
Box 47, File 12/6 Tobruk Enquiry	Telegram Theron to Van Ryneveld.	10 June 1946

Box 47, File 12/6 Tobruk Enquiry	Tobruk Poster	1942
Box 47, File 22	Radio Zeesen transcript.	20 July 1942
Box 47, File 4038	Bastin Letter in Defence of Klopper's Honour	1942
Box 173, File 25	Conversion to Armoured Division.	1942

10.1.4 Chief of General Staff Group 2 (CGS GP 2)

Box 589, File 1019/0/24	Notes on Desert Campaigning.	19 March 1942 - 21 August 1942

10.1.5 Diverse Archive Group I (DGI)

Box 10, File 6RG/19/0/1	Defence Policy of the Union.

10.1.6 Director General Technical Services (DGTS)

Box 35, File 5/20	Reports on Exercise with Bush Cart.

10.1.7 War Diaries (WD)

Box 21, File A1-4	5th South African Infantry Brigade	Jun - Oct 1940
Box 85, File B2-3	1 Regiment Botha	Jul, Aug 1941
Box 90, File B1-5	1st South African Irish Regiment	Jun - Oct 1940
Box 168, File B1	1st South African Infantry Division	Dec 1942 - Jan 1943
Box 198, File A1-5	1st South African Infantry Division HQ	Jan - Mar 1941
Box 199, File B1-5	1st South African Infantry Division	Jan - Mar 1941
Box 199, File C1	1st South African Infantry Division	Nov 1940 - Apr 1941
Box 220, File B1-5	1st South African Irish Regiment	Jan - Mar 1941
Box 348, File A1-2	1st South African Infantry Division Intelligence Section	May - Jun 1942
Box 351, File A1-2	2nd South African Infantry Division HQ	May - Jun 1942
Box 359, File A1-6	2nd South African Infantry Brigade	May - Oct 1942
Box 363, File A1-5	5th South African Infantry Brigade	Apr - Aug 1941
Box 363, File A6-9	5th South African Infantry Brigade	Sep - Dec 1941

Box 364, File A1-6	5th South African Infantry Brigade	Jan - Jun 1942
Box 396, File A1-8	2nd Regiment Botha	May - Dec 1941
Box 397, File A1-13	2nd Regiment Botha	Jan - Dec 1942
Box 406, File A1-13	1st South African Irish Regiment	Apr - Dec 1941
Box 411, File A1-6	3 Transvaal Scottish Regiment	May - Oct 1941
Box 412, File A1-7	3 Transvaal Scottish Regiment	Jun - Dec 1942
Box 486, File A1–3	1st South African Infantry Division Signals HQ	May - Jul 1942
Box 493, File A1-7	5th South African Infantry Brigade Signals Company	Jun - Nov 1941

10.1.8 Secretary for Defence (DC)

Box 356	Intelligence Report Mozambique

10.1.9 Operation Z Group (OZG)

Box 1, File A	The Z Plan–Narrative by the UWHS

10.1.10 Acquisitions Group

Box 46, Brink Papers	1 SA Division Middle East. Arrival of leading elements	
Box 48, Brink Papers	Brink's address to the Gunners Association	July 1966
Box 49, Brink Papers	1 SA Division Middle East Cyrenaica Operations	
Box 52, Brink Papers	1 SA Division fighting efficiency prior to occupation of Gazala line	Jun - Oct 1940
Box 55, Brink Papers	1 SA Division Operations Report Cyrenaica	18 November - 2 December 1941

10.2 National Archives Pretoria (NAP)

10.2.1 Jan Smuts Papers (JSP)

Box 94, f.153	Policy towards Portugal and Portuguese Possessions.	7 December 1940
Box 95-1, f.6	Smuts to Churchill, Empire Defence in New Situation After France Collapse and Strategic Role of Africa.	22 June 1940
Box 95-1, f.7	Churchill to Smuts, British Defence Priorities.	27 June 1940

Box 95-1, f.21	Churchill to Smuts, Operation Shrapnel and Brisk.	18 December 1940
Box 95-1, f.22	Smuts to Churchill, Strategy in the Wake of Wavell Victories.	8 January 1941
Box 95-1, f.23	Churchill to Smuts, Greece and Balkans	January 1941
Box 95-1, f.26	Smuts to Churchill, Ethiopia and Recognition of Selassie	28 January 1941
Box 95-1, f.28	Smuts to Churchill, Ethiopian Independence	31 January 1941
Box 95-1, f.35	Smuts to Churchill, Four Possible Fronts.	4 May 1941
Box 95-1, f.112	Churchill to Smuts, Churchill Encourages Initiative on eve of German attack.	17 June 1942
Box 95-1, f.114	Smuts to Churchill, Smuts Criticises Defensive Spirit of Allied Commanders	18 June 1942
Box 95-1, f.120	Smuts to Churchill, Conversion to Armour	6 July 1942
Box 95-1, f.145A	Churchill to Smuts, 1st Division Withdrawal from Egypt.	2 December 1942
Box 95-1, f.145B	Smuts to Churchill, Explanation of 1st Division Withdrawal from Egypt.	8 December 1942
Box 95-1, f.146	Smuts to Churchill, Service Beyond Africa	December 1942
Box 95-1, f.151	Smuts to Churchill, Preference for a Mediterranean Strategy	
Box 95-1, f.152	Smuts to Churchill, Elections 1943.	January 1942
Box 95-1, f.163	Smuts to Churchill, Capture of Rome.	July 1943
Box 95-1, f.164	Churchill to Smuts, Mediterranean theatre.	16 July 1943
Box 95-1, f.166	Smuts to Churchill, Washington - Mediterranean.	17 July 1943
Box 95-1, f.169	Churchill to Smuts, Election Congratulations.	4 August 1943

Box 95-1, f.174	Smuts to Churchill, Frustration at slow pace and Russian Dominance.	31 August 1943
Box 95-1, f.176	Smuts to Churchill, Invasion Italy and Balkans.	3 September 1943
Box 95-1, f.178	Smuts to Churchill, Italian Surrender and Balkan Front.	7 September 1943
Box 95-1, f.182	Churchill to Smuts, Commitment to Overlord.	11 September 1943
Box 95-1, f.191	Smuts to Churchill, Overlord and the Mediterranean Operations.	14 November 1943
Box 95-1, f.202	Smuts to Churchill, 6th Division Ready to deploy.	23 February 1944
Box 95-1, f.203	Churchill to Smuts, 6th Division Surplus to Requirements	28 February 1944
Box 95-1, f.206	Churchill to Smuts, Request for 6th Division to Deploy Italy.	10 March 1944
Box 95-1, f.207	Smuts to Churchill, Gratitude for Deployment of 6th Division	11 March 1944
Box 95-1, f.216	Smuts to Churchill, Objection to Operation Anvil.	4 July 1944
Box 95-1, f.222	Churchill to Smuts, Assessment Operation Dragoon.	25 August 1944
Box 95-1, f.223	Smuts to Churchill, Assessment Operation Dragoon.	30 August 1944
Box 95-1, f.226	Smuts to Churchill, Strategic Assessment and Post War Considerations.	26 September 1944
Box 132, f.66	Brigadier-General J. J. Collyer on the Union Defence Force 1939.	September 1939
Box 137, f.10	Smuts to Auchinleck, Armoured Car Output.	17 October 1941
Box 137, f.22	Auchinleck to Smuts, South Africans at Sidi Rezegh.	28 November 1941
Box 137, f.32	Auchinleck to Smuts, B Echelon at Sidi Rezegh	4 December 1941

Box 137, f.125	Auchinleck to Smuts, Addressing Smuts's Concern for Union Forces.	14 June 1942
Box 137, f.126	Auchinleck to Smuts, Informs Smuts of Withdrawal of 1st Division	15 June 1942
Box 137, f.128	Auchinleck to Smuts, Informs Smuts of Withdrawal of 1st Division to Egyptian Frontier	16 June 1942
Box 137, f.132	Smuts to Auchinleck, Encourages Auchinleck to Hold Tobruk.	18 June 1942
Box 137, f.133	Auchinleck to Smuts, Expresses confidence in Klopper.	19 June 1942
Box 137, f.138	Ritchie to Smuts, Condolences to Smuts on the loss of 2nd Division and praises Klopper.	21 June 1942
Box 137, f.139	Auchinleck to Smuts, Debrief on Fall of Tobruk.	22 June 1942
Box 138, f.173	Theron to Smuts, Reports High UDF Morale amongst 1st and 2nd Division Tobruk.	30 May 1942
Box 138, f.199	Lewis to Van Ryneveld, Klopper Upbeat Letter to Theron on Morale.	18 June 1942
Box 138, f.200	Theron to Van Ryneveld, Report on Klopper's High Morale.	19 June 1942
Box 138, f.206	Theron to Van Ryneveld, Klopper Looked Forward to Support of British Troops.	23 June 1942
Box 260, f.24	Thoughts on the New World. Address by Smuts to Empire Parliamentary Association.	25 November 1943
Box 260, f.31	Japie Smuts on UDF Morale	12 July 1943

10.3 South African Military History Museum Saxonwold

S. Monick Collection	Report by Lt. Maunsell regarding the events at Sidi Rezegh on 23 November 1941.	1942

10.4 Australian War Memorial

EF 940.5423BY N532 PT.1-2	The New Zealand Division in Cyrenaica and Lessons of the Campaign.

10.5 Hoover Institution Archives

Box 40, Folder 15	Performance SA 5th Brigade at Sidi Rezegh.	1942

10.6 National Archives United Kingdom (TNA)

10.6.1 Cabinet Papers (CAB)

Box 106/547	Wavell Despatch Somaliland.	1940
Box 106/638	Letter Armstrong to Deputy CGS, Brig. Armstrong objection to Auchinleck's Despatch.	1948
Box 80/106/15	Future Plans - Operation Menace.	13 October 1940

10.6.2 War Office (WO)

Box 32, File 10160	Auchinleck Despatch on Operations In The Middle East	1 November 1941 - 15 August 1942
Box 201, File 311	Wavell Despatch East Africa	May 1942
Box 201, File 2870	Martel Report on aftermath of Crusader	26 January 1942

10.6.3 Dominion Office (DO)

Series 116-1, f.8	HCT - Botha to Gladstone on Bechuanaland	12 March 1913
Series 116-1, f.9	HCT - Harcourt on Bechuanaland	2 May 1913
Series 116-1, f.10	Botha on Swaziland	
Series 116-1, f.17, 18	HCT - Hertzog on Bechuanaland and Swaziland.	June 1919
Series 116-1, f.22	HCT - The Earl of Athlone on Hertzog	20 October 1924
Series 116-1, f.35	HCT - Precis of conversation with Hertzog	24 February 1925

Series 116-1, f.45	HCT - Athlone to Secretary of State	25 January 1926
Series 116-1, f.60	HCT - Athlone to Hertzog on transfer of High Commission Territories	14 July 1926
Series 116-3, f.7	HCT - Buxton and others to Lord Passfield	8 November 1929
Series 116-5, f.3	HCT - Dominions Office Memorandum	July 1932
Series 116-5, f.7	HCT - Hertzog to Dominions Office	20 November 1932
Series 116-5, f.9	HCT - Smuts High Commission Territories	28 July 1933
Series 116-5, f.10	HCT - Thomas to Smuts	4 August 1933
Series 116-7, f.110	HCT - High Commissioner on Denys Reitz request for early transfer of HCT	12 October 1939
Series 116-7, f.113	HCT - Reaction to Smuts's request for transfer of HCT	18 October 1939
Series 116-7, f.114	HCT - Extract of discussion Eden/Reitz	23 October 1939
Class 35, P 1003/6, File WG3/4/1	Union Cooperation - Entry of Union into the War	12 September 1939
Class 35, P 1003/6, File WG3/4/11	Union Cooperation - Union Defence Requirements	December 1939
Class 35, P 1003/6, File WG3/4/32	Union Cooperation - Union Air Training Scheme	February 1940
Class 35, P 1003/6, File WG3/4/66	Union Cooperation - Future role of UDF	1 December 1942

Endnotes

Acknowledgments

1. D. B. Katz, 'The Greatest Military Reversal of South African Arms: The Fall of Tobruk 1942, an Avoidable Blunder or an Inevitable Disaster?,' *Journal for Contemporary History*, 37(2) (2012) (pp. 71–104).
2. D.B. Katz, 'A Case of Arrested Development: The Historiography Relating to South Africa's Participation in the Second World War,' *Scientia Militaria*, 40(3) (2012) (pp. 280–317).
3. David Brock Katz, 'Pre-war Military Planning and War Aims (Union of South Africa),' in 1914–1918-online International Encyclopedia of the First World War, ed. by Ute Daniel, Peter Gatrell, Oliver Janz, Heather Jones, Jennifer Keene, Alan Kramer, and Bill Nasson, issued by Freie Universität Berlin, Berlin, August 4, 2015. DOI: http://dx.doi.org/10.15463/ie1418.10695, and David Brock Katz, 'Historiography 1918-Today (Union of South Africa),' in 1914–1918-online International Encyclopedia of the First World War, ed. by Ute Daniel, Peter Gatrell, Oliver Janz, Heather Jones, Jennifer Keene, Alan Kramer, and Bill Nasson, issued by Freie Universität Berlin, Berlin, November 18, 2015. DOI: http://dx.doi.org/10.15463/ie1418.10772.

Introduction

1. J. A. I. Agar-Hamilton and L. C. F. Turner, *The Sidi Rezegh Battles, 1941* (Cape Town: Oxford University Press, 1957) and J. A. I. Agar-Hamilton and L. C. F. Turner, *Crisis in the Desert: May-July 1942* (London: Oxford, 1952).
2. J. Keegan, *The Face of Battle* (London: Pimilco, 1995) (p. 23).
3. N. Southey and F. A. Mouton, 'A Volksvreemde Historian: J. A. I. Agar-Hamilton and the Production of History in an Alien Environment,' *South African Historical Journal*, 44 (2001) (p. 72).
4. J. Grey, 'Standing humbly in the ante-chambers of Clio: the rise and fall of Union War Histories,' *Scientia Militaria*, 30 (2000) (p. 255).
5. I. van der Waag, 'Contested histories: Official history and the South African military in the 20th century,' in *The Last Word? Essays on Official History, in the United States and British Commonwealth*, ed. by J. Grey (Westport, CT, and London: Praeger, 2003) (p. 37).
6. L. Turner, H. Gordon-Cumming, and J. Betzler, *War in the Southern Oceans 1939–1945* (Cape Town: Oxford University Press, 1961). This is the third and final volume in the official history series.
7. Agar-Hamilton, *Crisis in the Desert.*
8. Van der Waag, 'Contested Histories,' (p. 37).

9. Agar-Hamilton, *The Sidi Rezegh Battles.*
10. Van der Waag, 'Contested Histories,' (p. 37).
11. In fact, two examples of these unpublished manuscripts have been published in *Militaria* since the demise of the UWHS. J. W. North, 'South African Army Postal Services, 1940–1946,' *Militaria*, 2(6) (1970) and F. J. Jacobs and R. Bouch, '6 Armoured Division Italy,' *Militaria*, 4(2) and 4(3) (1974).
12. 'Narratives and Reports Middle East' (Narratives and Reports, South African National Defence Force Documentation Centre [DODA], Union War Histories Section [UWHS], Box 119 to 173).
13. DODA, UWHS, Box 127 to 139.
14. DODA, UWHS, Box 127 to 139.
15. A. Stewart, *The Early Battles of the Eighth Army: Crusader to the Alamein Line, 1941–42* (Mechanicsburg, PA: Stackpole, 2002) (p. 7).
16. Two articles by Andrew Stewart give insight into the political sensitivities shortly after the war. Stewart demonstrates how the dispatches of Auchinleck were altered for political expediency while the efforts of General Klopper to clear his name were curtailed by Smuts. See A. Stewart, "The 'Atomic' Despatch: Field Marshal Auchinleck, the Fall of the Tobruk Garrison and Post-War Anglo-South African Relations," *Scientia Militaria*, 36(1) (2008), and A. Stewart, "The Klopper Affair: Anglo-South African Relations and the Surrender of the Tobruk Garrison," *Twentieth Century British History*, 17(4) (2006).
17. M. Montanari, *The Three Battles of Alamein (June–November 1942)* (Rome: Stato Maggiore Esercito, 2007) and M. Montanari, *Le Operazioni In Africa Settentrionale (Marzo 1941—Gennaio 1942)* (Rome: Ufficio Storico, 1993), II.
18. B. Stegemann, Detlef Vogel, and G. Schreiber, *Germany and the Second World War: The Mediterranean, South-east Europe, and North Africa 1939–1941* (Oxford: Oxford, 1995), III (p. 738).

CHAPTER 1

1. B. Nasson, *South Africa at War 1939–1945* (Pretoria: Jacana Media, 2012) (p.60).
2. P. B. Blanckenberg, *The Thoughts of General Smuts* (Cape Town: Juta and Co, 1951) (p.8).
3. R. Hyam and P. Henshaw, *The Lion and The Springbok: Britain and South Africa since the Boer War* (Cambridge: Cambridge University Press, 2003) (p. 14).
4. C. P. Stacey, *Arms, Men and Governments: The War Policies of Canada 1939–1945* (Ottawa: Minister of National Defence, 1970) (p. 5). In Quebec, there was massive opposition to a war in defense of the British Empire. Resentment was still fierce against Ottawa's imposition of conscription in the First World War, which had led to massive demonstrations, pitched battles with police, and widespread acts of resistance across Quebec. The Canadian government, headed by Mackenzie King, secured Parliament's adoption of a declaration of war on September 8, 1939, through a promise not to conscript men for overseas service.
5. T. J. Stapleton, *A Military History of South Africa: From the Dutch-Khoi Wars to the End of Apartheid* (Santa Barbara, CA: Praeger, 2010) (p. 113).
6. S. Miller, 'Lord Methuen and the British Advance to the Modder River,' *The South African Military History Society Military History Journal*, 10.4 (1996).

Methuen fought in the Boer War and was known for his preference for mobility. Throughout the war, the mobility of Methuen's troops set an example for the rest of the British Army.

7. B. C. Judd, 'Major General Sir Henry Timson Lukin, KCB, CMG, DSO.' *The South African Military History Society Military History Journal*, 7.3 (1987). When the Anglo-Boer War broke out in 1899, Lukin was in command of the Cape Mounted Rifles artillery and signals. Lukin was appointed to command the Cape Mounted Rifles in 1902, which he did, very ably, until the advent of Union in 1910, when he left on promotion. He was promoted to brigadier general and appointed Inspector General of the Permanent Force.
8. Stapleton, *A Military History*, 2010 (p. 114).
9. H. C. Hillegas, *With The Boer Forces* (London: Methuen and Co., 1900) (pp. 60, 81). The author was an American newspaper correspondent imbedded on the Boer side.
10. I. van der Waag, 'Smuts's Generals: Towards a First Portrait of the South African High Command, 1912–1948,' *War in History*, 18(1) (2011) (p. 40).
11. I. van der Waag, *A Military History of Modern South Africa* (Cape Town: Jonathan Ball, 2015) (p. 76). Van der Waag has produced a single volume of South Africa's modern military history. His chapter on the formation of the UDF is the best and most insightful to date.
12. Van der Waag, *A Military History of Modern South Africa* (p. 82).
13. Lettow-Vorbeck managed to survive with his small force despite the best attempts to annihilate him. He successfully eluded the attempts of successive Allied generals to end his skillful resistance. Smuts managed to remove the Germans from 80 percent of the German colony during his 1916 campaign.
14. S. Swart, 'Desperate Men: The 1914 Rebellion and the Politics of Poverty,' *South African Historical Journal*, 42.1 (2000). Swart offers a different interpretation from the norm in that she postulates that the 12,000 rebels were motivated mainly for economic rather than political reasons.
15. A. Garcia, 'Manoeuvre Warfare in the South African Campaign in German South West Africa During the First World War' (Masters thesis, Humanities, University of South Africa, 2015) (p. 4). Collyer served in the Anglo-Boer War as a captain when the Defence Act was drawn up from 1910 until mid-1912. He became chief staff officer during the German South West African campaign, with the rank of lieutenant colonel. He eventually retired as a brigadier general and chief of general staff.
16. I. van der Waag, 'The Union Defence Force Between the Two World Wars, 1919–1940,' *Scientia Militaria*, 30(2) (2000) (p. 186).
17. J. J. Collyer, *The South Africans with General Smuts in German East Africa 1916* (London: Imperial War Museum and Battery Press, 2004) (p. xv).
18. W. Churchill, 'Agreement with Portugal,' Hansard, vol. 392, cc716 (1943), http://hansard.millbanksystems.com/commons/1943/oct/12/agreement-with-portugal [accessed July 7, 2013]. Despite Portugal's long alliance with the United Kingdom and the unlikelihood of Portugal posing a threat to South Africa, in 1935 the Chief of General Staff Sir Pierre van Ryneveld seemed to think that Portugal would launch an invasion of the Union through Lourenço Marques with a modern expeditionary force. C. Birkby, *Uncle George: The*

Boer Boyhood, Letters and Battles of Lieutenant-General George Edwin Brink (Johannesburg: Jonathan Ball, 1987) (p. 95).

19. Such a threat became a reality in 1915 when the Germans, from their positions in German South West Africa, aided and perhaps played a role in inciting the Afrikaner Rebellion.
20. I. van der Waag, 'The Thin Edge of the Wedge: Anglo-South African Relations, Dominion Nationalism and the Formation of a Seaward Defence Force in 1939–1940,' *Contemporary British History*, 24:4 (2010) (p. 429).
21. The conferences were periodic gatherings of the leaders of the self-governing colonies and dominions of the British Empire. First convened to emphasize imperial unity, they became a platform for dominion governments to exercise ever-increasing independence.
22. Van der Waag, 'The Union Defence Force, ' (pp. 192, 193).
23. Dill was the Chief of the Imperial General Staff from May 1940 to December 1941, subsequently Chief of the British Joint Staff Mission in Washington, and then Senior British Representative on the Combined Chiefs of Staff.
24. Birkby, *Uncle George* (pp. 65, 66).
25. W. Goerlitz, *The German General Staff 1657–1945* (New York: Praeger, 1959) (p. 127). General von Seeckt described the task of the General Staff as not being to produce geniuses but to concentrate on the training of ordinary men who could display efficiency and common sense. The German General Staff sought to create a core of leaders who were able to ascribe to a common set of principles of operational thought.
26. Van der Waag, 'The Union Defence Force,' (pp. 192, 193, 199).
27. Hyam, *The Lion and the Springbok* (p. 112). Britain's concern for black interests was not completely altruistic, but rather more of a political expediency to counterbalance the threat of Afrikaner nationalism.
28. A. Stewart, *Empire Lost: Britain, the Dominions and the Second World War* (London: Continuum, 2008) (p. 9).
29. O. Pirow, *James Barry Munnik Hertzog* (Cape Town: Howard Timmins, 1958) (p. 109). Up to the signing of the Versailles treaty in 1919, it was generally accepted that the dominions, despite enjoying self-government, were subordinate to Great Britain and had little say in matters affecting foreign policy. Hertzog was at the forefront in acquiring equal status for South Africa within the empire and control over its foreign policy.
30. Stacey, *Arms, Men and Governments* (p. 2).
31. J. Ellis, 'Oswald Pirow's Five Year Plan for the Reorganisation of the Union Defence Force, 1933–1939,' *Scientia Militaria*, 30(2) (2000) (p. 222). The prevention and suppression of internal unrest was the priority of the Union Defence Policy formulated in 1926.
32. Van der Waag, 'The Union Defence Force,' (pp. 192, 193, 203).
33. Van der Waag, 'The Union Defence Force,' (p. 184).
34. Van der Waag, 'The Union Defence Force,' (p. 183).
35. O. Pirow, 'Oswald Pirow's Five Year Plan,' (p. 226).
36. A. C. Lillie, 'The Origin and Development of the South African Army,' *Scientia Militaria*, 12(2) (1982) (p. 13).
37. Van der Waag, 'The Union Defence Force,' (pp. 192, 193, 204).

38. The Fusion government was formed in 1934 when J. B. M. Hertzog was willing to cooperate with Gen. J. C. Smuts, and vice-versa, to form a coalition. The new cabinet, as had been agreed, had six Nationalist ministers and six members from Smuts's South African Party. Hertzog was the prime minister and Smuts was deputy prime minister.
39. J. Crwys-Williams, *A Country at War 1939–1945: The Mood of a Nation* (Johannesburg: Ashanti, 1992) (p. xix).
40. According to Brian Bunting, "Pirow's daughter Else caused some consternation on her arrival in England on June 6, 1939, when she was interviewed by the Daily Express: '. . . my father was a boy in Germany, my grandparents on both sides are German. I have heaps of relatives there. At home we speak German . . . though I have never been there I feel Germany is "home."' Miss Pirow was on her way to train in a German women's camp. 'I am going to try my best to be a good German—for a year at least,' she said." B. Bunting, *The Rise of the South African Reich* (London: Penguin Books, 1969) (p. 57).
41. Van der Waag, 'The Union Defence Force,' (pp. 192, 193, 186). The issue of the infamous bush carts receives kinder treatment by G. Bentz, who offers up two reasons for procuring the bush cart: it provided reliability in a country lacking infrastructure for a mechanized war, and was an economic necessity in a country recovering from the depression. G. Bentz, 'From El Wak to Sidi Rezegh: The Union Defence Force's First Experience of Battle in East and North Africa, 1940–1941,' *Scientia Militaria*, 40(3) (2012) (p. 181). Simpson is scathing in his attack on the bush cart episode, calling it a product of some nonmilitary brain. He cites the first trial of the bush cart on maneuvers, during which the oxen strayed during the night, the native drivers themselves being lost in any endeavor to find the oxen. "They reduced the whole Army the pace of an ox." J. S. M. Simpson, *South Africa Fights* (London: Hodder and Stoughton, 1941) (p. 62), and DODA, DGTS Group, Box 35, File 5/20, *Reports on Exercise with Bush Cart.*
42. O. Pirow, *James Barry Munnik Hertzog* (p. 219).
43. Lillie, 'The Origin and Development' (p. 13).
44. Lillie, 'The Origin and Development' (p. 15).
45. Simpson, *South Africa Fights* (p. 59).
46. Simpson, *South Africa Fights* (p. 60).
47. A. Stewart, 'The Klopper Affair: Anglo-South African Relations and the Surrender of the Tobruk Garrison,' *Twentieth Century British History*, 17(4) (2006) (p. 518).
48. H. J. Martin and N. Orpen, *South African Forces World War II- South Africa at War: Preparations and Operations on the Home Front, 1939/45* (Cape Town: Purnell, 1979), VII. (p. 10). Sir Pierre van Ryneveld, the UDF Chief of the General Staff, reiterated in 1936 that thinking, plans, organization, equipment, and training must be directed toward the highest possible efficiency in a campaign in tropical bush country. This policy he issued in the absence of a clear directive from government and DODA, DGI Group, Box 10, File 6RG/19/0/1, *Defence Policy of the Union.*
49. Van der Waag, 'The Union Defence Force' (p. 210).

50. It is interesting to note that on one issue there seemed to be general consensus, and that was the feeling that Italy posed a major threat to South African interests in Africa. South Africa was at the forefront in pressing for sanctions against Italy in 1936, on the occasion of the Italian invasion of Abyssinia. Hertzog is quoted as saying, "I contend that never before in the last 50 years have we become faced with such a menace to the freedom of Africa." Simpson, *South Africa Fights* (pp. 67, 68).
51. The eventual rejection of neutrality by Smuts on the eve of the war was seen as a betrayal by Hertzog and a breach of a cabinet agreement dated September 1, 1938. A general policy of neutrality was denied by Smuts on April 1, 1940, in a house debate, in which he said any agreement reached pertained to the Czechoslovakian situation in 1938 and had no bearing on the situation in September 1, 1939, when Germany had invaded Poland. *Selections From the Smuts Papers December 1934—August 1945*, ed. by J. van der Poel (London: Cambridge University, 1973), VI (pp. 190, 191).
52. A. Jackson, *The British Empire and the Second World War* (London: Hambledon Continuum, 2006) (p. 20). According to Jackson it is doubtful that the dominions would have gone to war over Czechoslovakia in 1938. Therefore, at that date South Africa was not alone in its reluctance to join a European war. With the exception of South Africa and Canada, who remained noncommittal, in the period after the Czechoslovakian crisis of 1938 the dominions had concluded that Germany posed a threat to world peace and the empire and were quite prepared to throw their lot in with Britain.
53. Van Ryneveld was trained as an engineer in London, where he entered a British regiment in August 1914 to be trained as a pilot. In July 1915 he joined the Royal Flying Corps and served in WWI as a war pilot and commanding officer in the mid-East and France. Smuts decided that South Africa must establish its own air force, and for this purpose Colonel van Ryneveld (at twenty-seven years old) was selected on February 1, 1920, as Director of Air Services, and was instructed to form an air arm that would be part of the army. He fought this idea and won, and consequently the South African Air Force (SAAF) was formed as an independent unit of the army. See *Dictionary of South African Biography Volume V*, ed. by C. J. Beyers and J. L. Basson (Pretoria: Human Sciences Research Council, 1987) (p. 827).
54. Ellis, "Oswald Pirow's Five Year Plan" (p. 225). Van Ryneveld ruled the UDF with an iron fist for the duration of the Second World War. He was the originator of the dubious Plan Z to invade Portuguese East Africa, and he was also the main instigator in ensuring that South Africa's black troops were only employed in a noncombative role. See the foreword to Martin, *Operations on the Home Front*.
55. Tilman Dedering has produced a fine article giving insight into the workings of the Fusion government, using the Italo-Ethiopian War of 1935 as a lens. T. Dedering, "South Africa and the Italo-Ethiopian War, 1935–6," *The International History Review*, 2013.
56. *The Cambridge History of Africa 1905–1940*, ed. by J. D. Fage and R. A. Oliver (Cambridge: Cambridge University, 2001), VII (p. 597). Smuts was determined that letting "Italy getting away with it" would lead to a continental war

within three years. *Selections From the Smuts Papers December 1934—August 1945* (p. 34).

57. Nasson, *South Africa at War* (pp. 70, 71). There was also a considerable submarine threat posed by the Italian navy operating from East Africa. Oswald Pirow was concerned with Italian bomber aircraft whose speed outperformed fighters of the South African Air Force. Martin, *Operations on the Home Front* (p. 9).
58. DODA, Notes on Minister's Outline of Defence Policy, June 15, 1935, Defence Policy 1935, Diverse Group 1, Box 10. The threat of an invasion was considered to be highly unlikely. The protagonists in that unlikely event were identified as France or Japan. The most serious menace was identified as an attack from the air, estimated at 100 enemy bombers. However, the possibility of "large scale native trouble in Africa" motivated by a "spirit of Bolshevism . . . and amongst those of the Mahommedan faith," was considered less remote. There were no qualms in coming to Britain's aid under these circumstances.
59. M. Roberts and A. E. G. Trollip, *The South African Opposition 1939–1945* (London: Longmans Green & Co., 1947) (p.4).
60. Stewart, *Empire Lost* (p. 22). Hertzog had stated his position clearly and publicly at the 1937 Imperial Conference, where he rejected his country's involvement in any future European war.
61. O. Pirow, *James Barry Munnik Hertzog* (p. 247).
62. O. Pirow, *James Barry Munnik Hertzog* (p. 218).
63. Stewart, 'The Klopper Affair' (p. 517). Stewart puts it less kindly, stating that, ". . . many within the large Nationalist Afrikaans speaking community, of which the country leader General J.B.M. Hertzog was one of the more moderate members, held sympathy for Germany and its actions in Europe."
64. The National Archives United Kingdom (TNA), DO, Class 35, P1003, File WG/3/4/1, *Union Cooperation—Entry of Union into the War*, September 12, 1939, and W.K. Hancock, *Smuts: The Sanguine Years 1870–1919* (London: Cambridge University Press, 1962) (p. 510). Smuts himself had urged moderation in the terms imposed on Germany in 1919 and predicted that, ". . . and Europe will know no peace hereafter. And in the coming storms these new States will be the first to go under."
65. D. W. Kruger, *The Making of a Nation* (Johannesburg: Macmillan, 1977) (pp. 195, 196).
66. Stewart, *Empire Lost* (p. 19). Jan Smuts, who was the deputy prime minister at the time, was one of the dominion leaders who were deeply unhappy with Britain's unilateral issue of a guarantee to Poland.
67. N. M. Stultz, *The Nationalists in Opposition 1934–1948* (Pretoria: Human & Rousseau, 1974) (p. 60).There were thirteen members of the cabinet in all, seven of whom opted for declaring war on Germany; the other six wished to remain neutral.
68. E. P. Hartshorn, *Avenge Tobruk* (Cape Town: Purnell, 1960) (p. 3).
69. Hartshorn, *Avenge Tobruk* (pp. 12, 13).
70. Kruger, *The Making of a Nation* (p. 197).
71. H. Giliomee, *The Afrikaners: Biography of a People.* (Cape Town: Tafelberg, 2003) (p. 440) and Stewart, 'The Klopper Affair' (p. 519).
72. Crwys-Williams, *A Country at War* (pp. 20, 21).

73. Pirow, *James Barry Munnik Hertzog* (p. 180). Pirow describes the period 1933 to 1939 as the ". . . happiest time South Africa has experienced since Union."
74. A significant proportion of the Afrikaner nationalist movement was influenced by Nazi ideology, which opposed similar adversaries, being among others, the British Empire, Jews, and capitalism. Radical right ideas appealed to Afrikaner nationalists such as Oswald Pirow and J. B. M. Hertzog. Support for Nazi Germany was at its strongest in the early parts of the war and waned with the decreasing fortunes of the Third Reich. S. Dubow, 'Introduction,' in *South Africa's 1940s: Worlds of Possibilities*, ed. by A. Jeeves and S. Dubow (Cape Town: Double Storey Books, 2005) (pp. 5, 6). Bill Nasson describes it thus, "a large portion of the dominant white minority was vigorously anti-war." The antiwar lobby was made up of those who were pacifist, those who were anti-British, and those who were pro-German. Nasson, *South Africa at War* (p. 15).
75. TNA, DO, Class 35, P1003, File WG/3/4/1, *Union Cooperation - Entry of Union into the War*, September 12, 1939. Hertzog had evolved a policy of "compromise neutrality," in which he planned to keep the Union out of the war and subject to the discharge of South Africa's obligations regarding Simonstown.
76. D. Visser, 'Anglo-South African Relations and the Erebus Scheme, 1936–1939,' *Scientia Militaria*, 35(1) (2007) (pp. 68–98). Visser, in his article, highlights the political divisions in South African society over participation in a 'British' war, using the *Erebus Scheme* as a lens with which to examine differing South African attitudes toward the war, as well as South Africa's fragile relationship with the United Kingdom. See also Simpson, *South Africa Fights* (p. 12). Simpson refers to two groups of Afrikaners other than those supporting the United Kingdom as isolationists and republicans.
77. A. Stewart, 'The "Atomic" Despatch: Field Marshal Auchinleck, the Fall of the Tobruk Garrison and Post-War Anglo-South African Relations,' *Scientia Militaria*, 36(1) (2008) (p. 79), and Stewart, 'The Klopper Affair' (p. 527).
78. O. Pirow, *James Barry Munnik Hertzog* (p. 252).
79. D. Reitz, *Adrift on the Open Veld: The Anglo-Boer War and its Aftermath 1899–1943* (Cape Town: Stormberg, 2011) (p. 519).
80. Birkby, *Uncle George* (p. 71). This was as a result of a report by General Brink born out of his study tour to Europe. Here he observed the strenuous physical training regime in Germany and other European armies.
81. Martin, *Operations on the Home Front* (p. 17).
82. A. Wessels, 'The First Two Years of War: The Development of the Union Defence Forces (UDF), September 1939 to September 1941,' *Military History Journal*, June 2000 (11/5) (p. 165).
83. National Archives Pretoria (NAP), Jan Smuts Papers (JSP), Box 132, f.66, *Brigadier-General J.J. Collyer on the Union Defence Force*, September 1939. See also Martin, *Operations on the Home Front* (p. 27).
84. TNA, DO, Class 35, P1003/6, File WG3/4/32, *South African Field Army - Notes on Lt. Col. Bishop's visit to South Africa*, January 1940. On a visit to South Africa in early 1940, Bishop identified the lack of leadership as acute and suggested filling the gaps with suitable British candidates. See also Martin, *Operations on the Home Front*, VII (p. 25). In contrast to the lack of staff officer training, a policy was established in 1926 that all would-be officers in the UDF had to

initially qualify as pilots and then go on to be trained in artillery and becoming "amphigarious" officers. Birkby, *Uncle George* (p. 70).

85. E. G. Malherbe, *Never a Dull Moment* (Cape Town: Howard Timmins, 1981) (p. 213).
86. Giliomee, *The Afrikaners* (p. 440).
87. Jackson, *The British Empire* (pp. 239, 242).
88. Giliomee, *The Afrikaners* (p. 443). These red tabs were given only to those in the military and police prepared to take the Africa Oath, and signalled the wearer's willingness to fight anywhere in Africa.
89. Giliomee, *The Afrikaners* (p. 441).
90. I. Rosmarin, *Inside Story* (Cape Town: W. J. Flesch & Partners, 1990) (p. 3).
91. P. J. Furlong, *Between Crown and Swastika: The Impact of the Radical Right on the Afrikaner Movement in the Fascist Era* (Johannesburg: Witwatersrand University Press, 1991) (p. 117). Refers to Alan Paton's biography on J. H. Hofmeyr, in which he noted that in 1938, one-third of Afrikaners were for Hertzog, one-third for Malan, and one-third for Smuts. The implication is that up to two-thirds of Afrikaners did not support a war against Germany, and many of those who supported Malan and even Hertzog where pro-German.
92. A. Grundlingh, 'The King's Afrikaners? Enlistment and Ethnic Identity in the Union of South Africa's Defence Force during the Second World War, 1939–45,' *The Journal of African History*, 40(3) (1999) (p. 354). E. G. Malherbe, Director of Military Intelligence, suggests that Afrikaans-speakers constituted at least 50 percent of the force.
93. Grundlingh, 'The King's Afrikaners?' (p. 361).
94. A. M. Grundlingh, 'South Africa and the Second World War,' in *South Africa in the 20th Century*, ed. by S. B. Spies and B. J. Liebenberg (Pretoria: J. L. van Schaik Academic, 1993) (p. 290). Nearly 80 percent of the black recruits came from "ravaged rural areas" affected by a devastating drought during 1941–1943.
95. F. L. Monama, 'The Second World War and South African Society,' in *Reflections on War*, ed. by I. Liebenberg and T. Potgieter (Stellenbosch: Sun Media, 2012) (p. 54).
96. B. Nasson, 'Battling for History: The Impact of War upon Modern South Africa,' *Scientia Militaria*, 31.1 (2003) (p. 113).
97. Nasson, *South Africa at War* (p.61)
98. Kruger, *The Making of a Nation* (p. 200).
99. The reluctance to arm, and therefore the relegation of "native" troops to support duties has precedence in the First World War, and found legal roots in the Defence Act (Act 13 of 1912). It was Article 7 of the Act that limited the participation of "non-Europeans" to noncombatant roles. I. Gleeson, *The Unknown Force: Black, Indian and Coloured Soldiers Through Two World Wars* (Johannesburg: Ashanti, 1994) (p. 9). Jan Smuts, a minister of defence at the time of the First World War, turned down an offer to raise a corps of "Coloured Boys" to fight against the Turks, as he could see no military value in the offer. This reluctance on the part of Smuts proved unfounded, as colored soldiers did eventually serve in the First World War in a combatant role with distinction. Gleeson, *The Unknown Force* (p. 12). The term "coloured" in a South African context refers to citizens of mixed race.

100. Martin, *Operations on the Home Front* (p. 72). The colored or mixed race community preferred to serve as combatants, as intimated to General Collyer, the Director-General of Reserves, by the chairman of the Association. The Minister of Defence was approached by the Coloured Welfare Association, which desired establishment of a battalion for service anywhere. The Cape Corps saw service in East Africa and Palestine as combatants in the First World War.
101. I. Gleeson, *The Unknown Force: Black, Indian and Coloured Soldiers Through Two World Wars* (Johannesburg: Ashanti, 1994) (p. 106). The Italians had little compunction in recruiting black troops for combatant duties, deploying 160,000 of them from Abyssinia and Somaliland.
102. There is an interesting account of the conditions encountered by Private Dick West on his induction into the UDF indicating that blacks were not alone in having to face appalling conditions in their training phase. Many white South Africans endured as bleak and as unhealthy conditions as their black compatriots, in an ill-prepared UDF overwhelmed with the task of raising a large army. Crwys-Williams, *A Country at War* (pp. 74–80).
103. L. Grundlingh, 'The Participation of South African Blacks in the Second World War' (Doctoral Thesis, Rand Afrikaans University, Arts/Humanities, 1986), pp. 111–48. Grundlingh has produced a monumental work, and his chapter "Conditions of Service" provides detailed and excruciating testimony of the appalling and discriminatory conditions suffered by blacks in rendering service to South Africa. On the question of the food ration, the army authorities saw fit to differentiate between the different racial groups, having different rations scales for whites, coloreds, and blacks. This was justified by drawing attention to the different standards of living of the different population groups. Furthermore, ". . . it is inadvisable to inculcate more than is necessary, habits which the individual may be unable to satisfy on his return to civil life."
104. J. A. I. Agar-Hamilton and L. C. F. Turner, *The Sidi Rezegh Battles, 1941* (Cape Town: Oxford University Press, 1957) (pp. 84, 85). Many well-qualified white volunteers had been recruited into the air force, engineers, and armored car units at the expense of the established regiments. Qualified partisans were being weeded from the infantry regiments to fill positions in the development of the engineering and ammunition industries. One thousand blacks had been posted to the 1st Infantry Division on the eve of the Crusader battles to replace white drivers and for some of the noncombatant roles. General Brink was not happy with their quality and was unable to train them in time for the operation. Due to manpower constraints, South Africa was only able to field a two-brigade division, which severely curtailed its fighting power.
105. Nasson, *South Africa at War* (pp. 51, 52).
106. Jackson, *The British Empire* (p. 239). Besides becoming fully self-sufficient, South Africa managed to contribute supplies to other parts of the empire and was especially important as an arms exporter before American and Canadian production came fully online in 1941.
107. Martin, *Operations on the Home Front* (p. 32).
108. NAP, JSP, Box 132, f.66, *Brigadier-General J.J. Collyer on the Union Defence Force*, September 1939.
109. Kruger, *The Making of a Nation* (p. 204).

110. Roberts, *The South African Opposition* (pp. 26, 27, 70). Hertzog, on his resignation as Prime-Minister, joined the Nationalists under Malan to become their leader. It was an uneasy alliance that was destined not to last. Malan was an out-and-out republican who believed in the dominance of the Afrikaner, while Hertzog believed in an independent South Africa for both Englishman and Afrikaner. His leadership of the reconstituted National Party (HNP) was short-lived, and he formed the Afrikaner Party on January 30, 1941. Hertzog began to increasingly embrace the principles of National Socialism and stated, "I regard National Socialism as suited to the moral and religious outlook of the Afrikaner . . ." See O. Pirow, *James Barry Munnik Hertzog* (p.259).
111. E. G. Malherbe, *Never a Dull Moment* (Cape Town: Howard Timmins, 1981) (p. 215). Although some of the worst offenders were interned, the great majority of those who sympathized with the Nazis were left at large because Smuts was reluctant to make martyrs of them, leaving military security to err on the side of leniency. South Africa was left literally waging a war on two fronts, one being a conventional one to the north of the border, and the other on the home front combating subversive activities and attempts to derail the war effort.
112. Roberts, *The South African Opposition* (p.75). The OB movement had been founded in Bloemfontein in October 1938 on the occasion of the centenary of the Great Trek. The Smuts government prohibited its employees from becoming members of the OB.
113. Roberts, *The South African Opposition* (p.79).
114. Bunting, *The Rise of the South African Reich* (p. 82).
115. Stewart, 'The Klopper Affair' (p. 525).
116. NAP, JSP, Box 95-1, f.6, Smuts to Churchill, *Empire Defence in New Situation after France Collapse and Strategic Role in Africa,* June 22, 1940. See also NAP, JSP, Box 95-1, f.7, Churchill to Smuts, *British Defence Priorities,* June 27, 1940 and I.S.O. Playfair, *A History of the Second World War: The Mediterranean and the Middle East*, ed. by J. R. M. Butler (Uckfield: Naval and Military Press, 2004), I (p. 127).
117. Playfair, *History of the Second World War,* I (pp. 166, 168).
118. Martin, *Operations on the Home Front* (pp. 84, 94, 95).
119. Pirow, *James Barry Munnik Hertzog* (p. 203). Hertzog was no less anxious than Smuts to incorporate the three protectorates of Swaziland, Basutoland, and Bechuanaland into the Union.
120. Hyam, *The Lion and the Springbok* (p. 102).
121. Hyam, *The Lion and the Springbok* (p. 32). ". . . Every Prime Minister from Botha in 1911 to Vervoerd in 1961 pestered Britain for the transfer of the High Commission Territories."
122. R. Hyam, *The Failure of South African Expansion, 1908–1948.* (London: Macmillan, 1972) (pp. 25–32, 186).
123. TNA DO A. Eden, 'Union Defence Requirements' DO 35-1003/WG3/4/11/2, October 23, 1939. The request was delivered through Denys Reitz, the Deputy Prime Minister, to Anthony Eden, Secretary of State for Dominion Affairs. NAP, JSP, J. Smuts, 'High Commission Territories,' Memorandum Smuts to Amery, Box 246(141), October 1939. Smuts felt that his hand would be greatly strengthened on the political front should the issue of the High Commission

Territories be resolved. TNA DO 'High Commission Territories' Telegram, DO 116/7/110, October 1939. Smuts felt that the House of Commons would take less interest due to the war. Hyam, *The Lion and The Springbok* (p. 107); P. Henshaw, 'South African Territorial Expansion and the International Reaction to South African Racial Polices, 1939 to 1948,' *South African Historical Journal*, 50(1) (2009) (p. 66).

124. TNA, DO 'High Commission Territories,' Memorandum to High Commissioner, DO 116/7/113, October 1939; Henshaw, 'South African Territorial Expansion,' (pp. 67, 68).
125. TNA, DO 'High Commission Territories,' Discussion Eden and Reitz, DO 116/7/114, October 1939.
126. NAP JSP, J. Smuts, 'Strategic role of Africa,' Memorandum Smuts to Churchill, Box 95-1 (6), 12/6/1940.
127. NAP JSP, W. Churchill, 'British Defence Priorities,' Memorandum from Churchill to Smuts, Box 95-1 (7), 27/06/1940.
128. M. Winslett, 'The Nadir of Alliance: The British Ultimatum of 1890 and its Place in Anglo-Portuguese Relations, 1147 -1945' (Thesis, University of Texas at Arlington, Master of Arts in History, 2008), p. 121. The British encouraged the Portuguese to enter the war on their side and demanded a contribution of 55,000 troops for the Western Front, of whom a staggering 10,000 became casualties.
129. DODA, UWHS, Pope-Hennessy, '"Z" Plan Narrative' 1949, Box 339. There were various plans designated W, X, Y, and Z for the occupation of the Portuguese African Colonies, should they become "hostile." Of the four plans, "Z" came the closest to execution.
130. I. van der Waag, 'Major J.G.W. Leipoldt, D.S.O. : A Portrait of a South African Surveyor and Intelligence Officer, 1912–1923,' *Scientia Militaria*, 25 (1995), 12-34 (p. 26).
131. Van der Waag, 'Major J.G.W. Leipoldt,' (p. 27).
132. DODA 'Plan Z,' Historical Narrative of Plan Z, Plan Z Box 1. According to the UWHS, ". . . the 'Z' plan was held in readiness and modified periodically in accordance with changing circumstances and the troops available in the Union at that time."
133. Nasson, *South Africa at War* (Johannesburg: Jacana Media, 2012) (p. 75).
134. DODA 'Plan Z,' Historical Narrative of Plan Z, Plan Z Box 1.
135. 'Operation Menace,' Memorandum Cabinet War Room, CAB 80/106/15, September 1940.
136. NAP, JSP, 'Operation Shrapnel and Brisk,' Memorandum Churchill to Smuts, Box 95-1 (21), December 1940.
137. TNA, DO, Harlech, 'Delagoa Bay,' Memorandum Harlech to Dominium Office, DO 35/1003/WG3/4/66, December 1942.
138. NAP, JSP, 'Portuguese East Africa,' Memorandum High Commissioner to Secretary of State, Box 94 (153), December 1940.

Chapter 2

1. C. Birkby, *The Saga of the Transvaal Scottish Regiment 1932–1950* (Cape Town: Hodder and Stoughton, 1950) (pp. 13–15). A speech by Smuts to his troops before departure to East Africa, July 14, 1940.
2. A. Wavell, *Despatch - Operations in East Africa, November, 1940—July, 1941* (*London Gazette*, 1946) (p. 3527). Smuts frequently impressed on Wavell the danger of reducing the forces in East Africa. This was in the face of pressure to release troops from East Africa for Egypt. There was a general sense of nervousness by the South Africans that the forces in East Africa were insufficient to prevent an Italian invasion of Kenya and even farther south.
3. This was an Italian designation for irregular forces, composed of foreigners or colonial natives, with some Italian officers and NCOs in command. The Banda were lightly armed and more suitable for policing duties than full-scale conventional war. Irregulars that were allied to the British were known as Shifta.
4. N. Orpen, *South African Forces World War II- East African and Abyssinian Campaigns* (Cape Town: Purnell, 1968) (p. 10).
5. Orpen, *East African and Abyssinian Campaigns* (p. 11).
6. E. Rosenthal, *General Dan Pienaar: His Life and His Battles* (Cape Town: Unie-Volkspers, 1943) and A. M. Pollock, *Pienaar of Alamein* (Cape Town: Cape Times, 1943).
7. Rosenthal, *General Dan Pienaar*, and Pollock, *Pienaar of Alamein.*
8. C. Birkby, *Uncle George: The Boer Boyhood, Letters and Battles of Lieutenant-General George Edwin Brink* (Johannesburg: Jonathan Ball, 1987) (p.75); Rosenthal, *General Dan Pienaar*; Pollock, *Pienaar of Alamein.*
9. A. Wavell, *Despatch - Operations in East Africa, November, 1940–July, 1941, First Report by Lieut. Gen. Sir Alan Cunningham, K.C.B., D.S.O.,M.C., on East Africa Force Operations Covering the Period From Ist November 1940 To The Fall of Addis Abeba, on Sth April, 1941.* (*London Gazette*, 1946) (p. 3557). Cunningham speaks of the reversal of poor morale on his entire force with the arrival of the South Africans in Kenya.
10. A. Wavell, *Despatch - Operations in East Africa, November, 1940–July, 1941* (*London Gazette*, 1946) (p. 3529). Early in 1941 the South Africans offered a second South African division for service in East Africa. Wavell considered, however, that he had sufficient troops in East Africa at that time and asked that the division might be reserved for use farther north.
11. A. Wavell, *Despatch - Operations in East Africa, November, 1940–July, 1941* (*London Gazette*, 1946) (p. 3531). Wavell acknowledged South Africa's contribution to the East African campaign in his dispatch. "I should like to add a special tribute to Field-Marshal Smuts for his unfailing support of the East African campaign; and to the generous response that the Union Government invariably made to any requests for assistance, either in personnel or material, during the whole period of my command in the Middle East."
12. Lieutenant-General Sir William Platt commanded the northern force that would attack from Sudan in the north through Eritrea. At this time General Sir Archibald Wavell was the Commander-in-Chief of the British Middle East Command.
13. Orpen, *East African and Abyssinian Campaigns* (p. 70).

14. Orpen, *East African and Abyssinian Campaigns* (p. 16). His Royal Highness Prince Amedeo of Savoy, the Duke of Aosta, had succeeded the hated Marshal Graziani as Viceroy of Ethiopia in November 1937 and had since done much to quench the flames of hatred kindled by the harshness of his predecessor. The duke was forty-two years old and enjoyed a credible record of service in both the army and the air force. He had earned the respect of the British in the Sudan as an administrator and he was liked as a neighbor.
15. Orpen, *East African and Abyssinian Campaigns* (pp. 19, 342, 343).
16. Orpen, *East African and Abyssinian Campaigns* (p. 19).
17. J. S. M. Simpson, *South Africa Fights* (London: Hodder and Stoughton, 1941) (p. 184).
18. Orpen, *East African and Abyssinian Campaigns* (p. 15).
19. Most narratives on Smuts's campaign in German East Africa in 1916 are less than flattering. The South African tactic of avoiding battle casualties through frontal attacks receives short shrift even among modern authors such as R. Anderson, 'World War I in East Africa 1916–1918' (PHD Thesis, University of Glasgow, Modern History, 2001). A more balanced view of Smuts and the South African way of war can be found in C. P. Fendall, *The East African Force 1915–1919: The First World War in Colonial Africa* (Leonaur, 2014).
20. Orpen, *East African and Abyssinian Campaigns* (p. 15).
21. Defeats on the Libyan-Egyptian border and Greece, in the battle of Britain, and at sea in the Mediterranean.
22. Birkby, *Uncle George* (p. 23).
23. Birkby, *Uncle George* (p. 11).
24. Birkby, *Uncle George* (pp. 53, 65).
25. *Dictionary of South African Biography Volume V*, ed. by C. J. Beyers and J. L. Basson (Pretoria: Human Sciences Research Council, 1987) (p. 809). Van Deventer joined the Boer Transvaal Republic State Artillery in 1896, which was one of the few formal formations existing in the Boer order of battle. As such he received formal training as an artilleryman with strong German influence. After the Anglo-Boer War he served with the UDF in the German South West Africa and German East Africa campaigns with distinction.
26. Birkby, *Uncle George* (p. 59).
27. Formed on May 1, 1933, under the patronage of Oswald Pirow, Minister of Defence. The object was to give training to youths, between the ages of seventeen and twenty-three, who, in the wake of the 1929 depression, could find no suitable employment on leaving school. In February 1940 a number of troops were transferred to the 1st and 2nd Field Force Battalions. These served with distinction in East Africa, Abyssinia, and the Middle East as part of 1st South African Infantry Division.
28. Birkby, *Uncle George* (pp. 70–75).
29. DODA, Acquisitions, Group 1, Box 48, File–Documents dealing with visit paid by Colonel Geo E. Brink to British, German, French and Italian Armies–1937. *Report to CGS (Chief of General Staff) on visits to Germany, Denmark, Italy, France and England–1937*, pp. 1–5. Thanks to Evert Kleynhans for drawing this to my attention.

30. DODA, Acquisitions, Group 1, Box 48, File–Documents dealing with visit paid by Colonel Geo E. Brink to British, German, French and Italian Armies–1937. *Report to CGS on visits to Germany, Denmark, Italy, France and England–1937*, p. 7 & Appendix A, pp. 4–5. Thanks to Evert Kleynhans for drawing this to my attention.
31. Birkby, *Uncle George* (p. 87–90).
32. Birkby, *Uncle George* (p. 97).
33. Platt became the GOC East Africa Command during December 1941.
34. Orpen, *East African and Abyssinian Campaigns* (p. 79) and Pollock, *Pienaar of Alamein* (pp. 69, 70).
35. DODA Reference Library, UWHS, *Narratives and Reports East Africa Volume V, East African Campaigns, Abridged Report on Operations at El Wak 14–18 Dec 1940* (p. 10461). The fact was highlighted that "perpetual rehearsal" may produce "stickiness" in mobile operations, and commanders need to be able to react quickly to new information received from the front that may not have formed part of the rehearsal.
36. DODA, WD, Box 300, File–12 AFR DIV, *Report on Operations at El Wak–30 December 1940* (p. 2).
37. Pollock, *Pienaar of Alamein* (p. 39). See also A. F. Hattersley, *Carbineer: The History of the Royal Natal Carbineers* (Aldershot: Gale and Polden, 1950) (p. 68).
38. DODA Reference Library, UWHS, *Narratives and Reports East Africa Volume V, East African Campaigns, Abridged Report on Operations at El Wak 14–18 Dec 1940* (p. 1049). The enveloping maneuver was designed to "fix" the elusive Banda, an enterprise that had not been accomplished to date.
39. DODA, WD, Box 300, File –12 AFR DIV, *Report on Operations at El Wak–30 December 1940 Part I* (pp. 5, 6).
40. DODA Reference Library, UWHS, *Narratives and Reports East Africa Volume V, East African Campaigns, Abridged Report on Operations at El Wak 14–18 Dec 1940* (p. 1050). The extraordinarily long approach march of 180 km was open to the danger of detection. The risk of being detected was somewhat abated by achieving local air superiority over the operational area.
41. DODA, WD, Box 300, File –12 AFR DIV, *Report on Operations at El Wak–30 December 1940 Part II* (p. 2).
42. DODA, WD, Box 300, File –12 AFR DIV, *Report on Operations at El Wak–30 December 1940 Part I* (pp. 3–5).
43. Klein, *Springboks in Armour* (pp. 7, 8).
44. Klein, *Springboks in Armour* (pp. 21).
45. DODA, UWHS, *Narratives and Reports East Africa Volume I, East African Campaigns, SATC in Action* (p. 196). See also Klein, *Springboks in Armour* (p. 24). Orde Winghate had a different opinion as to the usefulness of the armored car in East Africa. DODA, UWHS, *Narratives and Reports East Africa Volume II, East African Campaigns, Appreciation of the Ethiopian Campaign by Colonel O.C. Wingate* (pp. 142, 143). Operating with the irregular forces, Wingate found that ". . . armoured cars were the most useless of weapons; easily detected; confined to roads; and vulnerable to nothing more powerful than a Boys rifle."
46. C. Birkby, *Springbok Victory* (Johannesburg: Libertas, 1941) (p. 99). See also Klein, *Springboks in Armour* (pp. 26–30). This is an account of the entire battle from the perspective of the South African armor.

47. DODA, WD, Box 300, File–12 AFR DIV, *Report on Operations at El Wak–30 December 1940 Part III, Lessons Learned* (p. 2).
48. DODA, WD, Box 300, File–12 AFR DIV, *Report on Operations at El Wak–30 December 1940 Part II* (p. 9).
49. Birkby, *Uncle George* (p. 106).
50. Orpen, *East African and Abyssinian Campaigns* (p. 79) and Pollock, *Pienaar of Alamein* (p. 42).
51. Birkby, *Uncle George* (p. 110).
52. DODA, UWHS, *Narratives and Reports East Africa Volume IV, East African Campaigns, Narrative of the 1st SAI Brigade 3 Feb 1941–26 Feb 1941* (p. 659). Throughout the operation the brigade had to operate with one armored car company less a platoon, which reduced their effectiveness by one third and up to two-thirds on occasion. The same was true for the brigade engineers and some of the infantry. The ad hoc detachment of brigade assets to other formations most certainly affected the fighting power of the brigade, which was to have serious consequences later in the war.
53. Pollock, *Pienaar of Alamein* (p. 36). See also E. Kleynhans, 'Armoured Warfare: The South African Experience in East Africa, 1940–1941' (Master's thesis, Military Science, University of Stellenbosch, 2014) (pp. 46, 48). Brink was also concerned with the British tendency to break up formations and parcel them out on an ad hoc basis. Kleynhans has produced an important work that examines the development of South African armored doctrine through the exploits of the battles in East Africa in the Second World War.
54. Klein, *Springboks in Armour* (p. 47).
55. Kleynhans, 'Armoured Warfare' (p. 107). See also Klein, *Springboks in Armour* (p. 43).
56. The most comprehensive work on the role of the South African engineer is N. Orpen and H. J. Martin, *Salute the Sappers: The Operations of the SAEC in East Africa and the Middle East* (Sappers Association, 1981).
57. DODA, UWHS, *Narratives and Reports East Africa Volume I, East African Campaigns 2 SA Armd Car Coy* (pp. 140, 142).
58. Orpen, *East African and Abyssinian Campaigns* (p. 96).
59. Orpen, *East African and Abyssinian Campaigns* (p. 98).
60. D. Baker, *War, Wine and Valour* (Essendon: Baker Ebooks, 2005).
61. Orpen, *East African and Abyssinian Campaigns* (pp. 100, 101).
62. C. Birkby, *It's a Long Way to Addis* (London: Frederick Muller, 1943) (p. 133). Birkby describes the intense heat and how it sapped the troops' strength, who, despite "rigid water discipline," were at times without water.
63. Baker, *War, Wine and Valour.*
64. Orpen, *East African and Abyssinian Campaigns* (p. 102). See also C. Birkby, *Springbok Victory* (Johannesburg: Libertas, 1941) (p. 108–112) for a more sympathetic account of the battle.
65. J. Ambrose Brown, *The War of a Hundred Days: Springboks in Somalia and Abyssinia 1940–1941* (Johannesburg: Ashanti, 1990) (p. 112).
66. Birkby, *Uncle George* (p. 116). Buchanan would go on to display the same cautious behavior in the battle for Mega.

67. DODA, UWHS, *Narratives and Reports East Africa Volume I, East African Campaigns 2 SA Armd Car Coy* (pp. 142, 143). Some of the armored cars were used for secondary tasks such as escorting and guarding B Echelon on instruction from different officers at different times. The armored cars only had three wireless sets among them, which also made difficult the efficient use of command and control. See also Klein, *Springboks in Armour* (p. 38).
68. Orpen, *East African and Abyssinian Campaigns* (p. 104) and Birkby, *Uncle George* (p. 118). Brink in return scribbled a note on Cunningham's letter to the extent "but my object in using the Armoured Cars boldly was to put the fear of God into the enemy's native troops and in this we were most successful."
69. Birkby, *It's a Long Way to Addis* (p. 143).
70. Klein, *Springboks in Armour* (pp. 54, 55).
71. DODA, UWHS, *Narratives and Reports East Africa Volume I, Interview with* the *German Consul to Italian East Africa, 15 April 1941* (p. 85). The German Consul, Dr. Strohm, had a very low opinion of the Italian fighting abilities, which he put down to lack of "guts" or proper training and equipment, and above all to the demoralizing effect of the reversals suffered on the border in the first skirmishes at El Yibo and Mega.
72. Klein, *Springboks in Armour* (pp. 48, 49).
73. In the opening stages of the battle of Sidi Rezegh, elements of the 5th Brigade launched an attack on Axis positions without reconnoitering the positions first, resulting in a costly assault for little gain.
74. Orpen, *East African and Abyssinian Campaigns* (p. 125).
75. DODA, Reference Library, UWHS, *Narratives and Reports East Africa Volume V, East African Campaigns, 1 SA Div in East Africa* (p. 1106).
76. DODA, Reference Library, UWHS, *Narratives and Reports East Africa Volume V, East African Campaigns, 1 SA Div in East Africa* (p. 1106). It is also conceded that the South Africans failed to take adequate defensive measures when they decided to remain at the crossroads. See Kleynhans. 'Armoured Warfare,' (p. 178) for a slightly different viewpoint on the effectiveness of Italian armor in East Africa.
77. DODA, Reference Library, UWHS, *Narratives and Reports East Africa Volume I, East African Campaigns 2 SA Armd Car Coy* (p. 160); Birkby, *Uncle George* (p. 140).
78. DODA, Reference Library, UWHS, *Narratives and Reports East Africa Volume I, Interview with* the *German Consul to Italian East Africa, 15 April 1941* (p. 85). Confirmation of how close the Italians had come to routing the entire South African force manifested in an interview by South African intelligence officers of the German Consul to Italian East Africa, Dr. Strohm. The Consul believed that had the Italian reinforcements not been prevented from getting through to Mega from Yavello due to the engagement at the crossroads, the outcome of the battle would have been a completely different matter. He pointed out that the Italian tanks turned back at El Sad would have played havoc with the South African troops at the foot of Mega. For a less alarming account see Klein, *Springboks in Armour* (p. 70).
79. Birkby, *Uncle George* (p. 142).
80. Orpen, *East African and Abyssinian Campaigns* (p. 146).

81. Birkby, *Uncle George* (p. 143).
82. DODA, Reference Library, UWHS, *Narratives and Reports East Africa Volume V, East African Campaigns, 1 SA Div in East Africa* (p. 1107). Apparently the 2nd SAI Brigade ran out of water supplies and had to wait to be resupplied before they could move.
83. Klein, *Springboks in Armour* (p. 73).
84. DODA, Reference Library, UWHS, *Narratives and Reports East Africa Volume V, East African Campaigns, 1 SA Div in East Africa* (p. 1106). Buchanan's 35 km detour came about due to his belief that his primary task was to cut the Mega-Moyale road rather than launch an attack to the east of Mega as instructed.
85. DODA, Reference Library, UWHS, *Narratives and Reports East Africa Volume V, East African Campaigns, 1 SA Div in East Africa* (p. 1110).
86. S. Monick and O. E. F. Baker, 'Mega, February 1941: The Role of the 1st South African Irish Regiment,' *Scientia Militaria*, 20.4 (1990) (p. 42).
87. Birkby, *Uncle George* (p. 144).
88. DODA, Reference Library, UWHS, *Narratives and Reports East Africa Volume V, East African Campaigns, 1 SA Div in East Africa* (p. 1110). Buchanan was advised by "friendly natives" that the approaches were mined and not suitable for the use of troops. Buchanan may have done better to send his own reconnaissance for the correct picture.
89. Birkby, *Uncle George* (pp. 142, 143).
90. Monick, 'Mega, February 1941' (p. 45).
91. DODA, Reference Library, UWHS, *Narratives and Reports East Africa Volume V, East African Campaigns, 1 SA Div in East Africa* (p. 1110).
92. Birkby, *Uncle George* (p. 148).
93. DODA, Reference Library, UWHS, *Narratives and Reports East Africa Volume I, East African Campaigns 2 SA Armd Car Coy* (p. 162). See also Orpen, *East African and Abyssinian Campaigns* (p. 159).
94. DODA, Reference Library, UWHS, *Narratives and Reports East Africa Volume V, East African Campaigns, 1 SA Div in East Africa* (p. 1112).
95. Brown, *The War of a Hundred Days* (p. 124).
96. Klein, *Springboks in Armour* (pp. 76, 77); A. Wavell, *Despatch - Operations in East Africa, November, 1940–July, 1941* (*London Gazette*, 1946) (p. 3529). Throughout the swift campaign there was pressure to send the 1st SAI Division to Egypt, especially after the Axis re-conquest of Cyrenaica and the fall of Greece in April 1941. After the fall of Addis Ababa on April 6, 1941, Wavell was anxious the South African division and a large quantity of transports be sent to Egypt.
97. A. Wavell, *Despatch - Operations in East Africa, November, 1940–July, 1941* (*London Gazette*, 1946) (p. 3565). See also Pollock, *Pienaar of Alamein* (pp.47,48).
98. A. Wavell, *Despatch - Operations in East Africa, November, 1940–July, 1941* (*London Gazette*, 1946) (p. 3530).
99. DODA, Reference Library, UWHS, *Narratives and Reports East Africa Volume IV, East African Campaigns, Narrative of the events from the occupation of Addis Ababa 1st SAI Brigade* (p. 736). The excuse offered in the brigade narrative was that the captured Italian fuel was contaminated by sea water and the need to

mix two types of Italian fuel to achieve a workable mixture. See also DODA, Reference Library, UWHS, *Narratives and Reports East Africa Volume V, East African Campaigns, 1 SA Div in East Africa* (p. 1337). It is alleged that the South Africans were wasteful in their use and distribution of their fuel and that the staff of the brigade had failed to budget and had effectively lost control of the fuel situation.

100. Orpen, *East African and Abyssinian Campaigns* (p. 245). Pienaar would later be criticized for failing to close up with 5th Brigade at Sidi Rezegh and other similar instances of less than alacritous response to orders in the remaining actions of Operation Crusader. His reluctance to commit his force to the attack was again demonstrated in the Gazala battles, much to the frustration of his superiors. His initial negative attitude in the defense of Alamein once again drew the ire of the British command in 1942, who lost confidence in his offensive vigor.
101. Orpen, *East African and Abyssinian Campaigns* (p. 252).
102. Orpen, *East African and Abyssinian Campaigns* (p. 256) and A. Wavell, *Despatch - Operations in East Africa, November, 1940–July, 1941* (The London Gazette, 1946) (p. 3530).
103. E. P. Hartshorn, *Avenge Tobruk* (Cape Town: Purnell, 1960) (pp. 62, 63)
104. DODA, Reference Library, UWHS, *Narratives and Reports East Africa Volume I, Interview with Hartshorn 3 September 1941* (p. 73). It appears that the 1st SAI Brigade benefitted from having a few of its officers, among whom one was Hartshorn (See Chapter I), who received training in the First World War from the Indian Mountain Warfare School. The school was opened in May 1916 using innovative teaching methods specifically to train officers and NCOs in frontier fighting, who in turn would instruct their own units. See also DODA, Reference Library, UWHS, *Narratives and Reports East Africa Volume IV, East African Campaigns, Events in the battle of Amba Alagi from the viewpoint of the 1st SAI Brigade* (p. 593). At the end of the East African campaign Pienaar called for a training program for selected officers and NCOs to serve with the Indian Forces to gain insight and experience into the various methods of dealing with mountain warfare problems.
105. Orpen, *East African and Abyssinian Campaigns* (p. 272).
106. A. Wavell, *Despatch - Operations in East Africa, November, 1940–July, 1941, Report by Lt. Gen. Sir William Platt, K.C.B., D.S.O., On the Operations in Eritrea and Abyssinia* (*London Gazette*, 1946) (p. 3548).
107. DODA, DCS–CGS, Box 44, File–132(G) AFR DIV. *Lessons learnt in East African Campaign in Operations conducted by 1 SA Div* (p. 3).
108. DODA, Reference Library, UWHS, *Narratives and Reports East Africa Volume V, East African Campaigns, 1 SA Div in East Africa* (p. 1139).
109. DODA, Reference Library, UWHS, *Narratives and Reports East Africa Volume V, East African Campaigns, Abridged Report on Operations at El Wak 14–18 Dec 1940* (p. 1061).
110. DODA, DCS–CGS, Box 44, File–132(G) AFR DIV. *Lessons learnt in East African Campaign in Operations conducted by 1 SA Div* (pp. 1–4).
111. DODA, Reference Library, UWHS, *Narratives and Reports East Africa Volume V, East African Campaigns, Abridged Report on Operations at El Wak 14–18 Dec 1940* (p. 1063).

112. DODA, DCS–CGS, Box 44, File–132(G) AFR DIV. *Lessons learnt in East African Campaign in Operations conducted by 1 SA Div* (p. 4).
113. DODA, DCS–CGS, Box 44, File–132(G) AFR DIV. *Lessons learnt in East African Campaign in Operations conducted by 1 SA Div* (pp. 9, 10).
114. DODA, DCS–CGS, Box 44, File–132(G) AFR DIV. *Lessons learnt in East African Campaign in Operations conducted by 1 SA Div* (p. 24).
115. DODA, DCS–CGS, Box 44, File–132(G) AFR DIV. *Lessons learnt in East African Campaign in Operations conducted by 1 SA Div* (pp. 11–16).
116. DODA, DCS–CGS, Box 44, File–132(G) AFR DIV. *Lessons learnt in East African Campaign in Operations conducted by 1 SA Div* (p. 21).
117. DODA, Reference Library, UWHS, *Narratives and Reports East Africa Volume I, East African Campaigns, Signals* (p. 194).
118. DODA, Reference Library, UWHS, *Narratives and Reports East Africa Volume V, East African Campaigns, Abridged Report on Operations at El Wak 14–18 Dec 1940* (p. 1067).

CHAPTER 3

1. The operational level is the art of war, as opposed to tactics, which is the art of fighting. J. L. Romjue, 'The Origins of Contemporary Doctrine,' in *The Occasional (30)*, ed. by J. Gooch (Camberley: Strategic and Combat Studies Institute, 1997).
2. This definition is in part derived from the Canada Department of National Defence. The Conduct of Land Operations B-GL-300-001/FP-000, 1998.
3. J. Baily, *The First World War and the Birth of the Modern Style of Warfare* (Camberley, UK: Strategic and Combat Studies Institute, 1996) (p. 48).
4. James J. Sadkovich has gone some way to redressing the unbalanced viewpoint of the Italian contribution to the war effort in North Africa. His work provides refreshing insight into a period of history plagued with prejudice against Italian military ability. See J. J. Sadkovich, 'Understanding Defeat: Reappraising Italy's Role in World War II,' *Journal of Contemporary History*, 24(1) (1989) (pp. 27–61) and J.J. Sadkovich, 'Of Myths and Men: Rommel and the Italians in North Africa, 1940–1942,' *The International History Review*, 12(2) (1991) (pp. 284–313). See also I. Walker, *Iron Hulls Iron Hearts: Mussolini's Elite Armoured Divisions in North Africa* (Ramsbury: Crowood Press, 2006) for a more detailed explanation of Italian armored doctrine.
5. Most authors dealing with the subject attest to the special conditions that a desert provides in the conduct of mobile armored warfare. Two dedicated sources that deal with the geography of war are J. M. Collins, *Military Geography* (Dulles: Potomac Books, 2006) and H. A. Winters, *Battling the Elements: Weather and Terrain in the Conduct of War* (Baltimore: Johns Hopkins, 1998).
6. For a rare study of the fledgling UDF's first successful campaign using maneuver warfare see A. Garcia, 'Manoeuvre Warfare in the South African Campaign in German South West Africa During the First World War' (Master's thesis, Humanities, University of South Africa, 2015).
7. J. A. I. Agar-Hamilton and L. C. F. Turner, *The Sidi Rezegh Battles, 1941* (Cape Town: Oxford University Press, 1957) (pp. 33, 34).
8. J. F. C. Fuller, *Memoirs of an Unconventional Soldier* (London: Ivor Nicholson and Watson, 1936) (pp. 318–41). Plan 1919 exposed Fuller's thinking early in

his career. His vision gave precedence to the tank as a war-winning weapon rather than as part of a combined arms team. "Up to the present the theory of the tactical employment of tanks had been based on trying to harmonise their powers with existing methods of fighting, which is with infantry and artillery tactics."

9. One of the better books that debunks the link between the development of German armored doctrine and that of the British intellectuals is authored by Jonathan Mearsheimer. In his book he exposes Guderian's praise of Liddell Hart as being more as a result of duress than a factual account of Hart's contribution to German doctrine. J. Mearsheimer, *Liddell Hart and the Weight of History* (London: Cornell University, 1988).
10. J. Harris, *Men, Ideas and Tanks: British Military Thought and Armoured Forces 1903–1939* (Manchester: Manchester University Press, 1995) (p. 8). When Fuller is looked at on the subject of the role of the tank in future wars, his sentiments seem to be exactly mirrored in the objectives set for Operation Crusader. '. . . by the time the two armies are within striking distance, the infantry will be in rear of the tanks and the artillery in rear of the infantry. Tank will, consequently, engage tank, and a battle for tank supremacy will result.' J. F. C. Fuller, *The Reformation of War* (London: Hutchinson, 1923) (p. 157).
11. R. M. Citino, *The Path to Blitzkrieg: Doctrine and Training in the German Army, 1920–39* (Mechanicsburg, PA: Stackpole, 1999) (p. 10).
12. Harris, *Men, Ideas and Tanks* (p. 201). There are those who hold the opposite view. These advocates/proponents believed that the Germans owed much of their armored doctrine to the thinking of British intellectuals and theorists. One of the latest authors, attempting to resurrect the reputation of Liddell Hart, as well as define the debt owed by German mechanized doctrine to the British, is Azar Gat. A. Gat, *British Armour Theory and the Rise of the Panzer Arm: Revising the Revisionists* (London: MacMillan Press, 2000). Vardi believes that the German doctrine in the early and mid-1930s showed very little indication of British influence. There was a greater chance of a mutual learning process between the Soviets and Germany due to the joint training camp operated at Kazan before 1933. Gil-li Vardi, 'The Enigma of German Operational Theory: The Evolution of Military Thought in Germany, 1919–1938' (Doctoral Thesis, The London School of Economies, Philosophy, 2008) (p. 192).
13. The first time it appeared in the English press was in the September 1939 issue of *Time* magazine.
14. K. H. Frieser, *The Blitzkrieg Legend: The 1940 Campaign in the West* (Annapolis: Naval Institute Press, 2005) (pp. 4–11). Frieser deals extensively with demystifying the term *Blitzkrieg* and provides in-depth evidence as to the centuries-old evolution of German doctrine leading up to the Second World War.
15. L. Deighton, *Blitzkrieg* (London: Triad/Granada, 1980) (p. 173).
16. Harris, *Men, Ideas and Tanks* (pp. 201, 202).
17. The Royal United Services Institute for Defence and Security Studies (RUSI) is a British defense and security think tank founded in 1831 by the Duke of Wellington. RUSI describes itself as "the leading forum in the UK for national and international Defence and Security."
18. Fuller, *The Reformation of War* (p. 158).

19. Harris, *Men, Ideas and Tanks* (p. 206).
20. Harris, *Men, Ideas and Tanks* (pp. 207, 208).
21. There are those who see Hobart as a prophet and visionary of his time rather than misguided. See K. Macksey, *Armoured Crusader* (London: Grub Street, 2004). Shelford Bidwell places Hobart in correct historical context by observing that he was a full-fledged member of the radical school who propagated and to an extent instigated a completely new departure in the methods of war. The Fuller–Liddell Hart–Hobart teams were diametrically apart from those merely wishing to restore "audacity" to military doctrine. See S. Bidwell, *Gunners at War* (London: Arms and Armour Press, 1970) (p. 61).
22. C. Pugsley, 'We Have Been Here Before: The Evolution of the Doctrine of Decentralised Command in the British Army 1905–1989,' *Sandhurst Occasional Papers*, 2011 (p. 6). The British developed two distinct lines of tanks, infantry tanks (Valentine, Matilda, Churchill) and cruiser tanks (Cruiser, Crusader, Covenanter), each with its own distinct doctrine.
23. Citino, *The Path to Blitzkrieg* (p. 12). Seeckt's ideas on maneuver warfare and combined arms leadership were expounded in a tactical manual issued to the Reichswehr in 1921 titled *Fuhrung und Gefecht der verbunden Waffen*. H. von Seeckt, *Command and Combat Use of Combined Arms (German Field Service Regulations)*, trans. by Capt. P. B. Harm (Germany: United States of America Army War College, 1921). See also *On the German Art of War Truppenfuhrung: German Army Manual for Unit Command in World War II*, ed. by B. Condell and D. Zabecki (Mechanicsburg, PA: Stackpole, 2009). The 1934/1935 edition includes armored warfare. See also Frieser, *The Blitzkrieg Legend* (p. 331). Freiser states that Seeckt bequeathed to his successors a "gospel of mobility."
24. Citino, *The Path to Blitzkrieg* (p. 35).
25. Field Marshal Helmuth von Moltke was chief of staff of the Prussian army for thirty years.
26. Citino, *The Path to Blitzkrieg* (p. 43). *Bewegungskrieg* being a war of movement incorporating maneuverability with interarm combined warfare tactics.
27. Gil-li Vardi, "The Enigma of German Operational Theory: The Evolution of Military Thought in Germany, 1919–1938" (Doctoral Thesis, The London School of Economies, Philosophy, 2008) (p. 156).
28. Deighton, *Blitzkrieg* (p. 143). Lieutenant-General Sir John Monash, commander of the Australian Corps, France, 1918, likened a modern battle to an orchestral composition in which the units are the instruments and the tasks they perform the musical score.
29. K. H. Frieser, *The Blitzkrieg Legend: The 1940 Campaign in the West* (Annapolis: Naval Institute Press, 2005) (p. 330).
30. J. House, *Toward Combined Arms Warfare: A Survey of 20th-Century Tactics, Doctrine, and Organization* (Honolulu: University Press of the Pacific, 1984) (pp. 52, 53). German emphasis on combined arms warfare is embodied in their 1921 *Regulation on Command and Combat of the Combined Arm*. German doctrine allowed for technological advances to be incorporated and a freedom to develop doctrine based on their experiences.
31. K. H. Frieser, *The Blitzkrieg Legend: The 1940 Campaign in the West* (Annapolis: Naval Institute Press, 2005) (p. 332).

32. Vardi, 'The Enigma of German Operational Theory' (p. 29).
33. K. H. Frieser, *The Blitzkrieg Legend: The 1940 Campaign in the West* (Annapolis: Naval Institute Press, 2005) (p. 338).
34. 'Friction' is defined by Carl von Clausewitz as 'The intangible force that makes the apparently easy task so difficult.' Clausewitz acknowledges that friction creates enormous difficulties for the realization of any plan, and the *fog of war* hinders commanders from knowing what is happening. He went on to say that 'nothing is simple in war, the simplest thing is difficult.' Friction is the element that distinguishes real war from the war of the planners. C. von Clausewitz, *On War*, ed. by M. Howard and P. Paret (Princeton, NJ: Princeton University, 1976) (p. 119).
35. Citino, *The Path to Blitzkrieg* (p. 45). Seeckt found that written orders were too long and complicated, and thought that formations up to battalion size could function on nothing more than a short oral description of what was required.
36. Citino, *The Path to Blitzkrieg* (p. 57). An insightful comment from Seeckt in his *1925 Observations* illuminates German thinking on empowering the individual soldier and thus enhancing *Auftragstaktik*. "The principal thing now is to increase the responsibilities of the individual man, particularly his independence of action, and thereby to increase the efficiency of the entire army. . . . The limitations imposed by exterior circumstances cause us to give the mind more freedom of activity, with the profitable result of increasing the ability of the individual."
37. Vardi, 'The Enigma of German Operational Theory' (p. 31).
38. British military intellectuals of the period seemed to have little regard for the German doctrine of *Auftragstaktik*. An example of British difficulty in grasping the concept of mission command tactics is none other than J. F. C. Fuller, who in describing what he felt were defects in the Prussian staff system, writes, "Whereas Napoleon I led and controlled throughout, Moltke brought his armies to their starting points and then abdicated his command and unleashed them. . . . He never issued an order except for a few suggestions to General Blumenthal." J. F. C. Fuller, *A Military History of the Western World: From the American Civil War to the End of World War II* (New York: Da Capo, 1957), III (p. 134). In more modern times the situation has changed somewhat, with the United States and the United Kingdom endeavoring to incorporate *Auftragstaktik* into their military doctrine in an effort to capture what they believe is the essence of the excellent German command of tactics. The adoption of *Auftragstaktik* in the tactics of Germany's former enemies has proved to be more difficult than first envisaged because this doctrine was deeply ingrained for centuries in German military culture. A further complication is that *Auftragstaktik* is merely one component of the many that make up German doctrine, which have as their centerpiece the achievement of combined operations warfare.
39. Vardi, 'The Enigma of German Operational Theory' (p. 31). Quoting Moltke the elder, "no plan of operations can extend with any prospect of certainty beyond the first clash with the hostile main force. Only a layman can pretend to trace throughout the course of a campaign the prosecution of a rigid plan, arranged beforehand in all its details and adhered to the last. All successive acts

of war are therefore not premeditated executions but spontaneous acts guided by military tact."

40. DODA, UWHS, Box 138, Narrative and Reports 12, p. 1, *The Advance and Attack of German Armoured Formationsin Libya 1941–42 by Colonel H. B. Latham.* Although the natural German aggressivenes favored the attack, a defensive posture was often adopted as a tactic as part of an attack. Armored formations would immediately take up a defensive position in a meeting engagement and lure the opposing armored force onto the antitank guns. On the attack, a tactical feature would be seized that would entice a counterattack on the ground of German choosing.
41. A. Beevor, *Ardennes 1944: Hitler's Last Gamble* (London: Penguin, 2015) (pp. 88, 89).
42. The combined arms approach to warfare can be explained simply by equating it to the well-known game of roshambo (rock-paper-scissors). In this game rock smashes scissors, scissors cuts paper, and paper defeats rock. So too in warfare, infantry are vulnerable to artillery, tanks are vulnerable to antitank weapons and in turn, antitank weapons are vulnerable to artillery and infantry. Therefore, success is achieved on the battlefield by applying the most appropriate weapon system in a combined arms force to defeat a particular type of threat. Jackson describes the fundamental German philosophy as 'antitank guns to kill tanks, tanks to kill infantry, and artillery to kill antitank guns and infantry.' W. Jackson, *The Battle for North Africa 1940–1943* (New York: Mason/Charter, 1975).
43. L. H. Addington, *The Blitzkrieg Era* (New Brunswick: Rutgers University Press, 1971) (p. 26).
44. Citino, *The Path to Blitzkrieg* (p. 204).
45. The British tank brigade fielded almost the same amount of tanks as a German *Panzer* division. The fundamental difference was that the German *Panzer* division had a strong component of infantry and artillery, lacking in the British version.
46. This viewpoint is of course contentious. Many researchers believe that the German *Panzer* forces owed much in their creation to the British. W. Murray and A. R. Millet, *Military Innovation in the Interwar Period* (New York: Cambridge University, 2008) (p. 24). The authors give the reason for Fuller refusing to command the initial experimental force, ". . . because he disapproved of the decision to operate the experimental force in conjunction with the more traditional branches, the artillery and the infantry." In this refusal is the essence of the difference between British and German doctrine: The British scorned combined arms warfare and the Germans embraced it.
47. Vardi, 'The Enigma of German Operational Theory' (p. 249). A German study from late 1928 compared the "extreme wing" represented by Fuller and Liddell Hart to French armored doctrine, heavily criticized the British concept of pure armored formations containing no infantry, and favored the French doctrine to a great extent.
48. The force consisted of a medium tank battalion, an armored car and tankette battalion, a motorized machine gun battalion, an artillery brigade, a light artillery battery, and a field engineering company. Harris, *Men, Ideas and Tanks* (p. 217).

49. J. F. C. Fuller, *Lectures on FSR III* (London: Sifton Praed & Co., 1932) (pp. 15, 16, 95). In 1932 he stated, "To combine tanks and infantry is tantamount to yoking a tractor to a draft horse. To ask them to operate together under fire is equally absurd."
50. Fuller, *Lectures on FSR III* (pp. 15, 16, 95) and Harris, *Men, Ideas and Tanks* (pp. 226, 227).
51. Fuller, *The Reformation of War* (p. 157).
52. F. Von Mellenthin, *Panzer Battles* (London: Futura, 1979) (p. xv).
53. DODA, UWHS, Box 138, Narrative and Reports 12, p. 1, *The Advance and Attack of German Armoured Formations in Libya 1941–42 by Colonel H. B. Latham.* Latham identifies four German principles: 1. The primary role of the tank was to kill infantry. 2. The main weapon of the tank was thus the machine gun. 3. The tank can only be succesful when used with all other arms. 4. Tanks must be used en masse. As a result the Germans will not fight a tank-versus-tank battle if this can be avoided. Latham considered the British doctrine of seeking out and destroying enemy tank formations as disastrous.
54. House, *Toward Combined Arms Warfare* (p. 54). The Germans used the antitank weapon in an offensive role, often deploying them upfront to spearhead an attack against armor.
55. Harris, *Men, Ideas and Tanks* (p. 204). Harris believes that this practice was carried through to the Second World War and owed much to J. F. C. Fuller's influence and his analogies with naval warfare. One of his lecture titles in 1920 was *The Development of Sea Warfare on Land*, which drew strong analogies to naval warfare. In a report by Newton-King, he categorically states that "firing on the move" was seldom used and almost always ineffective accept as a tactic against a demoralized enemy. DODA, UWHS, Box 132, Narrative and Reports 6, File 3175, p. 4, *Colonel Newton-King commander of 4 S.A. Armoured Car Regiment in Crusader remarks on armour and armament, 1952.* However, the fact that the British trained to fire on the move is borne out in the Martel report which states, "We have spent much effort in training for this, and are probably ahead of the enemy in gunnery from a moving tank . . ." TNA, WO 201, File 2870, *Martel Report on Aftermath of Crusader, Part IV Summary of the main lessons, 26 January 1942.*
56. Jackson, *The Batte for North Africa* (pp. 159, 160).
57. Citino, *The Path to Blitzkrieg* (p. 44).
58. Von Mellenthin, *Panzer Battles* (p. xv).
59. It is interesting that in the early stages of the war in North Africa, tank brigades were the exclusive domain of the British. Dominion brigades made up the backbone of the British infantry component of the 8th Army.
60. Ian van der Waag has contributed much to our understanding of the formation of the UDF in 1912. Of the fifty-one officers nominated for the first course at the newly established Military School in Bloemfontein, twenty-six were Afrikaners. Many of them would hold high rank over the next decades and, as a group, were termed the "fathers" of the UDF. It is safe to assume that they carried much of the Boer Republican Army system into the UDF. See I. van der Waag, 'Smuts's Generals: Towards a First Portrait of the South African High Command, 1912–1948,' *War in History*, 18(1) (2011) (p. 41).

61. A. G. McKenzie, *The Dukes: A History of the Duke of Edinburgh's Own Rifles 1855–1956* (Cape Town: Regimental Council, 1956) (pp. 84, 85).
62. McKenzie, *The Dukes* (p. 74). His style of command was not dissimilar to that of another old "Boer," Jan Smuts, who displayed the same characteristics when he commanded the Imperial forces in East Africa in 1916. His personal disregard for safety and insistence on leading from the front drew little support from the British generals he commanded. His antics did earn respect from the men he commanded.
63. H. C. Hillegas, *With The Boer Forces* (London: Methuen and Co., 1900) (p. 111). An exception to this was the State Artillery of the Transvaal and Free State. These two organizations had foreign training, wore uniforms, and drilled regularly.
64. The British and US armies have tried to introduce mission command tactics (*Auftragstaktik*) into their doctrine with varying degrees of success. Frustration with British preference for direct command over mission command tactics, even as late as the 1980s in the Falklands Island campaign, was highlighted eloquently in S. Fitz-Gibbon, *Not Mentioned in Despatches: The History and Mythology of the Battle of Goose Green* (Cambridge: Lutterworth Press, 1995).
65. Hillegas, *With The Boer Forces* (pp. 114–119).
66. I. van der Waag, 'Boer Generalship and the Politics of Command,' *War in History*, 12(1) (2005) (p.25). "Boer veterans wore no medals, no uniforms, their status gauged by the all-important white beard. Age, often in combination with family credentials, brought respect . . . not young, innovative genius."
67. Hillegas, *With The Boer Forces* (pp. 80–82).
68. Hillegas, *With The Boer Forces* (p. 89).
69. Van der Waag, 'Boer Generalship,' (p.16). Van der Waag demonstrates how the initial crop of gentlemen farmer generals, many of whom were related through ties of kinship and economic interests, were replaced by "men of youth and competence, who achieved political influence through military ability." The new breed of leader also brought about a transformation in discipline.
70. Hillegas, *With The Boer Forces* (pp. 120–23). The obvious enemy referred to here is the British, who were cumbersome and predictable in their conduct of the war against the Boer armies.
71. Van der Waag, 'Boer Generalship,' (p.27). Van der Waag relates an incident in which a Boer general by the name of Joubert failed to exploit a victory and instead gave his staff a lesson in theology: " 'When God holds out a finger, don't take the whole hand.' This might have been sound theology, as one burgher, Isaac Malherbe, pointed out, but was no good in making war." See also *The German Official Account of the War in South Africa October 1899–February 1900*, ed. by W. H. H. Waters (London: John Murray, 1905) (p. 12).
72. Hillegas, *With The Boer Forces* (pp. 130–34).
73. J. J. Collyer, *The South Africans with General Smuts in German East Africa, 1916* (London: Imperial War Museum and Battery Press, 2004) (p. 273).
74. *The German Official Account of the War in South Africa October 1899–February 1900*, ed. by W. H. H. Waters (London: John Murray, 1905) (p. 14).
75. Hillegas, *With The Boer Forces* (p. 60).
76. Van der Waag, 'Boer Generalship' (p. 30).

77. R. A. Preston, A. Roland, and S. F. Wise, *Men in Arms: A History of Warfare and its Interrelationships with Western Society* (Orlando, FL: 1991) (pp. 228–29).
78. The same accusation may be leveled at the German way of war, which produced phenomenal results at the tactical and operational level but mixed results at the strategic level of combat. The opposite holds true for the British, who lost many battles but won many wars having mastered the strategic level of war, to the detriment of their opponents.
79. I. van der Waag, *A Military History of Modern South Africa* (Johannesburg and Cape Town: Jonathan Ball, 2015) (pp. 73–77).
80. I. van der Waag, 'South African Defence in the Age of Total War, 1900–1940,' *Historia*, 60(1) (2015) (p.135).
81. Van der Waag, *A Military History of Modern South Africa* (p. 105).
82. R. Williams, 'Historical Parallel or Historical Amnesia? The Formation of the Union Defence Force,' *South African Defence Review No. 2*, 1992. In considering the proposed nature of the UDF on its formation Smuts insisted, "The UDF should utilise the different military traditions of the white population in a constructive manner. Equestrian personnel should be drawn from the rural mainly Afrikaans-speaking districts (where such talents were well developed). Infantry complements should rely on the English-speaking South Africans in the towns and cities (where a reasonably developed Citizen Force Regimental system existed)."
83. E. P. Hartshorn, *Avenge Tobruk* (Cape Town: Purnell, 1960) (p. 162).
84. *Infantry Training* (London: War Office, 1902). The manual sets out its aim, contained in its first words, ". . . to secure, at the decisive moment of battle, the greatest development of fire, from the most effective direction, and under the strictest general control." These words, written by Field Marshal Lord Roberts in the preface to the manual, demonstrate a willingness to maneuver in order to fight.
85. I. Beckett, 'The Boer War: Army, Nation and Empire?: The 1999 Chief of Army/Australian War Memorial Military History Conference,' ed. by P. Dennis and J. Grey (Canberra: Australia Department of Defence Army History Unit, 2000) (p. 30). The significance accorded firepower and the methodical caution in attack apparent in the new manuals, Combined Training in 1902 and Infantry Training in 1905, was reversed in Field Service Regulations in 1909, which downgraded firepower and subordinated the defensive to the moral effect of the vigoros offensive. See also S. Jones, *From Boer War to World War: Tactical Reform of the British Army 1902–1914* (Norman: University of Oklahoma Press, 2012) (pp. 65, 66).
86. E. Kleynhans, 'Armoured Warfare: The South African Experience in East Africa, 1940–1941' (Masters thesis, Military Science, University of Stellenbosch, 2014) (p. 7). The Field Force comprised two squadrons of the 1st Regiment, South African Mounted Riflemen, and three batteries of the SA Field Artillery, with the 1st Regiment, SAMR, reorganized to include an Armoured Car Section of two vehicles.
87. I. van der Waag, 'South African Defence in the Age of Total War, 1900–1940,' *Historia*, 60(1) (2015) (p.149).
88. Van der Waag, 'South African Defence,' (p.153).

89. Hartshorn, *Avenge Tobruk* (p.61).
90. DODA, UWHS, Box 128, Narrative and Reports M.E. 2 (p. 15) *The Springbok troops were mishandled, Major-General E. Dorman O'Gowan in Outspan article 18 February 1955.*
91. C. Birkby, *The Saga of the Transvaal Scottish Regiment 1932–1950* (Cape Town: Hodder and Stoughton, 1950) (p. 574, footnote 5).
92. DODA, UWHS, Box 139, Narrative and Reports M.E. 13 (p. 3) *Interview with General H. B. Klopper 2 S. A. Division 6 May 1946.*
93. M. Carver, *Out of Step: The Memoirs of Field Marshal Lord Carver* (London: Hutchinson, 1989) (p.120).
94. Mearsheimer, *Liddell Hart and the Weight of History* (p. 33). J. F. C. Fuller, in an article submitted to the *Journal of the Royal United Services Institution* in 1920, proposed that highly mobile tanks would dominate future battlefields to the extent that land warfare would approximate naval warfare, with tanks fighting each other in the same manner as ships fight at sea.
95. A. Stewart, *The Early Battles of Eighth Army: Crusader to the Alamein Line, 1941–42* (Mechanicsburg, PA: Stackpole, 2002) (p. 63).
96. A quote erroneously attributed to Lieutenant-General in the Confederate Army, Nathan Bedford Forrest, by the *New York Times* in 1918 as, "Getting there firstest with the mostest," sums up the doctrine succinctly. 'Nathan Bedford Forrest,' in *Wikipedia* http://en.wikipedia.org/wiki/Nathan_Bedford_Forrest [accessed August 11, 2013].
97. Bidwell, *Gunners at War* (p. 180). Bidwell cites the period between Battleaxe and Auchinleck's stand at Alamein as the most costly period of British unorthodoxy.
98. Bidwell, *Gunners at War* (pp. 164, 165).
99. DODA, UWHS, Box 138, Narrative and Reports 12, p. 6, *Answers to questions by U. W. Hirt re tanks, antitank guns and general tactics, Fritz Bayerlein.*
100. The difference between a "Jock Column" and a *Kampfgruppe* was one of size. The British were incapable of forming a combined arms formation anywhere near the size that the Germans achieved.
101. R. L. Dinardo, *Germany's Panzer Arm in WWII* (Mechanicsburg, PA: Stackpole, 1997) (pp. 119–25).
102. R. Jarymowycz, *Tank Tactics from Normandy to Lorraine* (Mechanicsburg, PA: Stackpole, 2009) (pp. 205, 206). The author provides some interesting insights into British and American attempts to exercise combined arms warfare at a higher level as late as 1944. The Americans came the closest in emulating the German *Kampfgruppe* doctrine with their combat commands, but these structures, unlike the German version, tended to become permanent.
103. Rommel called his source *die gute Quelle* (the good source) and derived much information from its unwitting provider, Brevet Colonel Bonner Frank Fellers, the US military attaché in the Egyptian capital of Cairo. He also had his own 621st Signals Battalion mobile monitoring element commanded by Hauptmann Alfred Seeböhm, which took advantage of a lack of British battlefield radio discipline.
104. Stewart, *The Early Battles of the Eighth Army* (p. 18). See also B. H. Liddell Hart, *The Tanks: The History of the Royal Tank Regiment* (London: Cassel, 1959) (p. 94).

105. M. Carver, *Dilemmas of the Desert War: A New Look at the Libyan Campaign 1940–1942* (London: Batsford, 1986) (p. 52); P. Griffith, *World War II Desert Tactics* (Oxford: Osprey, 2008) (pp. 24, 26); and W. Murphy, *The Relief of Tobruk*, ed. by M. Fairbrother (Wellington: Historical Publications Branch, 1961) (p. 59).
106. Jackson, *The Batte for North Africa* (pp. 159, 160). The German Mark IV had a close-support 75mm gun that could fire a high-explosive shell to a maximum range of 3,000 m, which was lethal to both tank and antitank gun. The British had nothing similar either by way of tank armament or artillery that could deploy at even half this range. The British 3.7 inch antiaircraft gun, although possessing similar ballistics to the German 88mm, was not deployed in anything other than its intended role against aircraft, to the detriment of the 8th Army. See also DODA, UWHS, Box 132, Narrative and Reports 6, File 3175, p. 5, *Colonel Newton-King commander of 4 S. A. Armoured Car Regiment in Crusader remarks on armour and armament, 1952.* Newton-King was adamant that the lack of a high-explosive capability of the British 2-pounder was a crippling disadvantage in dealing with German antitank positions.
107. Liddell Hart, *The Tanks* (pp. 94, 95).The 88mm proved the ultimate tank killer, able to knock out British tanks 3,000 m away, while the British 2-pounder primary armament for the tanks and antitank guns, was effective out to a maximum of 500 m.
108. Carver, *Dilemmas of the Desert War* (p. 52); I. S. O. Playfair, *A History of the Second World War: The Mediterranean and Middle East*, ed. by J. Butler (Uckfield: Naval & Military Press, 2004), III (p. 100); and S. Bidwell, 'Indirect Fire Artillery as a Battle Winner/Loser,' in *Old Battles and New Defences* (Oxford: Brassey's Defence Publisher, 1986) (p. 123). The tendency of the British infantry to rely on the 25-pounder artillery in the antitank role was at the expense of the artillery effort, arguably the strongest arm the British had.
109. Carver, *Dilemmas of the Desert War* (p. 52).
110. *German Tank Maintenance in World War II*, Pamphlet 2 (Department of the Army, 1954). This pamphlet provides a rare insight into the extent of the measures employed by the Germans in tank recovery. It was mandatory for the Germans to recover a tank unless it was blown to bits. Heavily damaged vehicles were recovered in order to be cannibalized for parts.
111. TNA, WO 201, File 2870, *Martel Report on Aftermath of Crusader*, January 26, 1942. See also L. Friedli, *Repairing the Panzers: German Tank Maintenance in World War 2* (Heathfield: Panzerwrecks, 2013). An interesting study on the German vehicle repair units in the field.
112. B. H. Liddell Hart, *The Rommel Papers* (New York: De Capo Press, 1953) (p. 199). Eloquently put by Rommel himself as, "The main endeavour should be to concentrate one's own forces in space and time, while at the same time seeking to split the enemy forces spatially and destroy them at different times."
113. E. Echols, 'Military Dust,' *The Classical Journal*, 47.7 (1952) (p. 285).
114. A. Toppe, *Desert Warfare: German Experiences in World War II* (Report Paper, U.S. Army Command and General Staff College, Combat Studies Institute, 1952) (pp. 59–61).
115. *FM 90-3: Desert Operations* (Washington: US Marine Corps, 1993) (pp. 2–3).

116. TNA, WO 32/10160/337, *Auchinleck Despatch on Operations in the Middle East*, November 1, 1941 to August 15, 1942, and DODA, Brink Papers, Box 55, p.14, 15, *1 SA Division Operations Report Cyrenaica 1942*, November 18–December 2, 1941. Brink states in his debrief, ". . . night moves, unless of vital importance to achieve a most important object, should not be carried out over difficult and unknown terrain."
117. S. Bidwell and G. Dominick, *Fire-Power: The British Army Weapons & Theories of War 1904–1945* (Barnsley: Pen and Sword Books, 2004) (p. 228). Bidwell quotes a German commander: "A tacticians paradise but a quartermaster's nightmare."
118. M. Van Creveld, *Supplying War: Logistics from Wallenstein to Patton* (New York: Cambridge University, 2009) (p. 182).
119. Van Creveld, *Supplying War* (p. 183) and P. Griffith, *World War II Desert Tactics* (Oxford: Osprey, 2008) (p. 4).
120. Liddell Hart, *The Rommel Papers* (p. 328). Rommel's observations on the fundamental importance of supply are instructive. "The first condition for an army to be able to stand the strain of battle is an adequate stock of weapons, petrol, and ammunition. In fact, the battle is fought and decided by the Quartermaster before the shooting begins. The bravest men can do nothing without guns, the guns nothing without plenty of ammunition, and neither guns nor ammunition are of much use in mobile warfare unless there are vehicles with sufficient petrol to haul them around."

CHAPTER 4

1. Article in the *Evening Post*, Volume CXXXII, Issue 124, November 21, 1941, taken together with a BBC announcement on November 20, 1941, delivered at 9 p.m. leaves little to the imagination as to the purpose and scale of the Allied attack. *The 8th Army, with about 75,000 men excellently armed and equipped, have started a general offensive in the Western Desert, with the aim of destroying the German-Italian forces in Africa.*
2. M. Van Creveld, *Supplying War: Logistics from Wallenstein to Patton* (New York: Cambridge University, 2009) (pp. 184, 185).
3. B. H. Liddell Hart, *The Tanks: The History of the Royal Tank Regiment* (London: Cassel, 1959) (p. 99). Liddell Hart joined the long list of those underestimating the Italian military prowess in Crusader, stating, ". . . their obsolete equipment, shaky morale, and lack of mechanical vehicles largely nullified their value as an asset, while making them an actual handicap for mobile operations." See also P. Griffith, *World War II Desert Tactics* (Oxford: Osprey, 2008) (pp. 16, 17).
4. M. Carver, *Dilemmas of the Desert War: A New Look at the Libyan Campaign 1940–1942* (London: Batsford, 1986) (p. 23).
5. Liddell Hart, *The Tanks* (p. 102). For a view to the contrary see Carver, *Dilemmas of the Desert War* (pp. 51, 52). Carver denies German technological superiority as being a major factor.
6. S. Bidwell and G. Dominick, *Fire-Power: The British Army Weapons & Theories of War 1904–1945* (Barnsley: Pen and Sword Books, 2004) (p. 230). The 3.7 inch AA gun was dissimilar to the German 88mm in a number of aspects, especially for the fact that it was much heavier and had a sophisticated fire control system. These shortcomings could have been overcome with the correct will. Bidwell

also argues that there was a strong case for deploying the weapon in its original antiaircraft role.

7. Total South African battle casualties on land throughout the campaign had been only 270, of whom 73 had been killed. N. Orpen, *South African Forces World War II - East African and Abyssinian Campaigns* (Cape Town: Purnell, 1968) (p. 328).
8. N. Orpen, *South African Forces World War II - War in the Desert* (Cape Town: Purnell, 1971) (p. 6).
9. E. Rommel, *Infantry Attacks* (Brattleboro: Echo Point Books & Media, 2015).
10. C. Leroux, *Chicago Tribune*, in *Rommel May Guide U.S. In Desert Warfare* http://articles.chicagotribune.com/1991-02-19/news/9101160457_1_desert-warfare-military-history-petrol [accessed March 19, 2013].
11. Churchill himself proclaimed, "Before Alamein we never had a victory. After Alamein we never had a defeat." Thus he ignored the fact that Operation Crusader was a clear-cut British victory, although not as notable as O'Connor's campaign against the Italians the previous year. Carver, *Dilemmas of the Desert War* (p. 51).
12. Carver, *Dilemmas of the Desert War* (p. 51).
13. J. J. Sadkovich, 'Understanding Defeat: Reappraising Italy's Role in World War II,' *Journal of Contemporary History*, 24(1) (1989) (p. 28).
14. Sadkovich, 'Understanding Defeat,' (p. 43).
15. M. Montanari, *Le Operazioni In Africa Settentrionale (Marzo 1941–Gennaio 1942)* (Rome: Ufficio Storico, 1993), II. The relevant portions of the Italian official history have been translated using Google Translate, located at http://translate.google.co.za/.
16. J. A. I. Agar-Hamilton and L. C. F. Turner, *The Sidi Rezegh Battles, 1941* (Cape Town: Oxford University Press, 1957).
17. R. Humble, *Crusader: The Eighth Army's Forgotten Victory November 1941–January 1942* (London: Leo Cooper, 1987).
18. R. Kriebel, *Inside the Afrika Korps*, ed. by B. I. Gudmundsson (London: Greenhill, 1999).
19. K. Ford, *Operation Crusader 1941: Rommel in Retreat* (Oxford: Osprey, 2010).
20. R. Crisp, *Brazen Chariots* (London: Frederick Muller, 1959).
21. H. W. Schmidt, *With Rommel in the Desert* (Durban: Albatross, 1950).
22. Carver, *Dilemmas of the Desert War.*
23. A. Stewart, *The Early Battles of the Eighth Army: Crusader to the Alamein Line, 1941–42* (Mechanicsburg, PA: Stackpole, 2002).
24. C. Barnett, *The Desert Generals* (New York: Viking Press, 1961) (pp. 81, 82). See also Ford, *Operation Crusader.*
25. S. Bidwell, *Gunners at War* (London: Arms and Armour Press, 1970).
26. DODA, UWHS, Box 321, p. (1)8, Narrative prepared for UK Cabinet, *General Auchinleck's Offensive and the Relief Of Tobruch - The Planning Period,* June–November 1941.
27. Carver, *Dilemmas of the Desert War* (p. 27). The Germans invaded the Soviet Union on June 22, 1941. Operation Barbarossa dwarfed the North African campaign, effectively rendering it to the status of a sideshow.
28. DODA, UWHS, Box 138, Narrative and Reports 12, p. 1, *Lieutenant-General Willoughby Norrie narrative on Sidi Rezegh 1941.* According to Norrie the central position of Gabr Saleh afforded the British a position from which they could strike in any direction.

29. TNA, WO 32/10160/312, *Auchinleck Despatch on Operations in the Middle East,* November 1, 1941 to August 15, 1942.
30. Carver, *Dilemmas of the Desert War* (p. 33); DODA, UWHS, Box 321, p. (1)19, 44, Narrative prepared for UK Cabinet, *General Auchinleck's Offensive and the Relief Of Tobruch - The Planning Period,* June–November 1941; and TNA, WO 201, File 2870, *Martel Report on Aftermath of Crusader,* January 26, 1942.
31. DODA, UWHS, Box 132, Narrative and Reports 6, File 3175, p. 4, *Colonel Newton-King commander of 4 S. A. Armoured Car Regiment in Crusader remarks on armour and armament, 1952.* This assumption discounts the Italian armor in its entirety. This proved to be an expensive error for the 22nd Armoured Brigade when they met *Ariete* at Bir El Gubi with disastrous results.
32. DODA, UWHS, Box 138, Narrative and Reports 12, p. 1, *Lieutenant-General Willoughby Norrie narrative on Sidi Rezegh 1941.*
33. DODA, UWHS, Box 138, Narrative and Reports 12, p. 1, *Lieutenant-General Willoughby Norrie narrative on Sidi Rezegh 1941.* The code word to break out of Tobruk was "Pop" and it was not to be given until such time as the enemy armor was neutralized.
34. TNA, WO 32/10160/312,335, *Auchinleck Despatch on Operations in the Middle East,* November 1, 1941 to August 15, 1942. See also DODA, UWHS, Box 138, Narrative and Reports 12, p. 2, *Lieutenant-General Willoughby Norrie narrative on Sidi Rezegh 1941.*
35. DODA, UWHS, Box 321, p. (1)30, Narrative prepared for UK Cabinet, *General Auchinleck's Offensive and the Relief Of Tobruch—The Planning Period,* June–November 1941 and TNA, WO 32/10160/335,336, *Auchinleck Despatch on Operations in the Middle East,* November 1, 1941 to August 15, 1942.
36. The 7th Support Group under Brigadier J. C. "Jock" Campbell contained the 7th Armoured Division's artillery and a good portion of the infantry assets, and unlike the German *Panzer* division, the artillery and infantry were not integrated within division but formed a separate support group.
37. TNA, WO 32/10160/335, *Auchinleck Despatch on Operations in the Middle East,* November 1, 1941 to August 15, 1942.
38. Carver, *Dilemmas of the Desert War* (p. 27).
39. Liddell Hart, *The Tanks* (p. 104).
40. W. E. Murphy, *The Relief of Tobruk*, ed. by M. Fairbrother (Wellington: Historical Publications Branch, 1961) (p. 16). Freyberg was among the first to express his doubts. He was concerned that the dual role of one of the armored brigades—to co-operate with either the infantry or the armored corps as the situation demanded—was not in itself sufficient. "I made it clear," he says, "that I did not agree . . . to go out into the blue against unbeaten armored formations." That the armored brigade would be "in support," he added, "meant nothing to me, as they would be ordered away in a crisis and . . . unless we had tanks under our immediate command we should not be moved across the [frontier] wire until the armoured battle had commenced."
41. Liddell Hart, *The Tanks* (p. 103). Liddell Hart describes it as, "the advantage gained by the strategical outflanking maneuver, which had placed the enemy in a very awkward in danger situation, was forfeited in the tactical execution." The Germans had concentrated their forces into one compact force while the British introduced their armor brigades one at a time into the battle.

42. Liddell Hart, *The Tanks* (p. 105); Carver, *Dilemmas of the Desert War* (p. 33); DODA, UWHS, Box 321, p. (1)34, Narrative prepared for UK Cabinet, *General Auchinleck's Offensive and the Relief Of Tobruch - The Planning Period,* June–November 1941; and TNA, WO 201, File 2870, *Martel Report on Aftermath of Crusader,* January 26, 1942.
43. DODA, UWHS, Box 321, p. (1)36, Narrative prepared for UK Cabinet, *General Auchinleck's Offensive and the Relief Of Tobruch—The Planning Period,* June–November 1941. Norrie was keen to aim the 7th Armoured Division directly at Tobruk but was turned down by Cunningham at a conference held on October 29. TNA, WO 201, File 2870, *Martel Report on Aftermath of Crusader,* January 26, 1942 and DODA, UWHS, Box 138, Narrative and Reports 12, p. 2, *Lieutenant-General Willoughby Norrie narrative on Sidi Rezegh 1941.* Norrie favoured El Adem and Sidi Rezegh as the objectives that offered a position of strategic value.
44. J. Fuller, *The Foundations of the Science of War* (Kansas: US Army Command and General Staff Colledge Press, 1993) (p. 257). One of the cornerstones of *The Nine Principles of War* authored by J. F. C. Fuller relates to the seizing, retaining, and exploiting the initiative. Fuller maintains that, "Maintaining the initiative does not necessarily mean attacking and advancing. If the reserves be strong, it may frequently mean defending and retiring in order to create a situation in which their use may lead to decisive victory." See also Liddell Hart, *The Tanks* (p. 103) and Stewart, *The Early Battles of the Eighth Army* (p. 17).
45. Carver, *Dilemmas of the Desert War* (p. 33).
46. DODA, UWHS, Box 321, p. (1)23, 30, Narrative prepared for UK Cabinet, *General Auchinleck's Offensive and the Relief Of Tobruch—The Planning Period,* June–November 1941, and Agar-Hamilton, *The Sidi Rezegh Battles* (pp. 115, 116).
47. Liddell Hart, *The Tanks* (p. 107)
48. Agar-Hamilton, *The Sidi Rezegh Battles* (pp. 74, 75).
49. DODA, Brink Papers, Box 55, p. 2, *1 SA Division Operations Report Cyrenaica 1942*, November 18–December 2, 1941, and Carver, *Dilemmas of the Desert War* (p. 31). See also Agar-Hamilton, *The Sidi Rezegh Battles* (p. 90).
50. DODA, Brink Papers, Box 55, Part III, 2, *1 SA Division Operations Report Cyrenaica 1942*, November 18–December 2, 1941.
51. NAP, JSP Box 137, f.10, Smuts to Auchinleck, *Armoured Car Output,* October 17, 1942.
52. DODA, Brink Papers, Box 55, p. 3, *1 SA Division Operations Report Cyrenaica 1942*, November 18–December 2, 1941.
53. DODA, Brink Papers, Box 55, p. 4, *1 SA Division Operations Report Cyrenaica 1942*, November 18–December 2, 1941. Brink states, "By occupying well organized defended localities, tanks could be fought off."
54. DODA, Brink Papers, Box 55, p. 4, *1 SA Division Operations Report Cyrenaica 1942*, November 18–December 2, 1941. Brink was not alone in underestimating the worth of the Italian forces. Liddell Hart does the same in his monumental work on the history of the Royal Tank Regiment. Liddell Hart, *The Tanks* (p. 99). See also Agar-Hamilton, *The Sidi Rezegh Battles* (p. 112). See also Murphy, *The Relief of Tobruk*: "That an Italian armoured division might also have to be dealt with was scarcely considered; its tanks, the minutes broadly hinted, were inferior."

55. Murphy, *The Relief of Tobruk* (p. 41).
56. DODA, Brink Papers, Box 55, p. 5, *1 SA Division Operations Report Cyrenaica 1942*, November 18–December 2, 1941.
57. Orpen, *War in the Desert* (pp. 6, 15, 16).
58. DODA, UWHS, Box 131, Narrative and Reports ME 5, File 2715, p. 1, *2nd Reserve Motorised Company Unit History.*
59. DODA, Brink Papers, Box 55, p. 9, *1 SA Division Operations Report Cyrenaica 1942*, November 18–December 2, 1941, and Murphy, *The Relief of Tobruk* (p. 40).
60. Agar-Hamilton, *The Sidi Rezegh Battles* (pp. 89, 90).Brink originally requested twenty-one clear days once his transport was in hand in which to get ready for the operation. See also TNA, WO 32/10160/311,335, *Auchinleck Despatch on Operations in the Middle East,* November 1, 1941 to August 15, 1942.
61. E. P. Hartshorn, *Avenge Tobruk* (Cape Town: Purnell, 1960) (p. 81).
62. Hartshorn, *Avenge Tobruk* (p. 80).
63. Carver, *Dilemmas of the Desert War* (p. 32). Carver describes Brink relenting as a "pity for all concerned."
64. Agar-Hamilton, *The Sidi Rezegh Battles* (p. 92).
65. DODA, Brink Papers, Box 55, p. 15, *1 SA Division Operations Report Cyrenaica 1942*, November 18–December 2, 1941. Brink reported that the night move did indeed prove to be 'expensive,' and he concluded that, "night moves, unless of vital importance to achieve a most important objective, should not be carried out over difficult and unknown terrain." See also Agar-Hamilton, *The Sidi Rezegh Battles* (p. 120).
66. DODA, UWHS, Box 131, Narrative and Reports ME 5, File 2893, p. 2, *Battle Report Libyan offensive 18 November–2 December 1941, 1st SA Division.*
67. Murphy, *The Relief of Tobruk* (pp. 34, 35).
68. Murphy, *The Relief of Tobruk* (p. 32).
69. F Echelon vehicles are the fighting vehicles that go into battle as part of the action, such as command vehicles, armored troop carriers, and antitank guns. A Echelon vehicles meet the immediate needs of the battalion after the battle such as rations, extra ammunition, packs, and cooking equipment. B Echelon has the longer term stores and workshops.
70. The South African official history refers to provision being made to incorporate the "B" Echelon within the brigade perimeter in a diagram supposedly issued to units of 1st Brigade. Agar-Hamilton, *The Sidi Rezegh Battles* (p. 118). The 1st South African Infantry Division Order of Movement diagram also incorporates the "B" Echelon within the divisional perimeter. DODA, Brink Papers, Box 55, Appendix B, *1 SA Division Operations Report Cyrenaica 1942*, November 18–December 2, 1941.
71. DODA, Brink Papers, Box 55, Part III,1, *1 SA Division Operations Report Cyrenaica 1942*, November 18–December 2, 1941.
72. Previously known as the Western Desert Force, the name was changed to the Eighth Army at midnight September 26/27, 1941. DODA, UWHS, Box 321, p. (1)21, Narrative prepared for UK Cabinet, *General Auchinleck's Offensive and the Relief Of Tobruch—The Planning Period,* June–November 1941.
73. Barnett, *The Desert Generals* (pp. 81, 82). See also Ford, *Operation Crusader* (pp. 12–15).

74. Carver, *Dilemmas of the Desert War* (pp. 51, 52). Carver denies German technological superiority as being a major factor.
75. TNA, WO 32/10160/384, *Auchinleck Despatch on Operations in the Middle East,* November 1, 1941 to August 15, 1942.
76. Liddell Hart, *The Tanks* (p. 102).
77. DODA, UWHS, Box 321, p. (1)37, Narrative prepared for UK Cabinet, *General Auchinleck's Offensive and the Relief Of Tobruch—The Planning Period,* June–November 1941, and Carver, *Dilemmas of the Desert War* (p. 52). See also Murphy, *The Relief of Tobruk* (pp. 59, 60).
78. I.S.O. Playfair, *A History of the Second World War: The Mediterranean and Middle East*, ed. by J. Butler (Uckfield: Naval & Military Press, 2004), III (p. 30). General W. Norrie includes 5 captured Britsh "I" tanks and 55 "armoured gun carriers" in the German figures. He also seems to exclude the American Stuart tanks from the British figures describing them as "...only a tracked armoured recce vehicle!!" See DODA, UWHS, Box 138, Narrative and Reports 12, p.1, *Lieutenant-General Willoughby Norrie narrative on Sidi Rezegh 1941.*
79. DODA, UWHS, Box 131, Narrative and Reports ME 5, File 2723, p. 3, *Battle Report Cyrenaica 18 November–29 December 1941, 1st SA Infantry Brigade HQ, Notes Conclusions and Suggestions Based on Experiences.*

Chapter 5

1. Special Order of the Day HQ_70 Inf. Div. 18/11/41. Telegram sent to Auchinleck by Churchill.
2. W. E. Murphy, *The Relief of Tobruk*, ed. by M. Fairbrother (Wellington: Historical Publications Branch, 1961) (p. 32).
3. Murphy, *The Relief of Tobruk* (p. 32).
4. DODA, UWHS, Box 138, Narrative and Reports 12, p. 2, *Lieutenant-General Willoughby Norrie narrative on Sidi Rezegh 1941.*
5. J. A. I. Agar-Hamilton and L. C. F. Turner, *The Sidi Rezegh Battles, 1941* (Cape Town: Oxford University Press, 1957) (p. 128).
6. DODA, UWHS, Box 131, Narrative and Reports ME 5, File 2723, p. 1, *Battle Report Cyrenaica 18 November–29 December 1941, 1st SA Infantry Brigade HQ.* The orders to halt were received from 22nd Armoured Brigade. In light of the failed attack by 22nd Armoured Brigade, it would have been advisable to have launched the attack with the assistance of the 1st Brigade. See also I. S. O. Playfair, *A History of the Second World War: The Mediterranean and Middle East,* ed. by J. R. M. Butler (Uckfield: Naval and Military Press, 2004), III (p. 40). The British official history provides no clear answer as to the reason Gott felt it necessary to attack *Ariete* and offers that he may have thought it unwise to leave them unmolested on his left flank or that alternatively he felt he could inflict major damage at little cost.
7. Agar-Hamilton, *The Sidi Rezegh Battles* (pp. 133, 134).
8. Murphy, *The Relief of Tobruk* (p. 33).
9. DODA, UWHS, Box 139, p. 4, *7 Field Regiment SAA Narrative ME 12/8/1941–4/4/1942.* The regiment was attached to the 1st Infantry Brigade for Crusader and suffered thirteen wounded in the air attack.

10. DODA, UWHS, Box 138, Narrative and Reports 12, p. 2, *Lieutenant-General Willoughby Norrie narrative on Sidi Rezegh 1941.* These figures are confirmed by Norrie in his narrative.
11. Agar-Hamilton, *The Sidi Rezegh Battles* (p. 150).
12. DODA, UWHS, Box 131, Narrative and Reports ME 5, File 2749, p. 2, *Battle Report Cyrenaica 18 November–29 December 1941, 1st Transvaal Scottish.* The nondescript term "masking" is more thoroughly defined in the 1st Transvaal Scottish battle report as, "contain the enemy and prevent any movement against friendly supply lines."
13. Murphy, *The Relief of Tobruk* (p. 35).
14. I. Walker, *Iron Hulls Iron Hearts: Mussolini's Elite Armoured Divisions in North Africa* (Ramsbury: Crowood Press, 2006) (p. 86). The Italian armored division *Ariete* was equivalent to a British armored brigade in tank strength. The difference was that the Italians were able to build a more balanced division that contained integral infantry and artillery, unlike the British Brigade that was essentially a pure tank force. M. Knox, *Military Effectiveness: The Second World War*, ed. by A. R. Millet and M. Williamson (New York: Cambridge, 2010), III (p. 151). Italian doctrine was surprisingly predisposed to an all arms concept of warfare, not having been largely exposed to British "all tank" theorists. The Italians favored all arms cooperation. The few mobile Italian units apparently learned more quickly than the British the lesson that armor, artillery, and infantry must of necessity function as a team
15. M. Montanari, *Le Operazioni In Africa Settentrionale (Marzo 1941–Gennaio 1942)* (Rome: Ufficio Storico, 1993), II (p. 450).
16. Walker, *Iron Hulls Iron Hearts* (p. 83). *Ariete* had the advantage over the British 22nd Armoured Brigade. It had a similar amount of tanks to the British, but unlike them, it also had a balanced component of infantry and artillery in a combined arms division.
17. Montanari, *Le Operazioni In Africa Settentrionale* (p. 450).
18. Italian sources admit to the loss of thirty-four tanks and claim to have destroyed fifty British tanks. The British in turn admit to the loss of twenty-five tanks, which seems to be a low estimate. Walker, *Iron Hulls Iron Hearts* (p. 84). The Italian official history admits to forty-nine tanks lost (of which fifteen were repairable) as against fifty-seven British tanks. M. Montanari, *Le Operazioni In Africa Settentrionale* (p. 450). Richard Humble gives further perspective to the British defeat at the hands of *Ariete*, stating that a further forty-five tanks had been immobilized by battle damage or breakdowns. This meant that 22nd Armoured Brigade was down to 50 percent of its fighting strength after its clash with the Italians. Richard Humble, *Crusader: The Eighth Army's Forgotten Victory November 1941–January 1942* (London: Leo Cooper, 1987) (p. 98). Liddell Hart in his history of the Royal tank Regiment devotes but one sentence to the rebuff suffered by 22nd Armoured Brigade, describing it as a "series of gallant charges" that drove back the Italian tanks. Liddell Hart, *The Tanks* (p. 106).
19. DODA, Brink Papers, Box 55, p. 4, *1 SA Division Operations Report Cyrenaica 1942*, November 18–December 2, 1941. Brink writes, "I did not know at the time that the Italian tanks carried mixed German and Italian crews and were to put up such good fights." Auchinleck is more generous to the Italians in his despatch, TNA, WO 32/10160/3327, *Auchinleck Despatch on Operations in the*

Middle East, November 1, 1941 to August 15, 1942. "We counted on being able to oppose between 450 and 500 cruiser and American tanks to the enemy's 250. This latter figure did not include the 138 tanks of the Italian *Ariete* Division, which, although it lay to the south of Tobruk on the flank of our proposed line of advance, was believed to [be a] foe not very formidable." This estimate of its value, based on the experience of General Wavell's campaign of the previous winter, proved to be somewhat erroneous. British reports spoke of Italian tanks being reinforced by German tanks. DODA, UWHS, Box 321, p. (2)30, Narrative prepared for UK Cabinet, *General Auchinleck's Offensive and the Relief Of Tobruch—The Planning Period,* June–November 1941.

20. TNA, WO 32/10160/312, *Auchinleck Despatch on Operations in the Middle East,* November 1, 1941 to August 15, 1942.
21. Murphy, *The Relief of Tobruk* (p. 35).
22. Murphy, *The Relief of Tobruk* (pp. 85, 86). *Kampfgruppe* Stephan consisted of eighty-five tanks, twelve 105mm howitzers, and four 88mm antitank guns. The two sides were evenly matched in material.
23. A *laager* is used in South Africa to describe a historical encampment formed by a circle of wagons. It gained more universal acceptance as an entrenched position defended against opponents.
24. Murphy, *The Relief of Tobruk* (p. 86).
25. Agar-Hamilton, *The Sidi Rezegh Battles* (p. 153). See also A. Stewart, *The Early Battles of Eighth Army: Crusader to the Alamein Line, 1941–42* (Mechanicsburg, PA: Stackpole, 2002) (p. 20). Rommel's awareness of British intentions was no doubt heightened by a BBC broadcast at 2100 announcing a major British offensive in the Western Desert.
26. Agar-Hamilton, *The Sidi Rezegh Battles* (p. 159). Richard Humble estimates 4th Armoured Brigade losses in the encounter with 15 *Panzer*-Division as twenty-six tanks lost. The British claimed a further thirty German tanks destroyed, once again seriously overestimating the damage they had inflicted. Humble, *Crusader* (p. 108). See also Murphy, *The Relief of Tobruk* (p. 88). The official history estimated the 4th Brigade losses for the day at more than forty.
27. Agar-Hamilton, *The Sidi Rezegh Battles* (p. 162).
28. Playfair, *A History of the Second World War,* III (p. 42).
29. Murphy, *The Relief of Tobruk* (p. 89).
30. Agar-Hamilton, *The Sidi Rezegh Battles* (p. 163).
31. DODA, UWHS, Box 138, Narrative and Reports 12, p. 3, *Lieutenant-General Willoughby Norrie narrative on Sidi Rezegh 1941.* Norrie issued the code word "Pop" while directing the sortie from Tobruk.
32. Murphy, *The Relief of Tobruk* (p. 90). This has been described by the official New Zealand history as being a "haphazard" way of conducting the operation, in light of identifying, in the planning phase, that the neutralization of Axis armor was a prerequisite to any breakout attempt by the Tobruk garrison.
33. Playfair, *A History of the Second World War,* III (p. 42).
34. Murphy, *The Relief of Tobruk* (p. 89). See also Agar-Hamilton, *The Sidi Rezegh Battles* (p. 164).
35. Murphy, *The Relief of Tobruk* (p. 89). Described by the official history as being a "curious" role for infantry.

36. DODA, UWHS, Box 131, Narrative and Reports ME 5, File 2723, p. 1, *Battle Report Cyrenaica 18 November–29 December 1941, 1st SA Infantry Brigade HQ*, and Agar-Hamilton, *The Sidi Rezegh Battles* (p. 166).
37. DODA, Brink Papers, Box 55, pp. 27, 28, *1 SA Division Operations Report Cyrenaica 1942*, November 18–December 2, 1941.
38. DODA, Brink Papers, Box 55, p. 30, *1 SA Division Operations Report Cyrenaica 1942*, November 18–December 2, 1941.
39. DODA, UWHS, Box 131, Narrative and Reports ME 5, File 2725, pp. 2, 3, *Battle Report Cyrenaica 18 November–29 December 1941, 1st SA Infantry Brigade HQ*.
40. Agar-Hamilton, *The Sidi Rezegh Battles* (p. 169). The official history describes Brink's reluctance to move at night as an honest recognition of the low standard of training throughout the division. Playfair, *A History of the Second World War*, III (p. 43).
41. DODA, Brink Papers, Box 55, p. 34, *1 SA Division Operations Report Cyrenaica 1942*, November 18–December 2, 1941, and Agar-Hamilton, *The Sidi Rezegh Battles* (pp. 167, 169). In his dispatch Auchinleck incorrectly cites Armstrong as seeking permission to halt his brigade at nightfall, when in fact this was as per his instructions from Brink, and TNA, WO 32/10160/337, *Auchinleck Despatch on Operations in the Middle East,* November 1, 1941 to August 15, 1942. Armstrong protested against this in a letter to Auchinleck in which he attempted to put the record straight, and TNA, CAB 106/638, Letter Armstrong to Deputy CGS, *Objection to Field-Marshal Auchinleck's Despatch*, 1948.
42. Murphy, *The Relief of Tobruk* (p. 90).
43. Humble, *Crusader* (p. 111). See also Murphy, *The Relief of Tobruk* (p. 92).
44. DODA, UWHS, Box 138, Narrative and Reports 12, p. 5, *Lieutenant-General Willoughby Norrie narrative on Sidi Rezegh 1941.*Norrie quotes a figure of twenty tanks remaining after the day's action.
45. DODA, UWHS, Box 138, Narrative and Reports 12, p. 5, *Lieutenant-General Willoughby Norrie narrative on Sidi Rezegh 1941.*
46. The graphs have been created using figures from different sources, which must be noted, vary greatly in the numbers reported. The graphs are meant as an illustration to aid in better understanding the disproportionate attrition rate suffered by the British in the face of superior German tactics, as well as the state of the British armor just prior to the South African 5th Brigade being overrun on November 23, 1941.
47. Murphy, *The Relief of Tobruk* (p. 99).
48. DODA, UWHS, Box 138, Narrative and Reports 12, p. 5, *Lieutenant-General Willoughby Norrie narrative on Sidi Rezegh 1941.* Norrie describes it, "Up to now the whole brunt of the operation had been confined to XXX Corps."
49. Playfair, *A History of the Second World War*, III (p. 46).
50. Murphy, *The Relief of Tobruk* (p. 108). Once again the influence of " British prophets" on German doctrine has been grossly exaggerated in no less a publication as an official history. Playfair, *A History of the Second World War*, III (p. 45).
51. DODA, UWHS, Box 131, Narrative and Reports ME 5, File 2725, p. 2, *Battle Report Cyrenaica 18 November–29 December 1941, 1st SA Infantry Brigade HQ*.

52. DODA, Brink Papers, Box 55, p. 34, *1 SA Division Operations Report Cyrenaica 1942*, November 18–December 2, 1941.
53. TNA, WO 32/10160/313, *Auchinleck Despatch on Operations in the Middle East,* November 1, 1941, to August 15, 1942.
54. DODA, UWHS, Box 138, Narrative and Reports 12, p. 5, *Lieutenant-General Willoughby Norrie narrative on Sidi Rezegh 1941.* See also M. Carver, *Dilemmas of the Desert War: A New Look at the Libyan Campaign 1940–1942* (London: Batsford, 1986) (p. 37).
55. NAP, JSP, Box 137, f.32, Auchinleck to Smuts, *'B Echelon' at Sidi Rezegh,* December 4, 1941. South African divisions were ordered to reduce transport to British War Establishments. See Agar-Hamilton, *The Sidi Rezegh Battles* (p. 168). See also DODA, UWHS, Box 138, Narrative and Reports 12, p. 8, *Lieutenant-General Willoughby Norrie narrative on Sidi Rezegh 1941.* Norrie considers the retention of the B Echelon transport within the 5th Brigade leaguer as an "error of judgment."
56. DODA, UWHS, Box 132, Narrative and Reports 6, File 341/9, p. 1, *Report on Sidi Rezegh 21–23 November 1941 by Lieutenant-Colonel Dobbs OC 1 SA Irish.* See also Agar-Hamilton, *The Sidi Rezegh Battles* (p. 189). See also Murphy, *The Relief of Tobruk* (p. 99). See also TNA, CAB 106/638, Letter Armstrong to Deputy CGS, *Objection to Field-Marshal Auchinleck's Despatch*, 1948. See also DODA, Brink Papers, Box 55, p. 37, *1 SA Division Operations Report Cyrenaica 1942*, November 18–December 2, 1941.
57. Murphy, *The Relief of Tobruk* (p. 100).
58. Murphy, *The Relief of Tobruk* (p. 101).
59. Carver, *Dilemmas of the Desert War* (p. 38). Crüwell was under the false impression that his *Panzers* were surrounded by the British tank brigades, hence the withdrawal to allow more room.
60. Murphy, *The Relief of Tobruk* (p. 101).
61. DODA, UWHS, Box 138, Narrative and Reports 12, p. 6, *Lieutenant-General Willoughby Norrie narrative on Sidi Rezegh 1941.* See also Carver, *Dilemmas of the Desert War* (p. 38).
62. DODA, Brink Papers, Box 55, p. 39, *1 SA Division Operations Report Cyrenaica 1942*, November 18–December 2, 1941. See also DODA, UWHS, Box 132, Narrative and Reports 6, File 341/9, p. 2, *Report on Sidi Rezegh 21–23 November 1941 by Lieutenant-Colonel Dobbs OC 1 SA Irish.*
63. C. Birkby, *The Saga of the Transvaal Scottish Regiment 1932–1950* (Cape Town: Hodder and Stoughton, 1950) (p. 318).
64. DODA, UWHS, Box 132, Narrative and Reports ME 6, File 3371, p. 17, 5th SA Infantry Brigade HQ, *Detailed account of Sidi Rezegh November 1941.*
65. DODA, UWHS, Box 132, Narrative and Reports ME 6, File 3371, p. 17, 5th SA Infantry Brigade HQ, *Detailed account of Sidi Rezegh November 1941.* See also Murphy, *The Relief of Tobruk* (p. 107).
66. DODA, UWHS, Box 131, Narrative and Reports ME 5, File 2725, p. 3, *Battle Report Cyrenaica 18 November–29 December 1941, 1st SA Infantry Brigade HQ.* The entire distance required of 1st Brigade to move to the south of Sidi Rezegh consisted of 48 km. The reason for not attempting a night move was that it was feared there might be intervening enemy positions between the 1st and 5th Brigades.

67. Birkby, *The Saga of the Transvaal Scottish* (p. 351). See also Murphy, *The Relief of Tobruk* (p. 107).
68. Birkby, *The Saga of the Transvaal Scottish* (p. 339).
69. DODA, UWHS, Box 138, Narrative and Reports 12, p. 6, *Lieutenant-General Willoughby Norrie narrative on Sidi Rezegh 1941.* Norrie describes this as the biggest tank battle (250 tanks in all) thus far in the operation. See also Murphy, *The Relief of Tobruk* (p. 103).
70. Carver, *Dilemmas of the Desert War* (p. 39).
71. Murphy, *The Relief of Tobruk* (p. 106). The British in their wisdom and partly as a result of Battleaxe had relegated their I tanks (Matilda) to support the infantry while leaving the lighter and more mobile Cruiser tanks to tackle the enemy armor. The Cruisers failed in their task against the German tanks and it would be left to the infantry with their I tanks to do the job.
72. DODA, Brink Papers, Box 55, p. 45, *1 SA Division Operations Report Cyrenaica 1942*, November 18–December 2, 1941.
73. Carver, *Dilemmas of the Desert War* (p. 39). See also Murphy, *The Relief of Tobruk* (p. 156).
74. DODA, UWHS, Box 138, Narrative and Reports 12, p. 8, *Lieutenant-General Willoughby Norrie narrative on Sidi Rezegh 1941.* Brink failed to get personal contact with Armstrong as enemy tanks blocked the way.
75. DODA, Brink Papers, Box 55, p. 46, *1 SA Division Operations Report Cyrenaica 1942*, November 18–December 2, 1941. See also Murphy, *The Relief of Tobruk* (p. 156).
76. Agar-Hamilton, *The Sidi Rezegh Battles* (p. 231). See also Murphy, *The Relief of Tobruk* (p. 156).
77. Agar-Hamilton, *The Sidi Rezegh Battles* (p. 249).
78. DODA, Brink Papers, Box 55, Part III, 1, *1 SA Division Operations Report Cyrenaica 1942*, November 18–December 2, 1941.
79. Murphy, *The Relief of Tobruk* (p. 158).
80. Murphy, *The Relief of Tobruk* (p. 160).
81. Agar-Hamilton, *The Sidi Rezegh Battles* (pp. 233, 234).
82. DODA, UWHS, Box 131, Narrative and Reports ME 5, File 2725, p. 4, *Battle Report Cyrenaica November 18–December 29, 1941, 1st SA Infantry Brigade HQ.* The 1st Brigade history records that the Field Ambulance unit did take heavy casualties after it became embroiled with enemy formations in their night move. See also Agar-Hamilton, *The Sidi Rezegh Battles* (p. 239).
83. Agar-Hamilton, *The Sidi Rezegh Battles* (p. 242).
84. DODA, UWHS, Box 131, Narrative and Reports ME 5, File 2725, p. 4, *Battle Report Cyrenaica November 18–December 29, 1941, 1st SA Infantry Brigade HQ.*
85. DODA, Brink Papers, Box 55, pp.49, 50, *1 SA Division Operations Report Cyrenaica 1942*, November 18–December 2, 1941.
86. Murphy, *The Relief of Tobruk* (p. 160).
87. DODA, UWHS, Box 132, Narrative and Reports ME 6, File 3446, p. 1, *Report on Sidi Rezegh 20–23 November 1941 by Lieutenant-Colonel Mason, 2nd Regiment Botha.* Mason was instructed to send his 25-pounder battery to B Echelon as it was correctly anticipated that the attack would come from the south. See also Agar-Hamilton, *The Sidi Rezegh Battles* (pp. 244, 245). See also Murphy, *The Relief of Tobruk* (p. 163).

88. Agar-Hamilton, *The Sidi Rezegh Battles* (p. 245). See also Murphy, *The Relief of Tobruk* (p. 163). New Zealand official history estimates 16 instead of 12 25-pounders in the southern sector.
89. B. Stegemann, Detlef Vogel, G. Schreiber, *Germany and the Second World War: The Mediterranean, South-east Europe, and North Africa 1939–1941* (Oxford: Oxford, 1995), III (p. 738).
90. Agar-Hamilton, *The Sidi Rezegh Battles* (p. 245).
91. Playfair, *A History of the Second World War,* III (p. 46).
92. At 1215 Brink sent a message to Armstrong that 1st Brigade was near and that they were coming. In the absence of any other indication and due to the proximity of 1st Brigade to the south sector of 5th Brigade, the expectation that the arrival of 1st Brigade was imminent is not unfair. Agar-Hamilton, *The Sidi Rezegh Battles* (p. 252).
93. S. Bidwell, "Indirect Fire Artillery as a Battle Winner/Loser," in *Old Battles and New Defences* (Oxford: Brassey's Defence Publisher, 1986) (p. 123).
94. R. Kriebel, *Inside the Afrika Korps*, ed. by B. I. Gudmundsson (London: Greenhill, 1999) (p. 88).
95. Agar-Hamilton, *The Sidi Rezegh Battles* (pp. 246, 247).
96. DODA, UWHS, Box 132, Narrative and Reports ME 6, File 3373, pp. 21–25, *History of Sidi Rezegh by the 5th Infantry Brigade HQ, January 1942.*
97. Agar-Hamilton, *The Sidi Rezegh Battles* (p. 249).
98. DODA, Brink Papers, Box 55, p. 52, *1 SA Division Operations Report Cyrenaica 1942*, November 18–December 2, 1941.
99. DODA, Brink Papers, Box 55, p. 52, *1 SA Division Operations Report Cyrenaica 1942*, November 18–December 2, 1941.
100. Murphy, *The Relief of Tobruk* (p. 162).
101. Kriebel, *Inside the Afrika Korps* (p. 93). The Germans describe their normal methods as detailed reconnaissance, thorough preparation for an attack against prepared positions using narrow sectors and organization in depth, and advancing by bounds (fire and movement) of debussed infantry supported by tanks and especially strong formations of the Luftwaffe to paralyze the superior artillery and antitank guns.
102. Murphy, *The Relief of Tobruk* (p. 162).
103. Kriebel, *Inside the Afrika Korps* (pp. 87, 88).
104. DODA, UWHS, Box 321, p. (2)107 Narrative prepared for UK Cabinet, *General Auchinleck's Offensive and the Relief Of Tobruch - The Planning Period*, June–November 1941.
105. H. W. Schmidt, *With Rommel in the Desert* (Durban: Albatross, 1950) *(*pp. 108–10). See also Agar-Hamilton, *The Sidi Rezegh Battles* (p. 255).
106. Murphy, *The Relief of Tobruk* (p. 165).
107. Murphy, *The Relief of Tobruk* (p. 166).
108. DODA, UWHS, Box 132, Narrative and Reports ME 6, File 3446, p. 5, *Report on Sidi Rezegh 20–23 November 1941 2nd Battalion, Regiment Botha Regimental History from September 1941.*
109. DODA, UWHS, Box 132, Narrative and Reports ME 6, File 3446, p. 5, *Report on Sidi Rezegh 20–23 November 1941 2nd Battalion, Regiment Botha Regimental History from September 1941.*

110. DODA, UWHS, Box 132, Narrative and Reports ME 6, File 3446, p. 2, *Report on Sidi Rezegh 20–23 November 1941 by Lieutenant-Colonel Mason, 2nd Regiment Botha.*
111. Murphy, *The Relief of Tobruk* (pp. 168, 169).
112. DODA, Brink Papers, Box 55, p. 53, *1 SA Division Operations Report Cyrenaica 1942*, November 18–December 2, 1941.
113. Carver, *Dilemmas of the Desert War* (p. 40). See also Agar-Hamilton, *The Sidi Rezegh Battles* (p. 255). See also Playfair, *A History of the Second World War,* III (p. 50).
114. Kriebel, *Inside the Afrika Korps* (p. 92).
115. Stewart, *The Early Battles of the Eighth Army* (p. 25). Ronald Lewin, in *The Life and Death of the Afrika Korps*, describes it as "Crüwell cut the heart out of his command."
116. TNA, WO 201, File 2870, *Martel Report on Aftermath of Crusader*, January 26, 1942, and DODA, UWHS, Box 321, p. (2)109, Narrative prepared for UK Cabinet, *General Auchinleck's Offensive and the Relief Of Tobruch—The Planning Period,* June–November 1941. "The South African gunners had been magnificent."
117. Hal Denny was an American citizen and correspondent with the *New York Times*, captured on November 23 by the Germans with other correspondents and members of the 5th Brigade, and was witness to the events of that day. Hal Denny, "Performance SA 5th Brigade at Sidi Rezegh" (Letter Denny to Colonel Phillip Astley, Hoover Institution Archives, Box 40, Folder 15, 1942).
118. NAP, JSP, C Auchinleck, "South Africans at Sidi Rezegh" (Personal Memorandum Auchinleck to Smuts, Box 137/22, 25 November 1941).
119. DODA, UWHS, Box 132, Narrative and Reports ME 6, Folder 3287, *SAEC 5Fd Coy Middle East Reports on Sidi Rezegh November 1941, Memorandum of Corporal J. Wallis.*
120. J. L. Scoullar, *Battle for Egypt: The Summer of 1942*, ed. by H. Kippenberger (Wellington: Historical Publications Branch, 1955) (pp. 1, 2).
121. Scoullar, *Battle for Egypt* (p. 5).
122. C. Birkby, *Uncle George: The Boer Boyhood, Letters and Battles of Lieutenant-General George Edwin Brink* (Johannesburg: Jonathan Ball, 1987) (pp. 251, 252).
123. "Gen. Brink on Sidi Rezegh," *Sunday Times*, November 10, 1957, and DODA, Brink Papers, Box 55, p. 37, *1 SA Division Operations Report Cyrenaica 1942*, November 18–December 2, 1941.
124. S. Monick and O. E. F. Baker, *Clear the Way ('Faugh-A-Ballagh'). The Military Heritage of the South African Irish 1880–1990* (Johannesburg: South African Irish Regimental Association, 1991) (p. 258).
125. Agar-Hamilton, *The Sidi Rezegh Battles.*
126. J. A. I. Agar-Hamilton and L. C. F. Turner, *Crisis in the Desert: May-July 1942* (London: Oxford, 1952).
127. "*The Sidi Rezegh Battles*—An official history," *The Natal Daily News*, November 8, 1957.
128. Agar-Hamilton, *The Sidi Rezegh Battles* (p. 271).
129. Kriebel, *Inside the Afrika Korps* (p. 94).
130. Birkby, *The Saga of the Transvaal Scottish* (p. 333).

131. S. Monick and O. E. F. Baker, *Clear the Way ('Faugh-A-Ballagh'). The Military Heritage of the South African Irish 1880–1990* (Johannesburg: South African Irish Regimental Association, 1991) (pp. 270, 283).
132. A. Pollock, *Pienaar of Alamein* (Cape Town: Cape Times, 1943) (p. 84).
133. E. Rosenthal, *General Dan Pienaar: His Life and His Battles* (Cape Town: Unie-Volkspers, 1943).
134. Agar-Hamilton, *The Sidi Rezegh Battles* (p. 327). See also J., A. Brown, *Retreat to Victory: A Springboks Diary in North Africa* (Johannesburg: Ashanti, 1991) (pp. 40, 41).
135. Agar-Hamilton, *The Sidi Rezegh Battles* (p. 332).
136. Agar-Hamilton, *The Sidi Rezegh Battles* (pp. 327–35).
137. C. Birkby, *The Saga of the Transvaal Scottish* (pp. 356, 357).
138. Agar-Hamilton, *The Sidi Rezegh Battles* (p. 331).
139. "War History says Gen. Pienaar flouted orders," *Sunday Express*, November 11, 1957.
140. R. Crisp, *Brazen Chariots* (London: Frederick Muller, 1959) (p. 143).
141. Agar-Hamilton, *The Sidi Rezegh Battles* (p. 393). See also Brown, *Retreat to Victory* (p. 41).
142. N.S. Nash, *'Strafer'—The Desert General: The Life and Killing of Lieutenant General WHE Gott* (Barnsley: Pen and Sword, 2013) (p. 170).
143. DODA, Brink Papers, Box 55, *1 SA Division Operations Report Cyrenaica 1942*, November 18–December 2, 1941.
144. DODA, UWHS, Box 131, Narrative and Reports ME 5, File 2723, pp. 1–4, *Battle Report Cyrenaica 18 November–29 December 1941, 1st SA Infantry Brigade HQ, Notes Conclusions and Suggestions Based on Experiences.*
145. B. C. Freyberg, "The New Zealand Division in Cyrenaica and Lessons of the Campaign" (Report, Headquarters New Zealand Division, 1942), p. 27.
146. DODA, Brink Papers, Box 55, Part III, 4, *1 SA Division Operations Report Cyrenaica 1942*, November 18–December 2, 1941.
147. TNA, WO 201, File 2870, *Martel Report on Aftermath of Crusader*, January 26, 1942. Martel believed in a similar fashion to Brink that infantry armed with suitable antitank weapons were a formidable obstacle to German armor.
148. DODA, Brink Papers, Box 55, Part III, 14, 15, *1 SA Division Operations Report Cyrenaica 1942*, November 18–December 2, 1941.
149. TNA, WO 201, File 2870, *Martel Report on Aftermath of Crusader*, January 26, 1942. Martel, on the other hand, concedes a need for combined operations of all arms.
150. Freyberg, "The New Zealand Division in Cyrenaica" (p. 28).
151. DODA, Brink Papers, Box 55, Part III, 13, *1 SA Division Operations Report Cyrenaica 1942*, November 18–December 2, 1941.
152. DODA, Brink Papers, Box 55, Part III, 16, *1 SA Division Operations Report Cyrenaica 1942*, November 18–December 2, 1941.
153. Bidwell, "Indirect Fire . . .". The artillery being the greatest beneficiary of concentration at divisional level, and conversely, being less effective if parceled out at brigade level.
154. DODA, Brink Papers, Box 55, Part III, 2, *1 SA Division Operations Report Cyrenaica 1942*, November 18–December 2, 1941.

155. TNA, WO 201, File 2870, *Martel Report on Aftermath of Crusader*, January 26, 1942.
156. TNA, WO 201, File 2870, *Martel Report on Aftermath of Crusader, Part IV Summary of the main lessons, 26 January 1942.*
157. Playfair, *A History of the Second World War*, III (p. 99).
158. Bidwell, "Indirect Fire . . ." (p. 123).
159. DODA, UWHS, Box 138, Narrative and Reports 12, p. 8, *Lieutenant-General Willoughby Norrie narrative on Sidi Rezegh 1941.*
160. DODA, Brink Papers, Box 55, Part III, 17, *1 SA Division Operations Report Cyrenaica 1942*, November 18–December 2, 1941. "To destroy the enemy's armoured formations before operations for the relief of Tobruk were undertaken."
161. DODA, Brink Papers, Box 55, Part III, 2, *1 SA Division Operations Report Cyrenaica 1942*, November 18–December 2, 1941. "Night moves by big formations should be avoided at all costs except for urgent and immediate tactical necessity." Inexplicably, in the aftermath of Sidi Rezegh, Brink continued to avoid night moves and discouraged maneuvers under the cover of darkness.

CHAPTER 6

1. A. Stewart, *The Early Battles of the Eighth Army: Crusader to the Alamein Line, 1941–42* (Mechanicsburg, PA: Stackpole, 2002) (p. 50).
2. The 2nd Division consisted of three brigades, being the 2nd, 3rd, and 6th Brigades. The composition of the 2nd Division was somewhat different when it was besieged at Tobruk, consisting of the 4th and 6th Brigades.
3. R. J. M. Loughnan, *The Official History of New Zealand in the Second World War 1939–1945: Divisional Cavalry* (Wellington: Historical Publications Branch, 1963) (p. 160). See also C. Birkby, *The Saga of the Transvaal Scottish Regiment 1932–1950* (Cape Town: Hodder and Stoughton, 1950) (p. 371).
4. I. S. O. Playfair, *A History of the Second World War: The Mediterranean and Middle East*, ed. by J. Butler (Uckfield: Naval & Military Press, 2004), III (p. 94). The figures were given by Military Intelligence Service, *The British Capture of Bardia (December 1941–January 1942): A Successful Infantry-Tank Attack* (U.S. War Department, Information Bulletin No. 21, 1942). At the conclusion of the action, however, it was found that this estimate credited the Axis with only about 40 percent of actual strength, for, in addition to unannounced Axis battlefield casualties, the British reported the capture of more than 8,000 prisoners, of whom approximately 1,800 were German.
5. *The British Capture of Bardia (December 1941–January 1942): A Successful Infantry-Tank Attack* (Information Bulletin No. 21, U.S. War Department, WWII Military Intelligence Service). Opposed to the British attackers was an Axis force initially estimated at 4,120 defenders, of whom 1,310 were German and the remainder Italian. The defending force included infantry, engineers, cavalry, artillery (the British knew the positions of 86 guns of various calibers), a detachment of 13 tanks, and the necessary service troops.
6. N. Orpen, *South African Forces World War II: War in the Desert* (Cape Town: Purnell, 1971), III (pp. 76, 102).
7. Loughnan, *The Official History of New Zealand* (p. 162).
8. Orpen, *War in the Desert*, III (p. 92).

9. *The British Capture of Bardia (December 1941–January 1942): A Successful Infantry-Tank Attack* (Information Bulletin No. 21, U.S. War Department, WWII Military Intelligence Service). There were two battalions of infantry tanks (114 tanks).
10. Orpen, *War in the Desert*, III (p. 105). Three field artillery regiments, less one battery of 25-pounders (total, eleven batteries); four batteries of medium artillery (three 6 inch batteries; one 4.5 inch battery);
11. Orpen, *War in the Desert*, III (p. 106).
12. Birkby, *The Saga of the Transvaal Scottish* (p. 374). Ritchie directed that the task was to be carried out with the minimum of casualties "in view of the difficulty of providing reinforcements to replace wastage in the infantry of the Union Defence Forces." See also Orpen, *War in the Desert*, III (p. 108).
13. Although to be fair the attack was to follow similar lines to the one proposed by Rommel in the first siege and was only interrupted by Operation Crusader.
14. Loughnan, *The Official History of New Zealand* (p. 164). See also Orpen, *War in the Desert*, III (p. 107).
15. Orpen, *War in the Desert*, III (p. 107). Of the fifty tanks engaged, there were twenty tank casualties, mostly in the left column during the Phase 1 attack. During the night all but three of these were recovered, and all seventeen were in condition to continue in the operation by the morning of January 1.
16. Orpen, *War in the Desert*, III (p. 125).
17. Orpen, *War in the Desert*, III (p. 127).
18. The official New Zealand history claims that the New Zealanders were in fact the unofficial captors at Bardia and that the Divisional Cavalry "stole the South Africans' thunder." Loughnan, *The Official History of New Zealand* (p. 167).
19. Orpen, *War in the Desert*, III (p. 135).
20. *The British Capture of Bardia (December 1941–January 1942): A Successful Infantry-Tank Attack* (Information Bulletin No. 21, U.S. War Department, WWII Military Intelligence Service).
21. Playfair, *A History of the Second World War*, III (p. 139). See also H. Boog, W. Rahn, R. Stumpf, and B. Wegner, *Germany and the Second World War: The Global War*, ed. by Militargeschichtliches Forschungsamt, Vol. VI (Oxford: Claredon Press, 2001) (p. 636). According to the German official history the *DAK* was alloted fifty-one tanks (Panzer Mk III and MK IV) and sixteen armored cars.
22. R. Kriebel, *Inside the Afrika Korps*, ed. by B. I. Gudmundsson (London: Greenhill, 1999) (p. 223).
23. Kriebel, *Inside the Afrika Korps* (p. 226).
24. Boog, *Germany and the Second World War* (p. 652). The British had taken sixty-three days to advance 925 km in 1940–41. Rommel advanced 850 km in forty days in 1941 and 610 km in only fifteen days in this operation.
25. Orpen, *War in the Desert*, III (p. 187).
26. Orpen, *War in the Desert*, III (pp. 73, 74).
27. DODA, UWHS, Box 128, Narrative and Reports M.E. 2 (p. 15), *The Springbok troops were mishandled, Major-General E. Dorman O'Gowan in Outspan article 18 February 1955.*
28. C. Barnett, *The Desert Generals* (New York: Viking Press, 1961) (p. 113).
29. M. Carver, *Dilemmas of the Desert War: A New Look at the Libyan Campaign 1940–1942* (London: Batsford, 1986) (pp. 11, 12). Carver is more sympathetic

to Ritchie's predicament than earlier authors and feels Ritchie was unfairly treated. See also Barnett, *The Desert Generals* (p. 124). Barnett believes Auchinleck retained Ritchie so that he could directly shape the future conduct of operations when he should have replaced Ritchie with someone more senior and experienced.

30. W. Churchill, *The Second World War: The Hinge of Fate* (Middlesex: Penguin, 1985), IV (p. 260).
31. NAP, JSP, J. C. Smuts (Memorandum Smuts to Churchill December 1942, Box 95-1 [146], 1942).
32. B. H. Liddell Hart, *The Tanks: The History of the Royal Tank Regiment* (London: Cassel, 1959) (p. 153).
33. M. Carver, *Tobruk* (London: B. T. Batsford, 1964) (pp. 162, 163).
34. NAP, JSP Box 95-1, f.112, Churchill to Smuts, *Churchill encourages initiative on eve of German attack*, June 17, 1942. Churchill and Smuts were in agreement in their concern for the prevailing defensive spirit in the higher command.
35. Playfair, *A History of the Second World War*, III (p. 217).
36. Stewart, *The Early Battles of the Eighth Army* (p. 58). See also Carver, *Tobruk (*p. 164). See also Liddell Hart, *The Tanks* (p. 152).
37. Liddell Hart, *The Tanks* (p. 152).
38. Playfair, *A History of the Second World War*, III (p. 216). See also Stewart, *The Early Battles of the Eighth Army* (p. 63).
39. Playfair, *A History of the Second World War*, III (p. 216).
40. Stewart, *The Early Battles of the Eighth Army* (p. 63).
41. Stewart, *The Early Battles of the Eighth Army* (p. 63). Auchinleck felt that the brigade would be more flexible, although conceding its vulnerability.
42. Barnett, *The Desert Generals* (pp. 135, 136).
43. Carver, *Tobruk* (p. 168).
44. Playfair, *A History of the Second World War*, III (p. 216).
45. Carver, *Dilemmas of the Desert War* (p. 64).
46. Barnett, *The Desert Generals* (p. 134). It is interesting to contrast this with the German official history, which describes the Gazala defenses as nothing less than a "complete innovation in desert warfare. . . . Here in the desert the British had sought to construct a fortified line." Boog, *Germany and the Second World War* (p. 672).
47. Playfair, *A History of the Second World War*, III (p. 218).
48. Carver, *Dilemmas of the Desert War* (p. 71).
49. Carver, *Dilemmas of the Desert War* (p. 75).
50. Playfair, *A History of the Second World War*, III (p. 213). See also Stewart, *The Early Battles of the Eighth Army* (p. 63).
51. Playfair, *A History of the Second World War*, III (p. 214).
52. Liddell Hart, *The Tanks* (p. 154). "Only the 280 German medium tanks were of serious importance."
53. Boog, *Germany and the Second World War* (p. 651). Rommel's criticism of the Italian formations was not directed at their individual military achievements but more at their commanders' lack of initiative and strict adherence to out-dated orders.
54. Carver, *Tobruk*, (p. 166). See also Stewart, *The Early Battles of the Eighth Army* (p. 60). See also Playfair, *A History of the Second World War*, III (p. 220).

55. Liddell Hart, *The Tanks* (pp. 154–57).
56. Barnett, *The Desert Generals* (pp. 135, 136).
57. S. Mitcham Jr, *Rommels Greatest Victory: The Desert Fox and the Fall of Tobruk, Spring 1942* (Novato: Presidio, 2001) (p. 61).
58. H. W. Schmidt, *With Rommel in the Desert* (Durban: Albatross, 1950) (p. 149). The author served as Rommel's aide-de-camp from March 1941. Tobruk was the core target of the offensive launched by Rommel on May 26, 1942.
59. Boog, *Germany and the Second World War* (p.668).
60. Playfair, *A History of the Second World War,* III (p. 216).
61. A. Toppe, *Desert Warfare: German Experiences in World War II*, ed. by H. Heitman (Fort Leavenworth: Combat Studies Institute, 1952) (p. 44).
62. Toppe, *Desert Warfare*, Appendix 8 (p. 18).
63. Toppe, *Desert Warfare*, Appendix 8 (p. 18).
64. Boog, *Germany and the Second World War* (p.674).
65. Boog, *Germany and the Second World War* (p.672).
66. Boog, *Germany and the Second World War* (p.675).
67. Liddell Hart, *The Tanks* (p. 160).
68. Stewart, *The Early Battles of the Eighth Army* (pp. 68, 69).
69. I. Walker, *Iron Hulls Iron Hearts: Mussolini's Elite Armoured Divisions in North Africa* (Ramsbury: Crowood Press, 2006) (p. 114). Carver mistakenly refers to a mixture of German and Italian forces that overran the 3rd Brigade, which is incorrect according to the Italian war diaries. Carver, *Tobruk* (p. 177).
70. Liddell Hart, *The Tanks* (p. 160).
71. Stewart, *The Early Battles of the Eighth Army* (p. 69).
72. Liddell Hart, *The Tanks* (p. 160).
73. Stewart, *The Early Battles of the Eighth Army* (p. 70).
74. Playfair, *A History of the Second World War,* III. See also Stewart, *The Early Battles of the Eighth Army* (p. 71) and Boog, *Germany and the Second World War* (p. 678).
75. Carver, *Tobruk* (p. 186). See also Boog, *Germany and the Second World War* (p.681).
76. B. H. Liddell Hart, *The Rommel Papers* (New York: De Capo Press, 1953) (p. 207). See also Playfair, *A History of the Second World War,* III (p. 225).
77. Liddell Hart, *The Rommel Papers* (p. 208).
78. Liddell Hart, *The Rommel Papers* (p. 208).
79. Boog, *Germany and the Second World War* (p.681).
80. DODA, UWHS, Box 139, Narrative and Reports M.E. 13 (p. 2), *Interview with Col. W. Mc A Richards CRA 2 SA Div 23 November 1946.* Initially, before Tobruk was cut off, the inner perimeter was defended against an airborne attack, a seaborne landing, or a "smash grab attack by AFV" on the supply lines and base installations.
81. Carver, *Tobruk* (p. 186). See also Playfair, *A History of the Second World War,* III (p. 225).
82. Liddell Hart, *The Tanks* (p. 166).
83. Walker, *Iron Hulls Iron Hearts* (p. 118).
84. Playfair, *A History of the Second World War,* III (p. 226). See also B. H. Liddell Hart, *The Tanks* (London: Cassell, 1959) (p. 166).
85. Liddell Hart, *The Tanks* (p. 166).

86. Liddell Hart, *The Rommel Papers* (p. 211).
87. H. von Seeckt, *Command and Combat Use of Combined Arms (German Field Service Regulations)*, trans. by Capt. P. B. Harm (Germany: United States of America Army War College, 1921).
88. XXX Corps consisted of the 1st and 7th Armour Divisions containing all but two of the armored brigades (the 1st and 32nd Army Tank Brigades).
89. Liddell Hart, *The Tanks* (p. 166).
90. Boog, *Germany and the Second World War* (p. 686).
91. J. A. I. Agar-Hamilton and L. C. F. Turner, *Crisis in the Desert: May-July 1942* (London: Oxford, 1952) (p. 38). The South Africans too extracted a heavy toll on German armor at Sidi Rezegh on November 23, 1941, where the South African 5th Brigade was overun by concentrated German forces in Operation Crusader.
92. R. M. Citino, *Death of the Wehrmacht: The German Campaigns of 1942* (Kansas: University Press of Kansas, 2007) (p. 144).
93. A. Kesselring, *A Soldier's Record* (New York: William Morrow and Company, 1954) (p. 147). Kesselring supplies a further insight that may suggest that the coordination between air and ground forces was not always perfect. He suggests that the "omission to synchronize air and ground attacks was responsible for the failure of these and subsequent infantry assaults [on Bir Hakim]."
94. Liddell Hart, *The Rommel Papers* (p. 214).
95. Boog, *Germany and the Second World War* (p. 688).
96. The Free French Box at Bir Hakim measured 16.5 km along its triangular perimeter and was manned by a mixed force of Free French units of approximately 3,700 men. By all accounts the French positions were skillfully placed surrounded by minefields and well-placed antitank guns, and importantly, well camoflauged. See E. Bimberg, *Tricolor Over the Sahara: The Desert Battles of the Free French 1940–1942* (Westport: Greenwood, 2002) (p. 103). It is once again tempting although spurious to draw obvious parallels with the state of readiness and resistance offered and the successful evacuation of Bir Hakim to the much larger forces of the Tobruk garrison.
97. DODA, UWHS, Box 127, Narrative and Reports ME.1, p. 1, *Western Desert Campaign, Remarks passed by Colonel H. Cilliers onetime G11 SA Infantry Division, to E. Axelson 18 September 1947.*
98. Stewart, *The Early Battles of the Eighth Army* (pp. 73–75). See also S. W. Mitcham, *Rommel's Desert War: The Life and Death of the Afrika Korps* (Mechanicsburg, PA: Stackpole, 2007) (pp. 67–71).
99. Mitcham, *Rommel's Desert War* (p. 65).
100. Mitcham, *Rommel's Desert War* (p. 69).
101. Mitcham, *Rommel's Desert War* (p. 71).
102. Stewart, *The Early Battles of the Eighth Army* (pp. 73–75). See also Mitcham, *Rommel's Desert War* (p. 69). "The Allies also violated every principle of control in battle. Their control arrangements can best be described as strange."
103. Mitcham, *Rommel's Desert War* (p. 73).
104. Boog, *Germany and the Second World War* (p. 690).
105. DODA, UWHS, Box 127, Narrative and Reports ME.1, p. 1, *Western Desert Campaign, Remarks passed by Colonel H. Cilliers onetime G11 SA Infantry Division, to E. Axelson 18 September 1947.*

106. NAP, JSP, Box 137, f.125, Auchinleck to Smuts, *Addressing Smuts' Concern for Union Forces,* June 14, 1942. Auchinleck saw the situation as "serious but by no means irretrievable." This was in response to the growing alarm in the South African camp.

Chapter 7

1. W. Churchill, *The Second World War: The Hinge of Fate* (Middlesex: Penguin, 1985), IV (p. 344).
2. DODA, UWHS, Box 127, Narrative and Reports ME.1, p. 1, *Western Desert Campaign, R. V. Davis 4th Bty 2nd Fd Regt from Gazala to Tobruk Feb-June 1942*
3. A. Stewart, *The Early Battles of the Eighth Army: Crusader to the Alamein Line, 1941–42* (Mechanicsburg, PA: Stackpole, 2002) (p. 50).
4. NAP, JSP, Box 137, f.132, Smuts to Auchinleck, *Smuts encourages Auchinleck to hold Tobruk,* June 18, 1942.
5. TNA, WO 32/10160/318, *Auchinleck Despatch on Operations in the Middle East,* November 1, 1941 to August 15, 1942. In Note on the Western Front by the Commander in Chief, M. E. F. (for Middle East Defence Committee) dated 4th February, 1942.
6. TNA, WO 32/10160/380, *Auchinleck Despatch on Operations in the Middle East,* November 1, 1941 to August 15, 1942. This viewpoint became Eighth Army Operational Instruction No. 46, dated February 16, 1942, in which this paragraph was repeated verbatim. DODA, UWHS–Civil, Box 371, Operations in the Western Desert, Part I, p. 14, Report of Tobruk Court of Enquiry, May 27–July 2.
7. Operational Order No. 23, code-named "Freeborn" and dated May 10, 1942, states in the opening paragraph that should the defense of the Gazala line become untenable the entire corps was to withdraw to the Egyptian frontier. Further on in paragraph 4(d) it emphasis that the "thorough demolition of Tobruk is an essential part of the scheme." Allowance was made for the withdrawal of the Tobruk garrison to Bir El Hariga close to the Egyptian frontier. DODA, UWHS–Civil, Box 371, Operations in the Western Desert, Part III, p. 31, *Report of Tobruk Court of Enquiry,* May 27–July 2.
8. In Auchinleck's own words as per his despatch, "I was determined that the Eighth Army should not yield more ground than was absolutely necessary. I therefore ordered General Ritchie not to allow Tobruk to become besieged but to hold a line through Acroma and El Adem and thence southwards." TNA, WO 32/10160/360, *Auchinleck Despatch on Operations in the Middle East,* November 1, 1941 to August 15, 1942.
9. TNA, WO 32/10160/360, *Auchinleck Despatch on Operations in the Middle East,* November 1, 1941 to August 15, 1942.
10. NAP, JSP, Box 137, f.132, Smuts to Auchinleck, *Smuts encourages Auchinleck to hold Tobruk,* June 18, 1942. As has been pointed out, it seems that this was a position that Smuts encouraged.
11. J. A. I. Agar-Hamilton and L. C. F. Turner, *Crisis in the Desert: May-July 1942* (London: Oxford, 1952) (p. 107).
12. Agar-Hamilton, *Crisis in the Desert* (p. 72).
13. E. P. Hartshorn, *Avenge Tobruk* (Cape Town: Purnell, 1960) (p.110).
14. Agar-Hamilton, *Crisis in the Desert* (p. 148).

15. Agar-Hamilton, *Crisis in the Desert* (p. 125).
16. Corelli Barnett is an example of a revisionist author. He sought to resuscitate the tarnished reputation and generalship of Ritchie at the expense of Auchinleck, and then later, in a similar exercise, that of Auchinleck over Field-Marshal Montgomery. Barnett attempts to redress some of the patently unfair criticism they both received at the hands of historians and especially in the case of Auchinleck at the hands of Field-Marshal Montgomery. C. Barnett, *The Desert Generals* (New York: Viking Press, 1961).
17. One of the few good biographies written on a UDF General is C. Birkby, *Uncle George: The Boer Boyhood, Letters and Battles of Lieutenant-General George Edwin Brink* (Johannesburg: Jonathan Ball, 1987). Another, although less satisfactory, is on Major-General D. H. Pienaar. A. Pollock, *Pienaar of Alamein* (Cape Town: Cape Times, 1943). The lack of biographical material has been addressed by Ian van der Waag, who, using a prosopographical approach, analyzed sixty-one men who held general or flag rank in the Union Defence Force (UDF). I. van der Waag, "Smuts's Generals: Towards a First Portrait of the South African High Command, 1912–1948," *War in History*, 18(1) (2011) (pp. 33–61).
18. Van der Waag, "Smuts's Generals," (p. 60).
19. DODA, Personal Records H. B. Klopper "Plea for Active Service" (Memorandum Klopper to Beyers, 1944).
20. H. B. Klopper, "Voorsmaak van die Stryd!" *Huisgenoot*, June 1950.
21. See also A. Stewart, "The 'Atomic' Despatch: Field Marshal Auchinleck, the Fall of the Tobruk Garrison and Post-War Anglo-South African Relations," *Scientia Militaria*, 36(1) (2008). The article delves into the behind the scenes shenanigans of the British and South African governments to stifle and discord in Klopper's attempts to clear his name.
22. DODA, Personal Records, *Record of Sevice H. B. Klopper* (1926–1945).
23. S. Monick, "A Man Who Knew Men: The Memoirs of Major M. G. Ind," *Scientia Militaria*, (20)1 (1990). Monick, in describing the term "amphigarious," states, "In December 1930 the first 6 'amphigarious' officers had been commissioned as airmen—artillerymen—infantrymen. Greek gave the amphigarious officers their 'earth-and-air-together-in-one' title, and those who survived the wastage rate of 50% wore the coveted badge of eagle and gun. Economic depression made it necessary for cadets to qualify both as army and air force officers in order to enter the Permanent Force."
24. DODA, Personal Records, *Record of Sevice H. B. Klopper* (1926–1945).
25. DODA, Personal Records, *Record of Sevice H. B. Klopper* (1926–1945).
26. DODA, Personal Records, *Record of Sevice H. B. Klopper* (1926–1945).
27. "Klopper's Wife Deceased" (Memorandum Personal Records, DODA, Personal Records H. B. Klopper, 1941).
28. DODA, UWHS–Civil, Box 366, File PMH62N/3, *Narrative on the Crisis at Tobruk.*
29. DODA, UWHS, Box 127, Narrative and Reports ME.1, p. 2, *Western Desert Campaign, Statement by Colonel Du Plessis on the fall of Tobruk 14 June 1943.*
30. DODA, UWHS–Civil, Box 366, File PMH62N/3, *Narrative on the Crisis at Tobruk.*

31. M. Carver, *Out of Step: The Memoirs of Field Marshal Lord Carver* (London: Hutchinson, 1989) (p.116). At a conference on June 16 attended by Klopper, Ritchie, and Gott, Gott suggested that he should stay in Tobruk and command the garrison, but Ritchie disagreed.
32. B. H. Liddell Hart, *The Rommel Papers* (New York: De Capo Press, 1953) (p. 96). Again on page 119, "A commander's drive and energy often count more than his intellectual powers."
33. These defenses are explained in the South African official history Agar-Hamilton, *Crisis in the Desert* (p. 112).
34. Agar-Hamilton, *Crisis in the Desert* (p. 114).
35. Agar-Hamilton, *Crisis in the Desert* (p. 130).
36. Hartshorn, *Avenge Tobruk* (p. 101), and again in the ofiicial British history, although here the author allows for less certainty as to the extent of the disrepair. I. S. O. Playfair, *A History of the Second World War: The Mediterranean and Middle East*, ed. by J. Butler (Uckfield: Naval & Military Press, 2004), III (p. 261) and again in Barnett, *The Desert Generals* (p. 159). A dissenting source as to the state of the Tobruk defenses is A. Heckstall-Smith, *Tobruk: The Story of a Siege* (London: Anthony Blond, 1959) (pp. 217, 218), who raises doubt that the defences were in as bad a state of repair as "legend" has it.
37. Hartshorn, *Avenge Tobruk* (pp. 112–14). The description of the run down nature of defenses of the fortress portrayed by the author is typical.
38. DODA, UWHS–Civil, Box 371 Operations in the Western Desert, Part II, p. 56, *Report of Tobruk Court of Enquiry,* May 27–July 2. However, see Agar-Hamilton, *Crisis in the Desert* (p. 141). The South African official history disagrees with these comments and finds them "surprising in view of the common knowledge that the Tobruk minefileds were regarded as a legitimate source of mines."
39. DODA, UWHS–Civil, Box 371, Operations in the Western Desert, Part II, p. 50, *Report of Tobruk Court of Enquiry,* May 27–July 2.
40. He attributes the German breakthrough largely to the detonation of the minefields by German bombing. A position not agreed to by the official historians of the UWHS, DODA, UWHS–Civil, Box 363, File PMH62C, Reports of South African Officers, *Interview with Brigadier H. B. Klopper (Notes on Major Turner's Interview)*, May 6, 1946.
41. TNA, WO 32/10160, *Auchinleck Despatch on Operations in the Middle East,* November 1, 1941 to August 15, 1942. This contrasts with Brigadier Anderson, who says, "On inspection being made it was found that portions of the minefields were non-existent. Mines which had been lifted and taken forward to the Gazala position had never been replaced. Records of lifted minefields were not avaialble." DODA, UWHS–Civil, Box 366, File PMH62N/3, *Narrative on the Crisis at Tobruk.*
42. NAP, JSP, Box 138, f.173, Theron to Smuts, *Reports High UDF Morale amongst 1st and 2nd Divisions at Tobruk*, May 30, 1942.
43. NAP, JSP, Box 138, f.200, Theron to Van Ryneveld, *Report on Klopper's High Morale*, June 19, 1942.
44. NAP, JSP, Box 138, f.206, Theron to Van Ryneveld, *Klopper Looked Forward to Support of British Troops,* June 23, 1942.

45. NAP, JSP, Box 138, f.199, Lewis to Van Ryneveld, *Klopper Upbeat Letter to Theron on Morale*, June 18, 1942. See also Agar-Hamilton, *Crisis in the Desert* (p. 129).
46. DODA, UWHS–Civil, Box 366, File PMH62N/1, *Narrative on the Decision to Hold Tobruk.*
47. DODA, UWHS, Box 127, Narrative and Reports ME.1, p. 2, *Western Desert Campaign, Remarks passed by Colonel H. Cilliers onetime G11 SA Infantry Division, to E. Axelson 18 September 1947.*
48. DODA, UWHS, Box 127, Narrative and Reports ME.1, p. 1, *Western Desert Campaign, Statement by Colonel Du Plessis on the fall of Tobruk 14 June 1943.*
49. DODA, UWHS–Civil, Box 366, File PMH62N/3, *Narrative on the Crisis at Tobruk.*
50. Agar-Hamilton, *Crisis in the Desert* (pp. 132, 133).
51. DODA, UWHS–Civil, Box 371, Operations in the Western Desert, Part II, p. 25, *Report of Tobruk Court of Enquiry*, May 27–July 2.
52. Agar-Hamilton, *Crisis in the Desert* (p. 138).
53. DODA, UWHS, Box 138, Narrative and Reports ME.12, p. 5, *Fritz Bayerlein: Answers to questions by UWH re tanks, antitank guns, and general tactics (German and British).*
54. DODA, UWHS–Civil, Box 371, Operations in the Western Desert, Part II, p. 25, *Report of Tobruk Court of Enquiry*, May 27–July 2.
55. DODA, UWHS–Civil, Box 366, File PMH62N/3, *Narrative on the Crisis at Tobruk.*
56. DODA, UWHS, Box 139, Narrative and Reports M.E. 13, p. 1, *Report on 1 Fd Regt 2nd Battery SAA by Major A. J. Morris for the period 12/6/42 to the fall of Tobruk.*
57. Agar-Hamilton, *Crisis in the Desert* (pp. 133, 134). This is based on the evidence of Major Tower, a battery commander of 25th Field Regiment.
58. Agar-Hamilton, *Crisis in the Desert* (p. 135).
59. Agar-Hamilton, *Crisis in the Desert* (p. 137). The official history omits these lines of Gooler's report. The full report is available at DODA, UWHS–Civil, Box 363, Tobruk Correspondence 1948–1950, Fannin to Agar-Hamilton, *Fannin on Klopper*, December 11, 1948.
60. Agar-Hamilton, *Crisis in the Desert* (p. 137).
61. DODA, UWHS, Box 127, Narrative and Reports ME.1, p. 2, *Western Desert Campaign, Statement by Colonel Du Plessis on the fall of Tobruk 14 June 1943.* DuPlessis's account (he was the Assistant Director Medical Services) carries weight due to his position within Klopper's headquarters.
62. UWHS, DODA, UWHS–Civil, Box 363, File PMH62C, Reports of South African Officers, *Interview with Brigadier H. B. Klopper (Notes on Major Turner's Interview)*, May 6, 1946. See also Horn, "Narratives from North Africa" (p. 97).
63. During the war a number of Störche were captured by the Allies. One became the personal aircraft of Field Marshal Montgomery.
64. DODA, UWHS, Box 139, Narrative and Reports M.E. 13, p. 2, *Interview with Col. W. Mc A Richards CRA 2 SA Div 23 November 1946.* Klopper is reported to have said that if the Australians could hold Tobruk, then the South Africans could.

65. DODA, UWHS–Civil, Box 366, File PMH62N/1, *Narrative on the Decision to Hold Tobruk.*
66. Agar-Hamilton, *Crisis in the Desert* (p. 129).
67. DODA, UWHS, Box 139, Narrative and Reports M.E. 13, p. 3, *Interview with General H. B. Klopper 2 S.A. Division 6 May 1946.*
68. DODA, UWHS, Box 139, Narrative and Reports M.E. 13, p. 2, *Interview with General H. B. Klopper 2 S.A. Division 6 May 1946.*
69. Agar-Hamilton, *Crisis in the Desert* (p. 150). According to the UWHS. DODA, UWHS–Civil, Box 366, File PMH62N/1, *Narrative on the Decision to hold Tobruk.*
70. DODA, UWHS, Box 139, Narrative and Reports M.E. 13, p. 2, *Interview with General H. B. Klopper 2 S.A. Division 6 May 1946.*
71. DODA, UWHS, Box 139, Narrative and Reports M.E. 13, p. 2, *Interview with Col. W. Mc A Richards CRA 2 SA Div 23 November 1946.*
72. DODA, UWHS–Civil, Box 366, File PMH62N/3, *Narrative on the Crisis at Tobruk.* See also DODA, UWHS, Box 139, Narrative and Reports M.E. 13, p. 2, *Report on 1 Fd Regt 2nd Battery SAA by Major A. J. Morris for the period 12/6/42 to the fall of Tobruk.* On the eveneming of June 19, Morris witnessed an RAF plane drop dispatches on the airfield, which he subsequently learned contained Rommel's plans for an attack on Tobruk.
73. R. M. Citino, *Death of the Wehrmacht: The German Campaigns of 1942* (Kansas: University Press of Kansas, 2007) (p. 147).
74. It is interesting to draw a contrast to numerous examples of the Allied forces being incapable or unprepared to perform simple maneuvers at night.
75. Agar-Hamilton, *Crisis in the Desert* (p. 158). See A. Toppe, *Desert Warfare: German Experiences in World War II*, ed. by H. Heitman (Fort Leavenworth: Combat Studies Institute, 1952) (p.45).
76. DODA, UWHS–Civil, Box 366, File PMH62N/1, *Narrative on the Decision to hold Tobruk.* This incident is acknowledged in the South African official history, but it goes on to paint an elaborate picture of confusing and obscure orders and the fact that a search was being conducted for the original orders that already seemed to be in the hands of the Intelligence Section at Tobruk. Agar-Hamilton, *Crisis in the Desert* (p. 157).
77. DODA, UWHS, Box 139, Narrative and Reports M.E. 13, p. 3, *Interview with Col. W. Mc A Richards CRA 2 SA Div 23 November 1946.*
78. H. Boog, W. Rahn, R. Stumpf, and B. Wegner, *Germany and the Second World War: The Global War*, ed. by Militargeschichtliches Forschungsamt, Vol. VI (Oxford: Claredon Press, 2001) (p. 698).
79. Liddell Hart, *The Rommel Papers* (p. 230). See also DODA, UWHS, Box 138, Narrative and Reports ME.12, p. 9, *Fritz Bayerlein: Answers to questions by UWH re tanks, anti-tank guns, and general tactics (German and British).*
80. The South African official history would have one believe that the minefields existed in name only. This despite Rommel's assertion as to the efforts to clear them the night before, and despite the evidence led by Brigadier Gaussen, who was the chief engineer of XIII Corps, that the policy was not to interfere with the perimeter minefields. Agar-Hamilton, *Crisis in the Desert* (p. 161). C. Birkby, *The Saga of the Transvaal Scottish Regiment 1932–1950* (Cape Town: Hodder and Stoughton, 1950) (p. 513).

81. DODA, UWHS–Civil, Box 366, *Tobruk Artillery Narrative.*
82. Agar-Hamilton, *Crisis in the Desert* (p. 163).
83. Agar-Hamilton, *Crisis in the Desert* (p. 163).
84. UWHS, DODA, UWHS–Civil, Box 363, File PMH62C, Reports of South African Officers, *Interview with Brigadier H. B. Klopper (Notes on Major Turner's Interview)*, May 6, 1946.
85. DODA, UWHS–Civil, Box 366, File PMH62N/3, *Narrative on the Crisis at Tobruk.*
86. There were apparently thirty-six guns available to bring down fire on the gap, but they appeared to have done little damage to the attacking force. DODA, UWHS–Civil, Box 366, *Tobruk Artillery Narrative.*
87. DODA, UWHS, Box 138, Narrative and Reports ME.12, p. 5, *Fritz Bayerlein: Answers to questions by UWH re tanks,anti-tank guns, and general tactics (German and British).* According to Bayerlein the Germans had 125 tanks available for the corps, of which half where available for the attack on Tobruk. The defenders had 77 Infantry tanks according to the Court Of Enquiry. See DODA, UWHS–Civil, Box 371, Operations in the Western Desert, Part II, p. 25, *Report of Tobruk Court of Enquiry,* May 27–July 2.
88. DODA, UWHS–Civil, Box 366, File PMH62N/3, *Narrative on the Crisis at Tobruk.*
89. Agar-Hamilton, *Crisis in the Desert* (p. 169).
90. Agar-Hamilton, *Crisis in the Desert* (p. 168).
91. DODA, UWHS–Civil, Box 366, *Tobruk Artillery Narrative.*
92. Agar-Hamilton, *Crisis in the Desert* (p. 169).
93. General Walther Nehring became Rommel's effective second in command after General Crüwell was captured. S. Mitcham Jr, *Rommel's Desert Commanders: The Men Who Served the Desert Fox, North Africa, 1941–42* (Mechanicsburg, PA: Stackpole, 2007) (p. 87).
94. Agar-Hamilton, *Crisis in the Desert* (p. 169).
95. A. Toppe, *Desert Warfare: German Experiences in World War II,* ed. by H. Heitman (Fort Leavenworth: Combat Studies Institute, 1952) (p. A-9-15).
96. Agar-Hamilton, *Crisis in the Desert* (p. 169).
97. Agar-Hamilton, *Crisis in the Desert* (p. 180).
98. DODA, UWHS, Box 139, Narrative and Reports M.E. 13, *Notes on an interview on 20 November 1946 with Major Wessels 2/c SA LAA Regiment.*
99. DODA, UWHS–Civil, Box 366, File PMH62N/3, *Narrative on the Crisis at Tobruk.*
100. Agar-Hamilton, *Crisis in the Desert* (p. 181).
101. DODA, UWHS–Civil, Box 366, File PMH62N/3, *Narrative on the Crisis at Tobruk.*
102. DODA, UWHS–Civil, Box 363, Reports of South African Officers, File PMH62C, *Written Comments of Lieutenant-Colonel Thompson 2nd Battalion TVL Scottish,* December 4, 1945.
103. NAP, JSP, Box 137, f.139, Auchinleck to Smuts, *Debrief on Fall of Tobruk,* June 22, 1942. See also Agar-Hamilton, *Crisis in the Desert* (p. 208).
104. Toppe, *Desert Warfare* (p. A-9-12).
105. DODA, UWHS, Box 139, Narrative and Reports M.E. 13, p. 2, *Notes on Interview on 18 Nov 46 with Major A. S. Hathorn ex B.M. CRA in Tobruk.*

Hathorn remembers the conference dragging on "interminably" on the night of June 20. Colonel Richards, the commander of the divisional artillery, was keen to take the breakout option. Brigadier Hayton said he did not have the transport to break out. Hathorn makes the comment that there were far too many people at the conference.

106. DODA, UWHS, Box 139, Narrative and Reports M.E. 13, p. 2, *Interview with Col. W. Mc A Richards CRA 2 SA Div 23 November 1946.*
107. DODA, UWHS–Civil, Box 366, File PMH62N/4, *Narrative of the Eighth Army and the Surrender of Tobruk.*
108. DODA, UWHS–Civil, Box 363, Tobruk Correspondence 1948–1950, Agar-Hamilton to Fannin, *Fannin on Klopper*, 18 November 1948.
109. DODA, UWHS, Box 139, Narrative and Reports M.E. 13, p. 2, *Interview with Lt. Col. G. L'Estrange OC Umvoti Mounted Rifles 22 November 1946.*
110. DODA, UWHS–Civil, Box 363, Tobruk Correspondence 1948–1950, Fannin to Agar-Hamilton, *Fannin on Klopper*, December 11, 1948.
111. DODA, UWHS–Civil, Box 366, File PMH62N/4, *Narrative of the Eighth Army and the Surrender of Tobruk.*
112. DODA, UWHS–Civil, Box 363, *Corrospondence file 4 SA Inf Bde HQ*, June 20, 1942.
113. Agar-Hamilton, *Crisis in the Desert* (p. 213).
114. DODA, UWHS, Box 127, Narrative and Reports ME.1, p. 3, *Western Desert Campaign, Account by Lt. A. N. Goldman and Sgt C. H. Spear, 2 RDL, Tobruk.*
115. DODA, UWHS, Box 139, Narrative and Reports M.E. 13, p. 2, *Interview with Lt. Col. Whyte 3 Fd Regt SAA 24 August 1946.* A somewhat different perspective is offered by Whyte. "There was no question of taking advantage of the confusion to escape. Lt. Col. Sherwell of 2 Fd Regt informed Col. Whyte that he had been in personal contact with the GOC [Klopper] and had been instructed by him to surrender."
116. DODA, UWHS–Civil, Box 363, File PMH62C, Reports of South African Officers, *Interview with Brigadier H. B. Klopper (Notes on Major Turner's Interview)*, May 6, 1946. Michael Carver is more specific, putting the figure at 2,000 tons of petrol, 2,000 servicible vehicles, 5,000 tons of food, and large quantities of ammunition. Carver, *Tobruk* (p. 248).
117. Boog, *Germany and the Second World War* (p. 698).
118. DODA, UWHS–Civil, Box 371, Operations in the Western Desert, Part I, p. 22, 23, *Report of Tobruk Court of Enquiry*, May 27–July 2.
119. DODA, UWHS, Box 138, Narrative and Reports ME.12, p. 5, *Fritz Bayerlein: Answers to questions by UWH re tanks,anti-tank guns, and general tactics (German and British).* Bayerlein admits to twenty German tanks put out of action in the assault on the southeastern corner of Tobruk.
120. The CGS file on Tobruk has a document on file that shows 6 South Africans killed out of a force of 12,395. DODA, CGS War, Box 47 Tobruk Enquiry, File 10/11, Casualties of South African Forces at Tobruk, 19 November 1942.
121. DODA, UWHS–Civil, Box 363, File PMH62C, Reports of South African Officers, *Interview with Brigadier H. B. Klopper (Notes on Major Turner's Interview)*, May 6, 1946.

122. DODA, UWHS–Civil, Box 363, File PMH62C, Reports of South African Officers, *Interview with Brigadier H. B. Klopper (Notes on Major Turner's Interview)*, May 6, 1946.
123. DODA, UWHS–Civil, Box 363, File PMH62C, Reports of South African Officers, *Interview with Brigadier H. B. Klopper (Notes on Major Turner's Interview)*, May 6, 1946.
124. DODA, UWHS–Civil, Box 363, Tobruk Correspondence 1948–1950, Agar-Hamilton to Fannin, *Fannin on Klopper*, 18 November 1948.
125. DODA, UWHS–Civil, Box 366, File PMH62N/4, *Narrative of the Eighth Army and the Surrender of Tobruk.*
126. DODA, UWHS–Civil, Box 363, File PMH62C, Reports of South African Officers, *Interview with Brigadier H .B. Klopper (Notes on Major Turner's Interview)*, May 6, 1946.

CHAPTER 8

1. H. Kippenburger, *Infantry Brigadier* (London: Geoffrey Cumberlege, 1949) (p. 138).
2. A. Danchev and D. Todman, (eds), *War Diaries 1939–1945 Field Marshal Lord Alanbrooke* (Los Angeles: University of California, 2001) (p. 269).
3. W. Churchill, *The Second World War: The Hinge of Fate* (Middlesex: Penguin, 1985), IV (p. 344). The words he uses are "Defeat is one thing; disgrace is another."
4. "Tobruk Disaster: Demand for Inquiry by British Press," *The Mercury*, June 23, 1942, accessed August 2, 2012, http://trove.nla.gov.au/ndp/del/article/25932389. This Tasmanian newspaper article gives a summary and an insight into the general feelings of the British press. See also D. B. Katz and K. Horn, 'The Surrender of Tobruk in 1942: Press Reports and Soldiers' Memories,' *Scientia Militaria*, 44.1 (2016) (pp. 190–208).
5. WO106/4946 June 22, 1942, National Archives United Kingdom.
6. Paardeburg was more of a battle in South African history than a South African battle. When comparing the magnitude of these South African defeats, one has to take note of the context in which these battles took place. One of the important considerations is the strategic impact of such a reverse in judging the scale of defeat. I am grateful to Lt. Col. (Prof.) D. Visser for giving me clarity on this issue.
7. A. Heckstall-Smith, *Tobruk: The Story of a Siege* (London: Anthony Blond, 1959). This appears on the inside dust jacket.
8. I. Rosmarin, *Inside Story* (Cape Town: W. J. Flesch & Partners, 1990) (p. 17). See also K. Horn, "Narratives from North Africa: South African Prisoner-of-War Experience Following the Fall of Tobruk, June 1942," *Historia*, 56, 2 (2011) (p. 100).
9. Quoted in M. Leigh, *Captives Courageous* (Johannesburg: Ashanti, 1992) (p. 3).
10. DODA, UWHS, Box 128, Narrative and Reports M.E. 2 (p. 15) *The Springbok troops were mishandled, Major-General E. Dorman O'Gowan in Outspan article 18 February 1955.*
11. H. Boog, W. Rahn, R. Stumpf, and B. Wegner. *Germany and the Second World War: The Global War*, ed. by Militargeschichtliches Forschungsamt, Vol. VI (Oxford: Claredon Press, 2001) (p. 718).

12. NAP, JSP, Box 137, f.125, Auchinleck to Smuts, *Addressing Smuts' Concern for Union Forces,* June 14, 1942.
13. J. A. I. Agar-Hamilton and L. C. F. Turner, *Crisis in the Desert: May-July 1942* (London: Oxford, 1952) (pp. 103, 104).
14. B. H. Liddell Hart, *The Tanks: The History of the Royal Tank Regiment 1939–1945* (London: Cassell, 1959) (p. 181).
15. Agar-Hamilton, *Crisis in the Desert* (p. 229). The Gazala Gallop described the headlong retreat of the British 8th Army during the six weeks following May 26, 1942, from the Gazala line in Cyrenaica to the Alamein line, 113 km (70 miles) west of Alexandria.
16. Agar-Hamilton, *Crisis in the Desert* (p. 229). Written by Lt. General Sir Francis Tucker in his book, *The Pattern of War.*
17. E. P. Hartshorn, *Avenge Tobruk* (Cape Town: Purnell, 1960) (p. 147). See also Agar-Hamilton, *Crisis in the Desert* (p. 230).
18. Agar-Hamilton, *Crisis in the Desert* (p. 232).
19. Agar-Hamilton, *Crisis in the Desert* (p. 234).
20. TNA, WO 32/10160/362, *Auchinleck Despatch on Operations in the Middle East,* November 1, 1941 to August 15, 1942.
21. TNA, WO 32/10160/327, *Auchinleck Despatch on Operations in the Middle East,* November 1, 1941 to August 15, 1942.
22. N. Orpen, *South African Forces World War II—War in the Desert* (Cape Town: Purnell, 1971) (p. 334).
23. Liddell Hart, *The Tanks* (p. 187).
24. M. Montanari, *The Three Battles of Alamein (June–November 1942)* (Rome: Stato Maggiore Esercito, 2007) (p. 63).
25. TNA, WO 32/10160/328, *Auchinleck Despatch on Operations in the Middle East,* November 1, 1941 to August 15, 1942.
26. Agar-Hamilton, *Crisis in the Desert* (p. 247).
27. Liddell Hart, *The Tanks* (p.189).
28. A. Stewart, *The Early Battles of Eighth Army: Crusader to the Alamein Line, 1941–42* (Mechanicsburg, PA: Stackpole, 2002) (p. 98).
29. S. W. Mitcham, *Rommel's Desert War: The Life and Death of the Afrika Korps* (Mechanicsburg, PA: Stackpole, 2007) (p.105).
30. Agar-Hamilton, *Crisis in the Desert* (p. 246).
31. TNA, WO 32/10160/363, *Auchinleck Despatch on Operations in the Middle East,* November 1, 1941 to August 15, 1942.
32. Agar-Hamilton, *Crisis in the Desert* (p. 248).
33. S. Bidwell, *Gunners at War* (London: Arms and Armour Press, 1970) (p. 176).
34. Stewart, *The Early Battles of the Eighth Army* (p. 96).
35. I. S. O. Playfair, *A History of the Second World War: The Mediterranean and Middle East*, ed. by J. Butler (Uckfield: Naval & Military Press, 2004), III (p. 335). The RAF flew close to 570 sorties every twenty-four hours at their peak intensity in July 1942. Auchinleck describes their contribution as decisive in the succesful defense of Alamein.
36. Agar-Hamilton, *Crisis in the Desert* (p. 252).
37. M. Carver, *Out of Step: The Memoirs of Field Marshal Lord Carver* (London: Hutchinson, 1989) (p. 121).

38. Agar-Hamilton, *Crisis in the Desert* (p. 258). The New Zealanders, together with a wounded Freyberg, made use of a bayonet attack to clear a way through the German lines for the whole division to pass through.
39. Agar-Hamilton, *Crisis in the Desert* (p. 260).
40. The Italian official history gives the figures as follows: 55 German medium tanks and 70 Italian tanks; 330 German and 200 Italian guns, including 50 captured 25-pounders; 15 armoured cars; and 2,000 German and 8,000 Italian infantrymen. Montanari, *The Three Battles of Alamein* (p. 99).
41. Montanari, *The Three Battles of Alamein* (p. 99).
42. F. W. Von Mellenthin, *Panzer Battles* (London: Futura, 1979) (p.160).
43. DODA, UWHS, Box 175, Translations No. 1 A (micro. 49786) *War Diary of the 90th Light Infantry Division 15 May 1942–5 July 1942.*
44. I. W. Walker, *Iron Hulls Iron Hearts: Mussolini's Elite Armoured Divisions in North Africa.* (Marlborough: Crowood Press, 2006) (p. 139).
45. Walker, *Iron Hulls Iron Hearts* (p. 139).
46. Agar-Hamilton, *Crisis in the Desert* (pp. 287, 288).
47. Liddell Hart, *The Tanks* (p. 194).
48. Boog, *Germany and the Second World War* (p. 722).
49. C. Barnett, *The Desert Generals* (Edison: Castle Books, 2001) (p. 197). See also Orpen, *War in the Desert* (p. 336).
50. E. Dorman O'Gowan, "Rommel Drives East," in *History of the Second World War* (London: Purnell, 1972) (p. 986). Pienaar openly criticized the decision to fight west of the Nile Delta.
51. DODA, UWHS, Box 130, Narrative and Reports M.E. 4 (p. 1) *Western Desert Campaigns, 18th Indian Infantry Brigade at Deir es Shein 28 June-2 July.* The brigade transport had not arrived in time and two of the battalions traveled by train to El Alamein. They reached the Deir El Shein box at dawn on June 29. See also Stewart, *The Early Battles of the Eighth Army* (pp. 105, 106).
52. Carver, *Out of Step* (p. 121).
53. DODA, FTV 38, Letters to CGS GAO/2/1. Letter Theron to Van Ryneveld June 29, 1942. See also Orpen, *War in the Desert* (p. 341).
54. Hartshorn, *Avenge Tobruk* (p. 152). Pienaar, contrary to his usual form, was apparently left speechless on this occasion.
55. Hartshorn, *Avenge Tobruk* (p. 152). The plan to remove people from danger who may have been of future use to South Africa was not Pienaar's alone. It seems Theron was also involved and it is likely Pienaar was acting under his instruction. See Orpen, *War in the Desert* (p. 341).
56. Carver, *Out of Step* (p. 120).
57. R. W. Tungay, *The Fighting Third* (Cape Town: Unie-Volkspers, 1947) (p. 239).
58. Orpen, *War in the Desert* (p. 343).
59. DODA, UWHS, Box 130, Narrative and Reports M.E. 4 (p. 1) *Western Desert Campaigns, 18th Indian Infantry Brigade at Deir es Shein 28 June-2 July.* According to the Indian narrative there were eighteen 25-pounders, sixteen 6-pounders, and twenty 2-pounders belonging to the 121 Field Regiment.
60. Playfair, *A History of the Second World War,* III (p. 340). See also Agar-Hamilton, *Crisis in the Desert* (p. 286).
61. Boog, *Germany and the Second World War* (p. 729).
62. Boog, *Germany and the Second World War* (p. 728).

63. DODA, UWHS, Box 175, Translations No. 1 A (micro. 49787) *War Diary of the 90th Light Infantry Division 15 May 1942–5 July 1942.*
64. Tungay, *The Fighting Third* (p. 242).
65. DODA, UWHS, Box 175, Translations No. 1 A (micro. 49789) *War Diary of the 90th Light Infantry Division 15 May 1942–5 July 1942.*
66. Playfair, *A History of the Second World War,* III (p. 341).
67. DODA, UWHS, Box 175, Translations No. 1 A (micro. 49789) *War Diary of the 90th Light Infantry Division 15 May 1942–5 July 1942.*
68. Von Mellenthin, *Panzer Battles* (p. 161). The panic is confirmed by the War Diary of the 90th Light and attributes the divisional commander and the adjutant with arresting the panic and rallying the troops. See DODA, UWHS, Box 175, Translations No. 1 A (micro. 49789) *War Diary of the 90th Light Infantry Division 15 May 1942–5 July 1942.*
69. Playfair, *A History of the Second World War,* III (p. 340). See also Agar-Hamilton, *Crisis in the Desert* (p. 291). The War Diary of the 90th Light reports a tank attack at 1700, which was successfully repelled by concentrating all the divisional artillery and breaking up the attack before it left its assembly area. DODA, UWHS, Box 175, Translations No. 1 A (micro. 49789) *War Diary of the 90th Light Infantry Division 15 May 1942–5 July 1942.*
70. Agar-Hamilton, *Crisis in the Desert* (pp. 293, 294).
71. Von Mellenthin, *Panzer Battles* (p. 161).
72. Agar-Hamilton, *Crisis in the Desert* (p. 296).
73. Montanari, *The Three Battles of Alamein* (p. 94).
74. Montanari, *The Three Battles of Alamein* (p. 108).
75. DODA, UWHS, Box 175, Translations No. 1 A (micro. 49791) *War Diary of the 90th Light Infantry Division 15 May 1942–5 July 1942.*
76. Agar-Hamilton, *Crisis in the Desert* (pp. 303, 304).
77. DODA, UWHS, Box 175, Translations No. 1 A (micro. 49791) *War Diary of the 90th Light Infantry Division 15 May 1942–5 July 1942.* The Germans estimated that they were up against seven to nine light and two heavy batteries of artillery from the northeast and two to four batteries from the east.
78. DODA, UWHS, Box 175, Translations No. 1 A (micro. 49793) *War Diary of the 90th Light Infantry Division 15 May 1942–5 July 1942.*
79. Agar-Hamilton, *Crisis in the Desert* (pp. 304, 305).
80. Agar-Hamilton, *Crisis in the Desert* (p. 306).
81. Agar-Hamilton, *Crisis in the Desert* (p. 307).
82. Playfair, *A History of the Second World War,* III (p. 342).
83. Hartshorn, *Avenge Tobruk* (pp. 157, 158). See also Agar-Hamilton, *Crisis in the Desert* (p. 307). See also C. Birkby, *The Saga of the Transvaal Scottish Regiment 1932–1950* (Cape Town: Hodder and Stoughton, 1950) (p. 571).
84. N. Barr, *Pendulum of War: The Three Battles of Alamein* (London: Jonanthan Cape, 2004) (p. 90). Most of the inside take on Auchinleck's feelings about the South Africans comes from Dorman-Smith's recollections of the events, which Neil Barr admits "shows clear evidence of a clouded memory." Nevertheless, on balance it can be assumed that Pienaar's general negative attitude was ringing alarm bells in the higher echelons of British command.
85. Montanari, *The Three Battles of Alamein* (p. 110).

86. DODA, UWHS, Box 175, Translations No. 1 A (micro. 49792) *War Diary of the 90th Light Infantry Division 15 May 1942–5 July 1942.* See also Agar-Hamilton, *Crisis in the Desert* (pp. 309, 310).
87. *The Rommel Papers*, ed. by B. H. Liddell Hart (New York: Da Capo, 1953) (p. 248).
88. Agar-Hamilton, *Crisis in the Desert* (p. 311).
89. Walker, *Iron Hulls Iron Hearts* (p. 140). The Italian prisoners were described as a dirty, greasy, and unkempt mob without fighting spirit. This is testament to the poor state of the Axis forces, which had been fighting since May 26. See also Agar-Hamilton, *Crisis in the Desert* (p. 312).
90. *The Rommel Papers*, ed. Liddell Hart (p. 249). See also Montanari, *The Three Battles of Alamein* (pp. 115, 116).
91. Montanari, *The Three Battles of Alamein* (p. 115).
92. Walker, *Iron Hulls Iron Hearts* (pp. 141, 142). *Littorio* arrived in Tripoli in early January 1942, but had to wait until March for the complete division to arrive. *Littorio* did not participate in the battle of Gazala. The division was a part of the investing force at Mersa Matruh, and pursued the Eighth Army in its retreat to El Alamein.
93. Agar-Hamilton, *Crisis in the Desert* (p. 313).
94. Stewart, *The Early Battles of the Eighth Army* (p. 110).

POSTSCRIPT

1. I. S. O. Playfair, *A History of the Second World War: The Mediterranean and Middle East*, ed. by J. Butler (Uckfield: Naval & Military Press, 2004), III (p. 367). See also N. Orpen, *South African Forces World War II—War in the Desert* (Cape Town: Purnell, 1971) (p. 388).
2. N. Orpen, *South African Forces World War II—War in the Desert* (Cape Town: Purnell, 1971) (p. 391).
3. E. P. Hartshorn, *Avenge Tobruk* (Cape Town: Purnell, 1960) (p. 167).
4. Hartshorn, *Avenge Tobruk* (p. 168).
5. Orpen, *War in the Desert*, III (p. 393).
6. Orpen, *War in the Desert*, III (p. 393).
7. H. Boog, *Germany and the Second World War: The Global War Volume VI* (Potsdam: Militargeschichtliches Forschungsampt, 2001) (p. 760).
8. B. H. Liddell Hart, *The Tanks: The History of the Royal Tank Regiment 1939–1945* (London: Cassell, 1959) (pp. 217, 218).
9. Boog, *Germany and the Second World War* (p. 765).
10. Orpen, *War in the Desert*, III (p. 404).
11. M. Carver, *El Alamein* (New York: Macmillan, 1962) (p. 85).
12. Boog, *Germany and the Second World War* (p. 766). See also Carver, *El Alamein* (p. 99).
13. Carver, *El Alamein* (p. 84).
14. Liddell Hart, *The Tanks* (p. 227).
15. Orpen, *War in the Desert*, III (p. 414).
16. Carver, *El Alamein* (p. 104).
17. Carver, *El Alamein* (p. 133).
18. Orpen, *War in the Desert*, III (p. 415).

19. J. Latimer, *Alamein* (Cambridge: Harvard University Press, 2002) (p. 239). See also Orpen, *War in the Desert*, III (pp. 438, 439).
20. Orpen, *War in the Desert*, III (p. 417).
21. J. C. Smuts, "Elections 1943" (Memorandum Smuts to Churchill January 1943, National Archives Pretoria, Jan Smuts Collection Box 95-1 [152], 1943). Smuts was reluctant to become a "second Ireland" due to South Africa's strategic importance to the Allied cause.
22. *Selections From the Smuts Papers December 1934–August 1945*, ed. by J. van der Poel and W. K. Hancock (London: Cambridge University, 1973), VI (p. 407).
23. *Selections From the Smuts Papers December 1934–August 1945*, ed. by J. van der Poel and W. K. Hancock (London: Cambridge University, 1973), VI (p. 402). Similar riots occurred in Johannesburg in December 1941.
24. Orpen, *War in the Desert*, III (p. 459).
25. J. Bourhill, *Come Back to Portofino* (Johannesburg: 30 Degrees South, 2011) (p. 31). C. Birkby, *The Saga of the Transvaal Scottish Regiment 1932–1950* (Cape Town: Hodder and Stoughton, 1950) (p. 629).
26. W. Churchill, "1st Division Withdrawal" (Memorandum Churchill to Smuts 2/12/1942, National Archives Pretoria, Jan Smuts Collection Box 95-1 [145A], 1942).

Epilogue

1. "My Family History, Bertie," http://familyhistory.desertbloom.co.za/?page_id=41, accessed June 13, 2016.
2. Popski's Private Army was an unconventional unit formed in the Western Desert during the Second World War to raid behind enemy lines. The unit performed the same task in Italy.
3. V. Peniakoff, *Private Army* (London: Jonathan Cape, 1950) (p. 394).
4. B. Nasson, *South Africa at War 1939 -1945* (Pretoria: Jacana, 2012) (p. 110).
5. H. B. Klopper, "Voorsmaak van die Stryd!" *Huisgenoot*, June 1950.
6. A. Stewart, "The 'Atomic' Despatch: Field Marshal Auchinleck, the Fall of the Tobruk Garrison and Post-War Anglo-South African Relations," *Scientia Militaria*, 36(1) (2008) and A. Stewart, "The Klopper Affair: Anglo-South African Relations and the Surrender of the Tobruk Garrison," *Twentieth Century British History* 17(4), no. 4 (2006).
7. I. Uys, *South African Military Who's Who 1452–1992* (Germiston: Fortress, 1992) (p. 122).

Index

Page numbers in *italics* reference figures, tables, and maps.